JOHN

PREACHING THE WORD
Edited by R. Kent Hughes

(((PREACHING *the* WORD)))

JOHN

THAT YOU MAY BELIEVE

R. KENT HUGHES

WHEATON, ILLINOIS

Library of Congress Cataloging-in-Publication Data

Hughes, R. Kent
   John : that you may believe / R. Kent Hughes
      p. cm.—(Preaching the word)
   ISBN 13: 978-1-58134-101-0 (alk. paper)
   ISBN 10: 1-58134-101-6
   1. Bible. N.T. John Commentaries. I. Title. II. Series:
Hughes, R. Kent. Preaching the word.
BS2615.3.H77   1999
226.5'07—dc21   99-25801

Crossway is a publishing ministry of Good News Publishers.

VP		33	32	31	30	29	28	27	26	25	24	23
17	16	15	14	13	12	11	10	9	8	7	6	5

For
Paul and Trudy Ogren

These are written so that you may believe that
Jesus is the Christ, the Son of God, and that by
believing you may have life in his name.

John 20:31

Contents

Acknowledgments

I must thank my beloved wife Barbara who has twice attentively listened to my expositions on the Gospel of John, which is a remarkable feat of endurance! Even more, she interacted with me over the text, always praying that God's Word would be clear. Also I want to thank Mrs. Sharon Fritz for her usual professional expertise—this time going the second mile to research long-disappeared footnotes—and for her good humor at all times. I must also express my thanks to my colleague Adam Rasmussen, who composed the Index of Sermon Illustrations. And, of course, thanks to Crossway editor Ted Griffin, who has expertly edited all the volumes in the Preaching the Word series—and has improved them all.

A Word to Those Who Preach the Word

There are times when I am preaching that I have especially sensed the pleasure of God. I usually become aware of it through the unnatural silence. The ever-present coughing ceases and the pews stop creaking, bringing an almost physical quiet to the sanctuary—through which my words sail like arrows. I experience a heightened eloquence, so that the cadence and volume of my voice intensify the truth I am preaching.

There is nothing quite like it—the Holy Spirit filling one's sails, the sense of his pleasure, and the awareness that something is happening among one's hearers. This experience is, of course, not unique, for thousands of preachers have similar experiences, even greater ones.

What has happened when this takes place? How do we account for this sense of his smile? The answer for me has come from the ancient rhetorical categories of *logos*, *ethos*, and *pathos*.

The first reason for his smile is the *logos*—in terms of preaching God's Word. This means that as we stand before God's people to proclaim his Word, we have done our homework. We have exegeted the passage, mined the significance of its words in their context, and applied sound hermeneutical principles in interpreting the text so that we understand what its words meant to its hearers. And it means that we have labored long until we can express in a sentence what the theme of the text is—so that our outline springs from the text. Then our preparation will be such that as we preach, we will not be preaching our own thoughts about God's Word, but God's actual Word, his *logos*. This is fundamental to pleasing him in preaching.

The second element in knowing God's smile in preaching is *ethos*—what you are as a person. There is a danger endemic to preaching, which is having your hands and heart cauterized by holy things. Phillips Brooks illustrated it by the analogy of a train conductor who comes to believe that he has been to the places he announces because of his long and loud heralding of them. And that is why Brooks insisted that preaching must be "the bringing of truth through personality." Though we can never *perfectly* embody the truth we preach, we must be subject to it, long for it, and make it as much a part of our ethos as possible. As the Puritan William Ames said, "Next to the Scriptures, nothing makes a sermon more to pierce, than when it comes out of the inward affection of the heart without any affectation." When a preacher's ethos backs up his *logos*, there will be the pleasure of God.

Last, there is *pathos*—personal passion and conviction. David Hume, the Scottish philosopher and skeptic, was once challenged as he was seen going to hear George Whitefield preach: "I thought you do not believe in the gospel." Hume replied, "I don't, but *he does*." Just so! When a preacher believes what he preaches, there will be passion. And this belief and requisite passion will know the smile of God.

The pleasure of God is a matter of *logos* (the Word), *ethos* (what you are), and *pathos* (your passion). As you *preach the Word* may you experience his smile—the Holy Spirit in your sails!

R. Kent Hughes
Wheaton, Illinois

1

The Greatness of Christ

JOHN 1:1–18

IT IS RIGHTLY SAID THAT each of the Gospels presents Christ with a distinctive emphasis. Matthew emphasizes his kingship, Mark his servanthood, Luke his manhood, and John his Godhood. Certainly all the Gospels present all four truths, but their separate emphases have allowed them unique functions in telling the story of Christ.

John is unique in his powerful presentation of Jesus as the great Creator-God of the universe. His massive vision of Christ has been used countless times to open the eyes of unbelievers to who Jesus is and the way of redemption.

This Gospel's continuing effect on Christians is equally profound because in John's account believers find an ongoing source for expanding their concept of the Savior's greatness. The serious student of John will find that each time he returns to the Gospel, Christ will be a little bigger—something like Lucy's experience with the lion Aslan (the Christ symbol in C. S. Lewis's Chronicles of Narnia) as she again gazed into his large, wise face.

"Welcome, child," he said.

"Aslan," said Lucy, "you're bigger."

"That is because you are older, little one," answered he.

"Not because you are?"

"I am not. But every year you grow, you will find me bigger."[1]

My hope is that as we work our way through the wonders of this book, we will find Christ bigger and bigger and bigger.

The prologue to John's Gospel (1:1–18) is considered to be one of the most sublime sections in all of Scripture. Some believe it was an early Christian "Hymn of the Incarnate Word," for Christ's incarnation is its subject, and it is marvelously poetic. Even more, it introduces us to some of the major ideas of the book: the cosmic Christ who came as light into the world, suffered rejection, but gave "grace upon grace" (v. 16) to those who received him. This hymn gives us a sense of the matchless greatness of Christ (vv. 1–3), the greatness of his love (vv. 4–13), and the greatness of his grace (vv. 14–18).

As John begins this introductory song, the force of what he says is so staggering that the words almost seem to bend under the weight they are made to bear. The opening three verses are an amazingly congealed expression of the greatness of Christ.

The Greatness of Christ (vv. 1–3)

> In the beginning was the Word, and the Word was with God, and the Word was God. He was in the beginning with God. All things were made through him, and without him was not any thing made that was made. (vv. 1–3)

Eternally Preexistent

"In the beginning was the Word." There never was a time when Christ did not exist because the word "was" is in the Greek imperfect tense, which means "was continuing." In fact, the entire first verse bears this sense. "In the beginning was continuing the Word, and the Word was continuing with God, and the Word was continually God." Or as one of my friends accurately (though ungrammatically) concluded, "Jesus always was wasing!" That is precisely it. Jesus Christ is preexistent. He always was continuing.

If you are like me, this kind of thinking makes for a super-headache. Our minds look backward until time disappears and thought collapses in exhaustion. Thus we begin our thoughts of the greatness of Christ. (The same thought can be found in 2 Corinthians 8:9, Philippians 2:6ff., and Colossians 1:17.)

Eternally in Relationship

Next the apostle adds, "And the Word was with God." Literally, "the Word was continually toward God." The Father and the Son were continually face-to-face. The preposition "with" bears the idea of nearness, along with a sense of movement toward God. That is to say, there has always existed the deepest equality and intimacy in the Holy Trinity.

Again our minds stagger as we think of Jesus as always having continued (without beginning and without end) in perfect joyous intimacy with the Father.

Eternally God

Moreover, as the final phrase of verse 1 adds, "And the Word was God."[2] The exact meaning is that the Word was God in essence and character. He was God in every way, though he was a separate person from God the Father. The phrase perfectly preserves Jesus' separate identity, while also stating that he is God. This was his continuing identity from all eternity. He was God constantly.

The simple sentence of verse 1 is the most compact and pulsating theological statement in all of Scripture. Jesus was always existing from all eternity as God, in perfect fellowship with God the Father and (though not mentioned) the Holy Spirit. He is the cosmic Christ.

Eternally Creator

Finally, Jesus is the Creator of the universe. "All things were made through him, and without him was not any thing made that was made." The fact of Christ's Creatorship is the consistent witness of the New Testament. Colossians 1:16, 17 says: "For by him all things were created, in heaven and on earth, visible and invisible, whether thrones or dominions or rulers or authorities—all things were created through him and for him. And he is before all things, and in him all things hold together." Hebrews 1:2, 3 adds: "In these last days [God] has spoken to us by his Son, whom he appointed the heir of all things, through whom also he created the world. He is the radiance of the glory of God and the exact imprint of his nature, and he upholds the universe by the word of his power." Revelation 4:11 states: "Worthy are you, our Lord and God, to receive glory and honor and power, for you created all things, and by your will they existed and were created." Also 1 Corinthians 8:6 says: "Yet for us there is one God, the Father, from whom are all things and for whom we exist, and one Lord, Jesus Christ, through whom are all things and through whom we exist."

There are about one hundred billion stars in the average galaxy, and there are at least one hundred million galaxies in known space. Einstein believed that we have scanned with our largest telescopes only one billionth of theoretical space. This means that there are probably something like 10,000,000,000,000,000,000,000,000,000 stars in space (ten octillion). How many is that? 1,000 thousands = a million; 1,000 millions = a billion; 1,000 billions = a trillion; 1,000 trillions = a quadrillion; 1,000 quadrillions = a quintillion; 1,000 quintillions = a sextillion; 1,000 sextillions = a septillion; 1,000 septillions = an octillion. So ten octillion is a 10 with twenty-seven zeros behind it. And Jesus created them all!

Not only is he the Creator of the macrocosm of the universe, but also of the microcosm in the inner universe of the atom. The text in Colossians explains that he holds the atom and its inner and outer universe together ("in him all things hold together").

We can trust such a God with everything. Because he is Creator, he knows just what his creation, his people, need. It was said of Charles Steinmetz, the mechanical genius and friend of Henry Ford, that he could build a motor in his mind, and if it broke down he could fix it in his mind. So when he designed it and actually built it, it ran with precision.

One day the assembly line in the Ford plant broke down. None of Ford's men could fix it, so they called in Steinmetz. He tinkered for a few minutes, threw the switch, and it started running again.

A few days later Ford received a bill from Steinmetz for $10,000. Ford wrote back, "Charlie, don't you think your bill is a little high for just a little tinkering!" Steinmetz sent back a revised bill: "Tinkering—$10. Knowing where to tinker—$9,990."

Only Jesus knows where the tinkering should be done in our lives to keep us in perfect running order. Christ always knows which screw to turn, which belt to loosen, and the most beneficial octane.

He is our Creator. Are you resting in him? Have you entrusted your life to him? Considering the greatness of Christ, nothing else makes any sense at all.

The Greatness of Christ's Love (vv. 4–13)

The greatness of Christ's love is apparent from the opening line of John where he is mystically identified as "the Word." Though much can be said about this term because of its rich history in Greek literature, its main significance here is that *Christ has always sought to reveal himself.* An interpretative paraphrase could well read, "In the beginning was the Communication." Ever since man's creation, Christ has sought to communicate with him in love. That Christ was always "the Word" should remind us that he has always loved us, for the nature of love is to express itself, to find an object.

In verses 4–13 the metaphor of Christ as light stresses the revelation, rejection, and reception of his love as it came to the world.

> In him was life, and the life was the light of men. The light shines in the darkness, and the darkness has not overcome it.
>
> There was a man sent from God, whose name was John. He came as a witness, to bear witness about the light, that all might believe through him. He was not the light, but came to bear witness about the light.

> The true light, which gives light to everyone, was coming into the world. He was in the world, and the world was made through him, yet the world did not know him. He came to his own, and his own people did not receive him. But to all who did receive him, who believed in his name, he gave the right to become children of God, who were born, not of blood nor of the will of the flesh nor of the will of man, but of God.

Light Revealed

In clearest terms, Christ is described as light: "In him was life, and the life was the light of men. The light shines in the darkness" (vv. 4, 5). There is ample Scriptural evidence that Christ is light in a physical sense, for he appears as such in his glory (see Matthew 17:2; Mark 9:2, 3; cf. John 17:5). But the emphasis here is on his being spiritual, life-giving light to a dark world. Verse 9 reveals that all humanity benefits from his light: "The true light, which gives light to everyone, was coming into the world." Romans 1:19, 20 explains that this happens through nature and conscience.

The thought of our Lord being spiritual light gives us a heartening insight into his loving attempt to reach the world. Where light goes, darkness is dispelled, revealing the true nature of life. No place with the slightest crack can withhold its presence. "The light shines in the darkness." Literally this means it shines *continually* in the darkness, meaning that Christ is continually bombarding every corner of our hearts of darkness through the work of his Holy Spirit in nature, conscience, and the Scriptures.

Whether you are with or without Christ, meditate upon Christ being light, and you will better understand how much he loves you.

But how was our Lord's loving light received?

Light Rejected

Sadly, the majority of mankind rejected the light. Verse 5 concludes, "And the darkness has not overcome it." Other translations read that the darkness did not "overpower" it. The light met with tremendous resistance. Verses 10, 11 round out the description in terms that are tragically absurd as we bear in mind the immense description of Christ that has gone before: "He was in the world, and the world was made through him, yet the world did not know him. He came to his own, and his own people did not receive him." Think of it! The One who said, "Let there be light," the One whose love constrained him to shine his saving light through creation and conscience, the One who mercifully sheathed his light in a human body so that he might bring light to men, the One who set aside a special people for himself to be a light to the nations, was rejected! Yet today he is still light and continues to seek to pry his way into hostile hearts. Amazing love!

And though many reject him, some respond.

Light Received

> But to all who did receive him, who believed in his name, he gave the right to become children of God, who were born, not of blood nor of the will of the flesh nor of the will of man, but of God. (vv. 12, 13)

Those who receive the light become children of God. This is a stupendous truth. Apparently John never got over it because when he was an old man he wrote, "See what kind of love the Father has given to us, that we should be called children of God; and so we are" (1 John 3:1). This ought to be the refrain of our lives if we have believed in him.

Furthermore, the future holds out to us the bright prospect of becoming like the risen Christ himself. John followed his statement of wonder with a statement of even greater wonder: "Beloved, we are God's children now, and what we will be has not yet appeared; but we know that when he appears we shall be like him, because we shall see him as he is" (1 John 3:2). C. S. Lewis, in his great sermon "The Weight of Glory," preached at St. Mary's, Oxford, elaborated on the implications of being children of God.

> It is a serious thing to live in a society of possible gods and goddesses, to remember that the dullest and most uninteresting person you talk to may one day be a creature which, if you saw it now, you would be strongly tempted to worship, or else a horror and a corruption such as you now meet, if at all, only in a nightmare. All day long we are, in some degree, helping each other to one or other of these destinations. It is in the light of these overwhelming possibilities, it is with the awe and the circumspection proper to them, that we should conduct all our dealings with one another, all friendships, all loves, all play, all politics. There are no *ordinary* people.[3]

A dizzy joy at our future as God's children should pervade all our ways.

Coming into this marvelous life is a matter of incredible simplicity. Becoming one of God's own comes by receiving Jesus, which verse 12 explains by saying, "all who did receive him, who believed in his name," which means believing on who Jesus is and receiving him as our own. In the language of John 1, the cosmic Christ, the eternal Creator who became one of us, took our sins upon himself and paid for them, was resurrected and now sits at the Father's right hand. Do you truly believe in his name, in him? That is the question. There is nothing to join, nothing to sign. Simply believe.

Oh, the greatness of Christ and his love. Receive it now if you have not done so before.

The Greatness of Christ's Grace (vv. 14–18)

As we close this study of John's prologue, the mention of grace becomes prominent. Verses 14–17 (excepting the parenthetical reference to John the Baptist in verse 15) all refer to grace:

> And the Word became flesh and dwelt among us, and we have seen his glory, glory as of the only Son from the Father, full of grace and truth. . . . For from his fullness we have all received, grace upon grace. For the law was given through Moses; grace and truth came through Jesus Christ. (vv. 14, 16, 17)

John explains that when Jesus became flesh and dwelt (literally, "pitched his tent") in the midst of humanity, men and women saw his glory, here characterized as "full of grace and truth."

John described this experience in this way: "For from his fullness we have all received, grace upon grace." Literally, the Greek for that last phrase says, "grace instead of grace." What does John mean? How do you get grace instead of grace? As the grace you receive is appropriated and allowed to work in your life, more grace will come, and then more grace, and even more grace. Some translations helpfully read, "grace following grace" or "grace heaped upon grace," attempting to convey the idea that grace continues to overflow. Martin Luther put it this way:

> The sun is not dimmed and darkened by shining on so many people or by providing the entire world with its light and splendor. It retains its light intact. It loses nothing; it is immeasurable, perhaps able to illumine ten more worlds. I suppose that a hundred thousand candles can be ignited from one light, and still this light will not lose any of its brilliance. . . . Thus Christ, our Lord, to whom we must flee and of whom we must ask all, is an interminable well, the chief source of all grace. . . . Even if the whole world were to draw from this fountain enough grace and truth to transform all people into angels, still it would not lose as much as a drop. This fountain constantly overflows with sheer grace.[4]

For those without grace, this grace is readily available. As Paul said, "But where sin increased, grace abounded all the more" (Romans 5:20). There is more than enough grace to cover your sins and give you an overflowing, victorious life.

For those who know Christ, our text makes it clear that "from his fullness we have *all* received, grace upon grace." We have it now, and grace is heaped upon grace as we walk with him.

Conclusion

John concludes his prologue with the sentence, "No one has ever seen God; the only God, who is at the Father's side, he has made him known" (v. 18). Jesus is the explanation (the exegesis) of God the Father.

The greatness of Christ explains the greatness of the Father. The greatness of Christ's love explains the greatness of the Father's love. And the greatness of Christ's grace explains the greatness of the Father's grace. May we continue to have our concept of God raised! As Aslan said to Lucy, "Every year you grow, you will find me bigger."

2

The Extended Christ

JOHN 1:4, 5, 9–14

OUR SPIRITUAL GROWTH is inextricably bound up with the size of our vision of Christ. Once we get away from a one-dimensional or overly narrow picture of Christ, once we see the fullness and glory of Christ in the Scriptures, our lives will be enlarged. I believe most of us need a bigger vision of Christ. We need to see what John 1:1–3 reveals—that he is eternal, that there never was a time when Christ did not exist. We need to see that he was with God, was always coming together with God, always was God in every aspect. We need to see the drama of his being Creator:

> All things were made through him, and without him was not any thing made that was made. (John 1:3)
>
> Uphold[ing] the universe by the word of his power. (Hebrews 1:3)

The universe is held together by Jesus' word. He is the force that holds all things together—from the smallest atom to the greatest galaxy.

If believers were to recapture the greatness of Christ, it would make an enormous difference in this world. A progression takes place in our spiritual lives, for as we see the greatness of Christ, we grow stronger in him. As a result, we will see more of the greatness of Christ and will grow even more. Growth to greatness, greatness to growth—this is an ascending spiral that, according to Ephesians 3, never ends.

We know from our creeds and the teachings of Scripture that God did not create us because he was lonely. God was all sufficient in the Godhead. Rather, he created us for his glory. The Westminster Confession of Faith states, "The chief end of man is to glorify God and to enjoy him forever."

We were created for the glory of God. But I believe there is also another reason for our creation—his love. Love has to have an object. James points this out in 2:15, 16 when he says, "If a brother or sister is poorly clothed and lacking in daily food, and one of you says to them, 'Go in peace, be warmed and filled,' without giving them the things needed for the body, what good is that?" Love has to have an object, and God's love brought creation into being.

Some time ago I discovered from the Scriptures that God accomplished his creation to music. Job 38 gives us God's response when he was finally fed up with all the dialogue and rhetoric of Job and his "comforters" and spoke out of the whirlwind:

> Who is this that darkens counsel by words without knowledge?
> Dress for action like a man;
>   I will question you, and you make it known to me.
>
> Where were you when I laid the foundation of the earth?
>   Tell me, if you have understanding.
> Who determined its measurements—surely you know!
>   Or who stretched the line upon it?
> On what were its bases sunk,
>   or who laid its cornerstone,
> *when the morning stars sang together*
>   *and all the sons of God shouted for joy?* (vv. 2–7)

As God spoke the world and the universe into being, the angels exclaimed with joy, and the stars burst into song. Music surrounded the creation of God!

There is a beautiful passage describing the beginning of the world in the sixth book of the Chronicles of Narnia (*The Magician's Nephew*). Lewis describes Aslan as standing with his face to the sun. His coat is shining and radiant. His mouth is wide open in song, and as he sings, green begins to form around his feet and spread out into a pool. Then flowers and heather appear on the hillside and move out before him. As Aslan begins to sing a more lively song, showers of birds fly out of the trees, and butterflies begin to flit about. Then comes great celebration as the song breaks into even wilder song. This is not mere fantasy—the creation was in fact done to music!

The first few verses of John, speaking of Christ's preexistence and his glorious creation, are beautiful. Creation was a joyous event filled with celestial music. In Proverbs 8:30, 31 Wisdom, a Christ image, says: "Then I was beside him, like a master workman, and I was daily his delight, rejoicing before him always." Then she adds, "Rejoicing in his inhabited world and delighting in the children of man." The wonderful, joyful love of God was spread throughout creation.

But the joyous love found in the creation of our universe is just a shadow of the joy God finds in the spiritual creation of his people. Focusing on the greatness of Christ as the Light and on the vast, bottomless, shoreless sea of his love will fuel our praise and service.

Christ, the Light Revealed (vv. 4, 5a, 9)

Verses 4, 5 tell us: "In him was life, and the life was the light of men. The light shines in the darkness, and the darkness has not overcome it." Christ is "the light." The Scriptures teach that such light is not only spiritual. There is a physical attribute to it. Moses went up Mount Sinai in the midst of thunderings, smoke, lightning, and luminescence at the peak. In Exodus 33:18 Moses asks God to "show me your glory." After God put him in the cleft of a rock and put his hand over the cleft, his glory passed by. Moses was only able to see the back of God, the afterglow of God. The effect on Moses was so intense that his face became so bright that his people could not look upon him. He had been in contact with the physicalness of God's glory. The Apostle Paul says in 2 Corinthians 3:7, "The Israelites could not gaze at Moses' face because of its glory."

There were many Old Testament images of God's glory—the *Shekinah* glory, the cloud, the pillar of fire by night, glory settling on the tabernacle, entering Solomon's temple at its dedication, filling the whole place. And then there came Ezekiel's lament that the glory departed from Israel. How sad when it was gone. *Ichabod* was written across the house of God.

Then after four hundred years of darkness Peter, James, and John were taken up a high mountain with Jesus, where he was transfigured before them. "His face shone like the sun" (Matthew 17:2). His raiment was as white as wool. There is a physicalness to God's glory.

John, however, is not talking about Christ's physical light but his spiritual light. Verse 4 says, "In him was life, and the life was the light of men." Life-giving light seeks out a world lost in darkness. What a rich image of our Lord! Light journeying endlessly, seeking a place to illuminate, a way to bring warmth and light. Penetrating any crevice or opening, the smallest light will reveal an object's true nature. In World War II during the blackouts in London, on a clear night a lighted match could be seen for twenty miles from the air. Our Lord is a light shining in the darkness. John says, "The light shines in the darkness" (v. 5), and the result is seen in verse 9: "The true light, which gives light to everyone, was coming into the world." Not only does the light shine in darkness—it enlightens every man. There is not a single person who has not been enlightened by that light!

Paul, in the first chapter of Romans, tells us that light's enlightenment is extensive, but men hold it down and suppress it. He says in verse 20, "they are without excuse." Some say God sheds this light just so he can hold mankind accountable. But there is another reason: love. "The light shines in the darkness." "Shines" in verse 5 is literally "shines on" or "continually shines." This is an image of our Lord shining upon every crevice of man's darkened heart, trying to reach into his being. If we have come to Christ, we have come not only because of his greatness in creation, but because of the greatness of his love.

Christ, the Light Rejected (vv. 5b, 10, 11)

How was the Lord's love received? Notice the last part of verse 5: "And the darkness has not overcome it." Some translations render this, "The darkness could never extinguish it." The light of Christ came into the world, and darkness pounced upon the light and tried to strangle it.

Verse 10 adds, "He was in the world, and the world was made through him, yet the world did not know him." That statement sounds absurd, but how man responded to Christ *is* absurd. John could have said, "He made their mouths. He held their tongues together by the very word of his power. But they refused to acknowledge him." Jesus was in the world that he created, and it did not even know who he was. Then John states the ultimate indignity in verse 11: "He came to his own, and his own people did not receive him."

A poor family was farming some land during the Depression. There was one son in this family, and his parents wanted the best for him. So they scrimped and saved so they could send him to college. After he had been gone for a year or so, his parents, who loved him very much, wanted to see him again. Again they saved, sold some things, and went to visit their son. They arrived on campus, poorly dressed in their farm clothes. Seeing their son with some other boys, the father ran over to him. "Son, son, it's your father," he said. The son looked at his father without showing any sign of recognition. The father said again, "Son, it's your father and mother. We've come to see you." The boy, perhaps embarrassed by his parents' poverty, turned to the other students and said, "I don't know who this is. He must be crazy." How absurd, how horrible.

But how much more incredible is the truth of verse 11: "He came to his own, and his own people did not receive him." He was rejected by those who would have been incinerated had he not veiled his glory in flesh. He was rejected by those whom he spoke into existence with his word, those for whom for thousands of years he had been preparing the way. His own people rejected him. Incredible! It is even more amazing that after two thousand years of the Spirit's witness in history and in the lives of godly men, people still reject him today.

What is most amazing is Christ's love, a bottomless sea of love that overflows to us. We need to see the greatness of Christ and the greatness of his love as he extends himself to us.

Christ, the Light Received (v. 12)

Not everyone rejected Christ. Some responded, and the result is astounding: "To all who did receive him, who believed in his name, he gave the right to become children of God" (v. 12). That statement is incredible. It is incomprehensible that God, the Creator of all things, the One who upholds all things by the word of his power, should enable me, one who has rejected him, to become his child. We need to hold this New Testament teaching close to our heart at all costs. We need to marvel not only at the greatness of Christ but at the absurdity of his love to us.

Being God's "children" (v. 12) means we can call God Father. More specifically, we can address him as "*Abba*, Father" or "dearest Father." We can call God, if we do not say it flippantly, Daddy. That is what my children called me long ago when they toddled to the front door and I took them in my arms. It is what they called me when they were hurting. It is the word my girls used when they wanted something from me. Calling God Daddy is a precious privilege. And before Jesus came, it just was not possible.

In the Old Testament God is called Father, in reference to Israel, fourteen times. Only one or two of those refer to intimacy. However, Paul, in Galatians 4:6, says: "And because you are sons, God has sent the Spirit of his Son into our hearts, crying, '*Abba*! Father!'" That cry is implanted in our hearts. When things are not quite right and I cannot sleep, I find myself repeating this great truth over and over and over again and finding comfort in it. Men are sometimes independent and macho, but they need to avail themselves of the precious, blessed fact that God is their Father. We all do.

Are you lonely? Insecure? Are you without God and Christ in this world? God says, "I, the light, have extended myself and my love from all eternity, and I am speaking to you through your conscience, through nature, and through the revelation of the cross. Will you respond?"

God has made everything so simple. Verse 12 is framed by two phrases: "But to all who did receive him" and "who believed in his name." All we have to do is believe. Jesus' "name" stands for all that he is. He is the eternal Christ who became incarnate flesh (v. 14) and so displayed God (v. 18). He is the One in whom we must believe in order to receive him. Once we ask Christ into our life, we can cry in our heart, "*Abba*, Father, I have come home."

Christ the Light—this is a love story from beginning to end. Zephaniah 3:17 tells us:

> The LORD your God is in your midst,
>   a mighty one who will save;
> he will rejoice over you with gladness;
>   he will quiet you by his love;
> he will exult over you with loud singing.

When God is pleased with his people, he sings over them. Has God sung over you lately? Has Christ? They want to.

Christ is the Light—the extended Light who shines on, trying to penetrate our conscience, our moral convictions, revealing himself in the stars, in the leaves, in the change of seasons. On one hand there is the greatness of Christ, which is far beyond any comprehension. Ten octillion stars are in the universe, and he knows them by name and holds them together. But he is also the Light who desires to penetrate human hearts.

3

The Greatness of the Good News

JOHN 1:12, 13

JOHN'S PROLOGUE presents the greatness of Christ and the greatness of the love of Christ, but also the greatness of the gospel.

In the spring of 1966 I was youth pastor in a large church in Southern California. Each year during Easter break we would minister to the scores of high schoolers and collegians who flocked to the beaches. However, in 1966 we decided to go to the Colorado River instead. So we got our camping gear together, recruited about twenty high schoolers, and set off.

What a sight when we got to our destination—Parker, Arizona. The Colorado River from Parker to the dam was packed with people getting as much sun as they could. We looked for a safe place to camp and thought one particular place looked very good. It was not. Later we found out alcohol was sold more cheaply there than anywhere else along the river. We had quite a week as we attempted to love the students and share our faith. And something especially beautiful happened that week. Five high school boys camped next to us. They lived about thirty miles from us in Southern California. Those boys had a great time that week, joking with us and drinking themselves into oblivion. Late in the week they ran out of money, so they ate with us. One meal I will never forget. It was Thursday night of Easter week. One of the boys had brought along his bottle, and he was drinking. He said to us, "You know, I think maybe you people are for real." That remark precipitated some serious conversation that evening. The next day, sitting on a boat trailer with all the boats roaring by, all five of those boys made a serious move toward Christ.

After the week was over, we all returned to Southern California. I convinced the boys to come to church, and they were as outrageous as they could possibly be. Because they lived thirty miles away, I did not see too much of them, even though I tried to keep in contact. A year later one of the boys got in trouble with the law. At any rate, we started a Bible study where they lived, and they all came. One by one they began to commit their lives to Christ. But there is more to the story. As long as we lived in California, every Christmas we would have a second Christmas at our home on December 26, and four of these fellows would come to our house with their wives. One became assistant to the dean at Biola College. Another replaced me as youth pastor at the church I had served for ten years. Another had a ministry at a Christian counseling center in that area. Another went to Capernwray Bible School and became an elder in a fellowship in the Long Beach area. All four men went on to actively serve Christ. All four became good, Christian husbands. Christ's gospel is indeed a great gospel!

The Greatness of Its Power

I am not ashamed of the gospel, for it is the power of God for salvation to everyone who believes, to the Jew first and also to the Greek. (Romans 1:16)

The word that Paul uses in that verse is the Greek word from which we get our English word *dynamite*. "I am not ashamed of the explosive power of the gospel." The gospel should permeate all of our thinking. Next to the cardinal pursuits of loving God and wanting to glorify him, the conviction of the power of the gospel to change lives ought to be the driving motivation of our lives. Take that away and Christian ministry would be like a stale glass of ginger ale. The gospel brings life!

One night a man stopped by our house for some business. He knew I was a pastor, and from what I could tell he was not a believer. But he turned the conversation around to spiritual matters. For an hour and a half we talked about who Jesus Christ is. Trying to avoid typical Christian verbiage, Barbara and I attempted to cut through everything else and talk about Christ. During the evening one of my daughters had brought chocolate-chip cookies to us. Our visitor made a big deal about them, saying they were his favorite cookies. After we had finished our conversation, when he went to get his coat, he put his hand in his pocket and pulled out a big bag of chocolate-chip cookies. The most significant thing that happened that evening was an act of kindness from my daughter. In any and all relationships, the smallest kindness, the gentlest word, a bag of cookies given in the name of Jesus—all have the potential of helping someone accept the gospel.

And how potent is that gospel! It is like the core of a nuclear reactor. When it is let loose with all of its power and creativity, you never know what it will do. Unfortunately, *gospel*, even in Christian circles, is often used in a pejorative sense. When we hear the word, we think of an out-of-tune piano and one more verse of "Just As I Am." We forget all about its power. We forget that when it is rightly loosed and rightly used, it is the supreme social force, as history has shown again and again. John 1:12, 13 and its context vibrates with a pulsating picture of the cosmic Christ who upholds all things by the word of his power and bombards our lives with his light through our consciences, nature, the witness of the saints, and the witness of the cross.

"But to all who did receive him, who believed in his name, he gave the right to become children of God" (v. 12). Astounding! The apostle John, the same man who composed this prologue, wrote 1 John at the end of his life. He says there: "See what kind of love the Father has given to us, that we should be called children of God; and so we are" (3:1). It was as if he were saying, "I can't believe it! We are children of God!" We say with those in *Fiddler on the Roof*, "Wonder of wonders! Miracle of miracles!" What is most amazing is that Christ was not obligated to bring us into the family of God. God did not have to adopt us. But because he loved us, he made us his children. Wonder of wonders!

John Bunyan, in his last sermon, preached on John 1:12.

> You that are called born of God, and Christians, if you be not criers, there is no spiritual life in you; if you be born of God, you are crying ones; as soon as he has raised you out of the dark dungeon of sin, you cannot but cry to God.

What do we cry? "Dear Father, *Abba*, Father." The power of the gospel makes us children of God!

Because of the power of the gospel, we not only become children of God but in one sense take on the nature of God. When families sit together at church, I often notice a family resemblance. Second Peter 1:4 says:

> He has granted to us his precious and very great promises, so that through them you may become partakers of the divine nature.

And we have done just that, through Christ. The love of God has been shed abroad in our hearts. When we came to know Christ, the wisdom of God came into our lives. We began to understand things we never understood before. Holiness began to develop in our lives. The same thing was true with my friends at the Colorado River. They became criers. *"Abba*, Father!" became their heart shout. The divine nature was imparted to them. Their lives were changed. "I am not ashamed of the gospel, for it is the power of God for salvation to everyone who believes." The key is not only to live in the greatness of Christ and his love but to possess the greatness of his gospel. That is the dynamic that brings effervescence to life. When you realize that Christ's love can radically change a life, life really becomes exciting!

The Greatness of Its Simplicity

The greatness of the good news comes not only from its power, but also from its simplicity. I am glad that when I met those high schoolers in 1966 I did not come with a system of spiritual perfection. You know what I mean: "If you will just join up and do this, we can help you climb the ladder. One day you can ascend and be God yourself." That is not good news. That is bad news! The true gospel is simple. In the thirteenth verse John makes this clear, saying that we are "born, not of blood nor of the will of the flesh." John was literally referring to what happens within the womb, to physical relationships. That is not the way to become a child of God. A person may able to trace his genealogy back to James, the brother of our Lord, through St. Augustine, to Martin Luther, then up to John Wesley and Charles Spurgeon, but that will not save him. Spiritual life does not come through "the will of the flesh," physical desire, or some procreative process. John adds that salvation does not come by "the will of man." It is not the result of determination or willpower. Jonathan Livingston Seagull may get to be president of IBM. The little choo-choo may finally get his load up the hill by saying, "I think I can, I think I can." You can accomplish a lot that way, but not eternal life.

True, there is a place for discipline in the Christian life, but John knows man's potential for creative volitional structures and building ladders for spiritual attainment, and he says spiritual life cannot be achieved in that way. The simplicity of the gospel is seen in the last three words of verse 13: "But of God." Salvation is all of God. James 1:18 says, "He brought us forth by the word of truth." And Ephesians 2:8, 9 says, "For by grace you have been saved through faith. And this is not your own doing; it is the gift of God, not a result of works, so that no one may boast."

Often the simplest concepts are the most profound. Look at the phrase, "To all . . . who believed in his name." "Name" here is the name of Christ, the cosmic name that vibrates throughout this passage. This name calls us to repentance because we see Christ in all his greatness. We see ourselves and all our sin. When we believe in the name of Christ, we receive him into our lives. The greatness of the gospel can be seen, first of all, in its power and, second, in its simplicity.

The Greatness of Its Benefits

Third, we can see the greatness of the gospel in its benefits. Remember John's abiding wonder at what Christ did:

> See what kind of love the Father has given to us, that we should be called children of God; and so we are. (1 John 3:1)

Now look at the next verse:

> Beloved, we are God's children now, and what we will be has not yet appeared; but we know that when he appears we shall be like him, because we shall see him as he is. (1 John 3:2)

In other words, when we see him, we are going to be like him! That is the outgrowth of being children of God. Because we are children of God, we are going to be like him spiritually—delivered from our sin, perfect in love and holiness, growing in our knowledge of him. But even more than that, we will be like him in glory. In Old Testament times God's glorious luminescence shone forth like the sun. And in Matthew 13:43 Jesus says, "Then the righteous will shine like the sun in the kingdom of their Father. He who has ears, let him hear." One day we are going to shine like the sun as we partake of his luminescence. We will be glorious beings!

We are again reminded of C. S. Lewis's great words:

> It is a serious thing to live in a society of possible gods and goddesses, to remember that the dullest and most uninteresting person you talk to may one day be a creature which, if you saw it now, you would be strongly tempted to worship, or else a horror and a corruption such as you now meet, if at all, only in a nightmare. All day long we are, in some degree, helping each other to one or other of these destinations. It is in the light of these overwhelming possibilities, it is with the awe and the circumspection proper to them, that we should conduct all our dealings with one another, all friendships, all loves, all play, all politics. There are no *ordinary* people. You have never talked to a mere mortal. Nations, culture, arts, civilization—these are mortal, and their life is to ours as the life of a gnat. But it is immortals whom we joke with, work with, marry, snub, and exploit—immortal horrors or everlasting splendours.[1]

The gospel can turn the dullest person into an immortal, glorious being beyond description or imagination.

Conclusion

I think about my young friends mentioned earlier. If their lives had not been changed, diverted from involvement in narcotics and the sensuality of the time, if they had remained without Christ, what a terrible tragedy that would have been—for themselves and for their families and society. Today those men have four good marriages, and their children are growing up in the shadow of the gospel.

Even their parents have been influenced. One of the boys, Tom Lighthight, was burdened for his father. Tom called his father Big Jim, not because he was tall, but because he was an intimidating, almost terrifying personality. He was a powerful, hard-driving, self-sufficient man. His father was one of the founders and architects of the Southern California Edison Company. Big Jim at age sixty-three had spent forty years as an executive with that company. He was also the scourge of the city council of Long Beach. I remember Tom saying that if his dad could become a Christian, anybody could!

As Tom grew in grace, his witness at home became more and more profound. After a time his mother professed Christ. Eventually Tom asked me to share Christ with his father. I remember that hot summer evening. Big Jim was sitting in a chair, wearing a silly hat. We talked for a couple of hours. Finally Jim said to me, "Pastor, I am no _____ good, but if Christ will have me, I want him." Tears were running down his face. Big Jim honestly and repentantly asked Christ into his life. He gave way to the power of the gospel.

After that Jim started coming to church, and he was rough around the edges. After church, no matter who was standing around, if Jim liked the sermon, he would shake my hand and say, "Pastor, that was a _____ of a sermon!" But he became involved in our church. For a time he drove thirty miles from his home almost every day because we were putting up a new sanctuary, and he was an expert in electricity. He had been fired from his job with the Edison Company, so he could be out there all the time. His help saved us thousands of dollars. My favorite picture of Jim is of him wearing his cutoffs and a silly hat, sitting in the dirt. He was sunburned and peeling and having the time of his life. I remember saying to him, "Jim, you have to stop working so hard." He would reply, "I can't. I owe the church my life!" After we finally finished the sanctuary, the chief elder and I, with our wives, decided to take him out to dinner. As we went to telephone Jim to invite him, we received another call telling us Big Jim had passed away in his living room, sitting in the same chair in which he had received Christ. His funeral was not a funeral—it was a coronation!

> I am not ashamed of the gospel, for it is the power of God for salvation to everyone who believes. (Romans 1:16)

Do you believe in the cosmic Christ incarnate? If not, will you receive him now?

4

The Greatness of Grace

JOHN 1:14, 16, 17

THOSE WHO HAVE READ C. S. Lewis's science fiction novel *Perelandra* have been amused and enlightened by the author's fantastic re-creation of a new world. This world had a great golden canopy. Underneath it was an emerald sea, and floating on the sea were pink islands. A person had to get his sea legs to walk on them. Foresting the island were bubble trees, and as one walked under the bubbles, they would burst, providing indescribable refreshment. Also on the planet were interesting animals—porpoises one could ride and little dragons with red and green scales who liked to have their white tummies scratched. Lewis's world is inviting and entertaining. It is also very instructive, giving us an idea of what our world was like before the fall. Lewis helps us understand the great tragedy that took place when Adam and Eve sinned.

If we were to read the first chapter of Genesis for the first time, we would undoubtedly find it just as fantastic as Lewis's world. There we read, "God saw everything that he had made, and behold, it was very good" (Genesis 1:31). What God had created was perfect. God's creatures made to fly in the air were good. The universe all around was good. The earth was good. The animals on the earth were good. His creation was perfect, and that includes our original mother and father. Adam and Eve were perfect. They were the prototype of man and woman. They stood as king and queen over all creation—perfect in health, unfallen.

Along with the physical perfection there was social perfection. The early chapters of Genesis tell us that Eve was taken out of Adam's side, that she was "bone of my bones and flesh of my flesh" (Genesis 2:23). That denotes intimacy. Adam and Eve had no sins to come between them, no complexes, no social hang-ups. The relationship our original mother and father had was a perfect relationship. Not only that, but they walked with God. Their perfect social relationship was paralleled by their upward spiritual relationship. Adam and Eve walked unclothed, innocent before God. This is an inviting, beautiful picture. All of us long for what Adam and Eve had and represent. We long for restoration from sin. We know too well the effects of the fall. Given what Adam said, "The woman whom you gave to be with me, she gave me fruit of the tree," we know that Adam and Eve did not have 930 years of conjugal bliss (Genesis 3:12). We know Adam's relationship with God went downhill as well. After having that refreshing relationship with God, Adam could never quite get enough air as he went through life. And ultimately, because of the fall, death came. We must not minimize the tremendous drama and implications of what happened in the garden.

We learn a great deal about sin in Genesis 3, and we learn much about grace in the first chapter of John. Grace, God reaching out to us in our sin, is best understood when we contrast it with the dark tableau of the garden. It is tremendously important to understand grace since it is the pipeline through which we receive all of God's tremendous benefits—the greatness of Christ, the greatness of his love, the greatness of the gospel. Grace is an ennobled New Testament revelation.

John introduces the subject in verse 14:

> And the Word became flesh and dwelt among us, and we have seen his glory, glory as of the only Son from the Father, full of grace and truth.

John is saying, "We had a glimpse of his grace and his truth, and in it we saw the glory of God." John saw the glory of God when Christ was transfigured, but he is not referring to that here. John saw grace and truth revealed in the glory of Christ's *incarnation*. John's enthusiastic observation gives us an image of grace that is very inviting.

Overflowing Grace (vv. 14b, 16a)

Notice verse 16: "For from his fullness we have all received, grace upon grace." John suggests here a fountain brimming over with grace, a spiritual reality. Colossians 2:9 tells us how this can be so: "For in him the whole fullness of deity dwells bodily." Paul is saying that in the humanity of Christ dwelt all the fullness of the Holy Trinity. This is not a theological deduction. It is a statement of fact. It may be incomprehensible, but all God's "fullness" dwelt in Jesus. Colossians 2:9 throbs with the energy, the power, and the reality of our Lord's humanity plus all the fullness of deity.

Colossians 2:9 is a thrilling verse because, when related to grace, it associates God's presence with his love. Grace is God's love coming to sinners. It is God's ultimate love communicated to us in Christ. Christ overflows with grace. We need to hold that truth before us as reality. It is not something just to discuss, not a mere theological nicety, but truth. Christ wants to overflow in the lives of those who do not know him. Likewise he wants believers continually to overflow with his love and grace.

When grace is poured out, it is more than adequate. Notice verse 16 again: "For from his fullness we have all received, grace upon grace." In other words, when we received grace, we were given all we would need. Grace is abundantly adequate. In the seventeenth century a young boy was born into a Christian home. For the first six years of his life, he heard the truths of the gospel and was dearly loved. Sadly, though, his parents died. The orphan boy went to live with his relatives and was maltreated, abused, and ridiculed for his interest in Christ. The orphan couldn't tolerate that situation and, though still a boy, fled and joined the Royal Navy. In the Navy the boy's life went downhill. He became known as a brawler, was whipped many times, and participated in the keelhauling of some of his comrades. Finally, while he was still young, he deserted the Royal Navy and fled to Africa, where he attached himself to a Portuguese slave trader.

There his life reached its lowest point. There were times when he actually ate off the floor on his hands and knees. He escaped, then became attached to another slave trader as the first mate on his ship. But the young man's pattern of life had become desperately depraved. He stole the ship's whiskey and got so drunk that he fell overboard. He was close to drowning when one of his shipmates harpooned him and brought him back on board. As a result, the young man had a huge scar in his side for the rest of his life. He could not get much lower. Finally, in the midst of a great storm off the coast of Scotland, after days and days of pumping water out of the boat, the young man began to reflect on verses he had heard as a boy and was marvelously converted. The new life he found is reflected in these famous words:

> Amazing grace—how sweet the sound
> That saved a wretch like me!
> I once was lost but now am found;
> Was blind but now I see.

This young man, John Newton, became one of the great preachers of the seventeenth century—all because of the amazing grace of God.

In the first chapter of his Gospel, the apostle John is talking about the amazing sufficiency of God's grace. No one is beyond the power of God's grace, even if he or she thinks he or she is. The Scriptures proclaim that Christ died for the ungodly. "Where sin increased, grace abounded all the more" (Romans 5:20). The Greek word used is the same used for "fullness" in John 1. God's grace is adequate for anyone.

Grace is one of the precious words of our faith. The word originally meant charm and beauty, and, scholars tell us that throughout all its shades of meaning, grace maintains that basic idea. Grace is not only sufficient for salvation; it brings beauty to life. And when grace enters our lives, death flees. Remember the words of D. L. Moody: "You may read in the paper one day that D. L. Moody is dead, but don't you believe it." The body dies, but the soul lives on.

When grace enters our lives, we are again able to breathe as we were created to breathe. And our social relationships will show the difference. John Newton was known for his godly marriage. That is remarkable considering the sin, the philandering, the wandering, the sensuality he had earlier experienced. When the grace of God entered his life and he matured in Christ, he enjoyed a marriage that was an example to all. In fact, it was one of the greatest aspects of his ministry. When we experience grace, we begin to enjoy the restoration of what our life should have been like.

Grace also brings physical changes. We often forget that our physical existence is meant to be immortal. When we die our bodies begin dissolving in the ground, but they will be resurrected one day. They will be gloriously transformed into something far beyond our imagination, and they will be immortal. In this world we only enjoy partially what sin has ruined. In Colossians 2:10 (NASB) we read, "And in Him you have been made complete" or full, referring to the fullness of Christ. When the grace of God enters our lives and we allow it to become transcendent, our lives become rich and overflowing. We enjoy the creation about us and those closest to us. We begin to live as we are supposed to live. Part of the discarded image of God begins to be restored in our lives.

Acts 4 says there was "great power" and "great grace" (v. 33) in the early church. Then the passage describes grace's effect upon the church. First of all, the early believers began to give. When grace flows into one's life, grace also begins to flow out. Furthermore, those early believers began to exercise their spiritual gifts, to reach the potential God had given them. Take Barnabas, for example. His name means "son of encouragement," and his life showed it. Grace is not just for salvation. It is an overflowing fountain that brings richness to *all* of life.

Again, John 1:16 says, "From his fullness we have all received, grace upon grace." Literally, John is saying, "Grace instead of grace." As the grace you receive flows out to others, more grace will come, and then more grace, and then even more grace. Some translations say, "Grace following grace," or "grace heaped up upon grace," all trying to convey the idea that grace keeps flowing over and over. When John said, "From his fullness we have all received [grace]," he was not merely making an observation but was speaking of his own experience. That has been our experience too. Martin Luther said:

> This spring is inexhaustible, it is full of grace and truth from God, it never loses anything, no matter how much we draw, but remains an infinite fountain of all grace and truth; the more you draw from it, the more abundantly it gives of the water that springs into eternal life. Just as the sun is not darkened by the whole world enjoying its light, and could, indeed, light up ten worlds; just as 100,000 lights might be lit from one light and not detract from it; just as a learned man is able to make a thousand others learned, and the more he gives, the more he has—so is Christ, our Lord, an infinite source of all grace, so that if the whole world would draw enough grace and truth from it to make the world all angels, yet it would not lose a drop; the fountain always runs over, full of grace.

Life is continual growth. The more grace we appropriate, the more grace we receive. And the more we do with that grace, the more we receive. Only through God's grace can we reach our potential. That is what John was talking about.

Overflowing Truth (vv. 14b, 17b)

At the end of verse 14 John mentions "grace and truth," and again at the end of verse 17. Much could be said about truth. Suffice it to say, however, that when grace comes, so does God's revelation of spiritual truth, and we begin to see things as they are. A little girl had a terrific fight with her brother. When her mother came in, the mother asked, "Why did you let the devil put it in your heart to pull your brother's hair and kick him in the shins?" The little girl thought for a moment and said, "Well, maybe the devil put it into my head to pull my brother's hair, but kicking his shins was my own idea." She had better theology than her mother. We begin to see things as they are when we through grace begin to understand ourselves, life, God, and salvation. The overflowing fountain of grace is a marvelous gift.

This "grace and truth" have ultimate consequences. For one thing, one day you and I will be physically perfect. According to the New Testament, we will have bodies that will not get tired. They will be more capable of enjoying whatever God has in store for us. As my son once said, those bodies will be "better than bionic." Socially all our relationships with one another will be clear eyed and continually face-to-face. We will be able to sit down and talk for fifty thousand years. I have the first fifty thousand reserved to spend with my wife—and that will not be enough.

Revelation picks up on the theme begun in Genesis and creates a striking contrast. Revelation 22:2 says, "On either side of the river [stood] the tree of life." There was a curse in the garden, but in Heaven there is no curse (Revelation 22:3). Adam and Eve merely walked with God, but in Heaven we will see the very face of God. These are the Alps of ultimate revelation. Alexander Peden, the old Puritan said, "Grace is young glory." "No eye has seen, nor ear heard, nor the heart of man imagined, what God has prepared for those who love him" (1 Corinthians 2:9). By ourselves we can have no conception of these things, but the Spirit has revealed them to us. Through Christ's grace we can see what will be. Our destiny, our possession, is the result of grace.

But grace is not only future—it is active now. If we bump a pitcher just a little, its contents will pour out. All who sincerely come to Jesus, whether for the first time for salvation or the millionth time for strength or nourishment, find all they need. This is amazing grace. "Though he was rich, yet for your sake he became poor, so that you by his poverty might become rich" (2 Corinthians 8:9). If we just say, "God, I want that grace. I want to yield to you. I want to turn around and throw myself completely on you," the pitcher will be poured out upon our lives.

Christians revel in verse 16: "For from his fullness we have all received, grace upon grace." Grace just keeps coming, but I doubt if any of us have as much grace as God intended. Why is this? Have we been defrauding ourselves, saying that "his fullness" is for a certain type of Christian but not for us? Scripture says we have "*all*" received "from his fullness." It is simply a matter of receiving grace upon grace upon grace, allowing God to put it to work within us. But at the same time receiving grace is not a matter of just lying there and saying, "Overflow me with your grace." We have to take hold of grace and believe that we will receive the promised abundance of divine favor and provision.

May we learn to receive grace upon grace, so our lives will become richer and more beautiful and more joyful through grace! May we be people who receive grace upon grace and who then give out grace upon grace in response to the effects of sin, misery, and horror in this world! God wants us to be filled with all his fullness and to possess it. Grace is ours. May God help us to appropriate this power!

5

The Essentials of Witness

JOHN 1:19–37

JOHN NOW ENDS his great prologue with its intense concentration of theological truth and begins to focus on the witness of John the Baptist.

We know from the other Gospels that John the Baptist had remarkable parents, Zechariah and Elizabeth, both of the tribe of Levi. They were elderly and childless. One day Zechariah was in Jerusalem because by lot it was his turn to perform his priestly duties, including the service of offering incense, considered the most sacred of all the priestly duties. On this fated day Zechariah had come to the temple of Herod and was ministering in the Holy Place where the table of incense stood. As he reverently performed his duties according to the instruction Jehovah had given to Moses, moving about the softly lit room, joy unspeakable filled his heart. It was a great day for Zechariah!

But in the midst of Zechariah's quiet worship, the angel Gabriel suddenly appeared in the sacred place and spoke to the old priest. Surely at that moment Zechariah was too stunned to comprehend the magnitude of what was happening. But later as he thought on these things he recalled that it had been *four hundred years* since the last angelic appearance. But now the angel Gabriel, one of the archangels, revealed himself to this humble priest.

That would have been enough in itself, but then Gabriel spoke. Even more remarkable were his words: "Your wife Elizabeth will bear you a son, and you shall call his name John . . . he will be great before the Lord . . . he will be filled with the Holy Spirit, even from his mother's womb. And he will turn many of the children of Israel to the Lord their God, and he will go before him in the spirit and power of Elijah" (Luke 1:13–17).

The records reveal that because Zechariah did not believe Gabriel's words, he was struck mute. A stunned man left the temple that day!

But that was not the end of the story, for we read later of a wonderful meeting between Elizabeth and her cousin Mary, the mother of our Lord, a meeting that overflowed in spontaneous joy. Elizabeth was in the fifth month of her pregnancy when Gabriel revealed himself to Mary also and told her, "You will conceive in your womb and bear a son, and you shall call his name Jesus" (Luke 1:31). When these two women met, Elizabeth said:

> Blessed are you among women, and blessed is the fruit of your womb! And why is this granted to me that the mother of my Lord should come to me? For behold, when the sound of your greeting came to my ears, the baby in my womb leaped for joy. (Luke 1:42–44)

Then Mary sang her beautiful *Magnificat*: "My soul magnifies the Lord. . . ." Mary praised the Lord, God her Savior, for his might, his holiness, his mercy. Of course, the story does not end there. John the Baptist was born, and as he was being circumcised, Zechariah wrote that his name was to be John. At that moment the old man's tongue was loosed, and he sang the *Benedictus*, that great blessing that includes the words:

> And you, child, will be called the prophet of the Most High;
>   for you will go before the Lord to prepare his ways,
> to give knowledge of salvation to his people
>   in the forgiveness of their sins." (Luke 1:76, 77)

There never has been anyone like John the Baptist! As he matured, he grew into his role as a prophet. He wore a camel-hair coat, fed on the wild honey and locusts of the land, and spent much time with God. He was a great man of God!

Finally, he burst on the scene as the supreme witness of all of history, for he knew who Jesus Christ was. While his life does not reveal everything about witnessing for Jesus Christ, it does give us the essentials.

The world in John the Baptist's day was in tremendous confusion. In John 1, John had been preaching for over a year. His ministry had thrown the Palestinian world into convulsions. Large multitudes, according to the Gospels, had come to hear him and be baptized. Matthew says that even Herod sought him and almost believed.

Just six weeks earlier John had been visited by Jesus. The prophet had first refused to baptize him but then deferred to Jesus' request. As he baptized Jesus, he saw the Holy Spirit come upon our Lord and heard God's words, "This is my beloved Son" (Matthew 3:17). So John's world was really whirling! It had only taken forty days to get the whirlpool going. The Lord had been in the wilderness. John had been ministering. Now the religious leaders in Jerusalem sent a delegation, sort of like a congressional fact-finding committee with religious and political motivations. They wanted to know who John was and what was going on.

The Messenger (vv. 19–28)

> And this is the testimony of John, when the Jews sent priests and Levites from Jerusalem to ask him, "Who are you?" He confessed, and did not deny, but confessed, "I am not the Christ." (vv.19, 20)

John knew exactly what they wanted to know because others had already been conjecturing about whether he was the Christ. He answered them formally and carefully (notice it says "confessed" twice in verse 20): "I am not the Christ." If John had said he was the Christ, thousands would have unfurled the banners of the Maccabeans, and the whole world would have been tossed into war. But he readily admitted he was not Christ.

So they asked him, "What then? Are you Elijah?" (v. 21). That was a fair question. After all, he looked like Elijah, and he came in the spirit and power of Elijah, and the Jews expected Elijah to come again. In fact, the final words of the Old Testament (see Malachi 4:5, 6) say Elijah will come again before the day of the Lord. But again John answered, "I am not."

Again they questioned him. "Are you the Prophet?" They were thinking about the one of whom Moses prophesied in Deuteronomy 18:15, 18: "The LORD your God will raise up for you a prophet like me." But John said, "No." He was very explicit in each denial.

Verse 22 goes on, "So they said to him, 'Who are you? We need to give an answer to those who sent us. What do you say about yourself?'" John's answer in verses 23–27 reveals what is of primary importance in the matter of witnessing. First, verse 23, he said, "I am the voice." He did not say, "I am the Word." He reached back seven hundred years to the words prophesied in Isaiah 40 (vv. 3–5) and said, "I am just a voice." He was not the substance but just the communicator. Borrowing the imagery from that Old Testament passage, he was saying, "I am merely a workman making a road for the Messiah." He moved the emphasis away from himself. Similarly, look at verses 26, 27: "Among you stands one you do not know, even he who comes after me, the strap of whose sandal I am not worthy to untie." He turned the conversation away from himself and pointed to Jesus Christ. Not only that, he claimed for Jesus a place so exalted that ordinary people like himself were unworthy to perform a task relegated to the lowest slave.

What humility! Yet Jesus said about John, "Truly, I say to you, among those born of women there has arisen no one greater than John the Baptist" (Matthew 11:11). Of all who ever lived, including Moses and Abraham, John the Baptist was the greatest of mortals.

The Scriptures tell us much about John's spiritual commitment. He was a Nazirite from the time he was born. In accordance with that vow, he never cut his hair, he never touched a dead body, he never drank the fruit of the vine. He lived a pure, physically uncontaminated life. He was filled with the Holy Spirit even before birth. His mother was likewise a Nazirite before his birth. John was the greatest of all men. If there was ever a man who had the temptation, especially as he saw Jesus' rising popularity, to exalt himself, John was that man. He could have talked about his miraculous birth or how it felt to live a solitary life of self-denial in the wilderness. He could have held forth on survival tactics in the wilderness or perhaps his grasshopper diet. He could have discussed his devotional regimen or published a manual of discipline for those who wanted to follow God. He faced great temptation, but to his everlasting credit, he would have none of it. In fact he said later, "He must increase, but I must decrease" (3:30). A witness never obtrudes himself into the picture of the one of whom he is witnessing. John was an excellent witness.

A seminary classmate of mine once shared a story with me about how he, then the pastor of a very large church, had been asked to lead a sunrise service at the Hollywood Bowl. That was a great honor. When he met with the planning committee, they asked him, "Where can the helicopter pick you up?" He answered that he did not think there was room in his neighborhood for a helicopter to land. They said, "The man we had last year had to have a helicopter." My classmate, however, said he would not need a helicopter. Then they offered a police escort. My friend could only imagine flashing lights and motorcycles in front of his house at 3 o'clock in the morning to escort his Volvo to the Hollywood Bowl! He turned down their transportation offers. When he arrived at the Bowl to prepare for the service, he noticed another participant dressed in a T-shirt and Levis. My friend's first thought was, "Well, if that's how he wants to relate to the people, that's fine." But before that man stepped onto the platform, he donned a robe that would make Home Shopping Network addicts green with envy!

All such behavior is completely removed from the pattern John the Baptist set. "He must increase, but I must decrease." The Apostle Paul, following in John's steps, wrote, "This is how one should regard us, as servants of Christ" (1 Corinthians 4:1). We should regard ourselves as servants, rowers in the galley. Paul set this truth down for all time in 2 Corinthians 4:5: "For what we proclaim is not ourselves, but Jesus Christ as Lord." The servant of Christ does not exalt himself.

One evening the great conductor Arturo Toscanini conducted Beethoven's *Ninth Symphony*. It was a brilliant performance, at the end of which the audience went absolutely wild! They clapped, whistled, and stamped their feet, absolutely caught up in the greatness of that performance. As Toscanini stood there, he bowed and bowed and bowed, then acknowledged his orchestra. When the ovation finally began to subside, Toscanini turned and looked intently at his musicians. He was almost out of control as he whispered, "Gentlemen! Gentlemen!" The orchestra leaned forward to listen. In a fiercely enunciated whisper Toscanini said, "Gentlemen, I am nothing." That was an extraordinary admission since Toscanini was blessed with an enormous ego. He added, "Gentlemen, you are nothing." They had heard that same message before the rehearsal. "But Beethoven," said Toscanini in a tone of adoration, "is everything, everything, everything!" This is the attitude we need toward ourselves and toward the Lord Jesus Christ. I am nothing, you are nothing, but he is everything! That was John's attitude, and it is the attitude of every authentic messenger of Christ.

The Message (vv. 29–37)
What was John's message?

> The next day he saw Jesus coming toward him, and said, "Behold, the Lamb of God, who takes away the sin of the world!" (v. 29)

In one sentence we have the essence of the Christian message. It is difficult for Western ears to appreciate the power of John's announcement, but these words brought an avalanche of meaning to the Jews' minds. A few years ago, while I was on a speaking engagement in San Diego, I decided to visit the Timkin Art Museum. I had heard they had an El Greco painting of *St. Peter Holding the Keys to the Kingdom*. I paid my money, walked into the museum, found the painting, and looked at the El Greco in admiration. Then I turned around. On the opposite wall was a small, walnut-colored painting—very ancient—1525. As I looked closely, I saw it was a lamb almost photographically rendered. Around the lamb's head, barely perceptible, was a halo. As I looked more intently, I saw that the lamb's legs were tied and that the animal, shrouded by the dark background, was lying on a cross. The title was *Agnus Dei*, Latin for "Lamb of God." I wanted to weep. I stood there and looked at that picture for a long time. It was not just the beauty that held me, but the theology of the atonement. John the Baptist's words kept running circles in my heart!

For centuries Israel's consciousness had been programmed with the idea of the sacrificial lamb. With John's statement, "Behold, the Lamb of God, who takes away the sin of the world!" their Jewish minds went as far back as Abraham and Isaac (Genesis 22:7, 8) when Isaac said, "Behold, the fire and the wood, but where is the lamb for a burnt offering?" Abraham replied, "God will provide for himself the lamb for a burnt offering, my son." John's hearers undoubtedly also thought of the Passover lamb, the application of its blood over the door, and those beautiful phrases from Isaiah 53:6, 7:

> All we like sheep have gone astray;
>   we have turned—every one—to his own way;
> and the LORD has laid on him
>   the iniquity of us all.
>
> He was oppressed, and he was afflicted,
>   yet he opened not his mouth;
> like a lamb that is led to the slaughter,
>   and like a sheep that before its shearers is silent,
>   so he opened not his mouth.

John's statement made it clear that Jesus would be a sacrifice for sin. God had provided the Lamb for their deepest need!

Our message too must be the sacrificial death of Christ! It is dangerously easy to move away from the blood of the atonement in our thinking. We love and sing William Cowper's great hymn, "There Is a Fountain Filled with Blood." Yet I have heard Cowper excoriated and that hymn almost spat upon by those who consider themselves to be Christians. How easy it is to abandon the essential! But the words of his hymn are true:

> There is a fountain filled with blood
> Drawn from Immanuel's veins,
> And sinners plunged beneath that flood
> Lose all their guilty stains.

Christianity is a bloody religion—the blood of Christ cleanses us of all sin! This reality must be primary in our witness and in our thinking! Yes, Christ came to give abundant life. Yes, Christ worked miracles, and he can work miracles in our lives today. But these are *benefits* of the gospel, not the gospel itself. The gospel centers upon Christ as the sin-bearer—"the Lamb of

God, who takes away the sin of the world!" Most of us understand what John is saying. However, our salvation does not depend on our formulation of the doctrine of the atonement, but on our experience of it! Is he *our* Lamb? Do we really believe he died for *us*? If we keep the wonder of the atonement before us, we will be different people!

The Lamb is our eternal message. The encounter between Abraham and Isaac *prophesied* his sacrifice. The Passover *applied* the principles of his sacrifice. Isaiah 53 *personified* his sacrifice. John 1 *identified* the sacrifice. And it is *magnified* in Revelation 5:9–14. The sacrificial death of Christ—this is the essence of our message.

But a faithful witness must also tell others *how* to appropriate the benefits of the Lamb. John the Baptist points this out in verses 31–33. In verse 31 he says, "I myself did not know him, but for this purpose I came baptizing with water, that he might be revealed to Israel." John's water baptisms were baptisms of repentance. That is how he prepared the way. People had to turn from their sins so that they might receive the Messiah and the benefits of his salvation. Christ brought a new, different baptism.

> And John bore witness: "I saw the Spirit descend from heaven like a dove, and it remained on him. I myself did not know him, but he who sent me to baptize with water said to me, 'He on whom you see the Spirit descend and remain, this is he who baptizes with the Holy Spirit.'" (vv. 32, 33)

John's preaching motivated the human will to change, but Christ's message brought the power to change! That marvelous word "baptize," which essentially means a dipping or submersion, here extends to the spiritual life. In 1 Corinthians 12:13 Paul says, "For in one Spirit we were all baptized into one body," referring to the saturation of the Holy Spirit that occurs at the time of salvation.

The power to change our lives—to leave our life of sin and enjoy the fullness of eternal life—comes only from a soaking or immersion in the Holy Spirit!

Conclusion

What is our message? It is, "Behold, the Lamb of God!"

Sarah Hale wrote the famous poem "Mary Had a Little Lamb." It is a nice little nursery rhyme, but I like to think of it theologically, completely out of its context. The Virgin Mary really did have a little Lamb—the *Agnus Dei*, the Lamb of God. And on the cross the Lamb took our sins upon himself as our sacrifice. "Worthy is the Lamb!" will be our eternal refrain. May we never move away from the centrality of his sacrificial death!

If you do not know the joy of having been soaked with the Holy Spirit and thus of knowing Christ personally, perhaps you have not personally experienced, first, the reality and greatness of Christ's sacrificial death and, second, the necessity of repentance. Possibly you give only lip service to the idea of his sacrificial atonement without fully depending on his shed blood. Just as the Jews needed John's baptism of repentance, perhaps you too need to repent. Many people miss Christ because they never have truly repented. Grace without repentance is cheap grace—not the real thing. A realization of what Christ has done must be coupled with a repentant spirit if we are truly to believe and be saved. We must say, "I am nothing, but he is everything, everything, everything!"

6

Angels Ascending
and Descending

JOHN 1:43–51

ON A DARK NIGHT about a hundred years ago a Scottish missionary couple found themselves surrounded by cannibals intent on taking their lives. On that terror-filled night the couple fell to their knees and prayed that God would protect them. It was a horrible time. Intermittent with their prayers, the missionaries heard the cries of the savages and imagined them coming through the door to take their lives. As the sun began to rise, to their astonishment they found that the natives were retreating into the forest. The missionaries were absolutely amazed and filled with joy. Their hearts soared to God. It was a day of rejoicing!

The couple bravely continued their work. A year later the chieftain of that tribe was saved. As the missionary spoke with him, he remembered the horror of that night and asked the chieftain why he and his men had not killed them. The chieftain replied in surprise, "Who were all those men who were with you?" The missionary answered, "There were no men with us. It was just my wife and myself." The chieftain began to argue with him, saying, "There were hundreds of tall men in shining garments with drawn swords circling about your house, so we could not attack you."

That story, recorded in Billy Graham's book *Angels*, is one of the greatest stories in missionary history. The missionary was the almost legendary John G. Paton of the New Hebrides. What a glorious story for the church — a story not often repeated or experienced, yet one that does have contemporary parallels.

Another vivid story was shared with me by a respectable Southern California pastor's wife. One evening she was driving down the Santa Ana

Freeway, which is always busy. As she drove down that freeway, somehow the car door opened, and her four-year-old child tumbled out onto the freeway amidst the high-speed traffic. With her heart pounding and with horrible expectations, she pulled her car to a screeching stop and ran frantically back along the freeway. But she did not expect to see what she saw. Her child was sitting up in the fast lane of the freeway amidst the glare of headlights, his only injuries a few abrasions. The first words that came out of his mouth were, "Mommy, Mommy, I saw Jesus put up his hands and stop the cars!" Was that a child's imagination? Possibly. None of the drivers saw anyone. They just managed to stop their cars and miss him. The boy had been raised in a pious home, so perhaps he was just parroting what he had heard others say. On the other hand, it may indeed have been angelic intervention, considering the incredible danger in that unusual situation.

Many of us today have miraculous stories to tell—some more incredible, some easier to believe than the two I have told. The question is, what are the day-to-day spiritual realities that surround us? John 1:43–51 will give us some answers.

Spiritual Life for Nathanael (vv. 43–51)

Our text opens with Jesus calling a new disciple named Philip.

> The next day Jesus decided to go to Galilee. He found Philip and said to him, "Follow me." (v. 43)

Jesus took the initiative, coming to Philip with a very simple command: "Follow me"—literally, "Keep on following me." And Philip did. In the following verses we see immediate incendiary results in Philip's life—he had a burning desire to share the gospel. One lighted torch lights another torch. So Philip went forth to share the gospel, and soon he found Nathanael.

> Philip found Nathanael and said to him, "We have found him of whom Moses in the Law and also the prophets wrote, Jesus of Nazareth, the son of Joseph." Nathanael said to him, "Can anything good come out of Nazareth?" Philip said to him, "Come and see." (vv. 45, 46)

Philip was excited! His words must have tumbled out of his mouth. Nathanael had not heard about Jesus, but he knew his Old Testament. He knew that Bethlehem was named as the birthplace of our Savior, not Nazareth. Besides, Nazareth was just four miles from Cana, which was Nathanael's hometown, and since there was a little rivalry between the two places, he had to challenge Philip. "Can anything good come out of Nazareth?" Philip gave him the best and only possible answer. He said, "Come and see." We need to make that response when we are tempted to argue.

The ensuing encounter between Jesus and Nathanael reveals the spiritual realities that were already at work.

> Jesus saw Nathanael coming toward him and said of him, "Behold, an Israelite indeed, in whom there is no deceit!" Nathanael said to him, "How do you know me?" (vv. 47, 48a)

Jesus emphasized that Nathanael was a transparent, honest man. That is probably why Nathanael reacted to Philip's news by saying, "Can anything good come out of Nazareth?" He said what he thought. I think that characteristic was confirmed by Nathanael's reaction to Jesus' words: "How do you know me?" Now, if Jesus said to me, "Behold, a believer in whom is no deceit!" I would probably say, "Me? Not me. But I guess if you say so, maybe I am." But Nathanael just owned up to it. He was in fact a guileless man.

Notice that our Lord said Nathanael was an *Israelite* in whom was no guile. He put deliberate emphasis on that word because Jacob, the Old Testament patriarch, was Israel, and he was full of guile—a scoundrel who loved God. God worked in his life until finally, after wrestling with God, Jacob was renamed Israel. Jesus was saying that Nathanael was an ideal Israelite because guile had gone out of his life. Temple's translation says, "Behold an Israelite in whom there is no Jacob." Nathanael was evidently an Old Testament believer, like Simeon and Anna, who was looking for God. The Lord knew Nathanael's character before he met him and said he was a guileless man. How could Jesus know? That thought must have flashed through Nathanael's mind. Beautiful revelation!

With Nathanael's mind whirling, our Lord continued to astonish him in verse 48b: "Before Philip called you, when you were under the fig tree, I saw you." This is one of the great cryptic statements of the New Testament. For centuries men have tried to decipher the symbolism of the fig tree. In some Scripture passages it is a symbol for peace. In many others it is a symbol for a home. Or it could be taken literally and just mean a fig tree. Exactly what it represents is not terribly important, but we will consider it as a fig tree. What is important is that Nathanael had a religious experience that no one but Jesus knew about. Maybe Nathanael had been reading the story of Jacob's ladder. Maybe he had been contemplating being baptized by John the Baptist. Maybe he was thinking about the Messiah. Maybe he had prayed that the Messiah would reveal himself to him. The point is, Nathanael had had a spiritual experience under a fig tree and Jesus was saying, "I know about the experience you had that you shared *only* with God." Jesus knew!

Nathanael was not only guileless—he was able to put two and two together quickly. He knew that God is omniscient, and he realized that Jesus' statement demonstrated omniscience. This man had to be God! Consider Nathanael's response in verse 49: "Rabbi, you are the Son of God! You are the King of Israel!" What an incredible answer! Because he was an Israelite with no guile, Nathanael was prepared to come to know God, and when he saw Jesus' omniscience, he responded and believed. He did a complete 180-degree turn and rapturously confessed that Jesus was the Son of God—all because he had experienced the reality of Jesus' omniscience.

> Jesus answered him, "Because I said to you, 'I saw you under the fig tree,' do you believe? You will see greater things than these." (v. 50)

In other words, "Nathanael, because you saw I am omniscient, you believe? You have not seen anything yet." Christ really took the lid off in verse 51 (it is significant that he switched from the second person singular to the second person plural, making his words universal in meaning):

> Truly, truly, I say to you, you will see heaven opened, and the angels of God ascending and descending on the Son of Man.

Spiritual Vision for Nathanael (v. 51)

That statement took Nathanael back almost two thousand years to the time of Jacob. To understand its meaning, we must first know its context—Genesis 28. Jacob had just stolen the birthright from Esau. He was a scoundrel, a rascal who also loved spiritual things. Because of his fear of Esau's wrath, Jacob, the conniver, was fleeing for his life. At this point it seemed that his only friend was his mother. That was not surprising because he was a mama's boy, not a man of the bush like Esau. Making such a sudden departure also meant he was not well prepared for traveling. Yet the distance he traveled that first day was about forty-three miles across the wilderness. Finally, at day's end, worn-out and tired, he came to a valley strewn with rocks. We pick up the story in verse 11:

> And he came to a certain place and stayed there that night, because the sun had set. Taking one of the stones of the place, he put it under his head and lay down in that place to sleep.

You are really tired when you can sleep on a stone! Jacob was in terrible shape. He felt wretched and alone, as if he didn't have a friend in the world. But even in his tremendous loneliness out in the wilderness, God loved him, rascal though he was. So God came and comforted him with a vision.

> And he dreamed, and behold, there was a ladder set up on the earth, and the top of it reached to heaven. And behold, the angels of God were ascending and descending on it! (v. 12)

Under that ominous Syrian sky God gave him a vision of encouragement. "Look, Jacob, do you think you are all alone out here? There is traffic between Heaven and earth on your behalf. Let that comfort you." That was the dream Jesus referred to when speaking to Nathanael, though he mentioned no ladder,

> Truly, truly, I say to you, you will see heaven opened, and the angels of God ascending and descending on the Son of Man. (v. 51)

The finest Greek scholars, from J. H. Bernard to C. K. Barrett say this means Jesus is the ladder. What a tremendous truth! The ladder is Christ! "Nathanael, you have not seen anything! As you enter into the fullness of your relationship with me, and as your spiritual vision is broadened, you are going to see swarming angels and hear the rustle of their wings as they move on that ladder between Heaven and earth for you." And this is actually what happens on behalf of believers today. We need to hold on to this and understand it and believe it until we can almost hear the rustle of their wings.

Jesus' words bring into our lives the stunning realities that were Jacob's! God is often the closest when he seems farthest away. Have you ever been out in the wilds of life, with stone pillows, so that it seemed as if God was far away? We learn from Jacob's vision that God is active in our lives when we are in the wilds. And we see that angels really do minister on our behalf! Hebrews 1:14 says, "Are they [angels] not all ministering spirits sent out to serve for the sake of those who are to inherit salvation?"

Heavenly hosts minister to us! Of course, sometimes angels get a little curious, as we know from 1 Peter 1:12: "It was revealed to them that they were serving not themselves but you, in the things that have now been announced to you . . . things into which angels long to look." They want to understand what is going on in this world. I love those old medieval pictures in which the sky is full of angels and fat cherubs. The artists aesthetically captured the reality. If our eyes could be opened, sometimes we would see the sky full of angels!

Missionary John G. Paton's experience was a repeat of what happened once in the Old Testament (2 Kings 6:14–17). Elisha and his servant were surrounded by the enemy, and Elisha prayed that his servant's eyes would be opened. Then his servant saw flaming chariots of fire and the armies of God all around. He saw the reality of ministering spirits. That same reality is ours. Someday we will actually see Heaven opened and "the angels of God ascending and descending on the Son of Man." In Christ we are brought very near to Heaven.

> But you have come to Mount Zion and to the city of the living God, the heavenly Jerusalem, and to innumerable angels in festal gathering, and to the assembly of the firstborn who are enrolled in heaven, and to God, the judge of all, and to the spirits of the righteous made perfect. (Hebrews 12:22, 23)

All who are in Christ live in the suburbs of Heaven. "But our citizenship is in heaven, and from it we await a Savior, the Lord Jesus Christ" (Philippians 3:20). We are fellow citizens with the saints who are already there.

> Blessed be the God and Father of our Lord Jesus Christ, who has blessed us in Christ with every spiritual blessing in the heavenly places. (Ephesians 1:3)

All those blessings are ours—the ministry of angels, our heavenly citizenship, the closeness of Heaven. There is also a promise of growth implicit in Christ's words to Nathanael: "You will see greater things than these." We will experience ongoing growth and increasing understanding of the heavenly realities all around us.

A certain woman had lived a long, circumscribed life of hard work. So busy with her labors, she had never gotten around very much. As the sun was setting on her life, she was taken to the ocean. As she looked at its apparently boundless expanse, she said, "Thank God there is enough of something." When we apply that to what we are going to have in Christ when the heavens open, we too will say, "Thank God there is enough of something!" He is infinite, and his infinite love will unfold for eternity. We will always be surprised and will keep growing into new knowledge of his love. His power, his mercy, his strength, his transcendence—all these things will keep unfolding for eternity. All these infinite experiences are bound up in Jesus' statement to Nathanael (and to us).

Christ's words make relevant to us both the tragedy and the ecstasy of

Jacob's life. Jacob's response to the vision of the heavens opened, the angels, and God's words to him (Genesis 28:16) was a very poignant and tragic statement: "Surely the LORD is in this place, and I did not know it." That is the tragedy of much of modern Christianity. We have de-supernaturalized life to the extent that we do not see God! God is in this place, and we do not know it! We go to work and do not know it. We go to school and do not know it. We have personal relationships and do not know it. All the time God is there, but we do not know it! This mentality even intrudes into church. We sing the great hymns, pray together, and worship together but do not really know he is there. Tragically, our Christianity thus becomes an empty, monochromatic Christianity that is not interesting to the world or to us.

On the other hand, there is the ecstasy of Jacob, seen in the following verses of Genesis 28:

> "Surely the LORD is in this place, and I did not know it." And he was afraid and said, "How awesome is this place! This is none other than the house of God, and this is the gate of heaven." (vv. 16, 17)

Jacob realized the truth of the spiritual realities. Verse 19 of Genesis 28 says, "He called the name of that place Bethel," which means "the house of God." How wondrous it is to know that wherever we are is Bethel, that there is intercourse between Heaven and earth on our behalf and the rustle of angels' wings in our lives. What a difference it would make if we appropriated those spiritual realities all the time. We believe it, but do we *believe* it? May God help us see and appropriate these realities.

Conclusion

If you do not know Jesus Christ, there is a promise to you if you will respond to him—you will begin to see the unseen. The heavens will be opened, and the angels of God will be ascending and descending upon our Lord Jesus Christ on your behalf. Jesus—our ladder—has his feet planted on the earth in his humanity and his blessed brow in the heavens. You can know that reality. Do you know how you can get it? The same way Nathanael did. "Nathanael answered him, 'Rabbi, you are the Son of God! You are the King of Israel!'" (v. 49). You can say those words and not believe. But if you can say them enthusiastically, with a heart full of faith, grace will be poured into your life. Your life will become alive, polychromatic, brilliant, exciting, effervescent, all because of Jesus. May God give us grace to receive the truth of his Word.

7

The Transforming Power

On the third day there was a wedding at Cana in Galilee, and the mother of Jesus was there. Jesus also was invited to the wedding with his disciples. When the wine ran out, the mother of Jesus said to him, "They have no wine." And Jesus said to her, "Woman, what does this have to do with me? My hour has not yet come." His mother said to the servants, "Do whatever he tells you."

Now there were six stone water jars there for the Jewish rites of purification, each holding twenty or thirty gallons. Jesus said to the servants, "Fill the jars with water." And they filled them up to the brim. And he said to them, "Now draw some out and take it to the master of the feast." So they took it. When the master of the feast tasted the water now become wine, and did not know where it came from (though the servants who had drawn the water knew), the master of the feast called the bridegroom and said to him, "Everyone serves the good wine first, and when people have drunk freely, then the poor wine. But you have kept the good wine until now." This, the first of his signs, Jesus did at Cana in Galilee, and manifested his glory. And his disciples believed in him.

One of the many benefits of being in the ministry is the repeated privilege of participating in the joy of a wedding. Counseling sessions invariably bring bright-eyed couples to my office, couples who seem barely able to touch the ground. Of course, at weddings I always have a front row seat, and I get to see things that are hidden to most people—like those universally nervous hands, sometimes barely able to manage the ring. Even better, I am just a few inches away from what the Scriptures teach is a sacred transaction. It is a privilege to be involved in weddings.

As a pastor, I also am privy to other things—some humorous, some even bordering on the bizarre. I remember a particular garden wedding. It was beautiful. The bride and groom were unusually relaxed. So I expected nothing irregular when we came to the time for the bride and groom to kneel in prayer. What a surprise it was when the bride's younger brother fainted and fell into the ivy. The story does not end there. Another wedding the following week was in a church that had a high platform area with a marble floor below it. Quite naturally I repeated the story at rehearsal and warned them, "Whatever you do, don't lock your knees. Stand on one leg or the other, or rock back and forth, but don't lock your knees." Guess what? At exactly the same place in the ceremony I heard not a crash but a thud. That bride's brother was out cold on the marble floor three steps down! I have also officiated at weddings that looked as if they had been scripted for Laurel and Hardy.

I think there are several reasons why weddings are like this, but one is primary. From the time we are little children, we see weddings idealized and dramatized, and stories are told and retold until finally, when it comes time for our wedding, very few of us are our normal selves. The bride has in her mind a clear picture of how the wedding should be and tells each member of the wedding party how he/she should walk, where he/she should stand, and what he/she should say, and this creates too much tension for young people who are participating in a formal occasion for the first time. I do not think there is anything particularly wrong with this. Weddings *should* be idealized. The simple fact is, a wedding day is typically a nervous event brimming with potential confusion.

The same emotions clearly applied to the little wedding in Cana of Galilee in John 2, especially in light of the Hebrew inclination toward drama and excitement. The wedding celebration was considered to be the most grand event in life, especially among the poor. Typically the Hebrew wedding ceremony took place late in the evening following a feast. After the ceremony the bride and groom were taken to their home in a torchlight parade complete with a canopy held over their heads. They were always taken along the most circuitous route possible so everyone would have the opportunity to wish them well. Instead of a honeymoon, they held an open house for a week. They were considered to be king and queen and actually wore crowns and dressed in bridal robes, and their word was considered to be law. In lives that often contained much poverty and difficulty, this was considered the supreme occasion. Many would plod all the way through life without ever again having a celebration like this. With this background in mind our text comes alive.

I do not think we can overemphasize the distress in Mary's words in verse 3: "They have no wine." In the Jewish wedding feast, wine was essential, not so the guests could drink to excess, but because it was a symbol of exhilaration and celebration. It was of such great importance that a lawsuit could be instituted if no wine was provided! Those who were behind the scenes at that little wedding in Cana were shattered by this breakdown in hospitality. Childhood dreams of the ideal wedding were about to dissolve in a nightmare. The drama of our text is very real.

This moment provides the setting for our Lord's first miracle, and it is full of spiritual meaning. Verse 11 tells us this was the beginning of Jesus' miraculous "signs." When John uses the word "sign," he always uses it with the idea of a miracle that conveys deeper teaching, and that is certainly true here. We not only see Christ showing his glory in his power to change the physical elements from water into wine, but in his power to change a life. This is what this is really all about. This is a bounding, joyous, leaping story of what Christ can do for *us*.

The Problem

"They have no wine" is not only a succinct statement of the young couple's problem but, as John saw, a spiritual condensation of human experience without Christ. Life without Christ is a life without wine. The Scriptures use wine as a symbol for joy, as in Psalm 104:15, "Wine . . . gladden[s] the heart of man," and in Isaiah 55:1, "Come, everyone who thirsts, come to the waters; and he who has no money, come, buy and eat! Come, buy wine and milk without money and without price." There is also a beautiful passage in Judges (9:13) where the vine says, "Shall I leave my wine that cheers God and men and go hold sway over the trees?" To the Jewish mind, wine symbolized joy. In fact, the rabbis had a contemporary saying: "Without wine, there is no joy." We could very well translate Mary's words, "They have no joy." At this precious time of life that should be filled with everything good, joy had run out.

Like these newlyweds, the universal experience of humanity, apart from Christ, is that there comes a time when the wine runs out, when the joy and exhilaration of life are gone. There probably has never been a more public example of this in our time than the life of Ernest Hemingway. From the time of his boyhood in Oak Park, Illinois, to his teenage summers in northern Michigan, he went after everything life could give him. He became a reporter with the Kansas City Star, served as an ambulance driver in World War I, spent years in Europe, and was intimately involved in the Spanish Civil War. His famous friendships ran all the way from the bullfighter Manolete to the novelist F. Scott Fitzgerald. In whatever he did—sports, warfare, romance—he went for all of it. And, of course, he was brilliant. His great stories—especially the greatest of all, *The Old Man and the Sea*—show his unique genius. He is a man who did it all. I have thought many times in reading *The Snows of Kilimanjaro* that it is largely autobiographical. When the wife of the dying hunter says, "Why, you're the most complete man I've ever met," she is saying what the author thought of himself. Hemingway went after the wine of life, but there came a time when the wine gave out. In his biography by Carlos Baker, we read these final words:

> Sunday morning dawned bright and cloudless. Ernest awoke early as always. He put on the red "Emperor's robe" and padded softly down the carpeted stairway. The early sunlight lay in pools on the living room floor. He had noticed that the guns were locked up in the basement. But the keys, as he well knew, were on the window ledge above the kitchen sink. He tiptoed down the basement stairs and unlocked the storage room. It smelled as dank as a grave. He chose a double-barreled shotgun with a tight choke. He had used it for years of pigeon shooting. He took some shells from one of the boxes in the storage room, closed and locked the door, and climbed the basement stairs. If he saw the bright day outside, it did not deter him. He crossed the living room to the front foyer, a shrinelike entryway five feet by seven, with oak-paneled walls and a floor of linoleum tile. . . . He slipped in two shells, lowered the gun butt carefully to the floor, leaned forward, pressed the twin barrels against his forehead just above the eyebrows and tripped both triggers.

No matter who you are, no matter what wines you have tasted, there comes a time when the exhilarations and excitements of life wear out. For some it comes sooner, for others later. Often it is when life is at its very best that the wine gives out. We are full of health; money increases; friends multiply; we have an abundance to eat, plenty to drink, and a warm place to sleep. But somehow the wine fails, and life loses its sparkle. It can happen in the teenage years. It is epidemic in the college years. It is endemic to the middle years. And ultimately it catches everyone. That is what makes this miracle so important. Every one of us will find that if the exhilarations of life are our focus, failure is inevitable. Young persons who hear, "You only go through life once. Get all you can get out of it! Live life with gusto!" need to hear this message. People cope in different ways, though most are not as extreme as Hemingway. Many settle for "gray days," clench their fists, and determine to go on with life. Others become bitter and sour. Some fight. Some give up all hope. All need the joy of knowing Jesus.

There is nothing intrinsically wrong with the natural joys of life, but a time can come when you have seen and done everything, and there is nothing else to bring exhilaration to life. The wines of the intellect are in some ways much more enduring, but they have a built-in defect too. The writer of Ecclesiastes talks about this in 1:16–18:

I said in my heart, "I have acquired great wisdom, surpassing all who were over Jerusalem before me, and my heart has had great experience of wisdom and knowledge." And I applied my heart to know wisdom and to know madness and folly. I perceived that this also is but a striving after wind.

> For in much wisdom is much vexation,
> and he who increases knowledge increases sorrow.

Intellectual pursuits are like a double-edged sword. They can bring great joys, but they can also bring an early end to the wine. Sensate wines also run out. Even Disneyland can get old! Visit enough times and the Magic Kingdom becomes tiresome. Lobster and steak are terrific, but not 365 days a year! It is an axiom of life that the greater the sensual focus, the greater the tendency to boredom. This has been the testimony of thousands down through the years. That is what makes the story in John 2 so wonderful!

The Solution

When the wine ran out, the mother of Jesus said to him, "They have no wine." And Jesus said to her, "Woman, what does this have to do with me? My hour has not yet come." His mother said to the servants, "Do whatever he tells you." (vv. 3–5)

Jesus had brought several disciples with him, and I think their presence caused Mary to speculate that it was time for his ministry to begin. Hence the statement, "They have no wine." Volumes have been written on Jesus' response, "Woman, what does this have to do with me?" Although it sounds harsh to our ear, he was actually making a courteous remark. He addressed her as "woman" again when he was on the cross and was tenderly giving Mary to John's care. At any rate the miracle is now set in motion. We read in verses 6, 7 that they took the six waterpots that were there for purification, and they filled them to the brim. Each of the waterpots held twenty or thirty gallons, so we are talking about as much as 180 gallons of wine! What a great wedding gift to the couple! That gift would provide them with money for quite a long time. The message to Jesus' Jewish listeners was particularly pointed, for we know from the Dead Sea Scrolls that such stone pots were used for ritual purification, confirming verse 6 ("rites of purification"). By performing his miracle in those stone urns, our Savior was testifying that the old religious rituals were dead and that he was filling the urns with new life. F. F. Bruce says, "Christ [is] changing the water of Jewish purification into the wine of the new age."

Jesus was saying that he brings joy to life, and the joy he gives is abundant and overflowing, with the best coming last! That teaching is for all of us! At the

very beginning of his ministry the Lord Jesus provided that great joy! Galatians
5:22 says, "But the fruit of the Spirit is . . . joy." Later in his life on earth, just a
few hours before his death, our Lord said, "These things I have spoken to you,
that my joy may be in you, and that your joy may be full" (John 15:11). The
Lord does not take away the natural joys of life but lifts them up and ennobles
them and makes them far more enjoyable. That is exactly what is suggested by
the broader picture in our story. We have here a wedding—something of the
earth, primal, basic. But what does Jesus do? He attends the wedding, partici-
pates in the happiness, averts disaster, and then supplies the joy! Admittedly
life has its sorrows. The Scriptures say our Savior was "a man of sorrows,
and acquainted with grief" (Isaiah 53:3). He knew all about sorrow, but the
overall tenor of his life was joy! We, too, will have many sorrows. There will
be times when the grace of God will seem distant, but overall our lives can be
lives of joy. Ephesians 5:18, 19 says, "Do not get drunk with wine, for that is
debauchery, but be filled with the Spirit, addressing one another in psalms and
hymns and spiritual songs, singing and making melody to the Lord with your
heart." That is joy! That is the way life is meant to be!

John here implies that life gets better as it goes on (see v. 10). I think
the master of the banquet made his statement jokingly: "Everyone serves the
good wine first, and when people have drunk freely, then the poor wine. But
you have kept the good wine until now." Although the natural wines of life
tend to lose their sparkle, the wine Christ gives—the joy we find in him—
increases as life goes on. I have found this to be true. He is serving delicacies
at my table now that I knew nothing of in my early years of Christian life.
Jesus is always giving us something better, and our taste is constantly being
refined. This is a promise of growth.

> The righteous flourish like the palm tree
> and grow like a cedar in Lebanon.
> They are planted in the house of the LORD;
> they flourish in the courts of our God.
> They still bear fruit in old age;
> they are ever full of sap and green. (Psalm 92:12–14)

Do you know anyone like that? Do you know someone who, as life has
gone on, has become more joyous, more vigorous and effervescent? Full of
Christ's wine? I do. What a positive outlook on life! Teenagers can have joy.
For those going through midlife, life can effervesce on into their final years on
earth and on into eternity—always increasing—saving the best for last. Get
all you can out of life! Live it with gusto! But do it God's way.

Conclusion

We must not overlook the context of all this. It was a wedding. By implication we see that all these joys come through the blessing of betrothal to Christ. We must understand that the wine of carnal life does run out, or perhaps has already. The sensual, visual, and intellectual joys of life will not endure. But Christ can change everything. Isaiah says our Lord gives "a beautiful head-dress instead of ashes, the oil of gladness instead of mourning" (61:3).

How do you think the people reacted to Christ's miracle at that wedding? Do you think they were blasé? I doubt it. There was probably a lot of jumping and hollering—Jewish style. They were having a great time! Can you see it? The bride and groom with their crowns in place—a torchlight parade—all the celebration complete with the overflowing joy of Christ! Consider in this regard these words recorded by the apostle John in Revelation:

> And the angel said to me, "Write this: Blessed are those who are invited to the marriage supper of the Lamb." And he said to me, "These are the true words of God." (19:9)

8

The Cleansing
of the Temple

JOHN 2:12–22

THERE IS A MEMORABLE PASSAGE IN C. S. Lewis's *Voyage of the Dawn Treader* that touches on John 2:12–22. Lucy and Edmund are engaged in their adventure when they come to a large grassy expanse. The sensuous green of the grass spreads off into the blue horizon except for a white spot in the middle of the green expanse. As Edmund and Lucy look at this spot intently, they have difficulty making out what it is. Being adventurous, they travel across the grass until finally the white spot comes in to view. It is a lamb! The lamb, white and pure, is cooking a fish breakfast.

Author C. S. Lewis probably based this passage on the imagery in the twenty-first chapter of John, where we find Jesus cooking a fish breakfast for his disciples. The white lamb is a Christ figure.

The lamb gives Lucy and Edmund the most delicious breakfast they have ever had. Then ensues a wonderful conversation as they talk about how to get to the land of Aslan—Heaven. As the lamb begins to explain the way, a marvelous thing happens. As Lewis records it, "His snowy white flushed into tawny gold and his size changed and he was Aslan himself, towering above them and scattering light from his mane." What a picture!

Lewis was illustrating a great truth of our faith—the Lamb is the Lion. In Biblical terms, the Lamb of God who takes away the sin of the world is the Lion of the tribe of Judah. Qualities we consider to be lamb-like—gentleness and meekness—are indeed in Christ, but so are the regalness and ferocity of a lion. The book of Revelation speaks of "the wrath of the Lamb" (6:16).

The passage we will now study begins in the wake of the beautiful miracle in Cana of Galilee, and we must view it with that in mind. Jesus had been to a wedding, and when the wine ran out, he changed the water into wine. The message of that miracle is that when the natural joys of life wear out, our Lord brings new wine—new joys. When the steward tasted the wine, he said, "You have kept the good wine until now." That is how it is with the Christian life. The best comes at the last. As we grow in him, the joys and wines of life become more perfect and more satisfying.

Now notice verse 12:

> After this he went down to Capernaum, with his mother and his brothers and his disciples, and they stayed there for a few days.

Capernaum was about twenty miles from Cana, so it was not much of a journey to get there. It was probably a very delightful journey since it was then spring in Palestine. As they approached Capernaum, they saw low, rising hills, the deep blue of the Sea of Galilee, and finally beautiful Capernaum situated on the shore, sprawling back into the hills and framed from behind by the snowcapped majesty of Mt. Hermon.

It was an idyllic time for our Lord, his brothers, his mother, and his newfound disciples, especially in light of the excitement and freshness of the miracle. It was also almost Passover, and there was a spirit of expectancy across the land—probably very much like what we experience during the Christmas season. The Jewish tradition required an entire month for preparation. The roads were repaired, the bridges rebuilt or shored up, the sepulchers rewhitened. The entire land bustled with the spirit of Passover. Jerusalem, although not a big city by ordinary standards, would have as many as two and a quarter million people crowded into its confines at Passover. So it is very natural to read in verse 13, "The Passover of the Jews was at hand, and Jesus went up to Jerusalem."

We can surmise that as our Lord traveled south to Jerusalem, the roads became very congested. When he entered the gates of the city and approached the cream and gold of that great temple, the congestion became even worse, with sellers of trinkets and souvenirs on all sides. Some of that must have bothered our Lord, but not, I imagine, as much as what he saw at the temple. Notice verse 14: "In the temple he found those who were selling oxen and sheep and pigeons, and the money-changers sitting there."

From the Lord's point of view, what he saw in the temple was an outrage! The money changers claimed their business was a necessity—changing foreign currency into Jewish currency because foreign money was not acceptable for offerings in the temple. Authorities tell us that the money changers charged as much as two hours of a working man's wage to change a half shekel. They charged the same amount again for every half shekel they gave in return for a larger coin. So if a man came in with a two-shekel piece, he would have had to pay an entire day's wage just to change his money! This brought a lot of money into the temple. In fact, some years before, when a man came in and ravaged the temple, he took the equivalent of $20 million and did not come close to depleting the treasury of the temple!

Furthermore, the sellers and inspectors in the temple sold all the sacrifices. Rabbinical literature tells us that inspectors spent eighteen months on a farm to learn to distinguish between clean and unclean animals. They even learned to identify an animal that would one day become unclean, even if it was clean at the time! The inspectors had a good thing going. If they did not approve an animal, it would not be approved. Extortion was common in the temple confines. To make things worse, Annas, the high priest, was behind the whole thing! Sarcastic commentators in those days dubbed the temple the "Bazaars of Annas." They knew the high priest actually sold franchises for money-changing booths and animal sales.

So when our Lord came to the temple, he found a religious circus! As his eyes scanned the great Court of the Gentiles, he saw sheep, oxen, fowl, and everything that goes with them. There was huckstering, bartering, and haggling over the weight of a coin. The commotion that must have been within the temple is almost beyond our imagination. It was certainly unacceptable to our Lord!

The following verses only give a glimpse of the drama that occurred. Jesus reached down, picked up some cords, and quickly knotted them together. Then he began to cleanse the temple. One commentator said he must have appeared to be seven feet tall as his whip began to fly. Tables crashed and money jangled across the floor as our Lord drove the money changers, the sellers, and the inspectors out of the temple. Jesus' words were, "Take these things away; do not make my Father's house a house of trade" (v. 16). The Lamb was a Lion!

In my imagination I see Jesus' heaving silhouette in the portico as the temple cleared out. He was indignant and angry, and it was a burning, white-hot anger. Some people have tried to water down Christ's intensity. For instance, one man said, "Catching up some of the reeds that served as bedding for the cattle, he twisted them into the semblance of a scourge, which could hurt neither man nor beast. He did not use it." Frankly, Scripture does not say who felt the sting of Jesus' whip. But when the accounts of the second cleansing of the temple are considered along with the drama of this situation, it is unthinkable that our Lord did *not* use the whip.

Gentle Jesus, meek and mild, is a concept that has been so overworked that many today preach and follow a Christ who has no resemblance to the Christ of the New Testament. That Jesus is an idol, drained of his deity—a weak, good-natured deity whose great aim is to let us off the hook.

Do not get me wrong. Jesus *is* meek and mild. In fact, he describes himself in that way in Matthew 11:29 when he invites those who have burdens to come to him. Dozens of Scriptures in the New Testament testify to his gentleness. But we need to balance this with other descriptions of our Lord. For instance, in Mark 3:5, the passage describing the man with the paralyzed hand, Jesus looked around at all those who were questioning whether or not he would heal on the Sabbath, and "he looked around at them with anger." Jesus' anger was a swelling wrath. There was nothing gentle in the fierce message he sent to Herod either: "Go and tell that fox . . ." (Luke 13:32), or in his response to Peter: "Get behind me, Satan!" (Matthew 16:23). I am sure the Pharisees in the temple saw nothing of his gentleness, meekness, and mildness when he said, "You are like whitewashed tombs" and "You serpents, you brood of vipers, how are you to escape being sentenced to hell?" (Matthew 23:27, 33). The scene described in our text is a wild scene! Men were grasping at their moneybags and tables as Jesus applied the whip to those not moving.

But the fact is, Jesus was as Godlike here as he was when he hung on the cross. He was revealing as much of God on this occasion as he did at Calvary. He was displaying a great underlying truth: Love presupposes hatred. A love for the downtrodden, the poor, and the oppressed also brings about a hatred for the conditions that caused their suffering. That truth has been evident in the lives of Shaftesbury, the Wesleys, Fox, and other great men of the church down through the centuries. Men and women of great love have always also been people of great hatred. In fact, you can tell as much about a person by his hatreds as by his loves. So what has been revealed through Christ's anger is very important. What are the hates and loves of God? In particular, what is the root of Christ's hatred and anger in this passage? And how should it affect our lives?

The Root of Christ's Anger

Christ's anger was rooted in his reaction against the religious irreverence of the Jews toward God the Father. But we must first realize the significance of the setting in this passage. First Kings 8:10, 11 describes the great temple of Solomon when the ark of the covenant was brought in. A thick cloud so filled the temple that the priests could no longer minister there. That was the glory of God! To glorify God was the very purpose of the temple. Therefore the sin of the money changers and the religious authorities lay in the fact that while they loudly proclaimed the holiness and otherness of God, they denied it in practice. Our Lord's whip opposes anything that detracts from the communication of God's glory, especially in worship.

There is scarcely anything more relevant than this truth to the twenty-first-century church. Even professing Christians sometimes reduce God to much less than he is. Many have made a valid attempt to present the humanity of Christ so men and women can see him as a God who relates to them, but this attitude has sometimes been carried to the extreme. It has been so perverted that Jesus has been effectively and functionally emptied of his deity. For many, Christ has become a pop Jesus who lies back with his headphones in place, reading *Sports Illustrated*. It is easy to fall into a flippancy of which an angel would never be guilty. The result is contemporary idolatry that at its core is a distortion of God into man-made and mental images. Our irreverence reflects an idolatrous concept of God. The flip phrase "the Man Upstairs" is an idolatrous statement, born out of ignorance and a wrong understanding of God. "The Big Man in the sky" is not the God we worship. No wonder Jesus was so indignant about the irreverence he saw!

When the loss of the knowledge of who God is settles in, an irreverent spirit begins to take root in our lives, and such an attitude restricts our ability to worship. A. W. Tozer, in the preface of his wonderful book *The Knowledge of the Holy*, explains why he wrote that book:

> With our loss of the sense of majesty has come the further loss of religious awe and consciousness of the divine presence. We have lost our spirit of worship and our ability to withdraw inwardly to meet God in adoring silence. Modern Christianity is simply not producing the kind of Christian who can appreciate or experience the life in the Spirit. The words, "Be still, and know that I am God," mean next to nothing to the self-confident, bustling worshiper in this middle period of the twentieth century.[1]

Our hearts can become like that outer court of the temple of Jerusalem. Even while we sit in church, the bazaars of suburbia can be spinning through our heads. We may be thinking about the next business deal we are going to close, athletic events that await us, shopping trips, or bridge parties. Solomon said it all when he said in Proverbs 5:14, "I am at the brink of utter ruin in the assembled congregation." It is possible to be almost in "utter ruin" even while we are part of a Bible-based church.

When we become sufficiently desensitized to the greatness and holiness of God because of the irreverent spirit and the idolatrous concept of God affecting our lives, our manner of service is also affected. Just as in the temple, the profit motive moves easily into the religious life of the church. Since in our view God is impotent, effete, and obsolete, we rationalize that we need to bring in the things of the world to help him out. D. L. Moody used to preach a sermon titled "If Christ Came to Chicago" about the return of Christ. It was a great sermon, but an even greater sermon for us would be, "What If Christ Came to the Temple of Our Lives?" What would he do?

The authenticity of our reverence is important because it indicates what we think of God. It affects what happens in our worship, and ultimately it affects what we do in our service for God. No wonder our Lord was indignantly passionate!

More important, the ultimate source of our Lord's anger was love—the love of God. As his disciples were standing there dumbfounded at their Lord, possibly while he was still breathing hard after driving the men out, the whip still in his hand, the Spirit brought Psalm 69:9 to the mind of one of the disciples. That Psalm is about David but had prophetic fulfillment in Christ. "His disciples remembered that it was written, 'Zeal for your house will consume me'" (John 2:17). The word "consume" in Greek means to be eaten up. When Martin Luther tried to explain this text to his congregation he said, "You know how it is when something is eating us." The Germans must say it just like the English! The Hebrew word for "consume" means "in a flame." Jesus was consumed with zeal for God's glory and his house. The full meaning of this word can be seen in the second half of Psalm 69:9: "And the reproaches of those who reproach you have fallen on me." David and our Savior identified so closely with God that when someone defamed the Lord, they too were defamed. What a wonderful thought for all of us— to be so identified with God and so in love with him that when his name is defamed or his glory somehow tarnished, we feel it and experience that same holy anger.

It is a pity that we have been so tamed by our culture. Today we believe a fallacy—namely, that thoughtful and intelligent people are supposed to discuss the most outrageous matters without emotion. Today people in the media dispassionately discuss the rape of women in minority cultures abroad or imminent violence in the Middle East, but that is not the way it ought to be in any area of life, especially when it involves the glory due to God. Ruskin, when speaking of his own age, said, "The crowning wickedness of this age [is] that they have starved and chilled our faculty of indignation." Oh, to be like Christ and to become angry at the things that anger our Savior! We should be passionate people!

Application for Our Lives

What other significance does this passage have for our lives? For one thing, corporate worship is important. The way we worship reveals what we think about God. In the temple a Gentile could come to the Court of the Gentiles, the outer circle, to pray and consider the true God of Israel. If a Gentile had entered and saw what Jesus saw, what would have been his understanding of God? Perhaps a prosperity gospel or some other misconcept of God.

Irreverence toward God is only a symptom of an idolatrous image of God that is man made. Dry ritualism indicates that our God is far away and dead. Joyless performance reveals an arid Deity. But on the other hand, reverence for God indicates our belief that he is great, awesome, and powerful. Joyful worship makes known the living God. How wonderful it is to worship with God's people—hearing the call to worship, waiting reverently upon God, having our hearts lifted to him by singing glorious hymns—not just with our lips, but with our hearts—joining in corporate prayer, having the Word of Life taught to us. When I die, I want to die in church, worshiping God with a body of believers. We cannot overemphasize the importance of our worship.

We live in a narcissistic, individualistic society. Historically we have insisted on doing things ourselves, going our own way, and questioning everything. The Body of Christ is not to function that way. We need each other. If you are a new believer, learn now that you need older Christians. You need to be taught by them and to worship with them.

Ultimately we are talking about the condition of our hearts. When our Lord's detractors finally approached him, they questioned him, and we read this interesting dialogue in verses 18–21:

> So the Jews said to him, "What sign do you show us for doing these things?" Jesus answered them, "Destroy this temple, and in three days I will raise it up." The Jews then said, "It has taken forty-six years to build this temple, and will you raise it up in three days?" But he was speaking about the temple of his body.

Christ was talking about his resurrection, by which he would be gloriously vindicated. But there was also a secondary meaning. Our Lord, like no other man, was the temple of God. Colossians 2:9 says, "For in him the whole fullness of deity dwells bodily." He was full of Deity like no other temple has ever been. Christ has now gone into Heaven, but he has left us here on earth, and the following verse in Colossians says, "And you have been filled in him" (v. 10).

For we are the temple of the living God; as God said,

"I will make my dwelling among them and walk among them,
    and I will be their God,
    and they shall be my people." (2 Corinthians 6:16)

What a glorious thought!

With this second meaning in mind, the significance of what happened in the temple is even more apparent. Some of us are not cutting it, are we? There was once a time when there was such a fullness in our lives that we were excited and overflowing—like the Holy of Holies, filled with *Shekinah* glory. We had awesome visions of God. But something happened. Instead of our hearts being temples, they became something else. A savings and loan? Perhaps a playhouse? A recreational vehicle? Or perhaps a library full of arcane, irrelevant thoughts? A sty of sensuality? The fullness is gone. It happens so easily.

The glorious truth is, Jesus cares about his temples and comes with a whip in hand. John 2:12–22 looks at the first cleansing of the temple, but the other Gospels tell us that he came back to the temple to cleanse it again, toward the end of his earthly ministry. Likewise, he comes again and again to cleanse our lives if they are not what they are supposed to be—temples giving glory to him. When he comes, we should praise him for his whip and his wrath toward the sin in our lives.

Before I was afflicted I went astray, but now I keep your word. (Psalm 119:67)

It is good for me that I was afflicted, that I might learn your statutes. (Psalm 119:71)

Conclusion

Remember the lamb in the C. S. Lewis story? "As he spoke, his snowy white flushed into tawny gold and his size changed and he was Aslan himself, towering above them and scattering light from his mane." What marvelous twin images of God—the Lamb and the Lion. The hand that was stretched out on the cross and had that nail cruelly driven through it is the same hand that grasped the whip—the Lamb and the Lion.

Let us be known for our hatred of sin and idolatry. We must not apply the whip to others, for we are not Christ, but let us apply it to our own lives. Let us be people so zealous, so overflowing, so burning, so full of him that nothing else can intrude. Do you know what the effects will be? First of all, we will have reverence for God in our lives. People will see our *ethos*—that it is real. It will affect our worship wherever we are, and our own church will become a house of prayer for the nations. The grace of God will go forth. May God deliver us from idolatry—a lower concept of him than we see in our awesome, transcendent, omnipotent, omniscient Lamb and Lion.

9

On Being Born Again

JOHN 3:1–8

I CAN STILL VIVIDLY RECALL the thrill I felt when I heard presidential candidate Jimmy Carter announce that he was born again. I was driving my car, and I gripped the steering wheel more firmly and thought, "Well, how about that!" *Born again* was a wonderful phrase to me then, an evangelical password.

But today (and I assure you, this has nothing to do with President Carter) my response is not quite the same. When I heard Larry Flynt, publisher of the pornographic magazine *Hustler* proclaim he was born again, I was less than enthusiastic. History has subsequently, I think, verified my reserve since Flynt continues to publish his magazine preaching his own version of the situation ethic ("if it is love, it cannot be wrong"). He calls it "clean sex."

A publication I saw included a letter to the editor from a woman who claimed she was a born-again Christian. She explained that along with being born again she had experienced an increased capacity to love and that she and her husband were now sexually expressing their love to others, specifically to their pastor and his wife! Along similar lines, another young woman claims she is "stripping for Jesus." Her rationale is that since she has been born again, she has realized that the Lord has given her a beautiful body, and this is the best way to use her gift! Jim Jones sometimes claimed to be born again, and yet he led hundreds to death and sorrow.

The January 21, 1980 issue of *Forbes* magazine carried a feature article entitled "Born-again Companies," describing businesses that were experiencing new prosperity. The *Los Angeles Times* has also printed an article on the sports page captioned "The Steeler Who Was Born Again," about a player who had made a comeback. And the *Chicago Tribune* once told about a starlet who was changing her image so she could become the sex symbol of the eighties. It mentioned incidentally that she was born again. A born-again sex symbol! How wonderful!

One of the greatest of all Biblical terms has been stolen, emptied of its meaning, and dragged through the mire so that today *born again* can mean almost anything or nothing! We need to rescue it and return it to its proper place. John 3:1–8 relates our Lord's classic conversation with Nicodemus, in which he explained what he meant by being born again. There we find the essentials, the nonnegotiables, of the born-again experience.

Nicodemus

It is hard to imagine there could be a better person for our Lord to use in explaining this matter of being born again.

> Now there was a man of the Pharisees named Nicodemus, a ruler of the Jews. (v. 1)

He was a Pharisee. One of the primary characteristics of the Pharisees was their seriousness. They were so earnest about their faith that on the Sabbath they would carry no more food than the weight of a dried fig or no more milk than could be swallowed at one gulp lest they break the Sabbath-rest. They were serious about their faith! Of course, that got them into some rather ridiculous situations. For instance, it was determined that on the Sabbath one could not tie a knot in a rope, but a woman could tie a knot in her sash. So if a man wanted to get water out of a well and there was nothing tied to the bucket, he could tie his wife's sash to the bucket. Ridiculous? Yes, but desperately fervent! They were not religious dilettantes! Nicodemus was not playing games, and that was one of the reasons he was receptive to Jesus' explanation.

Nicodemus was "a ruler of the Jews." That means he was a member of the Sanhedrin, a group of seventy men, both lay and clerical, who had jurisdiction over every Jew on earth. In addition, our Lord's identification of Nicodemus in 3:10 as "the teacher of Israel" may mean Nicodemus was considered to be the greatest teacher in Jerusalem. There is some evidence that he came from a very aristocratic family that traced its bloodline back to the Maccabees.

Nicodemus was nobody's fool. He was an educated man and an aristocrat. These things—his earnestness, his position, and his education coupled with the fact that he ultimately did respond to Christ (see John 7:50–52; 19:38, 39)—make his life a perfect case study for learning the essentials of salvation. Our Lord could talk to Nicodemus in highly symbolic, compacted language that would have fallen futilely on the ears of the man on the street. Jesus here gives us a dynamic explanation that would perhaps not have been spoken to anyone except a man like Nicodemus.

On that quiet Palestinian evening, a perplexed man moved along the serpentine backstreets of old Jerusalem to talk to a young rabbi. It was the greatest meeting of his life—a supreme experience. He was about to be face-to-face with Jesus.

Nicodemus and Jesus—Face to Face

This man came to Jesus by night and said to him, "Rabbi, we know that you are a teacher come from God, for no one can do these signs that you do unless God is with him." Jesus answered him, "Truly, truly, I say to you, unless one is born again he cannot see the kingdom of God." (vv. 2, 3)

As Nicodemus approached Jesus, he came respectfully, using the honored title "Rabbi." He was prepared for an exchange of philosophical ideas, but he was not prepared for what followed. Jesus cut him off and went straight to the heart of the matter. In a glorious instant the vocabulary of our faith was given one of its greatest concepts—"born again." Nicodemus pondered one of the greatest subjects possible to man, and his wheels began to turn. Many commentaries paint Nicodemus as a theological dummy. But Jesus would not have confronted a dummy with this high thought. Nicodemus knew exactly what was going on when Jesus said he needed to be "born again." The rabbis had a saying: "A proselyte who embraces Judaism is like a newborn child." All things were thought to be completely new, and old connections destroyed. When Nicodemus heard Jesus' words, he knew what Jesus was saying.

Nicodemus and Jesus—Mind to Mind

Nicodemus was mind to mind with Jesus—engaged in the deepest thoughts. Nicodemus was not naively suggesting in his reply some sort of crude gynecological miracle. He was putting forth a deep sense of longing.

"How can a man be born when he is old?" Nicodemus asked. "Can he enter a second time into his mother's womb and be born?" (v. 4).

It was with wistful yearning that Nicodemus said, "You talk about being 'born again,' you talk about that radical, fundamental change that is so necessary. I know it is necessary, but what I question is *how*. There is nothing I would like more. But you might as well tell me that as a full-grown man I need to go back inside my mother's womb and be born all over again. Oh, how I long for the new birth! Oh, how I desire that." Tennyson caught the idea when he wrote:

> Oh, for a man to rise in me,
> that the man that I am
> might cease to be.

That is the heart cry of mankind. We desire to change. We want to be different. We want new minds and new personalities. We want to be born again, but it is as difficult as going back into our mother's womb.

Are you like Nicodemus? Do you want to change? Do you want your life renewed? Do you want to know what it means to be born again, to understand how it can really happen?

> Jesus answered, "Truly, truly, I say to you, unless one is born of water and the Spirit, he cannot enter the kingdom of God." (v. 5)

Again Nicodemus knew what Jesus meant. He realized that at that very time John the Baptist was baptizing people in water as a symbol of their inward repentance. We read about this in 3:23. What flashed across Nicodemus' mind was: "Except you are born of all that water baptism signifies, which is *repentance*, and that which Spirit baptism accomplishes, which is *regeneration*, you cannot enter the kingdom of God." In other words, Nicodemus saw very clearly that no one is born again if there is no repentance; and along with repentance comes a work of the Spirit in the heart. *These are the nonnegotiables of being born again.*

The December 1979 *Christianity Today* stated that according to a Gallup Poll 39.5 million Americans claimed to have asked Christ to be their Savior, and that one in every five adults eighteen years old and over in the United States were evangelicals. If these statistics were or are true, why has the sinful pace of our country not slowed down? With the exploding numbers of evangelicals, why is pornography on the upswing? Why is national and corporate immorality epidemic? How can these things be if one in five of all adults in the United States are evangelical? If one in five of all adults in the United States were Communists, we would all be Communists within a very short time!

I would like to focus on what I believe are the main causes. First of all, there is an incredible ignorance in the church of Christ. The same Gallup Poll indicated that of those who claimed to be evangelicals, three in ten did not think the devil was a personal being. That shows ignorance of Scripture! Only six in ten could correctly identify "You must be born again" as the words of Jesus to Nicodemus (v. 7).

In other words, only six in ten of the people who claimed to be "born again" knew where the verse is or who said it! With this kind of ignorance, it follows that the moral and ethical teachings contained in Scripture are even less understood. Conclusion: It is conceivable that a new Christian, because of a lack of knowledge of what is right and wrong, may improperly repent. I remember a woman whom Barbara and I were instrumental in leading to Christ who, three months after she had her conversion, gave her father a *Playboy* calendar for his birthday. It never occurred to her that would be contrary to what the Lord wanted her to do! Things like this can happen because we live in a post-Christian era, an uninstructed time.

The second and far more important reason is that many people who claim to be born again know nothing of repentance. That means, according to our Lord's definition, that there are multiple thousands of people who claim to be born again but who really are not! Jesus says that unless one is "born of water"—that is, repents—it is impossible to enter the kingdom of God.

The Scriptures teach that there is no new birth without repentance. What does repentance mean? I can think of no better illustration than what happened to one of my sons while in college some years ago when he was playing football. At that time chewing tobacco was the "in" thing on his team, and just about all the men on the team "chewed." So one day after practice he stole up to another player's room and bit off a big "chew," slipping it into the back of his mouth. By mistake he swallowed a little bit, and it burned, and in his confusion he swallowed even more, so that he felt very sick! He could barely make his way out of the room and had to support himself by holding each side of the railing, and when he got down to the alley, everything came up. He was so sick that he lay down on the asphalt in the darkness and watched the moons—all three of them—whirl around! That night he repented! And he has not touched a flake of chewing tobacco since!

Repentance also involves a change of mind. The Biblical word comes from two words—one that means "after" and another that means "thought" or "mind." Chewing tobacco for my son is no longer fashionable. It is no longer the thing that occupies his mind. It is no longer the thing that he wants to do. Rather, it is repugnant to him. When there is repentance, there is a change of action coupled with a change of mind. It is not simply a new direction or an about-face. It is not education. It is not a religious experience. Did you know that being born again is not merely "asking Jesus into your heart"? If that happens *without* repentance, it will *not* bring regeneration and new life.

Being born again is a radical change that takes place in a person's life whereby through repentance and a work of the Spirit he is given a new nature. Second Corinthians 5:17 says, "Therefore, if anyone is in Christ, he is a new creation. The old has passed away; behold, the new has come." And 2 Peter 1:4 adds, "So that . . . you may become partakers of the divine nature."

Our Lord further explained this radical change in verses 6, 7.

> That which is born of the flesh is flesh, and that which is born of the Spirit is spirit. Do not marvel that I said to you, "You must be born again."

The radical change is not something that can be accomplished by human energy.

An Arabian Chicken Little story tells of a young Arab who was traveling along a road on his donkey when he came upon a small, fuzzy object lying in the road. He dismounted to look more closely and found a sparrow lying on its back with its scrawny legs thrust skyward. At first he thought it was dead, but closer investigation proved the bird to be very much alive. The young man asked the sparrow if he was all right. The sparrow replied, "Yes." Then the Arab said, "What are you doing lying on your back with your legs pointed toward the sky?" The sparrow responded that he had heard a rumor that the sky was falling, so he was holding his legs up to support it. The Arab replied, "You surely don't think you're going to hold it up with those two scrawny legs, do you?" The sparrow, after a very solemn look, retorted, "One does the best he can."

But of course our best will never suffice! That is what Jesus is saying in verse 6. "That which is born of the flesh is flesh, and that which is born of the Spirit is spirit." That which is vegetable is vegetable, that which is animal is animal, and that which is flesh remains flesh. There is no evolution from flesh to spirit! Jesus says, "You must be born again" (v. 7). You must realize you are a sinner and repent. You must receive the work of the Spirit in your life. "You must be born again." When Jesus says "must," we had better listen. Have you been born again according to the definition given in John 3? The question is not, have you had a religious experience, or have you had a transformation, but have you been born again?

Possibly as Jesus and Nicodemus were talking they heard the wind moaning along the narrow streets. Very possibly it stirred the leaves that overhung the window and came breathing in upon them.

> The wind blows where it wishes, and you hear its sound, but you do not know where it comes from or where it goes. So it is with everyone who is born of the Spirit. (v. 8)

"Nicodemus, being born of the Spirit is like your experience with the wind. You can see the wind's effect, but not the wind itself." With those who are born again, the effects of the Spirit are visible in their lives, even though the Spirit cannot be seen. One of the reasons we have not seen our country swept for Christ is that there has not been sufficient evidence of the Spirit in Christians' lives. In many cases "salvation" is a bogus experience.

Conclusion

Sometimes the wind of the Spirit is a raging power. Other times it blows gently so you can see it almost imperceptibly move a leaf. I think the winds of the Spirit were roaring for Nicodemus.

Is the wind of the Spirit at work in your life? Perhaps it is gently blowing, soothing your soul. From what you have heard, you feel affirmed. You are born again. You have turned from your sin, and the Spirit of God has washed you clean so that you have a new nature. "That which is born of the Spirit is spirit." If that is true in your life, then praise God!

Or possibly the wind of the Spirit is raging in your life right now. You clearly see the nonnegotiables. You see your sin, and you are repenting. You desire the Spirit to rush into your life and make you a new person. You believe Christ is the answer. If so, why not yield your life to him right now?

10

"How Can These Things Be?"

JOHN 3:9–21

OUR LORD BROUGHT NICODEMUS, the teacher of the Pharisees, face-to-face with the necessity of being born again, then confronted him with the nonnegotiables of the faith.

This encounter with Nicodemus is relevant for us today. The term *born again* has been pirated, emptied of its meaning, dragged through the gutter, and given back to us minus its power. Today when a person says he or she is born again we cannot be sure what he or she means. The mere use of the phrase tells us almost nothing. The truth, however, is that when one is really born again, there is a radical repentance, a radical work of the Spirit in that person's life, and a radical change so that the whole being is brought into new life. The results are discernible—they can be seen.

We see Nicodemus' final question in verse 9: "How can these things be?" That is, "Lord, I see your analogies, but how does this new birth happen? What is the force that lies behind being born again? Where does it spring from? What are its dynamics?" We might add for our own edification, "What does it mean in our lives?" As our Lord began to answer Nicodemus, he skillfully led up to the main thrust. Notice verse 10, where Jesus gently chides Nicodemus: "Are you the teacher of Israel, and yet you do not understand these things?" In other words, "You have all of this learning and yet you do not understand?"

> Truly, truly, I say to you, we speak of what we know, and bear witness to what we have seen, but you do not receive our testimony. (v. 11)

Then Jesus added, "If I have told you earthly things and you do not believe, how can you believe if I tell you heavenly things? No one has ascended into heaven except he who descended from heaven, the Son of Man" (vv. 12, 13). Jesus was saying, "My authority comes from the fact that I came from Heaven."

With that our Lord elected to give what is possibly the greatest illustration from the Old Testament of what the new birth means—the dynamics behind spiritual life.

The Great Illustration of the Cross

And as Moses lifted up the serpent in the wilderness, so must the Son of Man be lifted up, that whoever believes in him may have eternal life. (vv. 14, 15)

With those words Nicodemus' mind spun back thousands of years to what is recorded in Numbers 21. With this reference "the teacher of Israel" was on familiar ground.

From Mount Hor they set out by the way to the Red Sea, to go around the land of Edom. And the people became impatient on the way. And the people spoke against God and against Moses, "Why have you brought us up out of Egypt to die in the wilderness? For there is no food and no water, and we loathe this worthless food." Then the LORD sent fiery serpents among the people, and they bit the people, so that many people of Israel died. And the people came to Moses and said, "We have sinned, for we have spoken against the LORD and against you. Pray to the LORD, that he take away the serpents from us." So Moses prayed for the people. And the LORD said to Moses, "Make a fiery serpent and set it on a pole, and everyone who is bitten, when he sees it, shall live." So Moses made a bronze serpent and set it on a pole. And if a serpent bit anyone, he would look at the bronze serpent and live. (Numbers 21:4–9)

Scholars believe the serpents that are designated here as "fiery serpents" were so called because their bite inflicted a burning fever that, if not checked, brought death.

The picture is one of both horror and glory. It is horrible in that the Israelites were beset by a hoard of "fiery serpents," so many that the people could not escape, and as a result their bodies were inflamed with fever and they were on the verge of death. In fact, many died. What a hideous scene! But at the same time it is glorious because here we also see God's glorious provision of healing. Our Lord left no doubt about the application: "And as Moses lifted up the serpent in the wilderness, so must the Son of Man be lifted up." This is a picture of the dying, sinful world with the atoning cross raised high.

The details of the analogy are remarkable. The snakes are symbolic of sin—in fact, the perfect symbol of sin because it was a serpent that tempted Adam and Eve in the garden, thereby bringing sin into the world. Our very natures have been polluted. Paul says, "None is righteous, no, not one" (Romans 3:10; cf. Psalm 14:1–3). Then we see the likeness of a serpent lifted up on a pole. It is significant that Moses elected not to use an actual serpent. The symbolism would not have been so exact and perfect if he had. Our Lord became sin (or a serpent) for us. Romans 8:3 says, "God . . . sending his own Son in the likeness of sinful flesh and for sin . . . condemned sin in the flesh." Second Corinthians 5:21 adds, "For our sake he made him *to be sin* who knew no sin, so that in him we might become the righteousness of God." And Galatians 3:13 states, "Christ redeemed us from the curse of the law by *becoming a curse* for us."

With all the animal realm from which to choose, God chose the perfect symbol—the serpent. Our Lord on the cross took the sins of the world upon himself as symbolized by the writhing serpent.

We dare not miss the importance of the gaze of faith. Numbers 21:9 says, "And if a serpent bit anyone, he would look at the bronze serpent and live." The command to look to that uplifted serpent was a gracious foreshadowing of looking to Christ for our salvation. No wonder our Lord said, "As Moses lifted up the serpent in the wilderness, so must the Son of Man be lifted up." Moses raised that serpent up high in the camp, and all the dying Israelites had to do was look to that pole and be saved. No matter how horribly they were bitten, no matter how many times they had been bitten or how sick they were, the opportunity for salvation was there. Even the most degraded and miserable sinner who looks to Christ will be saved. That is why our Lord used this wonderful illustration.

Nicodemus had asked, "How can these things be?" How does the new birth happen? And our Lord answered in a way that Nicodemus would never forget. I do not think Nicodemus understood very much at that time, although he knew Jesus' illustration was from the Old Testament. But after our Lord was crucified, he put it all together, for it was Nicodemus who, along with Joseph of Arimathea, came to the Jewish leaders and claimed the Lord's body. Then he understood.

So Jesus has set down for all subsequent generations that the radical change, the new birth, is possible only when he takes our infected natures upon himself, bears the venom, and imparts a new nature to us. "Therefore, if anyone is in Christ, he is a new creation. The old has passed away; behold, the new has come" (2 Corinthians 5:17).

Christ is telling us that the new birth comes through the simple gaze of faith—not by a perfect faith. Perhaps you are hesitating to come to Christ because you are trying to work up enough faith. "I want to believe, I want to experience what these other people have, but I just do not have enough faith!" Some of those dying Israelites had doubts too. They procrastinated. They rationalized. Not all of them believed with the same quality of belief. But there came a time when they did exercise that look. Do not look at your look. Look to Christ. If you have a repentant spirit and you realize that Jesus Christ bore your sins on the cross, then all you need to do is look and be saved! What a great illustration our Savior used!

The Great Explanation of the Cross

The great illustration was followed by the greatest of explanations. Martin Luther called John 3:16 "the gospel in miniature."

> For God so loved the world, that he gave his only Son, that whoever believes in him should not perish but have eternal life.

D. L. Moody said this verse brought him to an understanding of the love of God. As Moody tells it, early in his ministry he had gone to England. While there he met a young minister by the name of Henry Morehouse, and in their conversation Morehouse said to Moody, "I am thinking of going to America." Moody responded, "Well, if you should ever get to Chicago, come down to my church and I will give you a chance to preach." Now Moody really did not mean that. He realized after he said it that he hoped this man did not come to America because he had never heard him preach.

Some time later Moody received a telegram that read, "Just arrived in New York. Will be in Chicago on Sunday. Morehouse." Moody did not know what to do. He had promised the man his pulpit, but he had never heard him preach! So after discussing the matter with his best counselor, his wife, and with the church leaders, he decided to allow him to preach one time. Then if he did okay, he could preach again. Moody had to go out of town, and Morehouse came.

After the week was over, Moody returned and asked his wife, "How did the young preacher do?" His wife responded, "He is a better preacher than you are. He is telling sinners that God loves them. You must go hear him!" Moody said, "What! He is telling sinners that God loves them? That's not true!" She said, "Well, he has been preaching on John 3:16 all week long." Moody made haste to get down to the church that night. Morehouse stood in the pulpit and began by saying, "I have been hunting for a text all week, and I have not been able to find a better one than John 3:16, so I will just talk about it once more." Later Moody testified that on that night he saw the greatness of the love of God as he had never seen it before.

John 3:16 shows us the greatness of God's love, that it is a vast, unbounded, bottomless sea! That is the heart of the gospel! It is not simply "God is love," but "God so loved the world, that he *gave*." That is what lies at the root of the new birth. "Nicodemus, do you want to understand how this can be? It is through the overflowing, unbounded love of God." Many churches sing F. M. Lehman's great hymn about the love of God. Interestingly, the last verse was not penned by him. He found it inscribed on the wall of an insane asylum next to the bed of a man who had evidently found the love of God before he passed away.

> The love of God is greater far
> Than tongue or pen can ever tell,
> It goes beyond the highest star
> And reaches to the lowest hell;
> The guilty pair, bowed down with care,
> God gave his Son to win;
> His erring child He reconciled,
> And pardoned from his sin.
> Could we with ink the ocean fill
> And were the skies of parchment made,
> Were ev'ry stalk on earth a quill
> And every man a scribe by trade,
> To write the love of God above
> Would drain the ocean dry,
> Nor could the scroll contain the whole
> Though stretched from sky to sky.

"Nicodemus, the new birth is possible because of the great, boundless love of God." That is the thrust of the words "God so loved the world."

This great love brings a great result: "That whoever believes in him should not perish but have eternal life." In Boothill in Tombstone, Arizona there is an epitaph for a man by the name of Les Moore. I do not think his friends really mourned his going because this is how the epitaph reads: "Here lies Les Moore. No Les—no more." Maybe that was true of poor Les Moore, but it is not true of those who know Christ! When we die we will be more alive than we have ever been! John 3:16 says that when we believe, we have eternal life as our *present* possession. As Bishop Westcott says, "We enter in qualitatively to that life." Eternal life is *now*, because "God so loved." Furthermore, he offers it to "the world," the *cosmos*, a word used 186 times in the Greek New Testament and always with a sinful connotation. Amazing—God loves the sinful world!

Next we see the condition for eternal life: "That whoever *believes* in him should not perish but have eternal life." Compare the first part of verse 18, "Whoever *believes* in him is not condemned." We receive eternal life by believing. So the greatest explanation follows the greatest illustration.

God	The greatest Lover
so loved	The greatest degree
the world	The greatest company
that he gave	The greatest act
his only Son	The greatest gift
that whoever	The greatest opportunity
believes	The greatest simplicity
in him	The greatest attraction
should not perish	The greatest promise
but	The greatest difference
have	The greatest certainty
eternal life	The greatest possession

In him, we have everlasting life.

The Great Necessity of the Cross

For God did not send his Son into the world to condemn the world, but in order that the world might be saved through him. Whoever believes in him is not condemned, but whoever does not believe is condemned already, because he has not believed in the name of the only Son of God. (vv. 17, 18)

Christ did not come into the world to judge the world, but judgment does come through him, and because of this there is a dynamic process going on that he described in verses 19–21:

And this is the judgment: the light has come into the world, and people loved the darkness rather than the light because their works were evil. For everyone who does wicked things hates the light and does not come to the light, lest his works should be exposed. But whoever does what is true comes to the light, so that it may be clearly seen that his works have been carried out in God.

How men respond to the light indicates how they relate to the new birth. How do *you* respond to the light?

We have been talking about what it means to be born again ("How can these things be?"), and we have seen the supreme illustration ("And as Moses lifted up the serpent in the wilderness, so must the Son of Man be lifted up")—i.e., the atonement. We have seen the greatest explanation ("For God so loved the world, that he gave his only Son, that whoever believes in him should not perish but have eternal life")—i.e., the atonement is possible because of God's great love.

Conclusion

Jesus' illustration about Moses is great not only because it tells us what the great necessity is, but because it suggests what the necessity is *not*. It would have been quite natural for the Israelites to attempt to concoct an antidote to counteract the poison. They could have occupied themselves trying to find a cure for the venom, and some of them would have been pacified right into death with the hope that a cure was imminent.

Similarly, in our own lives we sometimes try to eradicate the "venom" with hopeless rites and chastenings. The Israelites could have vowed to be more careful the next time, but there was no next time. Or as Dr. Barnhouse said years ago, they could have organized to fight the deadly serpents. They could have incorporated The Society for the Extermination of Fiery Serpents. They could have worn badges, issued cards, elected secretaries, had rallies, issued photographs of heaps of slain serpents, and played down the statistics of death. They could have even made offerings to the serpents. But none of these things would have availed. Nicodemus says, "How can this be? How can I be born again?" Through belief in Christ alone—looking to the cross. We must give up our dependence on ourselves—our cleverness, our self-improvement, our plans of becoming religious—and just look to him!

The new nature comes on the basis of the atonement of Christ. Have you looked to him? The Scriptures say, "Turn to me and be saved, all the ends of the earth! For I am God, and there is no other" (Isaiah 45:22). Look to him, believe, and so have everlasting life.

11

"He Must Increase,
but I Must Decrease"

JOHN 3:22–30

THIS PORTION OF JOHN'S GOSPEL opens with a note of intrigue. It is not the sinister kind that comes from premeditated evil, but rather the kind that sometimes sprouts from devotion to a good cause. The problem came from the fact that there were two groups administering the baptism of repentance. There was, first of all, the group that our Lord led.

> After this Jesus and his disciples went into the Judean countryside, and he remained there with them and was baptizing. (v. 22)

But the disciples of John were also baptizing.

> John also was baptizing at Aenon near Salim, because water was plentiful there, and people were coming and being baptized (for John had not yet been put in prison). (vv. 23, 24)

So two groups were publicly doing the same thing—baptizing. The only difference, according to 4:2, was that our Lord did not personally administer any baptisms.

The rub was that John's ministry was being eclipsed by the ministry of our Lord, and loyal disciples of John were jealous for John and felt threatened themselves as well. Things soon came to the surface.

> Now a discussion arose between some of John's disciples and a Jew over purification. (v. 25)

We do not know the details of that conversation, but apparently the Jewish detractor said, "Well, which baptism is superior? Is it John's or is it Jesus'?" Confusion was high among John's disciples.

> And they came to John and said to him, "Rabbi, he who was with you across the Jordan, to whom you bore witness—look, he is baptizing, and all are going to him." (v. 26)

This was an emotional exaggeration because not "all" were coming to Jesus. John was still performing the work of baptism, but his disciples were worried. "Rabbi, your star is sinking. Your ministry is diminishing. What are we going to do?" The implication was that they were not going to allow John to take a backseat to anyone else. The disappointment of watching the ebbing of a ministry that had once been a great flood tide, angry protests to those who were turning away, resentment over the success Jesus was having, largely by virtue of the words of John himself, embarrassment—it was all a very human reaction on the part of John's disciples, and it presented a temptation to John himself. He had spent many years of loneliness and self-denial in the wilderness, no doubt experiencing rejection and alienation from his culture. Now, having experienced headline success, he saw it suddenly begin to fade away. It would have been easy for John to yield to a very natural impulse to assert himself.

No matter who we are, no matter how much success we are having, sooner or later our lives or our ministries will be eclipsed. The most successful, competent, or famous will one day be asked to take a lesser role, and we all need to know how to react at such a time. The text we are studying in this chapter is important because there is a regrettable competition among Christians. The Bible itself records that this is inherent in the church down through history. One of the greatest examples is the experience the Apostle Paul had when he was under house arrest in Philippi. We read these words from the Apostle in Philippians 1:15–17:

> Some indeed preach Christ from envy and rivalry, but others from good will. The latter do it out of love, knowing that I am put here for the defense of the gospel. The former proclaim Christ out of selfish ambition, not sincerely but thinking to afflict me in my imprisonment.

While he was imprisoned, Paul, the missionary statesman of the early church, learned that some were proclaiming Christ out of "selfish ambition." The word translated "ambition" is literally "political ambition." There is a great deal of competition in the church of Christ. Years ago I heard Dr. Kenneth Chapin, pastor of the Main Street Baptist Church in Houston, Texas, a dynamic preacher, a man who at one time held the Billy Graham Chair of Evangelism at Southwestern Baptist Theological Seminary, say that when he was a professor of homiletics he gave a test to his young students—men who were going to be preachers. It was a scientifically designed word association test. Dr. Chapin said he was appalled to find so much bitterness and resentment in those men who were preparing for the ministry. Key words or phrases such as *truck driver* would invariably elicit derogatory responses such as "lazy." He said he came to realize through this test—and subsequent conversations—that very often those who go into the ministry are negative, highly competitive people. They particularly did not like preachers! This is a generalization, of course, but the pervasiveness of this phenomenon in church history has produced an exquisitely cynical Latin term, *odium theologicum*—hatred of theologians. Very few things give the enemies of Christianity an occasion for blasphemy like a jealous party spirit among Christians.

This passage has a contemporary impact, and I think it should be a mandatory study for all Christian workers. It is vital for everyone who names the name of Christ to understand what is taught here. Our competitive society is structured to compel us to measure our achievements against those of others.

As we go through the text, particularly verses 27–30, we will give passing reference to its primary or vertical significance, and then to its horizontal significance (i.e., how we are to relate to other believers).

The Proper Philosophy (vv. 27, 28)
John stood before his angry and excited disciples and quietly answered their resentful assertions with a proverb that is recorded in verse 27: "A person cannot receive even one thing unless it is given him from heaven."

That is, on a human level, if a man is displaying gifts superior to mine and having greater success than I am, it is because God has given those to him. That is the proper philosophy by which to evaluate the successes of others. Someone may have more education than I and may be prospering. He may have a nicer home, a larger or happier family, prestige. But the Scriptures say, "A person cannot receive even one thing unless it is given him from heaven."

At the same time, this is the proper way to evaluate our own successes. There is an unhappy human tendency to play down the successes of others and to uplift our own. If someone is doing well, we attribute it to a "golden spoon" or being at the right place at the right time. But if *we* happen to be particularly successful, it is because of our prowess, intelligence, and hard work! But the proper philosophy by which to evaluate our own successes is to remember that "A person cannot receive even one thing unless it is given him from heaven." The Apostle Paul says in 1 Corinthians 4:7 (TLB):

> What are you so puffed up about? What do you have that God hasn't given you? And if all you have is from God, why act as though you are so great, and as though you have accomplished something on your own?

So whether we are looking at ourselves or others regarding success, the proper philosophy is, "A person cannot receive even one thing unless it is given him from heaven."

John grounded his philosophy in a high view of God as the sovereign bestower of gifts. He could tolerate being outstripped by another because he knew that God does not make mistakes. I have seen this truth literally revolutionize people as they see that God has sovereignly created them with the gifts and abilities they have. They are set free!

Of equal importance is that John's philosophy, seen vertically, was grounded in an overwhelming desire for God's glory. Numbers 11:26–29 gives us a perfect example from the life of Moses. In the camp of Israel there were two men on whom the spirit of prophecy had come—Eldad and Medad—and they were prophesying in the camp, not at the Tent of Meeting.

> And a young man ran and told Moses, "Eldad and Medad are prophesying in the camp." And Joshua the son of Nun, the assistant of Moses from his youth, said, "My lord Moses, stop them."

Even Joshua, with all of his wisdom, was shaken by jealousy!

> But Moses said to him, "Are you jealous for my sake? Would that all the Lord's people were prophets, that the LORD would put his Spirit on them!

"Do you know what I wish? I wish everyone was prophesying for the Lord! How wonderful that would be!" Moses had seen God's glory, and it gave him great joy to see others catch a glimpse of that glory and exercise their spiritual gifts! I think it is no wonder that we read just a few verses later in Numbers 12:3:

> Now the man Moses was very meek, more than all people who were on the face of the earth.

The spirit of John the Baptist and the spirit of Moses were very much the same. They were two of the greatest men who ever lived. We can easily see that John applied this philosophy to his own life.

> You yourselves bear me witness, that I said, "I am not the Christ, but I have been sent before him." (v. 28)

John answered that he knew who he was (he had a good self-image). The overall tone of his response was freedom. He saw that God had sovereignly appointed differences between himself and the One who outshined him, the One he was free to serve. So in John's life there was no tinge of rivalry, no jealousy, no insecurity, no bitterness. Beautiful! Moreover, John kept on ministering. Although John and Jesus were only a few miles apart, and Jesus was having much larger crowds come to him, and greater things were being said about Jesus and his ministry, John stuck to his appointed task.

Do you feel outdone? Outclassed? Eclipsed? Has someone come into your life who is obviously more gifted or more effective, someone you are finding it difficult to accept? You need to remember, "A person cannot receive even one thing unless it is given him from heaven." When that heavenly philosophy is operating in our lives, it produces security, joy in God's work, humility, and freedom. How liberating it is to have a proper philosophy!

The Proper Attitude (v. 29)

> The one who has the bride is the bridegroom. The friend of the bridegroom, who stands and hears him, rejoices greatly at the bridegroom's voice. Therefore this joy of mine is now complete.

John portrayed his feelings toward the ministry of Christ in a superbly rich illustration—the Hebrew wedding. He said he was like the best man, like "the friend of the bridegroom." According to William Barclay:

> The "friend of the bridegroom," the *shoshben*, had a unique place at a Jewish wedding. He acted as the liaison between the bride and the bridegroom; he arranged the wedding; he took out the invitations; he presided at the wedding feast. He brought the bride and the bridegroom together. And he had one special duty. It was his duty to guard the bridal chamber and to let no false lover in. He would only open the door when in the dark he heard the bridegroom's voice and recognized it. When he heard the bridegroom's voice he was glad and he let him in, and he went away rejoicing, for his task was completed.[1]

John the Baptist said he found his fullness of joy in his Master's voice. We too are to find joy in Christ, but it has a double joy for us, because as members of the church we are the bride of Christ!

On a relational level, this suggests that the proper attitude toward fellow believers who outstrip us is to share the joy of their accomplishments just like a best man. It was a great event when I stood as best man for my closest friend, David MacDonald. We had been friends since we were teenagers. We had gotten into trouble together, double-dated together, and were college roommates. As I stood next to him at his wedding, I was not jealous. Although his bride was beautiful, I did not begrudge him. As a matter of fact, my joy was intimately tied up with my good friend. If something had gone wrong, I would have been greatly disturbed. His happiness was my happiness. My joy was made full.

We are supposed to rejoice in the successes of our brothers and sisters in Christ. This is rooted in one of the great metaphors of Scripture—the Body of Christ. The Apostle Paul says in 1 Corinthians 12:26, "If one member suffers, all suffer together; if one member is honored, all rejoice together."

Humanly speaking, John the Baptist faced a temptation that could have easily overcome him. He had been at the crest of his popularity. All segments of society had come out to hear him. Some people said he was Elijah incarnate. Herod himself was listening to John. But now his crowds had begun to diminish. Yet he rejoiced! No wonder we read in Matthew 11:11, "Truly, I say to you, among those born of women there has arisen no one greater than John the Baptist." His humility was the key to his greatness, just as it was with Moses, and it is the key to any greatness of ours, whether we serve in a great or small place. We should rejoice in the success of others, for we are bound together in Christ.

The Proper Conduct (v. 30)

He must increase, but I must decrease. (v. 30)

There is no other way to live for Christ! This is an operational imperative! It is a *must*, not an option. As William Carey lay dying, he turned to a friend and said, "When I am gone, don't talk about William Carey; talk about William Carey's Savior. I desire that Christ alone might be magnified." That was the spirit of John the Baptist as well. "He must increase, but I must decrease."

How are we to approach our eclipse, whether it is happening now or when it comes in the future? What is to be our attitude? There must be a volitional exalting of others' gifts and ministries and a rejoicing over the successes and growth of our brothers and sisters. The great preacher F. B. Meyer ministered in London at the same time that Charles Spurgeon was preaching in the great Metropolitan Tabernacle. As a young man, though dynamic and gifted, Meyer would stand on the steps of his church Sunday after Sunday and watch the carriages flow by to Spurgeon's church. That was difficult for him, but he did it. Another story comes from the end of Meyer's life, when he was preaching in Northfield at the invitation of D. L. Moody. G. Campbell Morgan was preaching there at the same time. Great crowds came to hear Morgan, but very small crowds came to hear Meyer. The latter was not in his prime, and Morgan was in the full bloom of his preaching power. Meyer came back to his cottage one day feeling very sad, and he began to pray. Later he was heard saying to people, "Have you heard Campbell Morgan preach? Did you hear that message this morning? My, God is upon that man!" "He must increase, but I must decrease." That is the proper conduct.

Conclusion

One of the most beautiful jewels in the treasury of the Old Testament is the story of Jonathan and David. After David's victory over Goliath, according to 1 Samuel 18:1, "The soul of Jonathan was knit to the soul of David, and Jonathan loved him as his own soul." That commitment grew with time, and Jonathan set himself to make David king, although as the oldest son of Saul, King of Israel, Jonathan was heir apparent to the throne. Rather than pursuing his own interests and advantage, Jonathan acted as a reconciler between his father and David and literally saved David's life. On the day David finally became king, Jonathan was not there, for he had died in battle along with his father. No one who has ever read David's mourning cry for his friend Jonathan can forget it.

> I am distressed for you, my brother Jonathan; very pleasant have you been to me; your love to me was extraordinary, surpassing the love of women. (2 Samuel 1:26)

Jonathan was a dramatic illustration of the selfless spirit of John the Baptist—a man who, seeing another who is anointed for a greater task, joyfully accepts God's appointed design.

Are we being eclipsed or in the process of being eclipsed? It will happen. Is someone or some group the focus of our envy? Is there someone whose success we secretly begrudge? God has called us to a proper philosophy— "A person cannot receive even one thing unless it is given him from heaven."

He has called us to a proper attitude—"The friend of the bridegroom, who stands and hears him, rejoices greatly. . . ." He has called us to proper conduct—"He must increase, but I must decrease."

Is God speaking to you about these things? William Law has suggested it is impossible to harbor animosity and jealousy toward one for whom we are praying.

> If . . . someone is leaving you behind, and you are becoming jealous and embittered, keep praying that he may have success in the very matter where he is awakening your envy; and whether he is helped or not, one thing is sure, that your own soul will be cleansed and ennobled, that you will grow a little nearer to the stature of the Baptist.

One more suggestion: Covenant before God to say something good either to the person or on behalf of the person you envy.

12

The Heart
That Ministers

JOHN 4:1–9

THOSE OF US WHO CLAIM the name of Christ must choose again and again between two very distinct courses. One is to cultivate a small heart. That is the safest way to go because it minimizes our sorrows. If our ambition is to avoid the troubles of life, the formula is simple: minimize entangling relationships and carefully avoid elevated and noble ideas and we will escape a host of afflictions.

Cultivate deafness, and we will be saved from the discords of life. Cultivate blindness, and we will not see the ugly. It is universally true for all of us that if we want to get through life with a minimum of trouble, we just have to reduce the compass of our hearts. This is how many people, even those who name the name of Christ, get through life with minimal tribulation. They have cultivated smallness of heart.

But another path is also open to us—namely, to open ourselves to others and become susceptible to a gamut of sorrows about which a shriveled heart knows nothing. Enlarge and ennoble your purpose and you will increase your vulnerability proportionately! A sentence in the diary of James Gilmour, pioneer missionary to Mongolia, written late in his life, must have been written in blood.

> In the shape of converts, I have seen no results. I have not, as far as I am aware, seen anyone who even wanted to be a Christian.

Painful words, are they not? Contrast now those words with what he wrote when he first arrived in Mongolia:

Several huts in sight! When shall I be able to speak to the people? O Lord, suggest by the Spirit how I should come among them, and guide me in gaining the language, and in preparing myself to teach the life and love of Christ Jesus!

I have not, as far as I am aware, seen anyone who even wanted to be a Christian.

James Gilmour would never have written those later pathetic lines if he had not decided to go for it all in his service for Christ. In fact, there is a very real sense in which James Gilmour's being in this position was his fault because he had decided to follow Jesus! If James Gilmour had never set out for Mongolia, he would never have experienced those hopes or disappointments.

Enlarge your heart, cultivate a ministering heart, and you will enlarge the potential for pain. Some are hurting specifically because they have enlarged their hearts. They have pursued elevated ideals and have given themselves to others, and that decision has left them prey to sorrows that otherwise would have been avoided.

Will you serve Christ and others, or yourself? Your decision will affect the kind of heart you will have. Little hearts, though safe and protected, never contribute anything. No one benefits from restricted sympathies and limited vision. On the other hand, ministering hearts, though vulnerable, are also the hearts that know the most joy and leave their imprint on the world. Cultivate deafness, and you will never hear the discords of life, but neither will you hear the glorious strains of a great symphony! Cultivate blindness, and you will never see the ugly, but neither will you see the beauty of God's creation. Cultivate a small heart, and you may have smooth sailing, but you will never know the heady winds of the Holy Spirit in your sails! You will never be borne along in power and exhilaration and will never see lives changed and great things happening for God.

We only have to glance at a daily newspaper to see there is a great need for ministering hearts—enlarged hearts—caring hearts. The story of our Lord and the woman at the well gives us insight into the ministering heart.

John 4 begins by indicating that Jesus decided it was time to conclude his disciples' baptizing ministry in Judea and move on up to Galilee by way of Samaria.

So he came to a town of Samaria called Sychar, near the field that Jacob had given to his son Joseph. Jacob's well was there; so Jesus, wearied as he was from his journey, was sitting beside the well. It was about the sixth hour. (vv. 5, 6)

They were journeying north about noontime, and they came to Jacob's well, near Sychar. There Jesus dispatched his disciples into town to get groceries, then sat down wearily by the well. Notice that "Jesus, wearied as he was from his journey, was sitting," just as any tired man would after a hard day's work.

A Ministering Heart Reaches Out Though Tired (vv. 1–6)

The ministering heart is a tired heart. Our Lord was weary in the service of souls. He reacted as any other exhausted man would at the end of the day. He was obviously more weary than his disciples because he did not accompany them into town. All we have to do is glance at the Gospels, and we see that our Lord could hardly find two minutes to rub together. He had to steal away to avoid the crowds. The disciples constantly asked him questions and needed him to minister to them and teach them by example. The multitudes were constantly pressing on him. When mental fatigue and physical weariness come together, we have a tired man! So our Lord was weary in his ministry to hearts. If he was more like me, he would probably have thought to himself, "If Peter asks me one more question . . . !"

Perhaps our Lord had his eyes closed as he reclined by the well when he heard the approaching footfall of another person. He looked up and saw a Samaritan woman! It would have been easy to rationalize in this situation. "I have been ministering to thousands, and I am tired. I just have to relax!"

That choice was available to Jesus, but that is not what he did! Our Lord went for the heart of this woman, and we have here one of the most glorious cases of spiritual aggression in all of Scripture! Jesus reached out to others even when he was at the edge of physical exhaustion. He had a ministering heart.

A ministering heart carries on when it is at the edge of its capacity. I think it was Oswald Sanders who said, "The world is run by tired men." I believe that is true. Though many Christian workers across the world are on the verge of collapse and need to take care of themselves and get some R & R, it is also true that the Christian world is run by tired men and women. I recall Anne Ortlund once saying, "Nowhere in the Bible are we told to slow down and take it easy." She then quoted various Scriptures. We are to "press on," "not grow weary of doing good," "run with endurance the race," etc. Our greatest rest and recreation will be ours in Heaven.

Most souls are won by tired people!

The best sermons are preached by tired men!

The best camps are run by exhausted youth ministers!

The Third World is being evangelized by tired missionaries!

Christian organizations are being run by tired men!

You show me a super VBS and I will show you some tired women!

We will never do great things for God until we have learned to minister when we are tired. In the sports world an athlete who endures and achieves his potential is one who learns to play with injuries. I am not talking about the wisdom of that, but the point is, in spiritual realities we need to learn to keep reaching out when we are tired. It has been my experience that quite often I have been most used when I was at the point of exhaustion. We will never do great things for God until we learn to minister when we have tired hearts!

Christ's example also teaches us that *a ministering heart is a working heart*. That was Paul's heart.

> For you remember, brothers, our labor and toil: we worked night and day, that we might not be a burden to any of you, while we proclaimed to you the gospel of God. (1 Thessalonians 2:9)

Paul was constantly working to proclaim the gospel. I always marvel at 2 Corinthians 11, the magnificent passage in which Paul presents his "credentials" to his detractors. He talks about the lashes he had received—195! "You want to know my credentials? There they are!" He talked about his shipwrecks and his being stoned in Lystra and the numerous things he had endured. He never hesitated when preaching to talk about dangers upon dangers upon dangers upon dangers. But the thing that most amazes me is his statement that "Apart from other things, there is the daily pressure on me of my anxiety for all the churches. Who is weak, and I am not weak? Who is made to fall, and I am not indignant?" (2 Corinthians 11:28, 29). A ministering heart is a working heart.

Luther said he worked so hard that when he went to bed, he literally fell into bed. In fact one account says he did not change his bed for a year! Now that's tired! Moody's bedtime prayer on one occasion was, "Lord, I am tired. Amen." Calvin's biographers marvel at his output. John Wesley rode sixty to seventy miles a day and on an average preached three sermons a day. When Alexander Maclaren went into his study he took off his slippers and put on working men's boots because he knew that a minister of God is to be a working man!

Our Lord's example calls us to expand our hearts and by doing so to be vulnerable to pain and disappointment as we reach out in love to others.

A Ministering Heart Overcomes Barriers (vv. 7–9)

> A woman from Samaria came to draw water. Jesus said to her, "Give me a drink." (For his disciples had gone away into the city to buy food.) The Samaritan woman said to him, "How is it that you, a Jew, ask for a drink from me, a woman of Samaria?" (For Jews have no dealings with Samaritans.)

The Samaritan woman responded to a heart that crossed barriers. She was absolutely amazed at Jesus' conduct. The bitter hatred between the Jews and Samaritans was long-standing—hundreds of years. In 721 BC the Assyrians swept through Israel, the Northern Kingdom, and took the inhabitants off to Assyria. During their years in Assyria, many Jews intermarried with the Assyrians and Cuthites.

In 587 BC Babylon took the people of the Southern Kingdom, Judah, captive into Babylon. But in Babylon there was no intermarriage, and when the Jews came back to their homes they were of unadulterated Jewish blood. As a result they refused to accept their northern kinsmen, and both sides developed an implacable, murderous hatred for each other. Jewish rabbis said, "Let no man eat the bread of the Cuthites [the Samaritans], for he who eats their bread is as he who eats swine's flesh." A popular prayer in those days said, "And Lord, do not remember the Samaritans in the resurrection." So it was truly amazing when Jesus crossed those lines.

In addition to that barrier, Jesus broke through another barrier by speaking to the person approaching the well, for she was a woman. Strict rabbis forbade other rabbis to greet women in public. There were even Pharisees who were called "the bruised and bleeding Pharisees" because when they saw a woman in public, they would cover their eyes and so bump into walls and houses as they walked about! Jesus not only spoke to this woman but asked to use the woman's drinking utensil and so become defiled. This is an utterly amazing story! Our Lord's ministering heart leapt across the conventional barriers of the day—a radical gesture.

Andrew Maclaren wrote:

> When these words were spoken, the then-known civilized world was cleft by great, deep gulfs of separation, like the crevasses in a glacier, by the side of which our racial animosities and class differences are merely superficial cracks on the surface. Language, religion, national animosities, differences of condition, and saddest of all, difference of sex, split the world up into alien fragments. A "stranger" and an "enemy" were expressed in one language, by the same word. The learned and the unlearned, the slave and his master, the barbarian and the Greek, the man and the woman, stood on opposite sides of the gulfs, flinging hostility across.

But then the gospel came! Then "the Barbarian, Scythian, bond and free, male and female, Jew and Greek, learned and ignorant, clasped hands and sat down at one table, and felt themselves 'all one in Christ Jesus.' They were ready to break all bonds."[1]

The world looked at the early Christians and accused them of sorcery and conspiracy because they could not understand what was going on. The great glory of the church is that the gospel of Christ crosses barriers!

Many believers today insist that pragmatically it is otherwise. Doctors best evangelize doctors, athletes best evangelize athletes, and ethnics best evangelize their own race, they say. Personally I believe the ideal is to have our hearts so filled with love that we are willing to go the extra mile and bridge social barriers.

Jesus calls us to have a ministering heart, to reach out to others regardless of the barriers, and that is the mark of an authentically enlarged heart—the heart of Jesus—the heart of Paul. That was the heart of Gilmour of Mongolia.

Perhaps we need to cross some barriers in our lives. Maybe we have never shared Christ with some people with whom we rub elbows because they are not like us. Perhaps our Lord is asking us to have a ministering heart.

A Ministering Heart Sees Providence in Relationships (v. 4)

The ministering heart is aware of divine arrangement in human acquaintances. Such a heart goes about its daily business, passing from person to person, proceeding from divine appointment to divine appointment. The idea is implicit in verse 4: "And he had to pass through Samaria."

The scholar Raymond Brown says, "This expression of necessity means that God's will or plan is involved." Jesus was aware of the sovereign ordering of his life so people would come his way. I have not forgotten the frustration of traveling 250 miles across the Mojave Desert to take some young people witnessing. When we got there, we could not find a place to camp. We drove up and down that stretch of river near Parker, Arizona, trying to find a place, and it was getting dark. Finally we pulled into a camp and found a place to pitch our tent—right next to five boys who eventually trusted Christ. Four of them are in the ministry today. I came to realize that my frustration was a prelude to God's sovereign appointment.

Stuart Briscoe has shared a story that is even more dramatic. When he was at Capernwray Bible School, he and his wife were separated from each other for a day. He had left her the car, but he had accidentally taken the keys with him. After a couple of hours, Jill borrowed another car, and as she was driving down the road she saw some girls hitchhiking, so she picked them up.

They turned out to be three German girls visiting England. She managed to persuade these girls to come with her to a conference for German Christian young people, and one of them was marvelously saved there. Afterwards Stuart Briscoe told that girl's story:

> She was a theological student in Germany. She had come under the influence of some teaching that, instead of leading her to an intelligent worship of God, had filled her with much doubt and confusion. She had delivered an ultimatum to the God whose existence she doubted. She told God that if he was there he should show himself to her in some way. He must do this within three months. If he didn't, she told him, "I'll quit my schooling, quit theology, quit religion, and I *think* I'm going to quit living because there's nothing to live for."
>
> After explaining this, she turned to my wife with great emotion and said, "The three months end today."

The ministering heart has an awareness of the sovereign ordering of life. It is indeed a sobering thing to realize that we never talk to a mere mortal. Never! Everyone we meet will live eternally, either as a glorious being or as a dreadfully lost soul. The ministering heart senses this and treats all encounters accordingly.

Conclusion

A ministering heart is an expansive heart that ministers when it is weary. A ministering heart is so filled with love that it crosses the normal barriers of life and reaches out. A ministering heart sees divine potential in its relationships. It is an enlarged heart, and it is remarkably vulnerable, just as Christ's was. This is not a safe path, but it is the only way to go. As C. S. Lewis wrote:

> To love at all is to be vulnerable. Love anything, and your heart will certainly be wrung and possibly be broken. If you want to make sure of keeping it intact, you must give your heart to no one, not even to an animal. Wrap it carefully round with hobbies and little luxuries; avoid all entanglements; lock it up safe in the casket or coffin of your selfishness. But in that casket—safe, dark, motionless, airless—it will change. It will not be broken; it will become unbreakable, impenetrable, irredeemable. The alternative to tragedy, or at least to the risk of tragedy, is damnation. The only place outside Heaven where you can be perfectly safe from all the dangers and perturbations of love is Hell.[2]

13

The Ministering Heart's Message, Part I

JOHN 4:1–15

IT IS A SPIRITUAL IMPERATIVE that we have ministering hearts. Having an enlarged heart will equip us to serve others. Jesus overcame his weariness and some difficult social and religious barriers, as discussed in the last chapter, because the Samaritan woman had a parched soul that had never found satisfaction, and our Savior knew that if he did not reach her, her soul would go on searching vainly and bitterly. From the brief exchange recorded in John 4:16–18 we can clearly see her problems.

> Jesus said to her, "Go, call your husband, and come here." The woman answered him, "I have no husband." Jesus said to her, "You are right in saying, 'I have no husband'; for you have had five husbands, and the one you now have is not your husband. What you have said is true."

Her life was a miserable chain of unfulfilling relationships. The pathetic fact that she had married five times indicates that she longed for fulfillment in her life and that she had sought it intensely. Our modern minds have no trouble imagining the course her life had taken. Her first marriage had probably begun with the racing exhilaration that is common to new love. She expected it would carry through her entire life. But something went wrong, and she had been left alone. Then came another man, and the fires began to flame again, though not quite as high as before, only to disintegrate into cold ashes. Then came another . . . and another . . . and another . . . and another. Now as she comes to the well at noon, so she can avoid the respectable people, she is worn down and despised. There are few abuses that have not been hurled at her by the people of Sychar. About the only things she has left are her quick tongue and her wits. Above all, she is filled with a deep longing, a thirst for something better.

It is fitting that as she comes to the well, she carries a pail so she can draw water to assuage her thirst. That Samaritan woman illustrates the longing of mankind and our thirst for something more fulfilling in life. In a local newspaper I read a review of a book on the life of George Sanders that contained his famous suicide note. George Sanders was at one time a leading man in Hollywood who had been married to Zsa Zsa Gabor and Benita Hume. He was a graduate of Cambridge University and was a brilliant mathematician. In sum, he was a man of exceptional mental and social abilities, but his note contained an element of Samaritan dissatisfaction and despair.

> I am committing suicide because I am bored. I feel I have lived long enough.
> I leave you all in your sweet little cesspool and I wish you luck.[1]

Ours is an age of thirst! Over the years I have heard with some regularity a popular song that keeps repeating the refrain, "Is that all there is?" The singer sings progressively about her experience and then wistfully says, "Is that all there is?" Such a sentiment could have been written by the writer of Ecclesiastes. Certainly it could have been written by the Samaritan woman. It is the song of all who try to slake their thirst with the world. Our text tells us what Christ prescribes for that thirst.

Our Lord's addressing the poor woman amazed her, producing the incredulous question, "How is it that you, a Jew, ask for a drink from me, a woman of Samaria?" (v. 9). That question gave Jesus the opportunity to meet the thirsting of her heart.

The Ingredient of Satisfaction (vv. 10–13)

> Jesus answered her, "If you knew the gift of God, and who it is that is saying to you, 'Give me a drink,' you would have asked him, and he would have given you living water." (v. 10)

On the surface it sounds like Jesus was simply saying that if she had known who he was and had asked him for a drink, he would have given her clean, sparkling, flowing water instead of the comparatively stagnant water of Jacob's well. It is possible on a literal level that this could be what he meant since the Greek words for "living water" mean "flowing water," as in a stream. However, I do not think that is the case for several reasons. First, when he used the term "living water," she probably understood something more than the physical because that phrase has many Old Testament associations. In Jeremiah 2:13 Jehovah calls himself "the fountain of living waters." Psalm 36:9 was an oft-quoted passage, as it is today: "For with you is the fountain of life." Similarly Isaiah 55:1 says, "Come, everyone who thirsts, come to the waters." Psalm 42:1, 2 states, "As a deer pants for flowing streams, so pants my soul for you, O God. My soul thirsts for God, for the living God." Furthermore, the messianic kingdom was talked about as a time when "living waters" would slake the thirst of mankind. So when Jesus used this expression, virtually everyone in the Hebrew or Samaritan tradition would have had an intimation of what he was saying. Taken together with the fact that he said in verse 10, "If you knew the gift of God, and who it is that is saying to you, 'Give me a drink,'" it is clear that the woman understood what he was saying and that her rejoinder was not just a simple statement.

> The woman said to him, "Sir, you have nothing to draw water with, and the well is deep. Where do you get that living water? Are you greater than our father Jacob? He gave us the well and drank from it himself, as did his sons and his livestock." (vv. 11, 12)

What the Samaritan woman understood him to say was that God was the only one who could satisfy her longing, but even more, Jesus was claiming to be the one who could give her the divine drink she needed. From our advantaged position we know he was talking about the impartation of life through the Holy Spirit. As we read a little later in 7:37, 38:

> If anyone thirsts, let him come to me and drink. Whoever believes in me, as the Scripture has said, "Out of his heart will flow rivers of living water."

What Jesus was saying to the woman was this: Nothing will ever satisfy our longings and dissatisfactions except for a long and continuous drink of God the Holy Spirit. In contrast:

> Everyone who drinks of this water will be thirsty again. (v. 13)

If unbelievers could be convinced to really believe Christ's claims, they would be saved from untold misery and would receive inexpressible joy into their lives. The truth is, those who drink of the natural wells of life will thirst again, and they can never quench their thirst with the natural waters of life.

Companionship and intimacy—the natural waters of life—will not satisfy people's longings. Jesus makes it clear, the whole body of Scripture makes it clear, and our experience makes it clear that companionship and sexual intimacy do not satisfy the thirstings of the soul. Notwithstanding the fact that these things are created by God and are given to us by him for immense pleasure and fulfillment in life, they do not quench our deepest longings. Many maintain a false courage that reasons that while this may be true for others—true for my parents (what do they know about these things?), true for my brothers and sisters, true for my relatives, true for the pastor—it is not true for them! Such a view is incredibly egocentric, naive, provincial, and foolish! George Sanders would tell us the same thing if he could do so today.

Sometimes we try to slake our thirst with materialism or exemplary achievement. In this regard, apart from the Bible itself, I do not think I could quote better wisdom than that which comes from Abd al-Rahman, an eighth-century monarch of Cordova:

> I have now reigned above fifty years in victory or peace; beloved by my subjects, dreaded by my enemies, and respected by my allies. Riches and honors, power and pleasure, have waited on my call, nor does any earthly blessing appear to have been wanting to my felicity. In this situation I have diligently numbered the days of pure and genuine happiness which have fallen to my lot; they amount to Fourteen: O man, place not thy confidence in this present world!

> He who loves money will not be satisfied with money, nor he who loves wealth with his income. (Ecclesiastes 5:10)

To try to quench our thirst with the things of this world is much like unfortunate sailors who, when they became famished, let themselves drink of the ocean, only to find themselves more wretched than they could have imagined possible.

For many the futile search for satisfaction manifests itself in the "when syndrome." When we are the age of a young child, we think life will come together when we become teenagers and get big and strong. When we are teenagers, we think life is going to shape up (from a boy's perspective) when we get a car. When we get our car, we expect life will be fulfilled when we graduate from high school. When we are in college, we think our needs will be met by marriage. When we are married, we think it will come through children. After that, it is when the children leave home. And finally, we pin our hopes on retirement. The fact is, trying to slake our thirst with the things of the world is like eating a Chinese dinner—no matter how much we eat, in a short time we are hungry again! Jesus says, "Everyone who drinks of this water will be thirsty again," and we need to believe his words!

The Completeness of the Satisfaction (v. 14a)

> But whoever drinks of the water that I will give him will never be thirsty again.

What a beautiful promise! Two things happen when we drink the water that comes from God. First, our thirst is *completely* satisfied, and second, it is *permanently* satisfied. I do not believe our Lord is saying we will never spiritually hunger or thirst again, but he is saying that within us is implanted such a supply of water that we never have to go thirsty. This is very much like the hungering and thirsting after righteousness by which we are filled (Matthew 5:6). Our capacity increases, and we are filled—a delicious spiral that goes on and on and on. So we never have to go thirsty again. Are you full, or is your life like a Chinese dinner?

The Character of the Satisfaction (v. 14b)

> The water that I will give him will become in him a spring of water welling up to eternal life.

This is a remarkable picture because the phrase used for "welling up" is rarely used of anything but living beings. It is typically used of the movement of bodies, for instance in Acts 3:8 where the lame man is healed and we read about him running and jumping in the temple praising the Lord. But here John applies it to the water that is within us. He is saying that when we have the divine spring, it is like a jumping, leaping, dancing fountain within us. What a picture of joy and effervescence! My own heart has experienced that bounding, leaping joy that comes from having the well of water within. I have been famished and thirsty and then had "living water" overflow my life.

Life with Christ is not stagnant but is full of motion and change. So often the world presents itself as exciting and energizing, but there is really nothing more boring than the pursuit of pleasures in an attempt to satisfy our souls. Real excitement, on the other hand, comes from drinking deeply at the well of water that springs up into everlasting life. "Out of his heart will flow rivers of living water" (7:38). Once God puts his fountain of life within us, our life streams out to others.

Not only is there an outwardness here but an upwardness. Jesus says in the last part of verse 14 that the well of water springs up into everlasting life. This image has a vertical thrust, as if the law of gravity were taken away so that when the water springs up, it keeps going eternally. Is that not an exquisite image? In Revelation 7:17 we read:

> For the Lamb in the midst of the throne will be their shepherd,
> and he will guide them to springs of living water,
> and God will wipe away every tear from their eyes.

This surging of water within us satisfies all our needs and ineluctably flows up into eternity. Our empty, parched lives are suddenly filled with living water—a dancing fountain—that springs up within us and continues right on into eternity.

Conclusion

Not long after the conversation we have been discussing, Jesus would attend the Feast of Tabernacles, the autumn harvest feast that commemorated the Israelites' sojourn in the wilderness. It was a colorful event because pilgrims came from all around the world to attend it. They came from the entire circle of the Mediterranean and from as far away as the steppes of Russia. When they arrived, they would build tiny shelters all over Jerusalem in remembrance of their wanderings for forty years. There were even construction rules for the shelters! The walls had to be constructed so as to give shelter but not shut out the sun during the day. The roofs were thatched so the stars could be seen at night. The purpose of these rules, of course, was to remind them that they were once homeless wanderers. It was a festive event, and everyone wore their brightest clothes. It was considered by some to be the most festive of all the festivals. For instance, we read in Zechariah 14:16 that the prophet dreamed of a day when the whole world would come to Jerusalem and build shelters at the Feast of Tabernacles.

The festivities featured a daily ceremony that began at the temple, where the people gathered together, then formed a processional on down to the Pool of Siloam. Alfred Edersheim, the great authority on Christ's life, tells us that as the people came, they brought palm branches and pieces of willow and cypress to make into wands that they carried in their right hands. In their left they carried a citrus fruit called a "paradise apple." The branches were meant to remind them of the desert, and the fruit was to remind them of the harvest. When all was ready, the music began, and the great throng headed down to the Pool of Siloam, shaking the branches and citrus fruit rhythmically to the music as they followed the white-clad priest carrying a golden pitcher. When they came to the Pool of Siloam, the priest dipped that pitcher with great joy and carried it back to the temple as the people continued singing and chanting Psalms. As they came to the gates of the temple, there could be heard three loud blasts from silver trumpets, and the priest would enter the temple confines to pour the water on the altar.

It was traditionally thought at that time that to see the water poured out on the altar was the high point of a dedicated Jew's life. Some considered it the height of joy. In fact, Edersheim records that a priest by the name of Alexander Janaeus once poured the water on the floor, and there ensued such a riot that around the environs of the temple 6,000 people were killed! As they chanted the *Hallel*, the great hallelujah Psalms together, there came a pause, and at that time the water was poured out on the altar. It is at that time, according to Edersheim's calculations, that Jesus stood and cried, "If anyone thirsts, let him come to me and drink. Whoever believes in me, as the Scripture has said, 'Out of his heart will flow rivers of living water.'" Now this he said about the Spirit" (John 7:37–39).

There could hardly be a more dramatic offer. It is essentially the same offer that Jesus made to the poor Samaritan woman. And it is an offer to us today—the offer of the Holy Spirit. The conditions upon which we may receive Christ's offer are twofold. First, we must thirst, then we must ask.

> If you knew the gift of God, and who it is that is saying to you, "Give me a drink," you would have asked him, and he would have given you living water. (v. 10)

And the woman did ask.

> The woman said to him, "Sir, give me this water, so that I will not be thirsty or have to come here to draw water." (v. 15)

At that point a process began that would culminate in her salvation.

Is your life a Chinese dinner? Are the delights that you pursue satisfying for a short time and then gone? Or is your life a well of living water, springing up, dancing within you, streaming up to eternal life, so that you will never thirst again?

If you are thirsting, why not ask for that spiritual water? Jesus always keeps his word.

14

The Ministering Heart's Message, Part II

JOHN 4:16–26

OVER THE YEARS it has been typical for preachers and commentators to imagine that the Samaritan woman's quick response to Jesus' devastating revelation that he knew she had had five husbands and the man she was living with was not her husband was a clever attempt to divert the conversation. They feel that when she stated, "Sir, I perceive that you are a prophet," she was attempting to deflect Jesus from the painful subject of her moral life.

But I do not think that view is correct. The Samaritans, as well as the Jews, at that time believed a prophet was sometimes given special insight into people's problems. For instance, there was the time when Jesus was having his feet washed by a penitent woman and the Pharisees snidely remarked, "If this man were a prophet, he would have known who and what sort of woman this is who is touching him, for she is a sinner" (Luke 7:39). The supposition is that true prophets have intuitive gifts. So it is reasonable to conclude that Jesus' knowledge of the Samaritan woman's condition, along with his claim to provide for her "a spring of water welling up to eternal life" (4:14), produced her sincere supposition that he might be a prophet. Then when she brought up the controversy about worship, she was asking a question that was the result of her dawning perception of who he was and of her sin and the knowledge that something needed to be done about it. She was evidently saying to herself, "I am a sinner before God. I must bring God an offering for sin. But where do I take it?" To her and her people, the cure for sin was sacrifice. But where was the sacrifice to be made? She was concerned about what God desired from her, and the answer was worship.

In the times in which we live there is epidemic confusion not only about the where and how of worship but about the function of Christianity in general. A feature article in *Harper's Magazine*, entitled "Trendier Than Thou," told how the Bishop of California, Kilmer Myers, welcomed Bay Area transcendentalists to Grace Cathedral for light shows, guitar liturgies, nature festivals, and pagan ceremonies.

> In 1971, during one nature ceremony in the cathedral, a decidedly ecumenical audience watched reverently as the poet Allen Ginsberg, wearing a deer mask, joined others similarly garbed to ordain Senators Alan Cranston and John Tunny as godfathers of animals (Cranston of the Tule elk and Tunney of the California brown bear).

As a native Californian, I do not want to see the Tule elk or the brown bear become extinct, but there seems to be something druidic about all this. The article continues:

> The cathedral dean was dimly seen through marijuana smoke, wrestling atop the high altar to remove a cameraman, while movie projectors simultaneously cast images of buffalo herds and other endangered species on the walls and ceilings, to the accompaniment of rock music. Although Episcopal priests had protested that this vigil would be a "profane employment of this sacred house of worship," Bishop Myers joined in nonetheless and offered prayers for a "renaissance of reverence for life in America."[1]

It is very significant that this exposé was written by Paul Seabury, professor of economics at the University of California, Berkeley and one of the descendants of Samuel Seabury, the first Episcopal bishop in America. The man knows what he is talking about.

A Chicago newspaper carried a church service review by its religion editor that mentioned, among other things, his surprise when the Communion service included the words "Today while the blossoms still cling to the vine, I'll eat your strawberries and drink your red wine."

But before we get too smug, one of the great evangelical spokesmen of our time once said:

> I wonder if there was ever a time when true spiritual worship was at a lower ebb. To great sections of the Church the art of worship has been lost entirely, and in its place has come that strange and foreign thing called the "program." This word has been borrowed from the stage and applied with sad wisdom to the type of public service which now passes for worship among us.[2]

The point of all this is that worship is a tremendously compelling and important subject! In Philippians 3:3 the Apostle Paul lists it as one of the three great distinctives of true belief. True believers "glory in Christ Jesus," they "put no confidence in the flesh," and they "worship by the Spirit of God." This is a tremendously important subject! In fact, in the book of John there are three "musts." John 3:7: "You *must* be born again"; 3:14: the Son of Man "*must . . .* be lifted up"; and 4:24: "God is spirit, and those who worship him *must* worship in spirit and truth." Practically and theologically, "Christian worship is the most momentous, most urgent, most glorious action that can take place in human life" (Karl Barth). It is the highest function in which our souls can be involved. The very highest!

In our text John reveals that our Lord views this matter of worship as of the utmost importance, and that is why he immediately answered the woman's questions, dispensing with the irrelevant and going to the heart of the matter.

> Jesus said to her, "Woman, believe me, the hour is coming when neither on this mountain nor in Jerusalem will you worship the Father." (v. 21)

In other words, the question of the *place* of worship is irrelevant.

> You worship what you do not know; we worship what we know, for salvation is from the Jews. (v. 22)

If Jesus gave her any further explanation, it undoubtedly included the fact that the Samaritans' worship was not adequate because they used only the first five books of the Bible, thus limiting themselves to an incomplete knowledge of the revelation of God. They worshiped in ignorance—"You worship what you do not know." Moreover, salvation is from the Jews—specifically, from the tribe of Judah.

But the real question, and this was the question Jesus answered, was, what does God require in worship? We find the answer in verses 23, 24.

> But the hour is coming, and is now here, when the true worshipers will worship the Father in spirit and truth, for the Father is seeking such people to worship him. God is spirit, and those who worship him must worship in spirit and truth.

What does God require? Worship "in spirit and truth." We will consider the last first.

God Seeks Those Who Will Worship Him in Truth (vv. 23, 24)

"Truth" means that we are to worship what is true about God. In other words, worshiping in "truth" occurs when we worship in accordance with what God has revealed about himself. That is true worship. The converse is also true—true worship does *not* take place when we do not worship in accordance with what God has revealed about himself. So what we think about God is of great importance. Subscribing to a Biblically based creedal statement is virtuous, though of course it is possible to mouth the words of a creed and mean something entirely different.

The truth is, the mightiest and most important thought man can entertain is, what is God like? What comes into our minds when we think about God? This is foundational. Our answer not only affects our worship but our living. Every failure in worship, or in doctrine or practice, can be traced back to wrong thoughts about God.

Going way back in history, we see that wrong thoughts about God were the source of Cain's failure to worship God as he should. Somehow Cain supposed God to be other than what he is, and he brought a sacrifice to fit his misconception. Some say Cain's error was one of sophistication. He thought, "Well, why in the world would God want an unattractive, bloody sacrifice instead of a beautiful sacrifice from the field?" Cain distorted the truth about God (his wisdom, his omniscience, and his goodness) and as a result brought the wrong sacrifice.

Likewise, in our times, to allow Allen Ginsberg in league with Transcendentalists to cavort around a great cathedral wearing a deer mask suggests a grave departure from the revelation God has given of himself in Scripture. When the church's concept of God in any way blurs, not only does worship suffer, but moral standards decline. I believe one of the answers to the divorce problem today is not just teaching on the family, though that is important, or teaching on relational aspects from Scripture, but teaching on who God is! When we see who God is and what he requires, and when we subscribe to these things in the very depth of our being, we will take seriously his plan for relationships in life.

Wrong thinking about God is in fact idolatry because an idolatrous heart assumes God is other than he is. In our sophisticated, civilized times we must not think we are free from idolatry just because we do not bow down to physical images. A wrong conception of God is the root of idolatry. "For although they knew God, they did not honor him as God" (Romans 1:21). Instead they created images. Idolatry begins with a wrong idea of who God is.

The pitiful truth is, the typical modern-day concept of God is decadent!

Some see him only as a cosmic force or the "ground of being." When we conceive of God in this way, we will worship him with an icy reverence. On the other hand, some conceive of God as a "God Pal." Everything in religious life is essentially centered on me and what God can do for me. God becomes a kind of cosmic slot machine, but instead of inserting quarters we put in Scripture verses to get what we want from him. This is by far the most popular concept of God today—the God who gives me whatever I want, the God who is my buddy. Gone is the awe and reverence of which he is worthy.

God wants his people to worship him in truth, as he really is.

> But the hour is coming, and is now here, when the true worshipers will worship the Father in spirit and truth, for the Father is seeking such people to worship him. (v. 23)

We must be people of the Word, because the clearest revelation of God that we have is in his Word. John would later record (17:17) Jesus' words in his High-Priestly prayer: "Sanctify them in the truth; your word is truth." God's Word contains truth about God! Charles Spurgeon, when he was talking about how we need to be full of the Word of God, said that when you cut a preacher the blood he bleeds should be "bibline." We are to be people filled with the Word of God. When that happens, the attributes and the metaphors and the words that so beautifully describe God become the music of our hearts.

Not only do we need to be people of the Word, but we need to be people who think. Worship is not a mindless activity. It includes mental interaction with the truth about God. We also need to develop the ability to hold contrasting truths about God in devotional tension. On the one hand we see him as the mighty, eternal, transcendent Creator who holds the universe together (Hebrews 1:3), while on the other hand we hold him to be the One who said, "O Jerusalem . . . How often would I have gathered your children together as a hen gathers her brood under her wings" (Matthew 23:37). We must see all we can of God through his Word if we are to worship him in "truth"! To worship only one attribute of God and ignore others is not worshiping him in truth. Worship must include the total revelation of who God is. When this happens, God is worshiped in truth, idolatrous hearts are purged, moral lives are elevated, and God is pleased.

God Seeks Those Who Will Worship Him in Spirit (vv. 23, 24)

God seeks those who will worship "in spirit." The Greek is quite clear here. It does not say "in the Spirit" but "in spirit." In other words, Jesus is not talking about worshiping in the Holy Spirit. He is talking about worshiping with or in the human spirit. What our Lord means is, he is not only looking for those who will worship him in the truth of who he is, but also in the very depth of their inner being—in spirit. Authentic worship happens only when the very core of our being is employed in worshiping God!

Outward performance may or may not be worship. As Spurgeon said, "God does not regard our voices, he hears our hearts, and if our hearts do not sing we have not sung at all." Sometimes we sing but do not worship. Sometimes we pray with our lips, but worship does not take place. Sometimes we give, but we do not worship. And sometimes we do none of these things but are in deepest worship! Outward circumstances cannot determine the authenticity of our worship. One could conceivably kneel in the most beautiful of cathedrals, listen to the most concise Biblical liturgy, and luxuriate in the strains of Evensong and still not be truly worshiping. This is not to say that externals are not helpful. Generally I think C. S. Lewis was right when he said that the best church service is the one we least notice.

> As long as you notice, and have to count the steps, you are not yet dancing but only learning to dance. A good shoe is a shoe you don't notice. Good reading becomes possible when you need not consciously think about eyes, or light, or print, or spelling. The perfect church service would be the one we were almost unaware of; our attention would have been on God.[3]

We need to realize that some of the most precious worship recorded in Scripture happened in the least likely circumstances. Remember how it was in Acts 16? Paul and Silas found themselves in a Philippian jail. "The magistrates tore the garments off them and gave orders to beat them" (Acts 16:22). They were thrown into prison. The jailer "fastened their feet in the stocks." It was "midnight." It is a scene of the most intense misery—their backs hanging in shreds, sitting in the inner dungeon of the Philippian jail, their feet in stocks so they could not even comfortably recline, sleepless with the insomnia of pain. I have sometimes imagined Silas and Paul conversing with one another and Silas saying to Paul, "Paul, I just can't take it any longer!" Paul turns to Silas and groans, "Silas, I can't either—I just have to sing!" And that is exactly what they did in that miserable Philippian jail! "About midnight Paul and Silas were praying and singing hymns to God, and the prisoners were listening to them" (Acts 16:25). They held a gospel service in that Philippian jail! Despite the difficult circumstances, there was such worship in their spirits that it inexorably bubbled into life! Those who worship God must "worship the Father in spirit and truth," and that can happen anywhere! This is one of the most wonderful things about worship.

There is something else we must never forget. Because as believers we have renewed spirits, our capabilities for worship have been infinitely expanded. Since the Holy Spirit has touched our human spirits, we have been renewed and have an expanded capacity and an enlarged hunger for worship. New believers cannot get enough of worship. That is the way we all should be. One of the major flaws of today's Christianity is that many times we do not make provision for worship, and as a consequence people sense an incompleteness in the church. Children who are raised in that kind of environment, where there is no real focus on worship, will sometimes later leave orthodoxy for empty forms that massage the need to worship. How wonderful it is to worship "in spirit"! May we be the kind of people the Lord seeks!

Conclusion

Our text suggests an intensity on God's part as well.

> For the Father is seeking such people to worship him. (v. 23)

The central reality in worship is not that we are seeking God, but that he is seeking us! This is a totally Christian idea. The Jews never thought of God this way. That is a wonderful thing about worship—the expectancy within us is just a shadow of God's expectancy! Zephaniah 3:17 says God "will exult over you with loud singing." God seeks worshipers!

Are we worshipers who worship him "in spirit and truth"? It is possible to attend a church from our youth, to fall into the habit of the liturgy (and every church has its own liturgy), to be a fairly diligent reader of the Word, and to do so for fifty or sixty years, and yet never once worship God the way Jesus described it. Tragic!

The Samaritan woman had no such privileged history, but she worshiped. The Samaritans had a belief that a prophet like Moses was going to be raised up and that he would explain the Law. They even had a name for him—the "*Taheb*"—and as a result the woman openly speculated about whether Jesus might be he.

> The woman said to him, "I know that Messiah is coming (he who is called Christ). When he comes, he will tell us all things." (v. 25)

In other words, "Are you the Christ?"

Jesus said to her, "I who speak to you am he." (v. 26)

Whether it was then or sometime in the future, that woman began to worship "in spirit and truth"—she believed what Christ said.

Perhaps it has never been your experience to actually worship "in spirit and truth." The first thing you need, of course, is the Messiah. You need to receive him just as that woman did, in the revelation of the truth of what he is—the God who holds the universe together, the God who became man and died and rose again for you. You need to be born anew. When that happens you will be able to worship "in spirit and truth." Whatever our condition, God wants us to be men and women who really understand how wonderful he is. God wants us to stand at his feet and be amazed at who he is and adore him in his awesome majesty. He wants to be worshiped "in spirit and truth." There is nothing more important than what we think of him and how we worship him. Nothing! May we heed his words and worship him "in spirit and truth."

15

Thinking Rightly about God's Love

JOHN 4:23, 24

WE LEARN FROM A STUDY OF Jesus' encounter with the Samaritan woman that there is scarcely anything more important in all our lives than what we think about God. Charles Spurgeon wrote over one hundred years ago:

> The proper study of God's elect is God; the proper study of the Christian is the Godhead. The highest science, the loftiest speculation, the mightiest philosophy that can ever engage the attention of a child of God, is the name, the nature, the person, the work, the doings, and the existence of the great God whom he calls his Father.[1]

If today's church would give itself to the serious study of God, it would cure itself of a multitude of ills because the study of God is the antidote to idolatry. Idolatry at its very core is a wrong conception of God. There never has been an idol fashioned by a man's hands that did not first exist as an image in his mind. In fact, mental idolatry is in some ways far more insidious than physical idolatry.

In order to think rightly about God, first of all we need to know the Word of God, because the Word of God is the ultimate revelation of the data about God. We also need to think and reflect upon the truths we receive. Worship is not only knowing facts about God, but thinking about that data and lifting it back up to him. We must appropriate the truth about God in our lives so it permeates our spirits and flows back up to him. When this happens, we are fulfilling what God is seeking—people who worship him "in spirit and truth."

In one sense it is impossible for mankind to know the truth about God. As

St. Augustine said, "When I am asked what God is, I think I know, but when I try to answer the question, I find that I know nothing." This is the dilemma all of us face—even preachers—when we tackle these great truths.

A more manageable question might be, where do we err the most in our understanding of God? Or what is the greatest evangelical error in our understanding of him? I would like to suggest it is in an area upon which there is great emphasis today—an area that is very popular in our generation. In fact, there are more lectures given on this topic, and more chapters in books dedicated to this subject, than any other. It is *the love of God*. It is my opinion that wrong thinking about God's love is the greatest source of unwitting idolatry and evangelical heresy in the church today. Not only that, I think when we fail to understand God's love, we fail to understand the entirety of God, for God's love programs and controls all the rest of his attributes. When we think wrongly about God's love, we think wrongly about all of God. So there could be nothing more important in our understanding of the truth about God than our understanding of "God is love" (1 John 4:8, 16).

What is the meaning of "God is love"? How do we conceive of God's love? How do we *think rightly* about this matter of God's love? We are going to answer these questions not so much from our text (John 4:23, 24) but from a broader Scriptural perspective.

The Problem: Errant Views of God's Love

Several years ago I performed a wedding I was sure would be a winner. The bride was a young woman who had grown up under my ministry. In fact, I had had her under my direction for about ten years—since she was a little seventh grader with bangs hanging over the top of her glasses. Now she was a mature woman. At the age of twenty-two she was an extremely attractive, marriageable young woman. I will never forget the hot summer night when at a church function she brought a young man to me who was *the* man for her. He had come to the area to study for the ministry (that always warms my heart). He was an excellent evangelist. He had a beautiful singing voice and was an exceptional songleader. He was handsome, good-natured, and very kind. In fact, my daughters (as little girls) would say, "Daddy, when I grow up, I want to marry a man just like him."

He was some catch! They had a beautiful wedding and ecstatically embarked on a life with high potential. He energetically attacked his work and his studies, and she went about her occupation. The young man was a great help to me in the church. He led songs and sometimes would preach if I was not available. He had a large home adult Bible study that people loved. They flocked to his study even when he was a seminary student. After a few years an opening came in a neighboring church, and I gave him the highest recommendation. In fact, I have never written a recommendation like that for anyone else! When he took that church, he was excited! He was a very effusive, outgoing man and was unusually thrilled for the opportunity to preach the Word and be a pastor. Everything was in his favor. I expected great things.

Of course he faced the typical problems everyone experiences—pressures of the ministry, budget problems, and so on—but nothing out of the ordinary. So it was a great shock when one day he came to me in tears and said, "My wife is divorcing me. She doesn't want to be a minister's wife. She will give no other reason."

Nothing could dissuade her—nothing. They are divorced today, and he is out of the ministry. Do you know what her rationale was? The rationale with which she fortified herself as she pursued the dissolution of her marriage, not listening to anyone—parents, friends, pastors, counselors? It was, "I'm not happy. God loves me and wants me to be happy. Therefore, this marriage is not God's will. A loving God wouldn't want me to spend my life with a man I don't love." That was the reason she gave for ending her marriage. Sadly, that story is coming from thousands of male lips today too—"I'm not happy, so I'm leaving."

Our understanding of God does affect the way we live! To be fair, we should also say the way we live affects our understanding of God. What we practice influences our theology. In this particular case, "God is love" somehow filtered through the grid of the young woman's mind and came out, "God exists to make me happy according to my definition of happiness." That is functional heresy! That is in essence idolatry!

A wrong concept of God permeates other areas of life as well—for example, parenting. Never before have parents been so convinced of their responsibility to make their children happy. The unfortunate thinking goes something like this: A loving parent will attentively do everything he or she can to make a child happy according to the child's perspective. That idea is so prevalent that the *Los Angeles Times* carried an article describing why young married couples were not having children. One of the major reasons was that they did not want to take on the obligation of making someone else happy. The *Times* also revealingly theorized that the problem stems from the fact that today's parents were brought up by parents who made them believe that *their happiness* was more important than anything. Whatever the reasoning, typically both children and parents today are subjected to the vicious accusation, "You have not made me happy as I desire. Therefore, you do not love me."

This misguided thinking is projected from our experience right back up to God the Father, so that he is imagined as nervously biting his celestial finger-nails as he tries to find creative ways to keep his children happy according to their own disposition and desires.

When we are in this frame of mind, our thinking can become even more bizarre. John 3:16 ("For God so loved the world, that he gave his only Son . . .") is mentally (and practically) appropriated to suggest that the sacrificial agonies Christ endured on the cross are an illustration of what he goes through to pro-cure our day-to-day happiness. "Christ is simply dying to make me happy!" From there one reasons, "I cannot be happy until I am financially successful. And it is God's will that I be successful because he loves me." There are also some today who believe that if you come to Christ and follow him, you will be comfortably well off. "I cannot be happy when I am sick. Therefore, it is not God's will that I be ill, because God loves me." The final absurdity says God loves me so much that his happiness is bound up with mine. When I am happy, God is happy. Whatever makes me happy makes God happy.

These perversions of God's love go hand in hand with the narcissism of our times. As you probably know, Narcissus was a Greek god who walked one day beside a pond, looked down, saw his reflection, and after that could never love anything besides himself. "Me-ism" is a malady of our contempo-rary culture. As Alexander Solzhenitsyn said in a controversial BBC speech:

> We have become hopelessly enmeshed in a slavish worship of all that is pleasant, all that is comfortable, all that is material. We worship "things." We worship products. . . .

He could well have added that *we worship happiness.* When "God is love" becomes in our minds "God is Santa Claus," we have reached the lowest point of Christian idolatry. We have become no better than the pagan who worships a god of his own making, one he thinks will supply him with a happiness of his own imagining. We have perverted the truth about God's love. What we think about God's love is one of the most important things in our lives.

What *do* we think of God's love? The antidote to idolatry is to think rightly about God and his love.

The Solution: The Truth about God's Love

The truth is, God's love is a holy love. God's love never conflicts with his holi-ness and his righteousness. His love is not regulated by sentiment but rather by *principle.* His love calls us to him, but so does, equally, his truth, virtue, goodness, and holiness. He is holy, so he seeks holiness in those he loves. He never condones actions that are not consonant with his righteousness. Never! He does not make the weak-minded errors of an overindulgent parent. He does not let himself be deceived by his children's foolish plans for temporary happiness. What my unfortunate friend failed to see is that God cares for our happiness in a far deeper way than she could possibly hope for. She failed to grasp that happiness is first found in God's character. God cares far more for our happiness than we do, and he is not going to let us settle for an inferior happiness. He wants the highest for us.

What does it mean to be a happy person? The formula for happiness is found in Jesus' Sermon on the Mount.

> Blessed [happy] are the poor in spirit, for theirs is the kingdom of heaven.
> Blessed are those who mourn, for they shall be comforted.
> Blessed are the meek, for they shall inherit the earth.
> Blessed are those who hunger and thirst for righteousness, for they shall be satisfied.
> Blessed are the merciful, for they shall receive mercy.
> Blessed are the pure in heart, for they shall see God.
> Blessed are the peacemakers, for they shall be called sons of God.
> (Matthew 5:3–9)

In other words, *happiness means having God's character in our lives.* That will be our ultimate happiness—having the character of God perfectly and completely when we are with him in Heaven. The pitiful irony in the story of the young lady is that if she does not repent, she has forsaken her only hope for true happiness in life.

All of this springs from the fact that God is *agape* love, the very highest form of love. *Agape* love has two aspects—God's intelligence and his will. God sees with greater intelligence and from a wider perspective than we ever could. He knows what real happiness is, and he wills that we be happy. Seeing this, we begin to think rightly about God's love.

Also, God is always good. Nahum 1:7 says, "The Lord is good." From the opening chapters of Genesis to the end of Revelation, we find the same testimony—God is good. He is *always* good, for he never changes. These thoughts naturally lead to the truth that his goodness has caused him to identify himself with our welfare. Those absurd statements—"God loves me so much that his happiness is bound up with mine. God is happy when I am happy. Therefore, whatever makes me happy makes God happy"—are deliriously true by *his definition* of happiness. He has indeed bound up his happiness with ours. J. I. Packer, in his book *Knowing God,* affirms this when he says, "God has in effect resolved that henceforth for all eternity his happiness shall be conditioned upon mine."[2]

Is that not a marvelous truth? God's happiness is bound up with my happiness and yours! Only, it is according to *his definition* of happiness. That is the nature of love. It attaches its happiness to the object it loves. For some reason known only in God's wisdom, he has attached his happiness to ours. That truth is beyond hope or belief! It is a logical implication of Christ's incarnation and death. To grasp this is to think rightly about God.

Remember too that his love is infinite. Paul says in Ephesians 3:19 that "the love of Christ . . . surpasses knowledge." Literally, it super-surpasses knowledge! Years ago a famous English preacher named Leslie Weatherhead recorded that on a Mediterranean cruise he witnessed the unexpected nocturnal eruption of the famous island volcano Stromboli. He beautifully described how the whole sky was aglow with a marvelous display—how he and the passengers watched this for four hours until it faded off beyond the horizon. Weatherhead, being a preacher, reflected upon what he had seen and concluded that for a few hours the fires that had been burning in the mountain's heart since the foundation of the world were revealed. Then he penned these words:

> I sometimes think about the Cross,
> And shut my eyes, and try to see
> The cruel nails and crown of thorns,
> And Jesus, crucified for me.
> But even could I see him die,
> I could but see a little part
> Of that great Love, which, like a fire,
> Is *always* burning in his heart.[3]

The measure of someone's love is how much he is willing to give. The measure of our Lord's love is the cross! Just like that volcano that momentarily flamed, revealing its inner fire, we must see the infinite fire of Christ's love.

> Because God is self-existent, his love had no beginning; because he is eternal, his love has no end. Because he is infinite, it has no limit. Because he is holy, it is the quintessence of all spotless purity. Because he is immense, his love is an incomprehensibly vast, bottomless, shoreless sea. . . .[4]

All his attributes are brought to clear focus in the infiniteness of his love.

If we could catch the truth about God's love and get it straight in our minds and hearts, it would make a profound difference in our lives. The truth of his infinity, the truth that he actually attaches his happiness to our happiness, and the stabilizing fact that he is always good must be balanced with the truth that God is holy, intelligent, has a will, and is not going to let any of us settle for a shabby imitation of happiness. He will lovingly pursue us and push us on to real happiness. That is God's love. That is thinking rightly about God. If we can learn to hold all of this in blessed devotional tension, we will be greatly blessed!

Conclusion

> But the hour is coming, and is now here, when the true worshipers will worship the Father in spirit and truth, for the Father is seeking such people to worship him. (v. 23)

God is seeking people to truly worship him. There is a divine poignancy in all of this, because the mere fact that God has to seek means there are few people who choose to worship God in truth and spirit. The question is, do *we*? Do we really worship him in truth? Do we worship him in spirit? Having the truth is not enough. In the seventeenth century every gentleman made it his hobby to study theology, very much the way Spurgeon urged just on hundred years ago. History reveals that although they knew the truth, many of them did not worship in spirit because the truth never penetrated their lives. We are to worship God in the reality of the love that has been poured out to us. "God's love has been poured into our hearts through the Holy Spirit who has been given to us" (Romans 5:5). And when that happens, true worship takes place in our lives.

"God is love," and he wants to be worshiped fully as such. He wants our human spirits to flow back up to him in adoration. I believe it is a passionate thing that he desires—he wants our hearts to be poured out, caught up in the truth of all that he is. God is seeking men and women in his church today to love him like that. May we love him with all our hearts.

16

The Ministering Heart's Approach to Life

JOHN 4:27–42

IN HIS CONVERSATION WITH THE Samaritan woman, our Lord had shown a ministering heart that was able to cross substantial barriers of race and social convention. Despite his utter weariness he was able to minister to the dear woman and to offer her "a spring of water welling up to eternal life" (4:14). Then the Lord explained what God requires from those who worship him.

Now we come to the final movement in our Lord's dealing with the Samaritan woman. It is framed with the two contrasting results of the probing dialogue. The first is very happy, the second regrettable. It is happy because Jesus, in response to the woman's questions, revealed that he was the Christ.

> So the woman left her water jar and went away into town and said to the people, "Come, see a man who told me all that I ever did. Can this be the Christ?" (vv. 28, 29)

She was so touched by her interaction with Christ that she indulged in a bit of pardonable exaggeration. It was impossible in such a short amount of time for the Lord to recite *everything* that she had ever done, but this is understandable in view of the circumstances and the difference Christ was making in her life.

Regrettably, the disciples evidently had not gotten beyond the social and cultural conventions about the woman, as we see in verse 27:

> Just then his disciples came back. They marveled that he was talking with a woman, but no one said, "What do you seek?" or, "Why are you talking with her?"

Knowing Jesus, the disciples probably surmised he was talking to her about spiritual things. Nevertheless they were amazed. Perhaps they shared the common opinion of the day, typified by this rabbinical comment:

> A man shall not be alone with a woman in an inn, not even with his sister or his daughter, on account of what men may think. A man shall not talk with a woman in the street, not even with his own wife, and especially not with another woman, on account of what men may say.[1]

To the disciples, conversation with the Samaritan woman was a grave breach of convention. One sage even went so far as to say:

> He that talks much with womankind brings evil upon himself and neglects the study of the Law and at last will inherit Gehenna.[2]

Such thinking is a radical departure from God's revelation on the subject.

So we have here a vivid contrast between the disciples' narrow incredulity and the woman's happy enthusiasm, all of which prompts our Lord to give some unforgettable instruction on what it is to have a ministering heart, not just in relationship to women, but in relationship to all people. In doing so, he gives us the secret of what our approach to life ought to be if we are followers of Christ.

A Transcending Priority (vv. 31–34)

> Meanwhile the disciples were urging him, saying, "Rabbi, eat." But he said to them, "I have food to eat that you do not know about." So the disciples said to one another, "Has anyone brought him something to eat?" Jesus said to them, "My food is to do the will of him who sent me and to accomplish his work."

Our Lord's intended thrust was that he was so engrossed with the woman's spiritual well-being that he cared little about anything else. Perhaps Jesus' thoughts were alternating between prayer and concern about what was going to happen to the woman as she went into the city. Perhaps our Lord was even thinking about the words he was going to say when she returned. "I have food to eat, and I am not hungry at this time because I am caught up in what will happen in this woman's life."

At the same time Jesus was directing his disciples to embrace the highest priority along with him. In fact, there was great purpose in his conversation. He could easily have deflected all the talk about his eating simply by courteously taking a morsel and making a kind remark, but instead he directed their attention to higher matters. He said in verse 32, "I have food to eat that you do not know about." The "I" and the "you" here are emphatic. "*I* have something that *you* do not have!" He was attempting to draw them to what he wanted to say and teach. When their curiosity was sufficiently aroused, he said, "My food is to do the will of him who sent me and to accomplish his work" (v. 34). "I wish," he implies, "that you had the same food I have. I put the highest emphasis on God's will and work in my life. That is my food." The transcending priorities in Jesus' life—serving God by doing his will and his work—were his sustenance in life.

I have a confession to make—I am a fisherman. From the time I was old enough to hold a pole I have loved fishing! The fishing instinct is a permanent part of my psyche. I even have catalogs and books on the subject beside my bed. I can tell you that for a fisherman, few thrills can equal searching all day for a marlin and then spotting in the distance those noble saber fins, easing the boat up to within fifty feet, presenting the bait, breathlessly watching the fish submerge, wondering if he really has the bait, feeding out the line, counting impatiently, and then striking! The experience is something I will never forget—the marlin sounding, his explosion from the water not thirty feet from the boat and, to use Hemingway's phrase, "falling back into the water like a horse," and then the leaping battle! At such a moment I am lost in heart-pounding euphoria!

The exhilaration of catching that marlin suspends my desire for other things. We have all found this phenomenon to be true in our own lives one way or another. There are some (a few) who have experienced similar feelings parsing a Greek verb. Others of us have found this feeling in our hobbies or favorite books. The point is, there are certain things that can become like food to us—suspending the conscious need for sustenance.

On a more elevated level, there are times when serving God becomes food and energy for the soul. I am reminded of the great William Wilberforce, the man who did so much to combat the evils of slavery in nineteenth-century England. He was not much in appearance. Barclay says, "When he rose to address the House of Commons the members at first used to smile at this strange little figure." He was sickly and unimpressive. But when he began to speak, the people soon realized a fire burned within him. Of Wilberforce it was beautifully said, "The little minnow became a whale." Serving God had become his food.

Historians say that John Knox, the great Scottish preacher, was so feeble as an old man that he had to balance himself on the pulpit. But as he began to preach, his voice, at first very weak, would regain the power of a trumpet call, and he was likely "to ding the pulpit into blads [to knock the pulpit into splinters], and leap out of it!" The message completely filled the man with divine power, and he experienced supernatural sustenance. That is what happened with our Lord.

When Jesus came to the well, he was weary. The long walk from the south to the north, the disciples' pressing him with endless questions, the incessant crowds, and the constant questions and badgering made him a tired man. Then the woman came to the well. After the initial verbal sparring, the conversation began to pick up, and so did he. He was exhilarated in the service of God. He was feasting on the potential he saw in that woman's life. He was so absorbed in what could happen to her that he forgot himself. Jesus found sustenance by being consumed by God's work. Just as I am consumed as I hold a fishing rod, forgetting everything else, our Lord was consumed with the welfare of his catch. His sympathy for a needy soul blotted out his conscious need for food.

I do not think our Lord was suggesting that when people are really spiritual, they go without food. Nor do I think that he was saying anything against the disciples for suggesting that he eat. As believers we need to realize that we are not angels. We have to eat and sleep. But Jesus was saying that we should have such a passion for God's work that we temporarily forget about our own physical welfare and say, "My food is to do the will of him who sent me."

The Lord was also teaching us that the believer who feeds on such food will grow and be nourished. Charles Spurgeon, the great Baptist preacher, challenged his own congregation with the teaching of this verse in a blunt confrontation.

> Some of you good people, who do nothing except go to public meetings, the Bible readings, and prophetic conferences, and other forms of spiritual dissipation, would be a good deal better Christians if you would look after the poor and needy around you. If you would just tuck up your sleeves for work, and go and tell the Gospel to dying men, you would find your spiritual health mightily restored, for very much of the sickness of Christians comes through their having nothing to do. All feeding and no working makes men spiritual dyspeptics. Be idle, careless, with nothing to live for, nothing to care for, no sinner to pray for, no backslider to lead back to the cross, no trembler to encourage, no little child to tell of a Savior, no grey-headed man to enlighten in the things of God, no object, in fact, to live for; and who wonders if you begin to groan, and to murmur, and to look within, until you are ready to die of despair?[3]

I would have liked to have been there for that sermon! There is spiritual sustenance in serving Christ by caring about others. It is very possible if you sense that something is not right in your life even though you have been studying the Word and having regular prayer and devotions that you simply need to be involved in his work, for where his will and work become part of your life, so will a sense of sustenance and well-being. We are made and redeemed to serve.

Our Lord shows us by example that spiritual sustenance comes from God's will and his work.

> Jesus said to them, "My food is to do the will of him who sent me and to accomplish his work." (v. 34)

Christ lived to do God's will. We read in Psalm 40:8 (a messianic Psalm), "I delight to do your will, O my God." Above all else, Jesus lived to do God's will. That was the key to his spiritual sustenance—and to ours. We can hold the most reverent thoughts about God and the tenderest feelings, but if we do not surrender our will to God, we will receive little of the spiritual food he provides. Until the will is right, nothing is right! People sometimes come to me asking how they can know God's will about marriage or about a job or about some other major life decision. I tell them that one of the first principles of life is to do his revealed will, to obey what we already know to be his will for us. His revealed will, first of all, is that we are *saved*. Is that true in your life? His revealed will is also for us to be *Spirit filled*. Are you filled with the Spirit? His revealed will is for us to be *sanctified*, that we live a holy life. Is that true in your life? His revealed will is that we are to live in *submission* to the authorities around us. What is your attitude toward authority? If those things are in line, then as St. Augustine stated, "Love God and do what you will." That is, if we obey his revealed will, his specific desires for us will begin to fit into place. Sadly, many people are seeking God's direction in their lives but are not conforming to his revealed will. When there is no authentic submission to what God has already revealed, we will be hungry and dissatisfied, for we do not have the divine food.

Jesus also said that in addition to doing God's will, he must do God's work. If we omit the middle phrase in verse 34, it reads "My food is . . . to accomplish his work." Jesus was anticipating the cross. In fact, the same word was used when Jesus cried from the cross, "It is finished" (19:30). Jesus ultimately accomplished God's work on the cross, and it will always be finished. Doing God's work should be the sustenance of our lives as well.

What is the secret of a genuine, fulfilling, godly life? Absolute submission to the divine will and the thrilling consciousness of doing it were the dynamics of Christ's life, and they ought to be evident in ours too. Are they? If not, perhaps we are feasting on empty pleasures—entertainment, food in excess, worldly amusements, fame, or success. We are then feeding on wind. The only food that will last is doing God's will and work. This must be our transcending priority if we are to be followers of Christ. We were saved to conform to his will and to serve.

A Sense of Urgency (vv. 35–38)

Another secret in our approach to following Christ is suggested in verse 35 and the following verses when our Lord speaks of the harvest.

> Do you not say, "There are yet four months, then comes the harvest"? Look, I tell you, lift up your eyes, and see that the fields are white for harvest. (v. 35)

Some years ago a famous Bible scholar, H. V. Morton, was sitting by that same Samaritan well and observed a fascinating incident.

> As I sat by Jacob's Well a crowd of Arabs came along the road from the direction in which Jesus was looking, and I saw their white garments shining in the sun. Surely Jesus was speaking not of the earthly but of the heavenly harvest, and as he spoke I think it likely that he pointed along the road where the Samaritans in their white robes were assembling to hear his words.[4]

I think that is very likely the case. In simplest terms, Jesus was saying: "You have a saying that correctly states there are four months between sowing and harvest, and agriculturally that is true. But spiritually that is not true. So, my disciples, lift up your eyes, look down the road at the approaching Samaritans, and you will agree that the fields are white unto harvest. This is the day of the harvest. The harvest is now! Men, if you follow me, you must know the secret of my heart—a sense of immediacy, even urgency, about the harvest." We need to have a sense of urgency because today too the fields are "white for harvest"! Though there is much sowing to be done and not all fields are able to be reaped, this is an age of harvest. Jesus was encouraging his disciples to see the urgency. "Already the one who reaps is receiving wages . . ." (v. 36). Wages were already being paid, and the master paid liberally: "And gathering fruit for eternal life." When we do the harvesting, there will be eternal results: "So that sower and reaper may rejoice together." There is joy in all of this, and our Lord says to get with it!

Jesus concluded his optimistic call to urgent evangelism in verses 37, 38:

For here the saying holds true, "One sows and another reaps." I sent you to reap that for which you did not labor. Others have labored, and you have entered into their labor.

Jesus was saying, "Your experience with the Samaritans is one of reaping where you did not sow," and that surely was the case. They had not sowed, but they reaped. In our age some of us may sow, and some of us may reap. The thrust of these verses is that there is going to be a good deal of reaping, but the implication also is that sometimes we may sow and never see the results. I am reminded of the story of George Müller who founded many orphanages in the last century. Early in his life Müller made the acquaintance of three men, and he began to pray for their salvation. Müller lived a long time, but when he died, none of those men had yet trusted Christ. It is recorded in his diary that he prayed for these men daily during all those years. But that is not the end! The glorious fact is that all three of those men did meet Christ—two of them in their seventies and one in his eighties! Müller sowed, but someone else reaped. Whether we find ourselves sowing or reaping, our lives are to be permeated with a sense of urgency. Jesus' harvest mentality was part of the secret of his life. We also are meant to be harvesting!

Conclusion

A miner once interrupted John Hutton, a famous Welsh preacher, by leaping to his feet in the middle of a sermon and leading the whole congregation in the Doxology. Hutton was taken aback and decided he would make the acquaintance of the man. Later the man explained that he had been a Christian only a few months and that it was all so gloriously different that he could not sit still while the Word was being preached! Then he said, "I was a bad lot. I drank. I pawned the furniture. I knocked my wife about. And now life is real life, and splendidly worthwhile." When asked how he fared among his fellows down in the pit, he laughed and replied, "Today they asked me, 'You don't seriously credit that old yarn about Jesus turning the water into wine?'" To which he had answered, "I know nothing about the water and wine, but I know this: that in my house Christ has turned beer into furniture; and that is a good enough miracle for me!"

I think there must have been something of this in the Samaritan woman's life. She could not give the townspeople all the right theological answers, but they saw that her life had changed—and they were interested.

Many Samaritans from that town believed in him because of the woman's testimony, "He told me all that I ever did." So when the Samaritans came to him, they asked him to stay with them, and he stayed there two days. And many more believed because of his word. They said to the woman, "It is no longer because of what you said that we believe, for we have heard for ourselves, and we know that this is indeed the Savior of the world." (vv. 39–42)

The Samaritans were the first to call Christ "the Savior of the world," and it came as a result of Jesus' approach to life. What was his secret? It was his sense of urgency: "Look, I tell you, lift up your eyes, and see that the fields are white for harvest." And they truly were, and are! Those disciples could have argued, "Lord, the Samaritans certainly are needy, but the field needs to be plowed, and the seed needs to be sown, and then we must wait for the harvest." But Jesus taught them that the age of the harvest is *now*. The interval between the sowing and the harvesting has been closed. Now is the time for harvesting. If we are following Christ, we will have a sense of urgency.

The other secret of Jesus' life was his priority: "My food is to do the will of him who sent me and to accomplish his work." Serving God is to be our very food. We are to be the kind of people who sometimes get so involved in ministry to others that we do not think of our own needs. It is wonderful to be the kind of people who partake of food about which world knows nothing. May we be followers of Christ and give the highest priority and urgency to his will and his work.

17

Growing Faith

JOHN 4:46–54

So he came again to Cana in Galilee, where he had made the water wine. And at Capernaum there was an official whose son was ill. When this man heard that Jesus had come from Judea to Galilee, he went to him and asked him to come down and heal his son, for he was at the point of death. So Jesus said to him, "Unless you see signs and wonders you will not believe." The official said to him, "Sir, come down before my child dies." Jesus said to him, "Go; your son will live." The man believed the word that Jesus spoke to him and went on his way. As he was going down, his servants met him and told him that his son was recovering. So he asked them the hour when he began to get better, and they said to him, "Yesterday at the seventh hour the fever left him." The father knew that was the hour when Jesus had said to him, "Your son will live." And he himself believed, and all his household. This was now the second sign that Jesus did when he had come from Judea to Galilee.

Verse 46 tells us, "At Capernaum there was an official whose son was ill." The word for "official" is the word *basilikos*, which can be translated "nobleman," "king's man," or "petty king." This man was evidently an official in Herod's court and was therefore a man of great influence and power. He was also a man of great wealth, as Herod's men were apt to be. Here was a man who by anyone's standards had everything he could possibly want, except for one thing—his young son was seriously ill. The child had contracted a fever, and his father had watched his life slowly drain away. The color had faded from the young face, the light in his eyes had begun to dim so that at times he stared but did not see, and finally he lapsed into an intermittent coma. Death was imminent. As a result the father's life was full of profound misery! When the Lindbergh baby was kidnapped, someone said, "Poor old

Lindy. Tonight he's worth $6,000,000, and he would give every cent of it to have his son back."

Nothing can shatter us more quickly or more completely than affliction falling upon our children. Nothing! Hearing the doctor's diagnosis, as I have, that your child has spinal meningitis, and then watching the doctor withdraw that huge hypodermic needle from your child's spine, your life turns gray and you wander from lab to clinic to doctor feeling like a useless character in a story no one wants to hear, thinking again and again, *This cannot be happening!* I understand how that nobleman felt! Behind his eyeballs burned an incessant fire, while on the outside he found himself enshrouded in grim darkness because the light of his life was about to expire. The tragic fact is, though children have a sense of immortality about them, children do die! All we have to do is visit a graveyard and look at the interminable gray monuments and we will see there are many who never made it to adulthood. In the history of mankind the first grave was dug for a young man!

Regardless of our station in life, trouble, sorrow, and death come to all! Death was knocking at the door of the house of that *basilikos*. Job 5:6, 7 was written by a man who was well acquainted with these realities:

> For affliction does not come from the dust,
>   nor does trouble sprout from the ground,
> but man is born to trouble
>   as the sparks fly upward.

As an open fire causes sparks to fly upward, even so mankind is inexorably consumed with trouble! The Hebrew is even more poetic because the two words that are used for "sparks" are literally "sons of flame." The idea is that men are born to endure the fires of this life and will eventually perish in burning. Everyone experiences sorrow! There are no exceptions!

There are many things money cannot buy. Money can buy a king-sized bed, but it cannot buy sleep! Money can buy a great house, but it cannot buy a home! Money can buy a companion, but it cannot buy a close friend! Money can buy books, but it cannot buy brains! Money can buy a church building, but it cannot buy entrance into Heaven! And as our text suggests, money cannot buy life and health. Wealth cannot buy the life of a loved one. The *basilikos* was in agony. Nothing could relieve him. Nothing! The end appeared inevitable.

We can surmise that at the news of Jesus' arrival in Cana (only about eighteen miles from Capernaum), the nobleman felt a glimmer of hope. He had undoubtedly heard of Jesus' miracle at a wedding in Cana earlier and had probably heard about Jesus from various people over time. So he quickly made preparations and set off in a gallop to Cana, the pounding of his horse's hooves a reflection of his inner heartbeat.

I like that nobleman. He went himself! He did not send a servant. He did not send his wife. In that nobleman we see a man who was involved with his family, who was so wrapped up in his children's destiny that he did not send someone else but went himself.

There could scarcely have been a greater contrast than that in verse 47—the *basilikos* and the Savior with his rough carpenter's hands. Add to this the crowds of people—the curious, the sensation-mongers—who were watching to see what would happen. Cap it off with the nobleman's actions, and we have a sensational encounter!

> When this man heard that Jesus had come from Judea to Galilee, he went to him and asked him to come down and heal his son, for he was at the point of death. (v. 47)

The word "asked" means he began to beg and kept it up. The *basilikos* was at the feet of Jesus begging repeatedly for him to heal his son. He was indifferent to the noise around him, unaware of the crowd. The idea is that he followed Jesus around. "Lord, Sir—heal my son!" He was desperately pleading for his son's life.

Jesus Grieves over an Imperfect Faith (v. 48)

Our Lord's reply is rather startling. "Unless you see signs and wonders you will not believe." That was Jesus' answer to the man's pathetic cry? On the surface it seems to be a detached, cold, unsympathetic response. The man had poured out his heart to the Lord—and now it looks as if the Lord throws a glass of cold water in his face! But actually Jesus' reply was full of grace. In C. S. Lewis's biography *Surprised by Joy*, he relates how he was brought kicking and struggling into the kingdom of God, his eyes darting every which way for a way of escape. Then he reflects, "The hardness of God is kinder than the softness of men, and his compulsion is our liberation."[1] Christ's words here are mercifully surgical. When he said, "Unless you [plural] see signs and wonders," he referred not only to the nobleman but also to the Galileans whose tendency the nobleman represented. Jesus' words would lift the man to new levels of faith—and likewise anyone else who would listen and respond. Later in John's Gospel (20:31) we are told that Christ's miracles were performed to make faith live.

With unerring accuracy our Lord put his finger on the weakness of the people's faith. They were following Jesus as if he were a religious sideshow. "Hurry, hurry, don't miss the latest miracle! Get your popcorn here. Crowd in close, folks, so you can see the new added-appendage miracle." There was such an extreme focus on signs and wonders that the people were missing his real identity. It seems that the poor, confused nobleman had this same idea because of his repeated emphasis on Jesus to "come down" to Capernaum to heal his son. He thought that if Jesus would work his magic, his son would be healed. Even today those who are constantly seeking signs and wonders and miracles to confirm their faith may be missing the intent of such things—to know Jesus himself! If we focus on sensationalism—miracles and signs—our focus is not on Christ himself who alone is sufficient. At the same time, our Lord was not deprecating signs and miracles because he was in fact going to heal the man's son. But that sign would lead the man to faith in him. The thrust of what Jesus was saying was, "Oh, that you would think less about the wonders and more about me!" He wanted them to go beyond signs and miracles to trust in him and believe in his word.

Jesus' penetrating words to that nobleman were not a rebuke but the beginning of grace in his life. It is very easy to hear what happened to the *basilikos* but never apply it to ourselves. It would be wonderful if the Holy Spirit who inspired this narrative would pen these words again in the fleshly tablets of our hearts!

Jesus Tests and Strengthens a Growing Faith (vv. 49–52)

We gain further insight into the nobleman's heart as we observe his response to Jesus. "The official said to him, 'Sir, come down before my child dies'" (v. 49). He did not deny Jesus' charge. More than that, he did not assert his own position. In fact, he seemed to maintain something of the spirit of the Syrophoenician woman—"Even the dogs eat the crumbs that fall from their masters' table" (Matthew 15:27). His spirit mirrored that exemplified by John Bunyan when he wrote:

> I was driven to such straits that I must of necessity go to Jesus; and if he had met me with a drawn sword in his hand, I would sooner have thrown myself upon the edge of his sword than have gone away from him; for I knew him to be my last hope.[2]

The nobleman would not go away from Jesus! Jesus was his last hope.

He also did not try to pull rank and say, "Now listen here, carpenter! This young boy has royal blood." Instead the nobleman grabbed hold of as much as he could comprehend of Jesus' character and pathetically cried, "Sir, come down before my child dies." He cried out for mercy!

Note Jesus' reply in the first part of verse 50: "Go; your son will live." These interesting words contain a partial granting and a partial denial. Jesus granted the healing, but he refused to go down to Cana. And he gave the man no sign! The only thing he gave the man was his word. Our gracious Savior was attempting to elevate the nobleman to a higher faith. Picture the scene. Jesus and the nobleman standing face-to-face—the pregnant silence that settled over the crowd surrounding them—Jesus saying to him, "Go; your son will live." What did that man think when he heard these words? How would he respond? "The man believed the word that Jesus spoke to him and went on his way."

There was no arguing, no pleading, no insistence on "just a little sign, please," no mind over matter—"I believe, I believe . . . I think I believe." He simply remembered what he had heard about the wedding miracle in Cana, looked at Jesus standing before him, added it all up—and believed!

Something radical happened inside that man that is the reverse of a very common phrase in our world today: "Seeing is believing." In that nobleman's life, believing was seeing. Even though there were eighteen miles between them, in his mind's eye he "saw" his little boy well and healthy again. The Scriptures testify to the relationship of faith and sight. Jesus says in 8:56, "Your father Abraham rejoiced that he would see my day." Through faith in what God said, Abraham saw the day of the gospel.

> These all died in faith, not having received the things promised, but having seen them and greeted them from afar, and having acknowledged that they were strangers and exiles on the earth. (Hebrews 11:13)

By faith they saw the promises! Notice Hebrews 11:27, speaking of Moses: "By faith he left Egypt, not being afraid of the anger of the king, for he endured as seeing him who is invisible." Moses' faith enabled him to see the unseen. He saw God by faith. Now look at the words with which that chapter begins, in verse 1:

> Now faith is the assurance of things hoped for, the conviction of things not seen. (NASB)

> Now faith is the substance of things hoped for, the evidence of things not seen. (KJV)

> And what is faith? Faith gives substance to our hopes, and makes us certain of realities we do not see. (NEB)

> Now faith means that we have full confidence in the things we hope for; it means being certain of things we cannot see. (PHILLIPS)

> Faith is the confidence that what we hope for will actually happen; it gives us assurance about things we cannot see. (NLT)

Faith sees the unseen! Believing is seeing. On the basis of Jesus' words, that nobleman saw his little boy healthy and well—the color back in his cheeks—in his mother's arms. He believed with such conviction that the Scripture records that "The man believed the word that Jesus spoke to him and went on his way."

It is by faith that we see the living colors of God's Word! Most of us are familiar with the promise of Romans 8:28: "And we know that for those who love God all things work together for good, for those who are called according to his purpose." Apart from the illumination of faith, that is just an ancient maxim, but seen through faith it bursts into life. Why? Because we see the unseen—our trouble resulting in good. By faith it becomes a living, leaping, bounding, flaming verse! The world says seeing is believing, but the immutable spiritual truth is that believing is seeing. Faith is "the confidence that what we hope for will actually happen . . . assurance about things we cannot see" (NLT).

The nobleman's subsequent growth in faith is amazing.

> As he was going down, his servants met him and told him that his son was recovering. So he asked them the hour when he began to get better, and they said to him, "Yesterday at the seventh hour the fever left him." The father knew that was the hour when Jesus had said to him, "Your son will live." (vv. 51–53)

Notice especially here the word "yesterday." I find this absolutely amazing because if the nobleman had left town at "the seventh hour" (one in the afternoon) and hurried back to Capernaum, he could have arrived at home by 5 p.m. (he surely traveled by horse). But actually he did not return to Capernaum until the next day. Personally, if I went off to get help for one of my children—say, to New York City—and while I was there received a call that my child had recovered, I would hop a red-eye special to get back home and see how he was doing. But not our nobleman. He believed so thoroughly in Jesus' healing answer that he stayed in Cana for a while longer. Perhaps he had a little business to take care of, or maybe he chatted with some of the disciples. Maybe he hoped for a further word with Jesus. What faith! Then when he met his servants on the road and was informed his son had recovered, he asked what time it had happened. When they replied that it occurred at 1 o'clock in the afternoon, he checked his sundial and said, "Just what I thought." What a difference between that breathless, pounding ride up to Cana and the leisurely ride back. The difference was faith. We all have problems and pressures, but if our lives are worried, frenetic, breathless, galloping, we have probably not learned to believe God's word to us.

Jesus Rewards a Tested Faith (v. 53)

The nobleman's faith was well rewarded. The Lord spoke only a few words to him, but in the little he said he took the man a million light-years ahead in his faith. The official had learned who Christ was, and he trusted fully in him. The more he reflected upon the circumstances, the more wonderful it all seemed. He became a convinced believer! Notice in verse 53 what happened when he got back to Capernaum: "And he himself believed, and all his household." There was an outburst of faith in Capernaum! When he returned he told his wife what had happened, recounting the details of the Lord's words, and then she said to him, "My dear, if you believe, I want to believe, too." Even his servants believed. If his son was old enough, he believed also (our text says that "all his household" believed)! Some people postulate that Chuza in Luke 8:3, a steward in the household of Herod, may be the very man who was converted here since Chuza's wife is mentioned as supporting the Lord's work. In any case we find believers in the very service of Herod. What a marvelous growth of faith!

Conclusion

Our passage clearly shows that two conditions bring forth faith. The first is to hear God's Word. Romans 10:17 says, "So faith comes from hearing, and hearing through the word of Christ." We must immerse ourselves in the Word of God so that we become fertile soil for faith's growth. It is fundamental to our spiritual lives. Colossians 3:16 gives beautiful expression to this need: "Let the word of Christ dwell in you richly."

The second condition is to exercise the faith that we have, because faith grows by exercise. Maclaren of Manchester said it well:

> The way to increase faith is to exercise faith. And the true parent of perfect faith is the experience of the blessings that come from the crudest, rudest, narrowest, blindest, feeblest faith that a man can exercise. Trust him as you can, do not be afraid of inadequate conceptions, or of a feeble grasp. Trust him as you can, and he will give you so much more than you expected that you will trust him more.[3]

Each one of us has opportunities to grow in faith as we find ourselves in difficult circumstances. In those trials, if we will turn to the Word of God, it will speak to us, and if we believe and act upon it, we will grow in faith.

Lewis's words are true: "The hardness of God is kinder than the softness of men, and his compulsion is our liberation." The *basilikos* had to be struck over the head so God could get his attention. Some of us may be experiencing emotions similar to those of the nobleman—a sense of closing darkness or a feeling of futility in life. If this is your experience, you may be on the verge of great blessing—if you turn to God. You have heard, as the nobleman did, that there is One who can meet your need. Fly to his feet. Hear his words. Obey him, and you will find life and a growing faith.

18

On Healing
Spiritual Paralysis

JOHN 5:1–18

A QUICK GLANCE AT religious history reveals that it is not difficult to gather people around reports of the miraculous. The shrines and holy places from Lourdes to Salt Lake City bear eloquent testimony to this. I have personally seen it happen. A housewife in California, near my former home, claimed to have had revelations from St. Joseph. Soon after she first shared her experience, large crowds began to gather around her house. In fact, people made pilgrimages from around the world to see her. In her community bumper stickers touting St. Joseph appeared. Just outside of town, 400 acres were purchased to build St. Joseph's Hill of Hope. Reports of miracles have also come from there—how St. Joseph appeared and revealed where water was to be found on someone's property, for example. The neighbors in surrounding housing developments became a bit nervous when devotees of this woman began buying houses in the neighborhood. There were even armed guards at the gate of the Hill of Hope.

All of this makes the legend described in John 5:1–18 very understandable. The ingredients are perfect. The Pool of Bethesda, the setting of this passage, was within the environs of Jerusalem. It periodically rippled because of a subterranean spring, and no doubt usually someone who had a disease was in the pool when the water moved. That individual probably concluded he had been healed, and the news of the "miracle" spread over the city and the surrounding countryside. With the Hebrew preoccupation with angelology, it is quite natural that a legend was born. In fact, we find this spurious teaching in the text of the older New Testament translations, though not in the earliest manuscripts. That doubtful addition reads, "An angel of the Lord went down at certain seasons into the pool and stirred up the waters, so that whoever first came in after the stirring might be healed."

As a result, hundreds of people came from the countryside to the Pool of Bethesda to be healed. Five porticoes were even built so that the infirm could keep out of the sun as they waited for the stirring of the waters. Probably someone thrilled with what was taking place donated the money.

What a pathetic sight the crowd around the pool must have been! According to verse 3, "a multitude of invalids" was there. Not just a few but hundreds of people gathered around those porches at Bethesda.

- The sick, including those with undiagnosed diseases
- Those who were so feverish they had to stay in the shade because the heat of the sun was unbearable
- The blind—some congenitally blind, some newly blind. The sightless huddled close to the edge of the pool, hoping someone would lead them into the pool when the waters quivered.
- The withered
- And the lame, who could not make it to the pool on their own. Their only hope to reach the waters was to crawl over others weaker than themselves.

What a pitiful crowd of broken humanity! It does not take much imagination to see those withered, wasted bodies, to smell the stench, to see the filth, and to sense the *pathos* of the old and young among that impotent, suffering humanity. It had to be a horrible, distressing sight—except for one thing— Jesus was there.

On this occasion our Lord was alone. Without his disciples Jesus could virtually travel incognito. He stood unnoticed, and his tender eyes surveyed those miserable heaps of humanity around the pool. Finally his gaze rested on one of the worst cases, a man who had been confined to his bed for thirty-eight years. He had never been able to reach the pool in time. But a few seconds later this man's life was changed. John 5:1–18 describes what happened, how the Lord engaged him in conversation, and how in just moments that man stood— *stood*—amid that crowd, completely whole, carrying his bed on his shoulder.

What do you think happened after this man was healed? Do you think he calmly rose to his feet, straightened his robe, and said, "Oh, yes, my bed" as he calmly rolled it up and walked off nonchalantly toward his home? I do not think there's a ghost of a chance that it was like that.

In the third chapter of the book of Acts, there is a healing parallel to this healing in John. Peter found a lame man by the Beautiful Gate. He was begging. Peter responded, "'I have no silver and gold, but what I do have I give to you. In the name of Jesus Christ of Nazareth, rise up and walk!' And he took him by the right hand and raised him up, and immediately his feet and ankles were made strong. And leaping up he stood and began to walk, and entered the temple with them, walking and leaping and praising God" (Acts 3:6–8).

What a scene that must have been! The man was leaping into the air! I think he shouted a few "hallelujahs" too!

With a little sanctified imagination I can picture what happened at the Pool of Bethesda. If this man's personality was anything like mine, when he stood to his feet and felt those muscles become firm and his legs enlarge, he let out a shout that rippled the water. He began to jump and say, "Look at me! Thirty-eight years a cripple, but now I'm healed!" Maybe he did that, maybe he did not, but I doubt that he was nonchalant.

The story of this man's healing is a marvelous story, and a true one, and there is much more in it than meets the eye. From a careful study of it we can learn much about ourselves and our Savior. Since we have already seen what our Savior did for this man, we need to see what he required and what our Savior got out of it.

What Christ Required of the Paralytic (vv. 6–9)

The first question Christ asked the paralytic was, "Do you want to be healed?" That is quite a question. The man had been crippled for thirty-eight years, and Jesus had the nerve to ask, "Do you want to be healed?" That sounds like a ridiculous question.

I have learned over the years there are some questions you just do not ask. For instance, when I am out in a boat looking for a spot where the fish are biting, I have learned never to ask fishermen if they are catching anything. If they are, they will say, "I've had a few bites," and if they are not catching anything, they will resent the question. Besides, fishermen by nature are not truthful. Similarly, you never ask a football coach, even during his most successful season and even if next Saturday's game is against the worst football team in the conference, if he is going to win the game. He will invariably give a glowing description of the opponents, saying their record is not indicative of their ability. He will follow that with a recitation of the injuries on his team. Finally he will make some statements like "We'll have to get off the ball a little quicker" or "We have to learn to execute," and to conclude he'll utter the cliché, "If everything comes together, we'll play competitive football."

I have also learned that when you see a car stalled at the side of the road and a man leaning under the hood, you do not say, "Is there something wrong with your car?" You are liable to hear something like "No, I'm just under here hugging my carburetor." Or something worse!

And I must confess that in all my years of hospital visitation I have never stood at the side of a bed and said, "Do you want to be healed?" I do not think I would have asked it of the paralytic either. If I had, I can imagine his response. "I have been confined to this loathsome shell for years. When the water ripples, I claw my way, and I crawl over others, but I have *never* been able to get to the water. Someone always shoves me back. I've been lying here because I want to be healed—and you ask me if I want to be healed?" A cruel, ridiculous question. But not when it comes from the lips of our Lord.

I believe that is the question Christ asks all of us. I believe it summarizes the great problem in our lives. *Do you want to be well?* Few things hamper the gracious work of Christ in our lives more than our response to this question.

We hear the promises of God, and at first our hearts are warmed and we respond to them, or at least we think we respond to them. But then we hear the promises again, and we again want to be warmed. This cycle continues in our life, but nothing ever happens. Why? Because although we think and say we want to be healed, in our heart of hearts we really do not. That is why this miracle is so relevant and important to us today.

For the paralytic, Jesus' query was an eminently significant question. J. A. Findley tells us that in the Middle East—and in some places today—a man who was healed would lose a good living. So, in fact, there are invalids whose situations are preferable. As the crippled man lay by the Pool of Bethesda, he was surrounded by misery and sorrow. But if the man looked out from those shaded porticoes, he saw men and women out in the sun carrying their burdens and working. He knew that if he were healed, his life would take on larger responsibilities. And so the question the Lord asked was very relevant: Do you really want to be healed?

That is a great question concerning the salvation of the soul. Pascal, the French philosopher, put it this way: "Men often mistake the imagination for the heart; and they believe they are converted as soon as they think of being converted." In other words, the thought of being converted is what many imagine to be conversion. Why does Pascal believe this? Because Christ and what he offers look so delicious from a distance, and yet when we look at it closely, it may appear in an entirely different light. We begin to see that Christ is an aggressive, requiring Lord. In my experiences I have seen people attend church, even sitting in the front row. They are very respectful, very excited about what they are hearing. They are not converted, but they are listening to the gospel. But there comes a time when they realize they do not want to be healed and they leave. Not to another faith or to another church. They just leave. They do not want to be healed.

That is the great question we must face. If you are not a believer, I am responsible to pass on to you Christ's question: Do you want to get well? Do you really want to be healed? Do you truly want to be forgiven and made new? Because if you want to, you can be healed right now. If you remain unconverted even though you have a knowledge of Christ in your life, it is because you choose to be lame. You really do not want to be healed. You haven't said yes to that tenderly aggressive question from Jesus Christ.

For those of us who are already Christians, there is also a question we must keep asking ourselves. Do we really know our own hearts? As we get to know ourselves, we find more and more that needs healing. But the question is, do we really want to be healed?

I am speaking primarily of bitterness, unresolved conflicts, and things that lie hidden within us. Sometimes when we experienced these things, we were aware of them but didn't deal with them. We cauterized them, layered them over. But they are realities within us, and they do affect our lives. Even though we cannot put a finger on them, they take their toll. As a result we do not feel God's power; we do not feel the authenticity of grace we know we ought to feel. We know we should be joyful in all the things we confess and while we are doing the right things—reading the Word and praying—but we have little power or inner peace. The question remains, do we really want to be healed? Do we really want to have those things resolved? I believe with all my heart that if we do and if we take the time to ask God to do his work within us, he will reveal to us the things that must be washed away—the refuse, the filth, the sin.

So the question that Christ asked the paralyzed man, the seemingly unnecessary, ridiculous question, was relevant for him and for us. It is the most insistent question people face if they do not know Christ, and it remains relevant in the lives of Christians. Do we want his continued healing? What a blessed thing to have the release, fullness, and joy that come with having things cleared with God, with being healed.

The paralytic wanted to be healed but responded, "Sir, I have no one to put me into the pool when the water is stirred up, and while I am going another steps down before me" (v. 7). He desired to be healed, but he realized he could not do it himself. Thirty-eight years of impotence, of not being able to get to the edge of the pool even though he longed to, had convinced him he was paralyzed, that he needed outside help. If it were only that way with our spiritual paralysis, but we just can't see it. So we imagine that although we want to be healed, there is something we can do for ourselves. Like the Burger King crowd, we want to have it our way. We want to fix ourselves.

The paralytic wanted to be healed, and he knew he could not cure himself. The third requirement for him was faith. When he realized he could not heal himself, he looked in obedience to Christ, trusting in him. The man stood up, and suddenly he found that his legs straightened out and he had the power to walk! We too, if we look to Christ in faith, can find the power in our lives to do the things we could never do otherwise. In Old Testament times faith healed those who were bitten by the fiery serpents. They were about to die but were obedient and dragged themselves out to look at a serpent impaled on a pole, and they then experienced healing power in their lives.

This is the progression Christ demands of us. First, do we want to be healed? And if we do, do we realize that we cannot heal ourselves? Lastly, are we willing to move to him, to cast ourselves upon him? With that faith comes joy. The paralytic experienced this. Whether he danced physically or not, he danced spiritually, leaping for joy in the Lord at the healing of his paralysis.

There are very few people whom I admire more than a woman known to us all—Joni Eareckson Tada, a quadriplegic who was at one time very bitter against God. But now she has the most liberated spirit—joyous, bounding, dancing. In one of her books she talks about how someday she is going to be glorified, and it is a great statement of faith.

> Being "glorified"—I know the meaning of that now. It's the time after my death when I'll be on my feet dancing.

And of course one day she will. She will have a new body, and she will be dancing. But the beautiful thing is that though she has not yet been healed physically, the paralysis of her soul is gone. Her words are dancing words. Every one of us can experience the same thing. We can be touched by faith, relieved of paralysis, and liberated to rejoice in God. All it takes is the willingness to be healed. Do you really want to be healed? Realize that you cannot do it yourself. Reach out to Christ in faith.

What Christ Got Out of It (vv. 10–16)

The other important question implicit in this passage is, what did Jesus get out of all of this? The paralytic got a great deal, but what did Jesus get out of it?

I would say that he got one thing out of it, and only one thing—a saved sinner. That's all. Many commentators are hard on this man. Leon Morris says he was an "unpleasant creature." That is not a nice thing to say, but I think that although that description may be a little harsh, the man really was not a very noble man. Verse 14 intimates that the reason he was paralyzed was because of some sin early in his life—maybe as a child or a young man. Verse 7 implies he was the kind of man no one wanted to put into the pool. He had been there all that time, and no one would help him into the pool. Maybe it was because he was so disagreeable. I may have to answer to him for that assumption, but I would also point out that we never find him thanking Jesus. He may have, but it is not recorded here that he did. And I think, above all, that we see his character as he goes out to the censorious, nitpicking Pharisees who are after Jesus' hide. Did he stick up for Jesus? Not really. He did not say a good word for him but just said Jesus was the man who healed him.

Still, to his credit, Jesus found him in the temple. But the words that Jesus spoke, "See, you are well! Sin no more, that nothing worse may happen to you" (v. 14), might indicate that our Lord was not confident this man was going to follow through with the new realities he had experienced. Through it all this individual seems to be a weak man without spiritual conviction.

Then again we may find that to be a great comfort. When we honestly look at ourselves, we say, "Oh, why did Jesus save me?" And after we have known Christ for a while and have come to see our inconsistencies and lack of thanksgiving, we marvel that he did not drop us along the way.

> I cannot pray, except I sin;
> I cannot preach, but I sin;
> I cannot administer, nor receive
> the holy sacrament, but I sin.
> My very repentance needs to be repented of;
> And the tears I shed need washing
> in the blood of Christ.

That is true. Those are the words of William Beveridge, but they are my words too. The amazing thing is that all Christ got out of his work was you and me—a bunch of saved sinners. But one day we are going to be glorious and radiant.

> Christ loved the church and gave himself up for her, that he might sanctify her, having cleansed her by the washing of water with the word, so that he might present the church to himself in splendor, without spot or wrinkle or any such thing, that she might be holy and without blemish. (Ephesians 5:25–27)

One day, paralytics all, we will be dancing with him. What a time that is going to be!

Now, when Jesus did this miracle on the Sabbath and commanded the paralytic to carry his bed on the Sabbath, he widened the breach between the Pharisees and himself. At that time the Pharisees decided they were going to have to do away with Jesus. So humanly speaking, our Lord sealed his death warrant with this miracle. It sent him to the cross. He loved the paralytic that much. He loves that much.

Matthew 13:45, 46, two marvelous verses, tell us: "The kingdom of heaven is like a merchant in search of fine pearls, who, on finding one pearl of great value, went and sold all that he had and bought it." To Jesus, the paralytic was the pearl of great value. We are the pearl of great price. Was that paralytic really a pearl? Maybe he was the beginning of one, a bit of sand, an irritation, an ignoble, faltering irritant to many people. But what happens to a bit of sand within an oyster? In the confines of its environment it is smoothed over with mother-of-pearl. In fact, I think the bigger and more irregular the irritation, the more chance the mother-of-pearl will surround that bit of sand until finally it becomes smooth. We are pearls of great price. We may be in a rough state now, but one day we are going to be the bride of Christ—beautiful, wonderful to the eye, pleasing to God in every way. The pearl of great price.

What do we need to experience this? The realization that we can't make ourselves into pearls. The realization that we have been lying here all these years in our sin and we cannot do it. Also, whether we are sixty, forty, thirty, or whatever, we have to want to get well. If you are not a Christian, the question is, do you really wish to get well? If you are a Christian, the question is still, do you wish to get well? Do you wish to be conformed to him? If so, reach out in faith. Obedience will bring the strength you need. May God grant this for each of us. May his Word bear fruit in our lives with power.

19

Conflict over the Sabbath

JOHN 5:1–18

I STILL REMEMBER THE DAY IN 1963 when pole vaulter Brian Sternberg broke his neck. I was an avid sports fan, and I followed Brian's career with great interest. His achievements were phenomenal. That year he'd had two great pole vaults at 16 7 and 16 8 . My friends and I were shocked that July day to hear that Brian had fallen on a trampoline at the University of Washington and broken his neck. For all these years he has hardly been able to move a muscle. Philip Yancey interviewed Brian in his book *Where Is God When It Hurts?* He describes him this way:

> Brian's head is of normal size, but the rest of his body has shrunk due to muscle atrophy. He can now make some motions with his arms. He can hit switches, turn knobs with difficulty, even type with a special contraption that holds back all but one finger.

Brian Sternberg wants to be healed. Since 1963 that has been the great desire of his life. When in the earlier days of his paralysis he would try mentally to get his body to move but could not, he would fall back exhausted and say things like "I've had it. I don't know what I'm going to do. Nothing is happening; I can't stand it lying tied up like this. I'm exhausted. I've tried too long to move, and I just can't. . . ." Then his voice would fade into tears and sobs. Brian Sternberg wanted to be healed.

Today he still wants to be healed. His family tenaciously holds onto that hope. His mother, a very articulate woman, says:

> No one in Brian's condition has ever walked. *No one.* Yet we still believe. I have no idea when God will heal Brian. It's conceivable this particular

battle will not be won here on earth. Some people you pray for are healed. Some aren't in this world. But that doesn't change God's desire for whole-ness—body, mind and spirit.

We won't give up. We're like doctors searching for a cure; we won't stop investigating. We think it pleases God for us to persevere.[1]

And there Brian lies.

Let's fantasize just for a moment, as Brian has done a thousand times. Let's imagine it is a beautiful sunlit spring morning. Brian has just finished his devotions. As the sun is shining through the window, he notices some feeling in his toes, some warmth that spreads up his withered legs to the tips of his fingers. He has feeling. He senses he has life. His arm does something it has not done for many years—it obeys him. He tears back the covers to reveal that his legs are fully restored. With a shout he leaps out of bed, grabs the pole off the wall, and steps out to the sunlit grass.

In this fantasy how do you think he would feel? Better yet, how do you think his family would feel? I think they would be rolling on the sunlit grass, embracing and weeping and praying on their knees, rejoicing in what God had done. It would be difficult to contain the emotion.

Amazingly, there are people who under certain circumstances could not share their joy. While we need to be careful with all the imagining we have done about Brian Sternberg, we must realize that the healed paralytic in John 5 experienced the same emotions as we imagined in Brian. Yet according to our text, some looked at him with disgust. John introduces them in verse 9 with the words, "Now that day was the Sabbath. So the Jews said to the man who had been healed. . . ." Their understanding of the Sabbath would not allow them to rejoice that a paralytic had been healed.

Our Lord's Conflict over the Sabbath

This inability to rejoice goes back to a very laudable attempt on the part of religious people within Israel to protect the Sabbath, in obedience to the Law. Some of the prohibitions given in the Scripture concerning this day include a ban on commerce and trade.

But eventually religious people began to "protect" the Sabbath by their own prohibitions, added to those of Scripture, eventuating in thirty-nine series of laws. These extra laws constituted a hedge around the Sabbath, but it was a man-made hedge! For example, looking in a mirror was forbidden. The rationale was that if you looked into the mirror on the Sabbath day and you saw a gray hair, you might be tempted to pull it out and thus perform work on the Sabbath. You also could not wear your false teeth because if they fell out, you would have to pick them up and you would thus be performing work. All kinds of obscure meanings and conversations centered around the Sabbath. You could not *carry* a handkerchief on the Sabbath, but you could *wear* one. That meant if you were upstairs and wanted to take a handkerchief downstairs, you would have to tie it around your neck, walk downstairs, and untie it. The Jews even debated about a man with a wooden leg. Namely, if his home caught on fire, could he carry his wooden leg out of the house on the Sabbath?

Because traveling was forbidden on the Sabbath, a journey was limited to one thousand yards. But if you wanted to extend your walk, you could tie a rope at the end of your street as much as one thousand yards away. You could then walk one thousand yards farther because you had extended your household by one thousand yards.

You could spit on the Sabbath, but you had to be careful where you spit. If you spit on the dirt and then scuffed it with your sandal, you would be cultivating the soil and performing work. Spirituality could be determined by where you spit.

By popular consent good religious people were considered list keepers, and, even better, list givers. But the Pharisees were the champion list givers.

Consider our story. For the first time in thirty-eight years, the paralytic was walking, his bed under his arm. There was a noticeable spring in his step. He might even have been skipping. Then he heard a voice asking, "Hey, what are you doing with that bed? Don't you know that is illegal?"

The healed paralytic stopped to reply, "Well, yes, but you see, I've just been healed! I was down by the Pool of Bethesda—I've been crippled for thirty-eight years. I was lying next to the pool, and a man walked by and asked me if I wanted to get well, and I told him I did. He asked me to stand up. I tried and found my legs strengthened—I can't tell you how great that felt—and now I'm walking!"

"Listen, fella, I don't want to hear about your medical record. The fact is, you're carrying your bed on the Sabbath. You're breaking the law, and you're in big trouble."

Does that conversation sound absurd? Look at verse 9 and following in our text:

> And at once the man was healed, and he took up his bed and walked.
> Now that day was the Sabbath. So the Jews said to the man who had been healed, "It is the Sabbath, and it is not lawful for you to take up your bed." But he answered them, "The man who healed me, that man said to

me, 'Take up your bed, and walk.'" They asked him, "Who is the man who said to you, 'Take up your bed and walk'?"

There was no question about the healing. Rather, all they asked was, "Who is the man who said to you, 'Take up your bed and walk'?" They were hard-hearted people.

This is what the spirit of legalism does. The Jews stopped persecuting the paralytic and started concentrating on Jesus because he had restored a man's body on the Sabbath. How dare he! These Jews experienced no joy over this miracle.

Some time ago a friend of my wife and myself was convalescing in the hospital. She was visited by the champion list giver in our part of the country, a person who had marvelously come to know Christ but had moved into a severe legalism. As they were talking, a nurse came in, and the patient began to talk with her. She was very attentive to the nurse, and it was obvious she was looking for an opportunity to witness. Her guest—the list giver—just sat there. After the nurse left, he turned to the patient and said, "You really care for her soul and are attempting to witness to her, aren't you? Well, I'm not, because God has called me to help Christians straighten out their lives." What an amazing but sad confession! The most vicious people in the Body of Christ are list makers who can find no joy in another soul healed if something in that changed person's life does not measure up to their rules.

Few things can break a pastor's heart or cause dissension in the body more than this. This is a pharisaic mentality—extra-Biblical requirements by which we judge others and set our own standards of spirituality. Donald Grey Barnhouse pointed out the Pharisees' fundamental motivation:

> Why all this viciousness? Why this desire to destroy the meek and lowly Jesus? Why this murderous attempt to do away with God? The answer is here in the Sabbath question. They wanted rules, they did not want God's grace. They wanted human merit. They did not want the simplicity of divine pardon. They wanted to do something for themselves.[2]

As believers we know we are saved by grace, but because of the human tendency of wanting to do everything ourselves, we create a list-giving, list-keeping Christianity that is far removed from the grace under which we entered into new life.

The Pharisees demanded to know who had healed the paralytic.

> Now the man who had been healed did not know who it was, for Jesus had withdrawn, as there was a crowd in the place. Afterward Jesus found him

in the temple and said to him, "See, you are well! Sin no more, that nothing worse may happen to you." The man went away and told the Jews that it was Jesus who had healed him. And this was why the Jews were persecuting Jesus, because he was doing these things on the Sabbath. (vv. 13–16)

Jesus was not caught unawares by their attack. In fact, he devastated them with his reply in verse 17: "My Father is working until now, and I am working." Jesus was saying that when God created the earth, he rested on the seventh day, but he kept working in order to hold the universe together. God kept working providentially in people's lives as well. "And," Jesus said, "I [too] am working."

Jesus' statement would have been fully acceptable to the rabbis except for one thing. He said, "My Father." In those days *no one* referred to God as his personal Father. The Pharisees' response to Jesus' statement was deep, lasting hatred.

This was why the Jews were seeking all the more to kill him, because not only was he breaking the Sabbath, but he was even calling God his own Father, making himself equal with God. (v. 18)

Jesus' statement was perceived as blasphemy. So they felt it was their duty to kill him.

What the Sabbath Is All About

The legalists had missed the whole point of the Sabbath. A key insight about the Sabbath comes from the second chapter of Genesis, which tells us that God created the earth in six days, but on the seventh he rested. Concerning the first six days Scripture tells us, "And there was evening and there was morning, and it was the first day," and so on. But there is no mention of evening and morning on the seventh day. God entered into his Sabbath-rest, and he is still in that rest, even while he is upholding the earth by his power. He works, *and* he remains in his Sabbath-rest.

Later when God gave the Law at Sinai he instituted the Sabbath as a reflection of his Sabbath-rest. The Sabbath's purpose was to help God's people elevate their lives. They set aside that time to practice the Sabbath-rest mentioned in Genesis. It also foreshadowed the Sabbath-rest that awaited them.

The Sabbath was a time of celebration. It was marvelously liberating because a man worked six days, but on the seventh he was free to focus upon God, to celebrate his presence and power. So the Sabbath was a time of joy. But when Christ came, the shadow or reflection was no longer needed.

Over twenty years ago I walked into a Tuesday night Bible study and saw the most beautiful girl I had ever seen sitting in the corner. It took me three months to get up enough nerve to ask Barbara Triggs for a date. Soon afterwards she gave me a photo of her. It was a sorority-type picture, and in it she looks like she is sitting in the midst of the clouds. Looking at that picture day after day is probably the closest I have ever come to idolatry. I would look at the picture in the morning and again in the evening and think about her. It was wonderful.

The day came when Barbara became my wife. Since then I have not spent a lot of time before that picture. I got it out recently and looked at it. She has not changed very much. She is still just as beautiful. But I find that picture incomplete and unsatisfying. Why? Because when the reality came, I had no more use for the picture—at least not on the same level.

When Jesus Christ, our Sabbath-rest, came, that reality did away with the need for the Old Testament Sabbath. The writer of Hebrews says in 4:9, 10, "So then, there remains a Sabbath rest for the people of God, for whoever has entered God's rest has also rested from his works as God did from his." God has ceased from his works, and so do we. God has rested in what Christ did, and so do we. We have entered the Sabbath-rest. Colossians 2:16, 17 says:

> Therefore let no one pass judgment on you in questions of food and drink, or with regard to a festival or a new moon or a Sabbath. These are a shadow of the things to come, but the substance belongs to Christ.

There is no longer any need to observe the Old Testament Sabbath. That need was removed when Christ died on the cross.

What Sunday Is All About

Where does Sunday fit into all of this? The Lord's Day, the first day of the week, has no intrinsic relationship to the Jewish Sabbath. God has set aside the *seventh* day as a day of rest. New Testament history and development reveals that the Holy Spirit set apart a special day, the *first* day, for God's church. That day was the day of resurrection. On that same day of the week our Lord would ascend into Heaven at the end of his earthly life. "Go to my brothers and say to them, 'I am ascending to my Father and your Father, to my God and your God'" (20:17). It was on Sunday that Jesus first appeared to his disciples. On Sunday he first broke bread with his disciples after the resurrection. On a Sunday Jesus gave a fuller understanding of the Scriptures to his disciples. On Sunday Jesus commissioned his disciples to the task of world evangelism. On Sunday Jesus breathed on his disciples so that they received the Holy Spirit.

Further, in the book of Acts it was on Sunday, seven weeks after the resurrection, that the Holy Spirit descended on the church at Pentecost. On Sunday Paul preached to believers gathered together for worship, as was their custom (Acts 20:7). Sunday was established by Paul as the day each Corinthian believer was to "put something [money] aside and store it up, as he may prosper, so that there will be no collecting when I come" (1 Corinthians 16:2). And lastly, on Sunday the Lord Jesus Christ appeared to John on the island of Patmos and gave him that great unveiling of himself in all his heavenly glory that we know as the book of Revelation. Sunday is resurrection day! It is the proper day on which Christian believers worship.

Not only that, but as James Boice mentions:

> Everything that we do in church on this day is based on these eleven great events [the ones we have just considered]. These are: the gathering together, the reading and interpretation of the Scriptures, the preaching and teaching of the Word of God, the collection of offerings, the observance of communion, and above all the remembrance and worship of the One who died for us and rose again. We do not do these things by accident or by whim. This is God's pattern.

For a full discussion of the Sabbath, see James Boice's commentary on John and also *Grace* by Lewis Sperry Chafer.

All this should dramatically affect how we approach the Lord's Day. It is easy to just think about the Pharisees' errors, but how do we regard our day of religious observance? As Christians, we do not *observe* the Sabbath, but we do *celebrate* it on the Lord's Day, and it is to be preeminently a time of joy. Sunday is our day to express our joy in the resurrection. Long faces should not characterize the Lord's Day. To be sure, sometimes when we come together we are greatly burdened, but overall we will experience bounding and leaping joy.

Along with *celebration*, the Lord's Day is a day of *activity*. The Lord's Day is not a day of passive rest. Dr. Lewis Sperry Chafer writes:

> The Lord's Day is not a day for selfish entertainment or amusement. It is not a day for idleness and rest. Its privileges should be, and will be, preserved by all who delight to do his will. It becomes an opportunity for many who are held by secular work during the days of the week, to offer the fullest service of prayer, worship, and testimony which belongs to their Lord. The instructed Christian no longer labors to be accepted of God,

which was the obligation under the law; but he, being accepted in grace, labors to glorify his Lord who saves him. He has ceased from his own works, and though ceaselessly active, is working in the power and energy of the Spirit.[3]

We may need to rest on Sunday if we had a frantic work schedule the other six days, but this should not be at the expense of active, holy service on the Lord's Day. That day is to be wonderfully filled with activity as we teach, minister, witness, and rejoice together.

Conclusion

Jesus' attitude toward and use of the Sabbath teaches us what to emphasize in our spiritual lives. Legalists do not celebrate—they observe. The Pharisees did not rejoice at the overflowing grace on that Sabbath day because something on their list was violated. The gospel for them was, "For God so loved the world that he gave a list, that whosoever might do the things on the list might have eternal life." Jesus disagreed.

What a privilege is ours—to celebrate the resurrection, to celebrate the Sabbath-rest. Jesus Christ within our hearts is that rest. We come on the Lord's Day rejoicing in the wondrous realities of that rest, and then we get to work. When Jesus said, "My Father is working until now, and I am working," he set an example for us. Our Lord is at Sabbath-rest, but he is working. And we are to be working and laboring for him. May these wonderful realities, the bounding joy, and the holy sense of celebration be ours and keep increasing, so that we will be a witness to the world, a balm to our own souls, and vehicles of glory to God.

20

The Claims of Christ

JOHN 5:19–30

IN HIS BOOK *PERELANDRA* C. S. Lewis describes the main character Ransom's view of the approach of angelic beings:

> Far off between the peaks on the one side of the valley there came rolling wheels. There was nothing but that—concentric wheels moving with a rather sickening slowness one inside the other . . . suddenly two human figures stood before him on the other side of the lake . . . they were perhaps thirty feet high. They were burning white like white hot iron. . . . Whenever he looked straight at them they appeared to be rushing towards him with enormous speed. Whenever his eyes took in their surroundings he realized that they were stationary. This may have been due in part to the fact that their long sparkling hair stood out straight behind them as if in a great wind. But if there were a wind it was not made of air, for no petal of the flowers was shaken.[1]

That is a wild and extravagant description. Lewis had one of the greatest imaginations in secular or religious literature in our time. But he would undoubtedly admit that his description does not come close to the prophet Ezekiel's vision, which is far more eloquent in its beautiful symbolism.

In the opening chapter of his prophecy, Ezekiel describes an approaching cloud. Fire flashes in it, and it is surrounded by a bright light. In the center of the cloud there appears to be gleaming metal. As the cloud rushes toward him, Ezekiel sees that the gleaming metal is really four human images, each having four faces and four wings. Each image faces north, east, south, and west, so that as those living images move, they never need to turn because they are already facing in all directions. Next to these fantastic images, Ezekiel sees great wheels of gleaming beryl rising into the heavens. The wheels have wheels within wheels, the inner wheel set crosswise, and thus they have the same liberty of movement as the human images have visually. Even stranger, the rims of the wheels are full of eyes. So wherever the living images move, the wheels move. Above this incredible sight, Ezekiel sees a crystal expanse, and above that is a sapphire throne, and on the throne sits a figure in human form surrounded by a glowing rainbow. That description is far more glorious than Lewis's description. Seen in its awesome magnificence, Stephen Spielberg would probably turn green with envy.

Ezekiel 1:1 says this blazing vision was a vision of God, expressed in symbolic form. The living beings who move wherever they want are a picture of God accomplishing his will. The eyes in the wheels and the rotating eyes represent his omniscience, his complete knowledge. The luminous expanse represents his ineffable glory.

That passage in Ezekiel 1 is one of the great foundational passages of Scripture concerning the doctrine of God and his character. With this background it is no wonder that when a Hebrew came to the name of God in Scripture he did not read it, but instead used a name that combined God's other names—the name Jehovah. Reverence for the divine name was so great among the Israelites that when the scribes came to it, they would wash their hands before writing it. And nothing was allowed to interrupt the writing of that name. If a king addressed them while they were writing the sacred name, they would not respond!

Knowing this background, we understand why Jesus' claims were considered blasphemous. The "blasphemous" claims recorded in this text were made in response to the furor that raged because Jesus performed miracles on the Sabbath. Jesus' reply had been, in part, "My Father is working until now, and I am working" (5:17). This answer was intolerable to the Jews, so intolerable that they decided to try even harder to kill him (5:18). No doubt some Jews could hardly believe what they were hearing. Readers might wonder, was Jesus really claiming to be equal with God? Yes, he was, and the audacious claims of Christ that we find in John 5:19–30 had colossal implications.

Christ's Claim: One with the Father in His Actions (vv. 19, 20)

Those colossal claims begin in 5:19. Jesus prefaced that first claim with "I tell you the truth" or "Truly, truly," or "Verily, verily," meaning "without possibility of contradiction." "You must hear and accept what I have to say."

> Truly, truly, I say to you, the Son can do nothing of his own accord, but only what he sees the Father doing. For whatever the Father does, that the

Son does likewise. For the Father loves the Son and shows him all that he himself is doing. And greater works than these will he show him, so that you may marvel. (vv. 19, 20)

Identity of action with God the Father is the first great claim of Christ. Some of the Jews shuddered at the thought, for Jesus was claiming equality with God! Equality is the inevitable result of identity of action. They are so closely related that one wonders how literate people can deny that Christ claimed to be equal with God the Father. But they do.

In the book *Donahue*, a best-selling autobiography, the celebrated talk-show host Phil Donahue explains why he left the faith.

> If God the Father is so all-loving, why didn't he come down and go to Calvary? Then Jesus could have said "This is my Father in whom I am well pleased." . . . How could an all-knowing, all-loving God allow his Son to be murdered on a cross in order that he might redeem my sins?[2]

Donahue's indictment of God's love comes from ignorance of the Scriptures, for Jesus' claims of equality with the Father make the Father a sharer in Jesus' sacrifice, pain, and love. As verse 19 says, "The Son can do nothing of his own accord, but only what he sees the Father doing."

Jesus' claim to equality with the Father demands that we see two hearts beating as one. That is a beautiful thought, and the opening words of verse 20 take us into the inner workings of this oneness: "The Father loves the Son and shows him all that he himself is doing." The word translated "loves" here is not the expected word, *agape*, normally used to describe love in the Godhead. Rather, it is the term for friendship love, *phileo*. From our human level we understand this as a personal love between friends who delight in sharing everything. Jesus is a separate person, he has power to act on his own, but by virtue of the love and identity within the Godhead, he does no action that the Father does not also do. So in essence in verse 20 he is saying, "Remember the great teaching of God in the Old Testament—those opening verses in Ezekiel? I am the incarnation of that vision and much more." Those who were with Christ saw the Father. They saw the Father's smile. They heard the Father's teaching. They observed the Father's tender touch and trembled before his wrath. If we want to see what the Father does, all we have to do is look at Christ. That is the answer to Donahue's question. In Jesus Christ we see the likeness of God the Father.

The colossal claim Jesus sets before us is that he is equal with the Father. Even if we have already embraced this truth, we must repeatedly affirm it.

We must daily appropriate the reality that Jesus is God! He is the King of kings and Lord of lords. That must be a constant reality in our lives. We as believers must affirm who Jesus Christ is. He is supreme.

To unbelievers he comes with the same claim—that he is King of kings and Lord of lords——and he will assert that for all time and eternity. This colossal claim continually confronts all mankind, and it demands a response.

Christ's Claim: The Power to Give Life (vv. 21, 24–26)

For as the Father raises the dead and gives them life, so also the Son gives life to whom he will. . . . Truly, truly, I say to you, whoever hears my word and believes him who sent me has eternal life. He does not come into judgment, but has passed from death to life.

Truly, truly, I say to you, an hour is coming, and is now here, when the dead will hear the voice of the Son of God, and those who hear will live. For as the Father has life in himself, so he has granted the Son also to have life in himself.

To his reeling hearers, Christ not only claimed equality and identity of action with God, but he claimed to be able to give life. "An hour is coming, and is now here," he said, "when the dead [that is, the spiritually dead] will hear the voice of the Son of God, and those who hear will live."

About forty-five years ago an eighth grade boy went to church camp. He was dead in his trespasses and sins. That boy was Kent Hughes. I had been raised in the church, and although I was spiritually unregenerated, I was fascinated with the church. Perhaps because of the beautiful building with stained-glass windows—I can remember looking at those windows and being attracted by the mystery of life they suggested. I loved my red-letter Bible, too, and treated it reverently. Also, the ecclesiastical jargon was mysterious and inviting to me. I have never been able to define just what the attraction was, but I was intrigued by spiritual things. And yet, even as a twelve-year-old, I knew I was on the outside, and I wanted to be inside, whatever the inside was.

Finally I was coerced into going to a church camp. For the first time I heard clearly what it means to be a Christian, and I asked Christ into my life. I wept a great puddle of tears on the floor. You would have thought I had committed every sin that could possibly be committed! I had not, but I knew I was a sinner. That night I was marvelously born again. I still have that little Bible, and I know which verses I marked inside that Bible as I lay inside my sleeping bag, using a flashlight late into the night. That little Bible had suddenly come alive for me! I felt free, my sins were gone, and I had purpose in life. I even felt the call to be a minister! Christ had given me life. That is exactly what he was talking about when he said, "An hour . . . is now here, when the dead will hear the voice of the Son of God, and those who hear will live."

Forty-five years ago I entered a new realm. My associations changed. My view of work, my relationships with other people, my relationship with my parents—all of these things entered into a process of transformation by virtue of what had happened in my life. As soon as I received Christ, I qualitatively began to experience eternal life. I know a tiny bit of what Heaven is going to be like because of what I experienced then and what I am experiencing now. My conversion experience is not normative for everyone. Those who receive Christ have wonderfully varied experiences. But at the same time I know that my experience of eternal life is similar to the experience of others who have it.

Years ago the great G. Campbell Morgan was preaching in Tennessee. During the sermon he stated, "By no means can every Christian remember the time when he was born again." At the end of the sermon someone challenged his statement. Morgan turned to him and asked the man, "Are you alive?" The man said, "Why, of course I am!" Morgan said, "Do you remember when you were born?" The man said, "No, but I know I am living." Morgan replied, "Exactly. Some Christians may not remember the moment of their new birth. But they are spiritually alive and know it and that is what counts." You can *know* you have eternal life. When the dead hear the voice of Christ, they enter into that relationship of life.

The new birth is a great mystery, but the process is very simple. "Truly, truly, I say to you, whoever hears my word and believes him who sent me has eternal life" (v. 24a). The process is simply hear and believe. When I as a twelve-year-old shed tears of repentance on that concrete floor, my pastor put his hand on my shoulder, took my little Bible, and opened it to these verses:

> If you confess with your mouth that Jesus is Lord and believe in your heart that God raised him from the dead, you will be saved. For with the heart one believes and is justified, and with the mouth one confesses and is saved. (Romans 10:9, 10)

As I read those verses, I heard, and I believed, and I was changed!

The process is simple. Christ claims to be able to give life. Verse 24 ends with this enticing thought: "[He who believes] does not come into judgment, but has passed from death to life." The tenses of the verbs indicate that when a man enters into this process, it remains his.

As a high school boy I wavered at times, but the fact remains that I was changed. My relationships were changed. My conception of life was changed.

I was re-created, redirected, and remade. Such are the results of the staggering claim that Christ makes. Sometimes when Christians repeat that claim, they are accused of being narrow and parochial. But they are speaking the truth. Christ made a very parochial statement when he said, "I am the way, and the truth, and the life. No one comes to the Father except through me" (14:6). That is the way it is. But at the same time Christ is infinitely liberal and accepting because the opportunity is for everyone, the process is simple, and the benefits are eternal. All may come to him.

Christ's Claim: The Authority to Judge (vv. 22, 27–30)

The last claim that Christ made on that occasion was that of being Judge.

> And he [the Father] has given him [Christ] authority to execute judgment, because he is the Son of Man. Do not marvel at this, for an hour is coming when all who are in the tombs will hear his voice and come out, those who have done good to the resurrection of life, and those who have done evil to the resurrection of judgment. (vv. 27–29)

A bugler could stand at the edge of a graveyard and play Reveille, but nothing would happen. He could travel to the greatest of our national cemeteries, where military men, noted for their obedience throughout life, lie buried. No matter how well or how loudly he played, nothing would happen. Those dead men need a far greater authority to bring them to life, and that authority is the voice of Jesus Christ. "An hour is coming when all who are in the tombs will hear his voice" (v. 28). It is not going to be the Father's voice or the Holy Spirit's voice but Christ's that will call believers and unbelievers to resurrection. Maybe he will use music too. First Corinthians 15:52 speaks of "the last trumpet." What will happen after he calls us to come forth? Will those whose bodies have been dissolved into the earth for hundreds of years be "beamed" into existence? Will it be like Ezekiel's valley of dry bones, with bones rattling together and sprouting sinew and skin? I have no idea, but I do know this—according to 1 Corinthians 15, we will receive new, immortal bodies. We will experience the fullness of what we have tasted here on earth.

At the end of Lewis's book *The Last Battle*, Aslan tells Peter, Edmund, and Lucy there has been a railroad accident and they are dead.

> And as he [Aslan] spoke he no longer looked to them like a lion; but the things that began to happen after that were so great and beautiful that I cannot write them. And for us this is the end of all the stories, and we can most truly say that they all lived happily ever after. But for them it was only the

beginning of the real story. All their life in this world and all their adven-
tures in Narnia had only been the cover and title page: now at last they were
beginning Chapter One of the Great Story which no one on earth has read:
which goes on for ever: in which every chapter is better than the one before.

The same is true for us if we believe in Christ as our Savior. The authority
of the voice of Christ will call us forth to a new life of which life on earth is
only the beginning chapter. Christ has made this claim, and he speaks truth.

The text we are considering also reveals that Christ will preside in judgment. "And he [the Father] has given him [Christ] authority to execute judgment,
because he is the Son of Man" (v. 27). In this statement Jesus reached back to
Daniel 7:13 and the term "son of man" used there and identified himself with it.
That title is beautiful and gracious in its context in Daniel, where the destruction
of the bestial empires of the world is followed by the coming of "a son of man"
who sets up a humane, gentle, and graceful government. Jesus uses the term to
tell believers that the one who comes in judgment is "the Son of Man." This is a
reminder of our Savior's humanity and the resulting understanding and sympathy he has for his own.

And yet those qualities that make him so precious to those who believe
are the very qualities that make him frightening to those who do not believe.
At the Great White Throne unbelievers will find themselves looking into the
face of One to whom they are completely accountable, and nothing will slip
by him. The same qualities that make Christ such a comfort for believers will
make him an awesome terror to the lost. "For the Father judges no one, but
has given all judgment to the Son" (v. 22).

Conclusion

Christ was the fleshly expression of Ezekiel's vision and much more. Many
years after Christ's death, John, on the island of Patmos, had a similar vision
that included the four living creatures and a similar throne. "He who sat there
had the appearance of jasper and carnelian, and around the throne was a rainbow that had the appearance of an emerald" (Revelation 4:3). The rainbow,
as elsewhere in the Bible, calls to mind God's faithfulness and grace. But the
white of the jasper and the red of the carnelian are new. They symbolize the
sacrifice of Christ's life. Jesus claimed to be God, and his death, resurrection,
and final exaltation prove it.

Again our Savior claims, "I have identity of action with the Father. I have
the power to give life, and I have the authority to judge." We must think on
these things. These claims are eternal, and they call for action.

That all may honor the Son, just as they honor the Father. Whoever does
not honor the Son does not honor the Father who sent him. (v. 23)

May we realize the riches we have in Christ. May we focus upon him
as one who expresses the action of God the Father, gives us life, and is our
Judge. If we do not know him, it is imperative that we give deep consideration to the claims of Christ, because they are the claims to which we will
have to answer.

21

Receiving the Witness of the Word

JOHN 5:37–47

SOME YEARS AGO one of the world's great classical scholars, D. E. V. Rieu, completed a marvelous translation of the works of Homer (*The Odyssey* and *The Iliad*) into modern English for the Penguin Classic series. He was then sixty years old, and he had been an agnostic all of his life. The same publisher soon approached him again and asked him to translate the Gospels. When Rieu's son heard this, he said, "It is going to be interesting to see what Father will make of the four Gospels. It will be even more interesting to see what the four Gospels make of Father." Rieu's son did not have to wonder very long. Within a year Rieu responded to the Gospels he was translating, became a marvelous, committed Christian, and joined the church. That is a great illustration of the power of the Word of God.[1]

> For the word of God is alive and powerful. It is sharper than the sharpest two-edged sword, cutting between soul and spirit, between joint and marrow. It exposes our innermost thoughts and desires. (Hebrews 4:12 NLT)

Dr. Rieu discovered that the Word of God does indeed pierce our very being, performing divine surgery and giving us life. There is great power in the Word of God.

Yet when some people read the Bible, they do not experience the impact of its power. In fact, I would say most people do not. Some people spend their entire lives studying the Word of God, yet do not have the transforming experience that Dr. Rieu had. Why do some people come to the Scriptures, read them, and say, "It is not that I *will not* but that I *cannot* believe?"

173

Our Lord directed that question (5:39, 40) to rabbis who rejected his witness. We will consider what the scribes did wrong and what we ourselves need to do as we come to God's Word. Thus we will discover how to receive the most out of the Word of God. The lesson came first to the Pharisees, but it is meant for us as well.

The Problem of Approach (vv. 39, 40)

"You search the Scriptures because you think that in them you have eternal life" (v. 39). The Pharisees regarded the Scriptures with such esteem that they thought that by studying the parchment and letters of Scripture they had eternal life. In actuality the Jews had a superstitious reverence about the Word of God that led to all manner of eccentric behavior among those who dealt with the Scriptures. Each letter of the Hebrew alphabet was given a numerical equivalent, and each word had a numerical equivalent. Each line thus formed a mathematical equation. In fact, the Jews numbered the center letter of each line of Scripture, the center letter in each book, and the center letter in the Old Testament.[2]

In copying the Scriptures, a scribe was not allowed to write more than one letter before looking back to the text. That eccentricity is wonderful for us because the transmission of the Scriptures was consequently so incredibly accurate, but it points to an underlying mistake in the focus of their faith. They really felt, as Jesus said, that in the Scriptures they had life. One of the greatest rabbis, Hillel, talks about this in a list of narrow maxims.

> More flesh, more worms; More wealth, more care; More maidservants, more lewdness; More menservants, more thieving; More women, more witchcraft; More Torah, more life.
>   Whoso hath gained a good name, has gained it for himself. Whoso hath gained the words of the Torah, hath gained for himself life in the world to come.[3]

In other words, life is found in the words of Scripture. The Jews believed this so firmly that some of them linked Scripture and memorization with salvation. All of this combined to create a misplaced enthusiasm and emphasis. The word used in the phrase "You *search* the Scriptures" in verse 39 is a technical word for scribes like those who labored at Qumran with such concentration and obsession. But tragically, although they always had their noses in the Scriptures, they seldom got beyond the paper and ink. Amazing! If we were to give these men titles today, we would say they were graduates of the Jerusalem Theological Seminary or the Law of Moses Training School or the Palestinian Missionary Society. They were the great Bible students of the day. And yet in spite of their knowledge of the Scriptures, they rejected Jesus when he came! Something was definitely wrong.

Let me illustrate their problem. Imagine you are standing on the observation floor of the Willis (formerly Sears) Tower in Chicago. You are overlooking the city, the sun is going down in the west, the lights are coming on along Lake Michigan. You are drinking it all in and are caught up in what you are seeing when someone tugs on your cuff. You turn to see a little man standing next to you. He says, "My! Isn't this a wonderful window! Do you see how it is set in steel and how the glass is tinted?" Then he unfolds his pocket knife and begins to scrape at a corner of the window, saying, "I'm going to do a chemical analysis of this window, and if you will give me your name and phone number, I'll call you and let you know what this window is made out of." Of course we would think the man was a little strange. He missed the whole purpose of the window. The window was created to show the great beauty of the city and the surrounding scenery, but all he saw was the frame.

The Bible is a wonderful window, but we must look through that window to see the beautiful realities of Christ and God. While I am committed to the need for detailed study of the Word of God, it must not be done just for the sake of literary analysis, graphs, or statistics. The Bible is not an end in itself but is a window through which we can learn marvelous truths about God and Jesus Christ. Those studious Jews had not gotten beyond the study of the window.

What does the Pharisees' problem have to do with us? It is very possible to make the same mistake that those ancient scholars made. In some homes the family Bible is used for two purposes—to record deaths and births and to press flowers. It is never opened, even though it is regarded as a holy book.

We can also err in the opposite direction. We can get caught up in the minutiae. When I was in seminary, I developed a studious taste that has never left me. I like things that have to do with the Bible. I like the feel of a Greek New Testament. I can be lost in the wonder of a critical commentary. I enjoy running my hands along its leaves and looking at the pages. I often pick up a book and savor its aroma. But that can be carried to an extreme. I think of long, serious discussions fellow students and I had about minutiae. Such behavior can lead to the trivialization of our faith.

What is the proper approach? In one way when we come to Scripture our approach is to be like that of the rabbis. We should immerse ourselves in the Scriptures. There are no substitutes for that today. Each believer (and not just the Christian professionals) should work at knowing the Bible. Dr. H. A.

Ironside, who ministered so mightily at Moody Church for many years, did not study formally beyond high school. He did, however, read everything in sight. One of the keys to his great power, I think, is found in this quotation from a short biographical sketch:

> Under his mother's guidance Harry began to memorize Scripture when he was three. By age 14 he had read through the Bible 14 times, once for each year. During the rest of his life he read the Bible through at least once each year.[4]

The biographer continued by recounting the story a pastor friend had told him about a Bible conference at which he and Ironside were two of the speakers. During the conference the speakers began to discuss their devotional life. The pastor told Dr. Ironside about what he had read for his devotions that morning and then asked the venerable preacher what he had read. Ironside hesitated, then humbly said, "I read the book of Isaiah." He was saturated with the Word of God, and it showed! This is the source of great power. Ironside literally, according to the account, read himself blind, and most of his reading was in the Word of God.

Once when Dr. Stephen Olford was talking about great preachers of this century, he noted that many of them have a Plymouth Brethren background. I asked why. Dr. Olford replied that they immerse themselves in the Bible. They know their Bibles. Regrettably, it is possible to go all the way through seminary and not have an exhaustive knowledge of the Word of God.

We need to be people of the Book. Unlike the rabbis, however, we are to be people who come to the Scriptures without preconceived programs or systems of interpretation that we try to force on God's Word. We must go beyond the frame and look to Christ. This is something we have to resolutely determine to do. When we come to God's Word, we must look beyond the letter for the principles, and then apply them to our lives.

The Problem of Motive (vv. 41–44)

Another problem also handicapped the Pharisees when they studied the Word of God—they had the wrong motive.

> I do not receive glory from people. But I know that you do not have the love of God within you. I have come in my Father's name, and you do not receive me. If another comes in his own name, you will receive him. How can you believe, when you receive glory from one another and do not seek the glory that comes from the only God? (vv. 41–44)

Christ's educated hearers fell short of believing because they were motivated by self-glory rather than a desire for God's glory. They wanted to receive glory from other scholars. One great authority would line himself up against another, and they would begin to argue about words. In the rabbinical schools the study of Scripture was a means to gain fame, to show off one's intellectual prowess. Biblical scholars dressed in such a way that everyone would recognize them. They prayed so they would be recognized. They were given prominence and position. But in all of this, they were lost! They knew the Word of God backward and forward, but they were unsaved! Our Lord exposed the state of their hearts in verse 42: "I know that you do not have the love of God within you." What did they love then? They loved their own opinions about the Word of God. And that wrong self-love kept them from loving God.

Jesus revealed more of their hearts in verse 43: "I have come in my Father's name, and you do not receive me. If another comes in his own name, you will receive him." That actually happened. Subsequent historical accounts tell us there were no less than sixty-three messianic claimants who attracted followers. These false prophets gained adherents because their claims corresponded with men's desires. They offered easy victory and political and material power, while Christ offered a cross.

Self-glorification was not only a problem for the Pharisees in Jesus' day. It tempts us in every area of our lives, and it is essentially a moral problem. Even a brief look at German theology in the eighteenth and nineteenth centuries will show us men holding on to theories about the Scriptures just like the rabbis did. And like the Pharisees, those German theologians thus missed the truth of Scripture. They were proud of their theories, they gloried in their methods, but they forgot to have a personal relationship with God through Christ. Hermann Reimarus presented a Jesus who was stripped of all supernatural elements. David Friedrich Strauss rejected most of the Gospels as mythology. Bruno Bauer denied the historical Jesus. These men knew the Scriptures backward and forward but still missed the message.

> Whatever light man finds they doubt it,
> They love not light but talk about it.
>
> John Masefield

There is more here than first meets the eye. Self-glorification will keep us from the truth, and in fact any moral deficiency is capable of doing so. Finding the truth is as much a matter of the heart as of the mind. A man may say, "I've read the Bible, and I want to believe it, but I just can't." But further conversation reveals he is having an affair or is short-changing his boss or is fudging on his income tax return. He *cannot* believe when he is in that state. Nor can the woman who comes and says, "I've been reading my Bible for years, and I cannot believe it," but she has an unforgiving spirit. The Lord's Prayer says we are to forgive as we have been forgiven and that an unforgiving person is an unforgiven person. So when we come to the Scriptures, there must be a yielding of our lives, a focus not on self but on God. Then we will be able to hear what the Scriptures have to say to us. Learning from the Scriptures depends on the motive and morality with which we come to them.

The Problem of Belief (vv. 45–47)

The Pharisees also had another problem—the problem of an incomplete belief.

> Do not think that I will accuse you to the Father. There is one who accuses you: Moses, on whom you have set your hope. For if you believed Moses, you would believe me; for he wrote of me. But if you do not believe his writings, how will you believe my words?

The purpose of the Law of Moses was to reveal man's need, his sinfulness. At the end of Moses' life, he called the Levites together and delivered the Law to them.

> Take this Book of the Law and put it by the side of the ark of the covenant of the LORD your God, that it may be there for a witness against you. (Deuteronomy 31:26)

In other words, the Law was a witness against our sins. The Ten Commandments were meant to bring us to the end of ourselves so we would come to Christ. If the Pharisees had understood and believed this, they would have responded to Christ just as Philip did in John 1:45 when he realized Jesus was the One pointed to in prophecy and believed in him. But the Pharisees did not *really* believe the Scriptures, even though they would have died for them. How about us? We may say we believe in the authority of the Word of God, but the way we put it in action or fail to do so reveals how much or how deeply we believe it. Often it appears that we believe part of it but not all. The solution to this anemia of the soul is to come with a receptive spirit, ready to accept and obey what our Lord says, eager to see God's truth.

Conclusion

John Broadus was one of the great men in American church history. At one time he was president of the University of Virginia. He left there to found Southern Baptist Seminary in Louisville. That work had a great start, but it was disrupted by the Civil War. When Broadus came back to Louisville, he only had seven students. But he was committed to doing his best for Christ, and he wrote one of the greatest books ever on homiletics—for the only student in that class, a blind man. Three weeks before he died, Broadus stood before the students. The Scripture reading for that day was Acts 18:24:

> And a certain Jew named Apollos, born at Alexandria, an eloquent man, and mighty in the Scriptures, came to Ephesus. (KJV)

Broadus went on to say, "Gentlemen, we must be like Apollos, mighty in the Scriptures." A student later said that a hush fell upon that class for the next few minutes as Broadus stood and repeated, "Mighty in the Scriptures. Mighty in the Scriptures. Mighty in the Scriptures!"

How do we become "mighty in the Scriptures"? How do we allow them to keep speaking to us? One final truth ties it all together. Our Lord, when he began his ministry, talked very simply, but as opposition increased and the religious leaders rejected him, he began to speak in parables. When his disciples asked him, "Why do you speak to them in parables?" (Matthew 13:10), Jesus responded:

> To you it has been given to know the secrets of the kingdom of heaven, but to them it has not been given. For to the one who has, more will be given, and he will have an abundance, but from the one who has not, even what he has will be taken away. (vv. 11, 12)

What did Jesus mean? If we do not use the spiritual understanding we have, it will be taken away. But if we act on it, we will receive more truth. We need to write this principle on our hearts. If we keep hearing the truth but do not respond to it, it is taken away. That is why I fear for any person who does not know Christ but complacently joins a congregation and hears the Bible taught but does not obey it. If he listens long enough and does not respond, the day will come when he cannot comprehend the truth. Believers too, when they hear the Word of God preached, must respond in some way. That is why when we are moved by something we hear, we must put into action the truth we receive. E. V. Rieu said of the Scriptures, "These words bear the seal of the Son of Man and of God, and they are the Magna Carta of the human spirit."

It is imperative that we pore over the Bible and that we respond to it. We must go beyond the frame of the words and respond to Christ and to God. We must believe what the Scriptures have to say and then act on our belief. If we want the Word of God to minister to us as it claims it can, we must come with the proper approach, the proper motivation, and the proper belief. If we do that, God's Word will speak to us and act upon us. But if we have been hearing the Word of God for years, yet have not responded to it, we must act on the truth we have heard. Our soul's salvation depends on it. We must respond to God as long as the truth is coming to us.

22

What Kind of Savior?

JOHN 6:1–26

JOHN 6 records Jesus' miraculous feeding of five thousand men plus women and children. However that multiplication took place—whether as Jesus spoke those words a great mound of bread and fish formed before the thousands, or whether as the bread and fishes were passed, they were multiplied—it was a stupendous act. And the people loved it! A man who could do that could do anything! In their mind's eye the masses probably saw the foot of Jesus upon the imperial eagles of the Roman legions. They could see the image of Caesar on their coins replaced with that of Jesus. Of course the people wanted Jesus to be their king. Who would not want to be subject to a man like that?

But our Lord immediately took steps to redirect the crowd. Verse 15 tells us that the people intended to "take him by force to make him king." So Jesus, knowing that the people's intentions were not of God, went onto a mountain to be by himself. We know from verses 16–21 and from the other Gospels that Jesus also sent his disciples, by boat, to the other side of the Sea of Galilee. While those disciples were out on the lake, a great storm came up, and those seasoned men of the sea were frightened. They thought they were going to perish. As they helplessly battled the storm, our Lord came walking phantom-like across the water to them and said, "It is I; do not be afraid" (v. 20). Jesus' words had special meaning to these disciples, who were undoubtedly disappointed that he had not set himself up as king. In essence he was saying, "Although I have not set myself up as an earthly king, I want you to know, my disciples, that you do not need to fear, for I am King!"

> On the next day the crowd that remained on the other side of the sea saw that there had been only one boat there, and that Jesus had not entered the boat with his disciples, but that his disciples had gone away alone. Other

181

boats from Tiberias came near the place where they had eaten the bread
after the Lord had given thanks. So when the crowd saw that Jesus was
not there, nor his disciples, they themselves got into the boats and went to
Capernaum, seeking Jesus. When they found him on the other side of the
sea, they said to him, "Rabbi, when did you come here?" (vv. 22–25)

The crowd was not easily put off. They had seen Jesus' great miracle.
They liked what they had seen. So they decided to follow him across the lake.
Notice Jesus' response to the mob in verse 26:

> Truly, truly, I say to you, you are seeking me, not because you saw signs,
> but because you ate your fill of the loaves.

In other words, "You are following me because of the things I have given
you, because you believe I am a material Savior." Christ's words have contemporary impact, as they have for two thousand years.

I once received a letter from two missionaries, Mal and Enid Forsberg.
(The conditions mentioned here also sometimes exist between Protestants or
even between Catholic orders.)

> Many changes have taken place here, not all for the better. The Catholics
> are setting up schools near Protestant groups. We have been getting church-
> es to be self-supporting, but some of the people are unhappy with us. They
> want us to do more for them. The Catholics have no such problem. They
> use their money to "buy" our people. It puts us into an unpleasant situation
> when we run into that. It is almost impossible to explain to our Christians
> why we do not hand out things. We trust we can be of help to our friends.

Wise missionaries know that Jesus is not essentially a materialistic Savior
and are careful not to make the people dependent on their material support.
But when someone else comes along with more money, many people switch
their allegiance. This is a modern-day example of verse 26.

The Oldest Problem between God and Man

Job was a man of great wealth, the greatest man in the East (Job 1:1). He
was also a man of integrity and spirituality. Job 1:5 tells us he would offer
sacrifices each day for his children in case they had sinned. He was eminently
pleasing to God. But there came a time when Satan asked the Lord:

> Does Job fear God for no reason? Have you not put a hedge around him
> and his house and all that he has, on every side? You have blessed the work
> of his hands, and his possessions have increased in the land. But stretch

out your hand and touch all that he has, and he will curse you to your face. (Job 1:9–11)

"God, the only reason Job is serving you is because of the things you have given him. But if you touch his possessions, he will curse you." Do you remember God's reply? "Behold, all that he has is in your hand. Only against him do not stretch out your hand" (Job 1:12).

Not many days afterward Job's children were gathered at the oldest brother's house to celebrate a birthday. At home Job was probably fondly thinking about the joyous time his children were having together when a messenger appeared on the horizon. He said, "Job, the Sabeans came and took away all your donkeys and all your oxen, and they have killed all your servants except for me." While Job contemplated his terrible loss, another messenger came. "Job, fire came down from Heaven, and it destroyed all your sheep and all your servants. I alone escaped." As Job was reeling from that second great material loss, a third messenger came. "Job, the Chaldeans came and took all of your camels and have killed all of your servants except for me."

In those few moments everything Job had gathered over the years was gone. As he saw a fourth messenger approaching, he trembled with dread. This time it was his children. "Job," the messenger said with difficulty, "as your children were dining and drinking together in celebration, a great wind came from the plains, flattened the house, and all of your children are dead." How would Job respond to such calamity? Would he indeed curse God? "Then Job arose and tore his robe and shaved his head and fell on the ground and worshiped" (Job 1:20). His first response was worship! Then he said, "Naked I came from my mother's womb, and naked shall I return. The Lord gave, and the Lord has taken away; blessed be the name of the Lord" (Job 1:21). In the midst of ultimate loss, Job did not sin by blaming God.

Again Satan came to God. This time he said, "Skin for skin! All that a man has he will give for his life. But stretch out your hand and touch his bone and his flesh, and he will curse you to your face" (Job 2:4, 5). In other words, "He still has his health, but touch his body and he will curse you."

> So Satan went out from the presence of the Lord and struck Job with loathsome sores from the sole of his foot to the crown of his head. And he took a piece of broken pottery with which to scrape himself while he sat in the ashes. Then his wife said to him, "Do you still hold fast your integrity? Curse God and die." But he said to her, "You speak as one of the foolish women would speak. Shall we receive good from God, and shall we not receive evil?" (Job 2:7–10)

In other words, "My God is not just a material Savior but a spiritual one. He's worth serving, no matter what the circumstances."

Over the centuries great men of God have shown similar devotion. Abraham was called by God to leave his home, and he obeyed God and went out to an unknown country. He stopped in Haran until his father, Terah, died. But in Genesis 12 God called him again and sent him on to Palestine, promising to make of him a great nation. Abraham obeyed God's command and traveled the length of Palestine, through the Gaza strip, down and back, in faithfulness to God. Eventually it became apparent that he might never have the things God promised—he had no nation and no land. At that point a conversation between God and Abraham could have gone something like this:

> "God, I have no nation."
> "You are going to have a son by the name of Isaac who will have two sons named Jacob and Esau. Jacob will have twelve sons, and they are going to father a great nation."
> "But when will that be?"
> "Five hundred years from now."
> "What about my land for the kingdom—the promised land—when is that going to happen?"
> "Five hundred years from now."
> "Lord, I have given up all of these things! What will you give me?"
> "What will I give you? 'Fear not, Abram, I am your shield; your reward shall be very great' [Genesis 15:1]. While I have not yet given you all these things, I do give you myself."
> "It is enough."

Jesus performed the feeding miracle in order to correct the people's mistaken beliefs. Perceptive Jewish observers should have recognized that the bread Jesus provided for the multitude was reminiscent of the manna God gave his people in the wilderness and that Jesus was claiming the power to supply every need—especially the spiritual. But they did not understand. Their perspective was clouded by a focus on the material. In fact, the crowd even asked for another sign (6:30, 31):

> Then what sign do you do, that we may see and believe you? What work do you perform? Our fathers ate the manna in the wilderness; as it is written, "He gave them bread from heaven to eat."

They tried to provoke Jesus to give them another sign, but he responded with the great Bread of Life discourse.

Jesus the Bread of Life

> Jesus then said to them, "Truly, truly, I say to you, it was not Moses who gave you the bread from heaven, but my Father gives you the true bread from heaven. For the bread of God is he who comes down from heaven and gives life to the world." They said to him, "Sir, give us this bread always."
>
> Jesus said to them, "I am the bread of life; whoever comes to me shall not hunger, and whoever believes in me shall never thirst." (6:32–35)

Jesus offered himself as the bread of life. The crowd wanted a material sign, but he offered himself. Sadly, that was not what they were looking for.

On the day of the miracle of the bread, the people chose rejection: "But I said to you that you have seen me and yet do not believe." At this the Jews began to grumble about him because he said, "I am the bread that came down from heaven" (6:36, 41).

Only twenty-four hours earlier these same people wanted to make Jesus king by force because of the multiplying of the loaves. But as soon as he began to talk about spiritual realities, they said, "Who is this? Is he not the son of Joseph?" (6:42).

Today God often blesses believers materially. But there has been false teaching about this. Some claim that if you receive Christ and commit your life completely to him, you will certainly have material wealth and good health. In fact, it is said that if you are not doing well materially, if you do not have good health, you probably are not right with God.

Some have made this false teaching part and parcel of the gospel. But this is not the gospel. Rather, it is an appeal to our hedonistic culture. When we self-consciously put ourselves first, it is no wonder that we mix Christianity with this popular, worldly philosophy. Many turn to God only because they have been told that God will bless them materially and give them health. They seek a material Savior.

But Jesus offers us himself. He does not promise us an easy life, but he does give life and peace and strength. During hardships and difficult times, as well as during wonderful moments of joy and victory, Jesus gives himself to us.

How to Get the Bread of Life

How do we receive the bread of life? "Do not work for the food that perishes, but for the food that endures to eternal life" (6:27). In other words, "Do not set your mind on the material but on the spiritual."

> "Which the Son of Man will give to you. For on him God the Father has set his seal." Then they said to him, "What must we do, to be doing the works

of God?" Jesus answered them, "This is the work of God, that you believe in him whom he has sent." (6:27–29)

The work God requires of us is to focus on him and on his Son. Faith in Christ is to be the basis of all our works.

> As the living Father sent me, and I live because of the Father, so whoever feeds on me, he also will live because of me. This is the bread that came down from heaven, not like the bread the fathers ate, and died. Whoever feeds on this bread will live forever. (6:57, 58)

We receive spiritual bread the same way we receive physical bread—by taking it into ourselves. Dr. H. A. Ironside wrote: "When we recognize that his precious blood poured out on the cross has atoned for our sins, then we are eating his flesh and drinking his blood."[1]

The New Testament phrase *believe in Christ* means not only believing in him but also interacting with him because when we believe, we enter into the spiritual realities symbolized by his flesh and blood.

The People's Reaction

What was the people's reaction to Christ's teaching? "When many of his disciples heard it, they said, 'This is a hard saying; who can listen to it?'" (6:60). When the people began to understand clearly what our Lord was saying, they began to turn away. The Apostle Paul described the same problem in Philippians 3:18, 19.

> For many, of whom I have often told you and now tell you even with tears, walk as enemies of the cross of Christ. Their end is destruction, their god is their belly, and they glory in their shame, with minds set on earthly things.

These people desired a Savior who would give them material blessings. Consider too the Prodigal Son, whose god was a god of materialism. He did receive material things, but only when he returned home in repentance. The clothing he desired, the sandals he wanted so badly, the jewelry that had glittered so brightly—all were his when he returned to his father. The "good times" that he pursued, he truly found when his father killed the fatted calf saying, "Let us eat and celebrate" (Luke 15:23). These are all ours when we receive the true Savior.

Conclusion

"After this many of his disciples turned back and no longer walked with him" (6:66). Then come some of the most poignant words in all of Scripture:

"So Jesus said to the Twelve, 'Do you want to go away as well?'" (6:67). Simon Peter, speaking for all who love Christ, answered, "Lord, to whom shall we go? You have the words of eternal life" (6:68). In history, in our personal lives, in our lives within the Body of Christ, our Lord is constantly coming to us and saying, "I want to give you myself." Sometimes he comes with great blessing as the kindness of God leads us to repentance. Sometimes he comes with difficulties or trials. But in all of life he wants to give us himself. As we pursue our Christian calling, how wonderful it is to realize that God loves us so much that he keeps driving us beyond the material to the spiritual, so that we will partake of him, eat of his flesh, and drink of his blood.

23

Appropriating Christ's
Power and Sufficiency

JOHN 6:1-14

MY WIFE AND MY CHILDREN and those who know me will tell you that I have "a thing" about the story of David and Goliath, one of the most dramatic stories in Scripture. I like to preach it. I like to refer to it in conversation. It is the height of drama—David, a teenager, alone, facing a danger so horrible that the bravest men of Israel would not face it but fled in fear. I love the story.

No one else faced a creature like Goliath, because Goliath was no ordinary man. The book of 2 Samuel tells us that Goliath had four brothers, one of whom had six fingers and six toes. Obviously Goliath's family was out of the ordinary. They were not of mankind's normal genetic stock. They were human all right, but there was something different about them. Scripture tells us that Goliath was six cubits and a span in height—almost ten feet tall! He would bump his head on a basketball goal!

Goliath was remarkable in other ways too. According to rabbinical commentary, he was a "champion" for ten years. That meant he had killed at least one hundred men a year for ten years! Even his armament was not ordinary. His spear was the length of a weaver's beam—some fourteen feet! Its tip weighed as much as a college shot put—sixteen pounds. He wielded a guided missile! Most of us could not even pick up the chain mail he wore—148 pounds of it. Think how intimidating it would be to have this spectacle towering over you in rage!

And yet no young man has ever attacked a problem with greater vigor than David did. When Goliath came out to David, the giant said, "Am I a dog, that you come to me with sticks? . . . Come to me, and I will give your flesh to the birds of the air and to the beasts of the field" (1 Samuel 17:43, 44). David answered that he was coming against Goliath in the name of the true God. "When the Philistine arose and came and drew near to meet David, David ran quickly toward the battle line to meet the Philistine" (1 Samuel 17:48).

As David ran toward the Philistine, he put his hand into his bag, took out a stone, and let it fly. The stone hit the Philistine right between the running lights, and down he came.

What was David's secret? Where did he get the courage for this confrontation? How was he able to attack the problem with such vigor? The answer to these questions can also be seen in John 6:1–14. The same thread runs through both passages—namely, the sufficiency and power that only Christ gives. Sooner or later each one of us will need this strength. This message is for all of us.

The Problem (vv. 1–9)

John 6 opens with a problem, a problem stemming from the success of Jesus' ministry. Jesus and his disciples were so popular that they drew unwieldy crowds. When Jesus saw how tired his disciples were, he instructed them to "Come away by yourselves to a desolate place and rest a while" (Mark 6:31). Mark then adds a parenthetical comment: "For many were coming and going, and they had no leisure even to eat."

In one sense it was great that they were so busy. The ministry was going well—so well that Jesus and the disciples could not even find time for lunch. They had been "peopled" to death—people after people, and more people. So Jesus and his disciples took a boat and crossed the sea to Bethsaida, hoping to rest their tired bodies and lift their drained spirits.

But now comes another problem—some of the people saw which direction the boat went. "Now many saw them going and recognized them, and they ran there on foot from all the towns and got there ahead of them" (Mark 6:33). In John 6:2 we read, "And a large crowd was following him, because they saw the signs that he was doing on the sick." As the boat headed north, toward the spot where the Jordan River empties into the Sea of Galilee, the crowd figured out that Jesus and his disciples were going to Bethsaida, two miles up the Jordan River. So the masses took off on foot and were waiting to welcome Jesus and company. So much for a vacation!

Mark notes that when the Lord saw the crowd, "He had compassion on them, because they were like sheep without a shepherd" (Mark 6:34). The word "compassion" tells us that he felt the needs of each person in that crowd. All day, according to the other Gospels, he ministered to the people, speaking about the kingdom. His ministry was a great success. Five thousand men, plus women and children, gathered around Jesus as he taught.

What a day that was! Jesus and the disciples were tired when they arrived at Bethsaida, then ministered that entire day. So as the shadows began to lengthen, Jesus drew his disciples aside, taking them a little further up the slope to discuss the situation. There was a problem. The people had come as far as ten miles to find Jesus, and in their excitement they had made no provision for food or lodging. They had been out in the hot sun all day long, and they were hungry and tired. Jesus summed up the problem in a question he put to the disciples, although he addressed it to Philip.

> Lifting up his eyes, then, and seeing that a large crowd was coming toward him, Jesus said to Philip, "Where are we to buy bread, so that these people may eat?" (v. 5)

The people would not die if they did not get something to eat right away, but the effect of the teaching might be lost if they were miserable and hungry as they made their way home. They had been pursuing spiritual things, and now they needed to have their bodies taken care of.

Jesus saw the people's problem, then gave it to the disciples. "He said this to test him, for he himself knew what he would do" (v. 6). Jesus knew what to do, but he asked the question in order to expand the disciples' spiritual understanding. He wanted them to see how to appropriate his power and sufficiency, to see how that could make a difference in their lives. In the disciples' responses we will see a shadow of ourselves.

> Philip answered him, "Two hundred denarii worth of bread would not be enough for each of them to get a little." (v. 7)

Philip did not really answer our Lord's question but just replied with statistics: 200 denarii would not be enough to feed the crowd. His answer revealed his problem—he was a bean counter. He had a slide rule for a brain. Now I am not saying we do not need to be practical people. Every family needs a practical person, and so does every church. But Philip was the kind of guy who decided everything with a calculator.

Other Scriptures confirm that Philip always looked at the external evidence. The first time we find him in the book of John, he wanted Nathanael to "come and see" Jesus (1:46). It was the same in the upper room where he made a very inappropriate statement: "Lord, show us the Father, and it is enough for us" (14:8). Philip required visual evidence. Just about every family has a person like this, and just about every business, and just about every church.

It is a good thing David did not use a calculator. "Ten feet tall at x number of pounds per inch. Why, Lord, he weighs at least 500 pounds. If he fell on me, he'd kill me! Lord, you've called the wrong man. I would need armor-piercing shells to beat him." Like Philip, some of us need to toss our calculators out and become more like David.

Next we see Andrew's problem, in verses 8, 9:

One of his disciples, Andrew, Simon Peter's brother, said to him, "There is a boy here who has five barley loaves and two fish, but what are they for so many?"

On the surface Andrew's response appears to be an improvement. At least he had been out in the crowd, looking in the brown bags, the sack lunches, and had learned what was there. He started out right, but unhappily he finished his statement with "What are they for so many?" When he came across that little boy with the five loaves and two fishes, he could have said, "Hey, son, let me borrow your lunch. You'll be amazed at what Jesus will do with it!" But instead he asked, "What are they for so many?" He did not look past the resources he had in his hand.

Andrew was very much like Philip. Philip calculated. Andrew simply looked at the resources and decided there was no way to solve the problem.

Then the rest of the disciples got together, as the other Gospels reveal, and they did not come up with any better outlook or plan. When you compile all the accounts, the story that emerges is something like this:

The Twelve came and said to him, "The place here is a wilderness, and the hour is already late. Send the multitude away so they can go into the villages and countryside to find lodging and buy themselves some food." But he answered and said to them, "They don't need to go away. You give them something to eat." And they said to him, "How can we buy 200 denarii worth of loaves?" So he said to them, "How many loaves do you have? Go and see." Upon finding out they said to him, "We have here just five loaves and two fish. What can we do with that?"

They could not possibly feed all those people. The disciples had calculated it and knew there was just no way. Anyone with common sense could see that. But as they found out, there is a time in life when common sense is very close to stupidity. To the disciples, the only answer was to send the multitude away. Someone else would have to help them. The disciples wanted to avoid the problem, ignore it, and let it just go away.

We have all felt that way at times. Psalm 55:6 says, "Oh, that I had wings like a dove! I would fly away and be at rest." Jeremiah 9:2 states, "Oh that I had in the desert a travelers' lodging place, that I might leave my people and go away from them!"

The disciples' problem was that they had grossly underestimated their wealth. They thought all they had was five loaves and two fish. What was wrong with that? They had been with the Lord. They had seen water changed into wine, a miracle similar to the one needed in this situation. They had seen the nobleman's son healed from a distance. Jesus had healed the paralytic lying by the pool of Bethesda. Why didn't they understand what Christ could do in this situation? The disciples had a defective view of Christ. That was their problem, and very often that is the root of our problem.

Thomas Carlyle spoke with deep insight when he said, "Men are like the gods they serve." We conduct our lives according to the concept of the God to whom we bow. That was precisely the difference between the nation of Israel and David. Years before David's time, Israel departed from what God had given them, a theocracy under judges, and decided they wanted to be like the other nations and have a king. They chose Saul, the tallest man in the nation (see 1 Samuel 9:2), to be their first king. They chose the giant in their nation to be their ruler, who then later cowered before the giant Goliath. Then along came David. He did not have a defective concept of his God. First Samuel 17 tells us that when he saw Israel retreating before Goliath, he said, probably in a soprano voice, "Who is this uncircumcised Philistine, that he should defy the armies of the living God?" (1 Samuel 17:26). Shortly afterwards he told King Saul, "Your servant has struck down both lions and bears, and this uncircumcised Philistine shall be like one of them, for he has defied the armies of the living God" (1 Samuel 17:36). David had the right concept of God.

> Then David said to the Philistine, "You come to me with a sword and with a spear and with a javelin, but I come to you in the name of the Lord of hosts, the God of the armies of Israel, whom you have defied. This day the Lord will deliver you into my hand, and I will strike you down and cut off your head. And I will give the dead bodies of the host of the Philistines this day to the birds of the air and to the wild beasts of the earth, that all the earth may know that there is a God in Israel, and that all this assembly may know

that the LORD saves not with sword and spear. For the battle is the Lord's, and he will give you into our hand." (1 Samuel 17:45–47)

"Men are like the gods they serve." What kind of God did David serve? What kind of God do we serve? The answer to that question is the continental divide in the practice of the Christian life. We can read the Apostles' Creed and subscribe to the vast, unfathomable doctrines of the greatness of our God and yet get into the fray and discover that our actual concept of God is something different. When we are in the battle we need a concept of God that is consistent with the God revealed in the Bible. That is what we need, but how can we achieve it?

The Solution (vv. 10–13)

The solution for the disciples came in a miraculous display of Christ's power. This was the most public of all of his miracles (recorded in all four Gospels), and in many ways it was the greatest, almost an *ex nihilo* miracle. Yes, he multiplied a few loaves, but it was almost as if he created them. During the last fifty years it has been very much in vogue to doubt this miracle. Some doubters say Christ did not really multiply the loaves and the fishes—the miracle occurred in the people's hearts because when that little boy pulled out his lunch, everyone else pulled out their lunch, and they shared. But that explanation does violence to the Biblical accounts. It simply is not what the Scriptures say. It is very interesting that in a passage that is trying to elevate our concept of Christ, this interpretation comes from a defective concept of Christ. The doubters have taken their Christ, a Christ who does not intrude himself into the supernatural, and imposed him onto this passage of Scripture. That is why they do not see a miracle here. Their problem is the problem the passage is trying to correct. The feeding of the five thousand was indeed a tremendous miracle.

Mark 6:39 says, "Then he [Jesus] commanded them all to sit down in groups on the green grass." It probably took some time to get them to do so. But finally they were seated, and then our Lord did something absolutely outrageous—he gave thanks. Can you imagine asking God's blessing on the food when there was no food? I imagine that some kept their eyes open, thinking, *What in the world is going on here?* Then the unthinkable happened. We read about the miracle in verse 11.

> Jesus then took the loaves, and when he had given thanks, he distributed them to those who were seated. So also the fish, as much as they wanted.

Mark tells us a little more: "[He] said a blessing and broke the loaves and gave them to the disciples to set before the people" (Mark 6:41). The loaves just multiplied. As the bread began to spread throughout those thousands, there began to be a murmur, and finally a roar—such a roar, so much excitement that the people wanted to make Jesus king. What an incredible miracle! Verse 12 tells us that the crowd ate until they were all filled. This was not just a snack. There was so much food that the disciples gathered twelve baskets full of leftovers, enough for the next day. God takes care of those who serve him.

Interestingly, the loaves were poor man's bread, the cheapest of all breads. The *Mishnah* talks about an offering a woman would bring if she had committed adultery. She was supposed to bring a bread offering, but the *Mishnah* qualifies it by saying it should be barley, the food of beasts, for the woman's sin was the sin of a beast. Barley is the bread of the poor.

Why would Christ use this food? He wanted his disciples to see that no matter what they had—even the tiniest or most menial thing—if they really gave it to him, he could use it. Little is much when God is in it. He wanted them to see that truth in a most dramatic demonstration.

What does this mean for us? Sometimes we feel like saying, "Lord, you do not understand my problem. If you only knew how I feel . . . I have calculated it all out, I have thought it all through, I have consulted the authorities, and there is nothing I can do." It is harder to give God our weaknesses than our strengths. If we are eloquent, it is easy to say, "God, here is my eloquence. Take it and use it." Or if we are good businessmen, we can say, "God, you can have my administrative ability. You can ennoble it and add grace to it—here it is." But to give God our weaknesses . . .

But the Lord says, "Give me whatever you have, including your weaknesses." Many of us have missed the great miracles God wanted to give us because we have been unwilling to do that because of our pride. If you have calculated all the angles of your difficult situation, if you just want to run away and hide, do you know what the solution is? First, realize that God wants to help you. He wants to pour his grace upon you. He wanted to help those disciples, and he wants to help you. Isaiah 30:18 promises, "The LORD waits to be gracious to you, and therefore he exalts himself to show mercy to you." Next, realize that God is big enough to help.

Do you believe God is big enough for your problem? Nothing much can happen if you do not. You need to have a correct concept of him. Then you must surrender your deficiency to him. A quotation from Elisabeth Elliot expresses this truth beautifully.

If the only thing you have to offer is a broken heart, you offer a broken heart. So in a time of grief, the recognition that this is material for sacrifice has been a very great strength for me. Realizing that nothing I have, nothing I am will be refused on the part of Christ, I simply give it to him as the little boy gave Jesus his five loaves and two fishes—with the same feeling of the disciples when they said, "What is the good of that for such a crowd?"

Naturally in almost anything I offer to Christ, my reaction would be, "What is the good of that?" The point is, the use he makes of it is none of my business; it is his business, it is his blessing. So this grief, this loss, this suffering, this pain—whatever it is, which at the moment is God's means of testing my faith and bringing me to the recognition of who he is—that is the thing I can offer.[1]

Do you have nothing to give? Then give that. *Your nothing plus God is everything.* We need to believe that God is big enough, that he wants to help us. Then we must give our problem to him. May we set aside our pride and give it all to him.

24

God's Children in the Storms of Life

JOHN 6:16–21

WHEN JESUS MIRACULOUSLY FED five thousand men plus women and children, some Jews wanted to make him king. Jesus realized their intentions and immediately departed. But before he left, he sent his disciples, by boat, to the other side of the Sea of Galilee. Then he withdrew to a nearby mountain to spend time alone. In 6:16–21 we read that Jesus joined the disciples by walking on the water to overtake their boat. The next day, on the other side of the lake, it looked very much as if Jesus' plan had worked. After all, they had the Sea of Galilee between the eager multitudes and themselves. Or did they? The multitude had boats too, and before long they too reached the other side and began questioning him, saying, "Rabbi, when did you come here?" (6:25). The crowd was not to be turned away. They liked the bread he had provided. They wanted a Savior who met their material needs. Our Lord's response is a penetrating indictment of religion without personal faith in Christ.

> Truly, truly, I say to you, you are seeking me, not because you saw signs, but because you ate your fill of the loaves. (6:26)

They continued seeking him only because they wanted a Savior who would supply material gifts. They did not want a spiritual Savior who would redeem them from their sins. Jesus did not deny that he was able to give material blessings, but he explained in the Bread of Life discourse that he was essentially a Savior who could give them unimagined spiritual gifts. How would his hearers react to his loving but strong words?

> After this many of his disciples turned back and no longer walked with him.
> So Jesus said to the Twelve, "Do you want to go away as well?" (6:66, 67)

Humanly speaking, the possibility of losing those disciples was very real. But Peter responded in a way we should all emulate when he said, "Lord, to whom shall we go? You have the words of eternal life" (6:68).

Why did Peter respond that way when most of the others were deserting Christ? The key is found in the crisis of the preceding night—when Peter and the rest of the Twelve were struggling to sail across the lake and our Lord came to them walking on the water and met the discouraged disciples and ministered to them. That made the difference in Peter.

By comparing Matthew 14, Mark 6, and John 6, we get the full picture of that awesome night.

This event has had many interesting, and many false, interpretations as theologians have attempted to explain away the miracle. One theory claims there were stones in the water and since Jesus was walking close to shore, he was walking on the stones. So why did Peter begin to sink? Another explanation translates the word "on" (Matthew 14:25; John 6:19) as "around," claiming Jesus walked around the lake. Neither the original text nor the obvious intent of the authors supports this view. What happened was presented in the Gospels as a miracle, and it is meant to be treated as such. Jesus intended for this miracle to teach the disciples deeper spiritual realities, and it can do the same for us. Note also that it is called a "sign" (see 20:30, 31, "signs," apparently including the feeding of the multitude and Jesus' walking on water). Whenever John speaks of a "sign," he is pointing us to deep spiritual truths that moves the reader toward believing that Jesus is the Christ. That night of struggle on the stormy sea is a picture of those who follow Christ through the storms of life.

Matthew 14:22, 23 gives us the setting for this miracle:

> Immediately he made the disciples get into the boat and go before him to the other side, while he dismissed the crowds. And after he had dismissed the crowds, he went up on the mountain by himself to pray. When evening came, he was there alone.

We can understand our Lord's actions. He was tired, and he needed to be alone for communion with his Father. But also, in Scripture a mountain is often used as a symbol of a place of authority. The picture of our Lord praying in a place of authority as his disciples struggled on the mission he had given them pictures his relating to those who faithfully follow him. In fact, it is a picture of God interceding for us while we, at his direction, are battling the storms of life.

The Miracle and Its Meaning

This is a story of faith from beginning to end. Matthew 14:22 tells us Jesus "*made* the disciples get into the boat." The word "made" could also be translated "compelled"—"to compel by force or persuasion or to constrain." The picture Scripture paints is one of disciples who did not want to go to the other side but who were persuaded, even compelled, by our Lord. He probably gave the boat a shove to get the Twelve going in the right direction. He deliberately sent them out into the lake.

The disciples were well on their way when the storm came. "But the boat by this time was a long way from the land, beaten by the waves, for the wind was against them" (Matthew 14:24). The disciples were several miles from shore, and their boat was being "beaten"—literally, "tormented." Scripture is very graphic at this point. "The wind was against them." That is, they were sailing straight into the wind. What terror they must have felt! The great preacher Clarence Edward Macartney described it like this:

> Peter, no doubt, took command; (and I am sure that he did) and you can see him there holding the tiller with his stalwart arm, and his beard anointed with the foam of the sea, as in stentorian tones he commands the disciples to trim the ship, lower the sails, and take to the oars. Where all was calm a little while ago, now all is tumult and confusion. As the tempest rages over the lake, the ship tosses like a cork up and down in the great waves, the white foam of the great rollers gleaming in the blackness of the night like the teeth of some monster of the sea.[1]

They were in trouble! Once I was in a twelve-foot boat in the Pacific Ocean and the waves got so big that we could not see over them. And when we were on top of the waves, we could see waves above those waves. Abject terror!

But why were the disciples in trouble? Because they had pointed their boat in the direction the Lord had told them to take. They would not have been in danger in the middle of the lake if they had disobeyed. Because they were obedient to Christ, they were in serious peril. How can this be?

In 1958, when I was a junior in high school, one of my high school buddies pulled up in front of my house in a '55 Chevy. He was towing a contraption he called a sailboat. Actually it was just a large surfboard with a sail. We took that misbegotten assemblage down to Newport Bay and decided we would try to sail it from one end to the other. Neither one of us had ever been sailing before, but we managed to get it rigged up and in the water. To reach the point we wanted, we had to sail into the wind. It took us four hours to sail a quarter of a mile, and in that four hours we capsized the boat eight times, the last time in front of a ferry loaded with cars and people! But when we turned the boat around and went back the other way, it only took us five minutes to get back to where we had begun.

The disciples were in trouble because they had encountered contrary winds. What is the meaning of this? Our Lord is saying, "Those of you who have decided to follow me as your Savior are going to be sailing your vessel into the winds of life. You are going to have trouble. But obey anyway." There are two ways to get into storms. One is to flee God's will, like Jonah did. A great storm blew up, and he ended up in a fish's belly. That is different from the disciples' situation. They were in the midst of a storm because they were obedient to God. Those who decide to follow Christ and give him their allegiance will face contrary winds, no doubt about it. Moses would never have felt rejected by a complaining people if at the burning bush he had decided not to obey Jehovah. Daniel would never have had to face a lion's den if he had not decided to be faithful to God. Just think of how much persecution Paul would have avoided if he had just stayed in Tarsus. But then these great men would have never known the refreshing winds of the Holy Spirit flowing through their lives. Yes, following Christ will take us into some fierce storms, but the rewards are even greater.

So there were the disciples, battling the gale, wondering if they would make it to shore. The storm was raging. The waves were immense. The spray kept dashing over the ship. The masts had begun to crack, and water was sloshing in the dark hold of their beleaguered ship. The disciples probably wondered, "Has the Lord forgotten us?" But Jesus had not forsaken them, even though it looked as if he had. Mark, in his parallel account (6:48), says Jesus "saw" them. John 6:17 says, "It was now dark." We do not know if Jesus saw the disciples in the midst of lightning or if he saw them because of his omniscience. Whichever it was, the point is that he knew their plight. In this dark age things can be so obscured by the secular winds of life and its problems that it looks as if Jesus has forgotten us, but he has not. He knows, he cares, and he will come to our aid. As Psalm 139:7–10 tells us:

Where shall I go from your Spirit?
    Or where shall I flee from your presence?
If I ascend to heaven, you are there!

If I make my bed in Sheol, you are there!
If I take the wings of the morning
and dwell in the uttermost parts of the sea,
even there your hand shall lead me,
and your right hand shall hold me.

Wherever we go, our Lord is there, and he knows all the details of our situation. When we are going through dark storms, it is easy to think he has forgotten us. But he is cognizant of it all. He knows when a sparrow falls to the ground, and he certainly knows the difficulties we are going through. Christ saw the disciples toiling and rowing helplessly, and yet he delayed coming to them. He knew their thoughts, he knew they were wondering where he was, and yet he chose to let that storm batter them for a while. Finally he came to them. Why did he delay? I do not think we can say for sure, but there is a hint in John 11, the story about Lazarus. Mary and Martha sent for Jesus, asking him to heal Lazarus because he was on the verge of death, but Jesus delayed and allowed him to die. Then Christ came, wept, and raised Lazarus back to life. Why? Perhaps to take his disciples to the very end of their strength, so they would rely fully on God. We cannot always know why God waits, but we can be sure that he knows everything and that he is ministering and caring for us and will never abandon us.

Matthew 14:25 adds another dimension to our story: "In the fourth watch of the night he came to them, walking on the sea." Our Lord came to the disciples, evidently taking the same course the boat had taken. After he had finished praying, he strode down that mountain to the same point on the shore and somehow, at least partially, followed the path they had taken. That is an incredibly encouraging aspect of Christ's incarnation—he understands our situation, he feels what we feel, he walks where we walk. So when we are being tossed about, he understands everything we are going through. Jesus experienced what the disciples were experiencing. What a scene to keep before us—our Lord walking across those waves, the angry waves the pavement for his feet.

That verse also tells us that Christ came to the disciples during "the fourth watch of the night," between three and six in the morning. Jesus came to his threatened followers during the darkest part of the night, when the disciples were exhausted, miserable, and tired, wondering if they were going to survive. Only then did the Lord come.

We have experienced the same thing. The check that came in the mail at the last minute. The house that sold at the eleventh hour. I experienced that "fourth watch" timing when I was in college. During my senior year my wife and I were expecting our first child. It was a difficult time in our lives because I was so busy. I was working full-time in a factory and taking a full load in school. All I was taking home was $73 a week for full time work. Two weeks before our child was due to be born, I calculated that by the time of Barbara's delivery I would have $160 on hand, but the doctor wanted $250 and the hospital another $250. We just did not have enough money. So we prayed in the eleventh hour.

Our baby came, but before that something happened. When my wife went for her final examination with the doctor, he looked over the charts and noticed for the first time that I was studying for the ministry. The man had no Christian background and was not interested in spiritual things, but he said, "I'm not going to charge you." Great! Now we owed only $250 to the hospital. When I went to the hospital to pick up our daughter, I was determined to bring her home. I had $163, and I was determined to pay that and walk out with my baby. Well, our timing had been just right, we had been charged for two days instead of three, and the bill was $160. I even had three dollars left over to buy flowers for my wife! Jesus came to us in the dark part of the night when we had been toiling and were fearful and uncertain of what was going to happen.

You may know Christ, but you will never know him deeply until he comes to you in the midst of the storms of life. Is that not what Job said when he had suffered everything? In Job 42:5 he said, "I had heard of you by the hearing of the ear, but now my eye sees you." Christ comes to us in the midst of storms.

Unfortunately, we also see the perverseness of the human heart in this event. Matthew 14:26 says, "When the disciples saw him walking on the sea, they were terrified, and said, 'It is a ghost!' and they cried out in fear." The disciples' fright is understandable. It was dark, the wind was blowing, and they were barely hanging on to their lives. Then they saw an apparition—a water demon—coming across the waters, looking like the Ancient Mariner without his ship! The disciples were ready to dive overboard. They were "terrified" by the help coming to them in Christ. Often the perversity of our hearts causes us to push God away when he comes to us in the storm. Perhaps this is partly because he often comes in ways we do not expect and that we (inexcusably) reject. Maybe his aid comes to us through someone we have rejected or through occupational tragedy or through a member of the family to whom we have felt superior. We must guard against rejecting what he is trying to do for us, whether through fear or pride or ignorance. Is he trying to help us in a storm but we are pushing him away?

As the disciples quaked with fear, some almost paralyzed, others falling over themselves, a voice pierced the storm. "Take heart; it is I. Do not be afraid" (Matthew 14:27). In an instant the disciples' attitude changed 180 degrees. A moment before, they had feared for their lives. Then they heard the voice of Christ. Note that he did not say, "Do not be afraid" before he said, "It is I." When we focus upon Christ, we begin to find and receive his help.

When the disciples saw it was Jesus, they became venturesome. Peter asked the Lord to call him, then stepped out and began to walk on the water. That is what faith causes us to do. Sometimes Peter is bad-mouthed by preachers, but how many of us have put a leg over the side of a boat and stepped onto water? Peter walked on water because of his faith and sank only when he began to take his eyes off Jesus. Fortunately, Peter had been around the Lord long enough to know what to pray at such a moment (Matthew 14:30): "Lord, save me." Then Jesus and Peter walked radiantly back to the boat.

"And when they got into the boat, the wind ceased" (Matthew 14:32). This is when Peter really got the point. Jesus had turned down the people's request that he be their Savior in the material world. He did not allow them to make him king, though he was obviously King over the material realm. Otherwise, how could he have walked on water and calmed the storm? Seeing all that gave Peter the grace to say, "Lord, to whom shall we go? You have the words of eternal life." "To whom shall we go?" That is the question for all of us. Only Christ has the words of life.

Master of the Storms of Life

"And those in the boat worshiped him, saying, 'Truly you are the Son of God'" (Matthew 14:33). They *worshiped*.

"Then they were glad to take him into the boat, and immediately the boat was at the land to which they were going" (6:21). Was that a miracle? Did the boat hydroplane frantically to shore? I do not think we can answer that with certainty, but I will make a suggestion. The times we spend with the love of our life fly by, and I think the disciples were so caught up in worshiping him that time ceased for them, and suddenly they found themselves on the shore. How wonderful it is to be so preoccupied with our wonderful Savior!

Conclusion

Following Christ will certainly bring us into contrary winds. That is inevitable. That is a promise. But it is comforting to know that he sees all. He understands and cares!

Are you going through the storms of life now? He sees. Believe that, rest in it, appropriate it. Rejoice that understanding help is on the way. Help was on the way for the disciples long before they saw it, and the same is true for you.

Are you filled with darkness? Do you wonder if there is a way out? Keep expecting him to come because he often comes in the fourth watch. Be open to the hand of God in your life. Focus the gaze of faith upon him.

Is your life filled with occupational uncertainty? Why not invite him into the boat? Insecurity? Invite him into the boat. Interpersonal struggle? Conflict with other believers? Invite him into the boat. An ethical dilemma? Invite him into the boat.

25

Dining on the Bread of Life

JOHN 6:26–35, 47–58

IN THE 1930S the most famous living author was William Somerset Maugham. He was an accomplished novelist, a great playwright, and a short story writer. In fact, his novel *Of Human Bondage* quickly established itself as a classic. His play *The Constant Wife* has gone through thousands of stagings.

In 1965 Somerset Maugham was ninety-one years old and fabulously wealthy. Royalties were continuing to pour in from all over the world despite the fact that he had not written a word in years. His fame seemingly was on the upsurge. He received an average of three hundred letters a week from his fans. He was experiencing incredible success. But how did Maugham respond to his success? What had it brought to his life? We gain an insight from an article written by Maugham's nephew, Robin Maugham, after he visited his uncle before his death at his uncle's fabulous villa on the Mediterranean.

> I looked round the drawing room at the immensely valuable furniture and pictures and objects that Willie's success had enabled him to acquire. I remembered that the villa itself and the wonderful garden I could see through the windows—a fabulous setting on the edge of the Mediterranean—were worth 600,000. (It cost him 7,000.) Willie had 11 servants, including his cook, Annette, who was the envy of all the other millionaires on the Riviera. He dined on silver plates, waited on by Marius, his butler, and Henri, his footman. But it no longer meant anything to him. The following afternoon, I found Willie reclining on a sofa, peering through his spectacles at a Bible which had very large print. He looked horribly wizened, and his face was grim. "I've been reading the Bible you gave me . . . and I've come across the quotation: 'What shall it profit a man if he gain the whole world

and lose his own soul?' I must tell you, my dear Robin, that the text used to hang opposite my bed when I was a child. . . . Of course, it's all a lot of bunk. But the thought is quite interesting all the same." That evening, in the drawing room after dinner, Willie flung himself down onto the sofa. "Oh, Robin, I'm so tired . . ." He gave a gulp and buried his head in his hands. "I've been a failure the whole way through my life," he said. "I've made mistake after mistake. I've made a hash of everything." I tried to comfort him. "You're the most famous writer alive. Surely that means something?" "I wish I'd never written a single word," he answered. "It's brought me nothing but misery. . . . Everyone who's got to know me well has ended up by hating me. . . . My whole life has been a failure. . . . And now it's too late to change. It's too late. . . ." Willie looked up, and his grip tightened on my hands. He was staring towards the floor. His face was contorted with fear, and he was trembling violently. Willie's face was ashen as he stared in horror ahead of him. Suddenly, he began to shriek. "Go away!" he cried. "I'm not ready. . . . I'm not dead yet. . . . I'm not dead yet, I tell you. . . ." His high-pitched, terror-struck voice seemed to echo from wall to wall. I looked round, but the room was empty as before. "There's no one there, Willie." Willie began to gasp hysterically.[1]

What a grim story! Maugham was one of the most famous and feted men of his generation—a man who had everything: not just money but fame. A man who dined with princes. But when he came to the time for reckoning, he found life empty and worthless and was afraid to die.

This is not what life is intended to be. God does not want anyone to come to the end of his life knowing it has been all futility and mistakes. The people in John 6:26–35, 47–58, though their situations were less dramatic, were headed in the same destructive direction as Maugham. Our Lord wanted to free them, just as he wanted to free Maugham. That's why he gave the Bread of Life discourse—to rescue us from the emptiness of life.

As we study this text, we will see, first, how Christ teaches his persistent followers they are empty. Once his followers understand their utter emptiness, he tells them how to receive the satisfaction he gives.

First, we will review the setting. Our Lord had become wildly popular, and there was such a crush around him and the disciples that they were exhausted. He sent the disciples across the lake to Bethsaida, where there was green grass, quiet, and the beautiful hope of relaxation. However, the crowds who were following him stormed after the disciples. They saw the direction the boat took, and sure enough, when Jesus got there the crowds were waiting for him. He responded by ministering all day, a day that culminated in the feeding of the five thousand. It also resulted in some very tired disciples. So that night he sent them across the lake in the boat. That was the night of the great storm when our Lord walked on the water. When the disciples finally arrived at the other side of the lake, it looked as if they had finally escaped the crowd—except the crowd had boats too. Sometime that next day men came to Jesus, saying, "Rabbi, when did you come here?" (6:25). It was almost as if he did not have any business eluding them!

Crowds wildly pursued Jesus because he had supplied them with the material things of life. They liked the idea of a fish maker and bread baker—someone who could give them the material things they wanted. They failed to take a step farther and realize that a man who could miraculously supply bread was also the One who could meet the deep spiritual needs of their lives. So he lifted their sights and brought them to a place where he could bless them.

Receiving Christ's Truth (vv. 26–35)

Jesus began with a confrontation.

> Truly, truly, I say to you, you are seeking me, not because you saw signs, but because you ate your fill of the loaves. (v. 26)

In other words, "You seek me only because you want full stomachs, because you are materially motivated." Today too some follow him hoping for a comfortable, soothing, indulgent Savior.

Our Lord continued:

> Do not work for the food that perishes, but for the food that endures to eternal life, which the Son of Man will give to you. For on him God the Father has set his seal. (v. 27)

With that statement he began to reveal the spiritual realities he wanted people to see. He was saying there are two kinds of bread, a material bread that perishes and a spiritual bread that lives eternally.

We all know that groceries perish. I can remember many times when my wife came home with a station wagon full of groceries, but by nightfall my boys were complaining there was nothing in the house to eat. Our Lord was reminding the crowd that we earn physical food by the sweat of our brow, but spiritual food is eternal life. That food does not come by our work. It comes from Christ.

In these verses our Lord began to elevate the people's defective view of what life is all about. We see this in the exchange that follows in verses 28, 29.

> Then they said to him, "What must we do, to be doing the works of God?" Jesus answered them, "This is the work of God, that you believe in him whom he has sent."

They asked what kind of work they had to do to get the bread they needed. Our Lord responded by saying there is no physical work we can do—we just need to believe in him. The bread that endures comes through faith.

Suppose you invited another family over for a Sunday afternoon dinner. It is a great meal. You really put on the spread for them. You fix their favorite meat, cooked just the way they like it. There is a big, tossed green salad, steaming baked potatoes with cheese sauce, a refreshing beverage, and then apple pie à la mode (just about everybody's favorite dessert). What a dinner! Soon everyone is sitting back, patting full tummies. And suppose, when it comes time for your guests to leave, they take out their wallets and ask, "How much do we owe you for this?" You would probably say, "You don't owe me anything!" But what if your guests respond, "We most certainly do! We are not freeloaders! How much do we owe you?" They even throw you a couple of twenty-dollar bills. Just a mention of payment in such a setting would be a grievous insult. Yet, we find ourselves going through life trying to pay for a free meal and in the process insulting our Lord. As Jesus says in verse 29, "This is the work of God, that you believe in him whom he has sent." In other words, the bread that endures unto eternal life is the bread that is freely given and that we freely receive. It comes through belief. We do not pay for it ourselves.

Unfortunately, the crowd did not catch on, and the evidence of their dullness is found in verses 30, 31. Instead of carrying this conversation on to its consummation and understanding the deep truths, the people tried to divert and test our Lord.

> So they said to him, "Then what sign do you do, that we may see and believe you? What work do you perform? Our fathers ate the manna in the wilderness; as it is written, 'He gave them bread from heaven to eat.'"

"Jesus, we're not really interested in all that. You did a great sign yesterday when you fed the five thousand, and now we want you to do a miracle on a par with Moses' miracle. He fed all of Israel six days a week for forty years with bread from Heaven."

To understand what they were saying and why, we need to consider Exodus 16:

> They set out from Elim, and all the congregation of the people of Israel came to the wilderness of Sin, which is between Elim and Sinai, on the fifteenth day of the second month after they had departed from the land of Egypt. And the whole congregation of the people of Israel grumbled against Moses and Aaron in the wilderness, and the people of Israel said to them, "Would that we had died by the hand of the LORD in the land of Egypt, when

we sat by the meat pots and ate bread to the full, for you have brought us out into this wilderness to kill this whole assembly with hunger." Then the LORD said to Moses, "Behold, I am about to rain bread from heaven for you, and the people shall go out and gather a day's portion every day, that I may test them, whether they will walk in my law or not." (vv. 1–4)

And the LORD said to Moses, "I have heard the grumbling of the people of Israel. Say to them, 'At twilight you shall eat meat, and in the morning you shall be filled with bread. Then you shall know that I am the LORD your God.'"

In the evening quail came up and covered the camp, and in the morning dew lay around the camp. And when the dew had gone up, there was on the face of the wilderness a fine, flake-like thing, fine as frost on the ground. When the people of Israel saw it, they said to one another, "What is it?" For they did not know what it was. And Moses said to them, "It is the bread that the LORD has given you to eat." (vv. 11–15)

You can imagine, as the sun came up, the buzz of conversation as people all around the camp asked, "What is it?" "What is it?" "What is it?" A father might have said to his daughter, "Tabitha, gather some of this white stuff—you know, the whatchamacallit." And she would say, "Sure, but what is it, Father?" We know that is what happened because Exodus 16:31 says, "Now the house of Israel called its name manna," which means "What is it?" So for the next forty years, six days a week, every morning the Jews ate "What is it?"

This was the idea running through the back of the minds of the people who were confronting Jesus. The Jews even had a fable that Jeremiah, at the destruction of the temple, had taken some of the manna and hidden it, and when the Messiah came, he would provide manna. So these people were saying to our Lord, "You did a great miracle yesterday. Now what we want is really a big one—bread from Heaven every day!"

There had just been a miracle the day before, but that miracle was not enough. We are the same way. We say, "God, if we can just have another miracle, if you would just do something else for me today . . . !" We forget what he has done in our lives already. One of the reasons David had so much power in his life was that he had not forgotten what God had done when he faced the lion and the bear, and that gave him the courage to face Goliath.

Jesus realized the crowd needed some correction, so he said in verses 32, 33:

Truly, truly, I say to you, it was not Moses who gave you the bread from heaven, but my Father gives you the true bread from heaven. For the bread of God is he who comes down from heaven and gives life to the world.

The crowd did not completely understand what Jesus was saying, but they understood part of it. He was correcting them. The bread they wanted did not come from Moses—it came from God. They understood that, and they understood that he was talking about something a little beyond the material. But they did not completely understand, so they continued to question. In fact, they really led with their chins in verse 34. "Sir," they said, "give us this bread always."

Now Jesus had them where he wanted them, so he could tell them what he could do for them. There are seven great "I am" sayings in the book of John—"I am the light," "I am the door," "I am the good shepherd," "I am the resurrection and the life," "I am the way, and the truth, and the life," "I am the true vine," and here in verse 35:

> I am the bread of life; whoever comes to me shall not hunger, and whoever believes in me shall never thirst.

What a statement! "I am the bread of life." It is no coincidence that Jesus was born in Bethlehem, "the house of bread," as prophesied hundreds of years earlier by Micah (Micah 5:2). The Word became flesh, and we broke it. There is no coincidence about that either. It was all planned by the Lord, for our redemption.

There are several similarities between manna and Jesus, "the bread of life." The manna typified Jesus, for it was white like fallen snow, just as Christ was without blemish or imperfection. Manna was also accessible. That was one of its main virtues. When a man walked outside the camp to gather it, he had a choice. He could either tread on it or he could pick it up. We can either tread upon Jesus or we can take him as our Savior. To change metaphors, the Scriptures say Jesus can either be a cornerstone or a stumbling block. How we respond to him makes all the difference.

Jesus is "the bread of life." He is our sustenance. Verse 35 says that he who comes to Christ will not hunger and he who believes in him will never thirst. Apart from Christ, nothing satisfies. The best of fishing trips must be followed by another fishing trip. The most exquisite meal still leaves you hungry. C. S. Lewis said, "I cannot find a cup of tea which is big enough or a book that is long enough." You can play the best racquetball game, be at your best, but it has to be followed by another game. You can have a great Sunday dinner, but it has to be followed by a good breakfast in the morning. You can wear the fanciest, most chic clothes, but you will have to have new clothes next year. All of these things are like a Chinese dinner—in just a few hours you are empty and ready to eat again. That is the way it is with the best things of life. Somerset Maugham dressed in his finest tuxedo and night after night played cards with the most famous people in all of the world. Dukes and duchesses sought his favor. He had the most exclusive of parties. But he found no lasting satisfaction.

But the bread of life satisfies. I would not agree with everything that Dietrich Bonhoeffer wrote, but I know that at the end of his life he was a man who was full of Christ. When he was transferred from the Nazi prison to the main Gestapo prison in 1944 and he knew his end was near, he calmly said good-bye to his prisoner friends. They said he seemed at peace, except "his eyes were quite unnatural." In all he was a remarkable testimony for Christ. One of the last messages received from him bore testimony to his marvelous spirit. It was a poem entitled "New Year 1945." The third stanza reads:

> Should it be ours to drain the cup of grieving
> Even to the dregs of pain, at thy command,
> We will not falter, thankfully receiving
> All that is given by thy loving hand.[2]

He was a man who was full of Christ, and he was satisfied. What a contrast with our pathetic millionaire on the Riviera. God says:

> Come, everyone who thirsts,
>   come to the waters;
> and he who has no money,
>   come, buy and eat!
> Come, buy wine and milk
>   without money and without price.
> Why do you spend your money for that which is not bread,
>   and your labor for that which does not satisfy?
> Listen diligently to me, and eat what is good,
>   and delight yourselves in rich food.
> Incline your ear, and come to me;
>   hear, that your soul may live. (Isaiah 55:1–3)

Jesus Christ essentially makes the same claim in John 6:35: "I am the bread of life; whoever comes to me shall not hunger, and whoever believes in me shall never thirst."

Having made his point, the Lord then discoursed on the mysteries of his grace in verses 36–46. In verse 51 he reiterated many of the same things he had just said, except he emphasized that there had to be a partaking of him as the bread of life. Because of that statement, the Jews asked a question (v. 52):

"The Jews then disputed among themselves, saying, 'How can this man give us his flesh to eat?'"

Misunderstanding Christ's words, they declared their shock at the suggestion of cannibalism! "What is Jesus talking about? Are we really to drink his blood and eat his flesh in order to get the bread of life?" Humanly speaking, if I had been the Lord, I might have backed off from that statement a bit, but the Lord did not. In fact, he issued an even stronger affirmation of what he was saying in verse 53.

Receiving Christ's Satisfaction (vv. 53–58)

So Jesus said to them, "Truly, truly, I say to you, unless you eat the flesh of the Son of Man and drink his blood, you have no life in you." (v. 53)

Our Savior meant there must be a deep partaking of him. How do we do that? We must live depending on him as the bread of life. As James Boice says:

Is he as real to you spiritually as something you can taste or handle? Is he as much a part of you as that which you eat? Do not think me blasphemous when I say that he must be as real and as useful to you as a hamburger and french fries. I say this because, although he is obviously far more real and useful than these, the unfortunate thing is that for many people he is much less.[3]

Is he substantially real to you? That is what is involved in treating him as the bread of life. This is one of the continental divides in the life of the soul, and this is where thousands flounder.

Paul had a vision of the risen Christ, and that is what set him apart from his contemporaries. He prayed that people's hearts might be opened so they could grasp the riches of their inheritance in Christ Jesus. He wanted his people to see that Christ is real. Is he real to you? Is he bread? Is he as real as meat and potatoes?

What else does *bread* suggest? Christ is absolutely indispensable. Since bread was the staple of life in those days, it was difficult for people to conceive of life without bread. Is it difficult for us to conceive of life without Christ? What if there were no Christ? How would that change our lives? The refrain from an old Peggy Lee song asks, "Is that all there is? Is that all there is?" What is your life like? Is that all there is? I cannot conceive of going on living without Christ. He is our bread. He is our all, our everything.

Joy Davidman, in her book *Smoke on the Mountain*, brilliantly commented on the first commandment ("Thou shalt have no other gods before me," KJV) by turning it around to positively read, "Thou shalt have me."[4] Is not that what it is all about? "You shall have me. I am the bread of life. Partake of me. I want you to have me. I want to be bread to you."

What else does bread suggest? A daily partaking. How often do we partake of Christ? Is he more than a hamburger and french fries to us? He wants to give us himself, which demands that we be constantly partaking of him, ingesting him into our lives.

Conclusion

Somerset Maugham did it all, but nothing satisfied him. The tragedy was dramatized when he took that large-print Bible in his wrinkled hands and read, "What shall it profit a man if he gain the whole world and lose his own soul?" and flippantly tossed it aside. What if he had read more? What if he had come to the book of John and read, "Jesus answered them, 'This is the work of God, that you believe in him whom he has sent'" (6:29). What would have happened to him if he had believed? The same thing that happened to the Prodigal Son. The ring would have gone on his hand, the sandals on his feet, the robe around his shoulders, and for the first time in that man's life he would have been satisfied.

All the people on earth can be divided into two groups. There are those who know the satisfaction Christ brings. They have partaken of him. Some in that group are more satisfied than others because they have been eating the Bread more consistently. There are others who know nothing of the satisfaction Jesus gives. They have never had true inner satisfaction. They know others who have the full and abundant life Christ offers, but they are on the outside looking in.

If that is true of you, you need to ask the question the disciples asked ("What must we do, to be doing the works of God?"), and you must hear Jesus' answer: "This is the work of God, that you believe in him whom he has sent." Very simply, if you believe and partake of the bread of Christ through his Word and prayer, he will change your life. This can happen to you.

'Twas battered and scarred, and the auctioneer
Thought it scarcely worth his while
To waste much time on the old violin
But held it up with a smile.
"What am I bid, good folks," he cried,
"Who'll start the bidding for me?
A dollar, a dollar—now two, only two—
Two dollars, and who'll make it three?

"Three dollars once, three dollars twice,
Going for three"—but no!
From the room far back a gray-haired man
Came forward and picked up the bow;
Then wiping the dust from the old violin
And tightening up the strings,
He played a melody, pure and sweet.
As sweet as an angel sings.
The music ceased, and the auctioneer
With a voice that was quiet and low,
Said: "What am I bid for the old violin?"
And he held it up with the bow.
"A thousand dollars—and who'll make it two?
Two thousand—and who'll make it three?
Three thousand once and three thousand twice
And going and gone," said he.
The people cheered, but some of them cried,
"We do not quite understand—
What changed its worth?" The man replied,
"THE TOUCH OF THE MASTER'S HAND."
And many a man with a life out of tune,
And battered and torn with sin.
Is auctioned cheap to the thoughtless crowd,
Much like the old violin.
A "mess of pottage," a glass of wine,
A game and he travels on.
He's going once and going twice,
He's going—and almost—gone!
But the MASTER comes, and the foolish crowd
Never can quite understand
The worth of a soul, and the change that's wrought
By the TOUCH OF THE MASTER'S HAND.

Myra Brooks-Welch

Has he touched you?

26

Rivers of Living Water

JOHN 7:1–39

IN ORDER TO UNDERSTAND THE Scriptures properly, we need to consider the actual *words* of Scripture. We have to know what the words mean in order to preach them. We also need to know the *context*. It has often been said, "Every text without a context is a pretext," and that is true. We have to know the total context. It is also helpful to understand the *historical and cultural setting*, which will give us the broader picture. Finally we need to understand why the writer wrote what he wrote—his *purpose*. Only when we have gathered all of this can we gain a full understanding of what a given passage of Scripture has to say.

But there is something else we need that is not so scientific but is just as important. We need to catch the *flavor* of the passage we are studying. To a great extent, how well we do that depends on us—how well we enter into the passage, whether we allow it to permeate our being, whether we permit our imagination to carefully interact with the passage, whether we as Christians allow the Holy Spirit to speak to us.

To understand John 7:1–39 we must catch its flavor. Although we are going to focus mainly on verses 37–39, we must first survey the context if we are to really appreciate what our Lord is saying.

Our Lord had just given the Bread of Life discourse. As a result, many of his disciples withdrew and did not walk with him anymore. The crowd was not interested in a Savior who was primarily spiritual. The drama of that rejection continues in the seventh chapter.

> After this Jesus went about in Galilee. He would not go about in Judea, because the Jews were seeking to kill him. (v. 1)

"The Jews" in John always represent Jesus' enemies. In other words, the religious leaders wanted to kill Jesus. So he stayed away from the high country of Judea and Jerusalem. The intensity continues to escalate as the passage continues. In the second verse we read, "Now the Jews' Feast of Booths was at hand." We must grasp the flavor here in order to understand the passage. The Feast of Booths or Tabernacles was a harvest feast. It took place when all of the harvest had been gathered. It was a joyous time of celebration, a very well-attended festival, for two reasons. It was an exciting festival to attend, and it was one of the three festivals that required the attendance of every Jewish male who lived within twenty miles of Jerusalem.

During the feast great throngs came to town. It was a colorful event. If it were to occur today, we would probably call it the Jerusalem Camping and Recreational Vehicle Convention! Shelters sprang up in the most unlikely places—on flat rooftops, down dark alleys, even in the courts of the temple—and all of the shelters followed the rabbinical building code. The walls were extra-thin so that light came through, and the roof had to show enough sky so the stars could be seen, thus reminding the Jews of how they had wandered in the wilderness and of how God had provided for them.

The feast was a wonderful and festive time. People dressed in their Sabbath best for the week. They called it "the season of our gladness." It was so festive that to Zechariah, it was a symbol of the glorious future of the people of God. In the fourteenth chapter of his book, he wrote of that golden age to come and of a future, universal Feast of Tabernacles.

At the heart of the celebration was a daily rite, a rite we must understand in order to catch the sense of John 7. Rabbinical literature tells us that each morning great multitudes would gather at the Temple of Herod. They would come with a citrus fruit in their left hands (an *ethrog*). The ethrog was a reminder of the land to which God had brought them and of their bountiful blessings. In their right hands the people would carry a *lulab*, which was a combination of three trees—a palm tree, a willow, and a myrtle, emblematic of the stages of their ancestors' journey through the wilderness. Each morning the people gathered together, and after the priest was sure everything was in order, he would hold out a golden pitcher. The crowds would then follow the priest to the Pool of Siloam, chanting some of the great Psalms and waving their *lulabs* in rhythm. As they approached the Pool of Siloam, the priest would dip his pitcher into the water, and the people would recite some beautiful words from Isaiah 12:3: "With joy you will draw water from the wells of salvation." Then the crowd would march back to the temple, entering through the Water Gate to the blast of the priests' trumpets. The priest would then circle the altar once, ascend with accompanying priests to the platform, and pour the water out. This was a daily event.

All of this was going on up at Jerusalem while Jesus remained in Galilee, where a conversation ensued between the Savior and his physical brothers, his own flesh and blood.

> So his brothers said to him, "Leave here and go to Judea, that your disciples also may see the works you are doing. For no one works in secret if he seeks to be known openly. If you do these things, show yourself to the world." (vv. 3, 4)

Jesus' brothers were egging him on. The reason for their contemptuous tone is given in verse 5—they did not believe in him. His own earthly brothers failed to embrace him as their Savior! How pitiful and tragic! First, the Jews wanted to kill our Lord, and now his own flesh and blood were urging him to go to the celebration at the risk of his life.

Our Lord's reply is a key to understanding the passage under consideration because it reveals our Lord's thoughts. "My time has not yet come, but your time is always here" (v. 6). Notice carefully the word Jesus used for "time"—*kairos*—a word that here, as often, carries the idea of opportunity. Our Lord meant that the opportune time had not yet come, though that time came shortly afterwards (see v. 10). Some commentators have misconstrued Christ's statement. For example, Schopenhauer said, "Jesus did of a set purpose utter a falsehood." But Jesus did not lie! He was simply saying that the right moment had not arrived, and he was waiting for that moment. Jesus was up to something very big. In fact, possibly, outside of the cross, it was the most visual, dramatic event of his life. The intensity was building.

After this interchange, Jesus' brothers went up to Jerusalem, but Jesus stayed behind (v. 9). "But after his brothers had gone up to the feast, then he also went up, not publicly but in private" (v. 10). Why was he not recognized by the crowds? When he did not have his disciples or family with him, he could travel incognito. So in the middle of the feast, our Lord chose to go to Jerusalem.

Once there, Jesus observed much agitation: "The Jews were looking for him at the feast, and saying, 'Where is he?'" (v. 11). The verb tenses in that verse are continuous. The Jewish leaders (his enemies) were continually asking, "Where is he?" not because they wanted to hear his teachings but because they wanted to put him to death. Even the multitudes felt the tension.

And there was much muttering about him among the people. While some said, "He is a good man," others said, "No, he is leading the people astray." Yet for fear of the Jews no one spoke openly of him. (vv. 12, 13)

Behind locked doors controversies raged about who Jesus was and what his powers were, and outside the discussions were carried on in hushed tones. No one wanted to speak too openly for fear of reprisal by the Jews.

At this point our Lord appeared at the temple, and it was a brilliant appearance. In brief, our Lord came into the temple and began to teach, and people realized that no one had ever taught like this. When they questioned him about it, he said, "My teaching is not mine, but his who sent me" (v. 16). He then accused them of being out to kill him. They responded by saying he had a demon or at least seemed to be a bit paranoid. With that, our Lord really set things in motion.

So Jesus proclaimed, as he taught in the temple, "You know me, and you know where I come from. But I have not come of my own accord. He who sent me is true, and him you do not know. I know him, for I come from him, and he sent me." (vv. 28, 29)

The drama definitely escalated at that moment, just the right moment for Christ to speak out. It was the final day of the feast, the seventh day, the day the priest would again come to the temple, followed by the great throng chanting their psalms and waving their *lulabs*. They would come in through the Water Gate. The trumpets would sound again. But this time the priest would circle the altar seven times in succession—just like at the walls of Jericho. And when he came around for the sixth time, he would be joined by another priest carrying the wine. They would ascend the ramp to the altar. There would be a pause as the priest raised his pitcher. The crowd would begin to shout to the priest to hold it higher, and he would try to do so. It was considered to be the height of joy in an Israelite's life if he could see the water being poured onto the altar.

It was in that hush and at that dramatic moment that Jesus acted.

On the last day of the feast, the great day, Jesus stood up and cried out, "If anyone thirsts, let him come to me and drink." (v. 37)

We do not serve an anemic Jesus. Our Lord was in control. He chose just the right psychological moment. His words were precise and powerful. What a beautiful, powerful, dramatic presentation of stupendous spiritual truth.

I wish I could continually keep the drama of this passage in front of me.

If we can read 7:37 with no emotion, no excitement, no sense of drama, what a pity! May we keep burning with the potency and vitality of our Lord's supreme words.

Are we satisfied, or are we thirsty? Is God's life flowing out of our innermost being and bringing satisfaction to others? Our Lord addresses these questions with his magnificent invitation.

"If Anyone Thirsts . . ." (v. 37a)

Jesus begins by saying (v. 37), "If anyone thirsts. . . ." Have you ever been thirsty? Really thirsty? Years ago when I was a youth pastor, we annually took our high schoolers on a trip from Southern California to Nevada to go water skiing on the Colorado River. I can still remember the trip over the Cajon Pass, across the Mojave Desert, through some of the beautiful "garden" spots of the Southwest—Barstow, Victorville, Baker (correctly named)—and then on to a place that is not even on the map: Searchlight, Nevada. For two days I was up all night, chasing young people. During the day I was subjected to the sun. I turned lobster red. I was in misery. As soon as the sun came up in the morning, I began to hurt.

I never will forget the trip back to Southern California either. We were in buses, and everyone was trying to stay away from the side of the bus where the sun shone in. The bus went down the road tilted to one side! Outside Baker we blew a tire, and for several hours we were without water. I was hot, sunburned, and uncomfortable. I have *never* been so thirsty and miserable in my life! When we finally came into Baker, I drank five glasses of water at Denny's. I know what it is like to be thirsty!

Our Lord uses a powerful image here, especially to those in the Middle East. They understood what he was saying. "If anyone thirsts, let him come to me and drink." They knew what it was to be thirsty—they understood. One of the tragedies of our age is that we twist the thirst for God into a desire for a new wardrobe, a new car, a new experience, or whatever. Or even if people realize they are thirsty, they take wrong measures to satisfy it.

> My people have committed two evils:
> they have forsaken me,
>   the fountain of living waters,
> and hewed out cisterns for themselves,
>   broken cisterns that can hold no water. (Jeremiah 2:13)

Somerset Maugham, at the end of life, was empty, miserable, and fearful of death. The final line of his autobiography, *The Summing Up*, is most revealing: "The beauty of life is nothing but this; that each should act in conformity with his nature and his business."[1] He is saying "the beauty of life" is just doing your own thing, and yet that philosophy brought tragedy to his own life. He had hewn a broken cistern that would hold no water.

Jesus encourages a healthy thirst. "If anyone thirsts, let him come to me and drink. Whoever believes in me, as the Scripture has said, 'Out of his heart will flow rivers of living water'" (vv. 37, 38). This invitation is open to anyone who thirsts. To receive this divine gift is spiritual health. To hunger and thirst for the water that Christ gives is to hunger and thirst for righteousness. May we each have a hunger and thirst for the things of God and for the fullness of the Holy Spirit. Are you thirsty? In the next line our Lord tells us how to be refreshed.

"Let Him Come to Me and Drink" (v. 37b)

That poor waitress in Baker, California, was undoubtedly annoyed with us because no matter how much water she brought us, it was not enough, and it could not come quickly enough as far as we were concerned. We wanted more water, and we wanted it sooner. But with our Lord there is no waiting for the water our souls require. "If anyone thirsts, let him come to me and drink." Anyone can drink the water of life he gives.

How are we to drink this water? Although the offer is free and open to all, there are yet some terms to be met. C. S. Lewis in his children's novel *The Silver Chair* puts his finger on this in the clearest of terms. Jill, seeing a lion, is scared out of her wits and runs into the forest. She runs so hard that she wears herself out and is just about to die of thirst, or so she thinks, when she hears the gurgling of a brook in the distance. She approaches it and is almost ready to go to the brook when on the grass before her is the same lion.

> "Are you not thirsty?" said the Lion.
> "I'm dying of thirst," said Jill.
> "Then drink, " said the Lion.
> "May I—could I—would you mind going away while I do?" said Jill.
> The Lion answered this only by a look and a very low growl. And as Jill gazed at its motionless bulk, she realized that she might as well have asked the whole mountain to move aside for her convenience. The delicious rippling noise of the stream was driving her nearly frantic.
> "Will you promise not to—do anything to me, if I do come?" said Jill.
> "I make no promise," said the Lion.
> Jill was so thirsty now that, without noticing it, she had come a step nearer.
> "Do you eat girls?" she said.

"I have swallowed up girls and boys, women and men, kings and emperors, cities and realms," said the Lion. It didn't say this as if it were boasting, nor as if it were sorry, nor as if it were angry. It just said it.

"I daren't come and drink," said Jill.

"Then you will die of thirst," said the Lion.

"Oh dear!" said Jill, coming another step nearer.

"I suppose I must go and look for another stream then."

"There is no other stream," said the Lion.

It never occurred to Jill to disbelieve the Lion—no one who had seen his stern face could do that—and her mind suddenly made itself up. It was the worst thing she had ever had to do, but she went forward to the stream, knelt down, and began scooping up water in her hand. It was the coldest, most refreshing water she had ever tasted.

Do you see what Lewis is saying? When you come to the water, you are coming to a Lion, you must come on the Lion's terms, and you have to yield yourself by faith in order to get the water. Some of us need to realize that we are thirsty, that we need that water so badly that we are going to die without it. We need to step out on faith, yielding to the Lion of the tribe of Judah, and receive the water of eternal life.

The Satisfying Results (vv. 38, 39)

Whoever believes in me, as the Scripture has said, "Out of his heart will flow rivers of living water ['out of his belly' KJV]." (v. 38)

Jesus is saying that the part of us that is never satisfied, the part of us that craves so much, becomes, when we receive this water, the part that is satisfied. Our unfulfilled desires can become fully satisfied by virtue of the indwelling Spirit of Christ in our lives.

Furthermore, not only does such satisfaction come to us in Christ, but it overflows to others. Notice that Christ does not say "river" but "rivers." Rivers of living water flow out of us by virtue of the indwelling Spirit of Christ. When a person comes to Christ and slakes his thirst as Christ would have him do, satisfaction flows out of him to others. Corrie ten Boom is a stirring example of this. Mother Teresa of Calcutta is another. One of the latter's favorite verses was, "Yet not I, but Christ liveth in me."[2] The love of Christ flowed out from her to the dying in Calcutta.

In the nineteenth century Billy Bray, a dynamic Christian and a Cornish miner, so overflowed with Christ that wherever he went, men trusted Christ. Each day as he went down into the mines—very dangerous in those days— he would pray with the miners as he went down, "Lord, if any of us must be killed or die today, let it be me. Let not one of these men die for they are not happy and I am, and if I die today I shall go to be in heaven."[3] It was rumored that at times when he got to the bottom of those mines, the other miners would all be on their knees.

Power and overflowing joy—these are the characteristics of great drinkers of the Spirit. But the sublime irony in this is that we *never* experience satisfaction as we are meant to until our lives give satisfaction to others. That is what Jesus was saying.

John Bunyan knew all about that and wrote, "There was a man, the world did think him mad, the more he gave away, the more he had." When our lives become stagnant and we begin to be introspective and focus upon ourselves, the remedy is not to concentrate on our own satisfaction but on satisfaction in Christ seeking to flow through us. When we come to a wall in our spiritual lives, we need to look for avenues of service. We need to drink of the Holy Spirit so much that he flows out to others.

Conclusion

Are you satisfied? Is your satisfaction flowing out to others?

We have seen that on the last great day of the feast, our Lord was in control. He was in control of the very syllables he spoke, the timing down to the millisecond, the effect of his words upon the people, the delicate precision of everything. It is beautiful.

During the desert wanderings that the Feast of Tabernacles portrayed, Moses smote a rock, and out of it came rivers of living water for the people. That was a picture of Christ, and our Scripture refers to this in verse 39:

> Now this he said about the Spirit, whom those who believed in him were to receive, for as yet the Spirit had not been given, because Jesus was not yet glorified.

Jesus had not yet been smitten on the cross and resurrected. Therefore the Spirit had not yet come to indwell believers. In the wilderness, the first time the Lord instructed Moses to *strike* the rock, Moses did, and God provided water. But the second time Moses made a grievous error. God told him to *speak* to the rock, but in his anger against the people Moses smote the rock. Water nevertheless came out graciously from God, but Moses paid heavily for his action because, though his whole life had been committed to leading the people to the promised land, he himself was not able to enter. Moses probably never suspected that he had ruined the type because Christ was not smitten twice but once. Again we see God's provision and his grace.

Our Lord is a Lion, the Lion of the Tribe of Judah, and we must come to him on his terms, though he graciously invites us to communicate with him, to speak to him. Are you satisfied? Have you drunk long and deep of that water so that out of your innermost being are flowing rivers of living water? Is your life a beatitude to others? Whether or not that has happened, speak to him about it now.

27

Christ the Divider

JOHN 7:40–52

THE MOMENT WHEN CHRIST STOOD AND CRIED, "If anyone thirsts, let him come to me and drink. Whoever believes in me, as the Scripture has said, 'Out of his heart will flow rivers of living water'" (John 7:37, 38) was one of the great moments in our Lord's life—in fact, one of the great moments in history. Our Lord knew just the right moment to speak those words. In that instant our Savior offered himself as the water that would *always* satisfy.

What a powerful, overwhelming image for the ancient world—and for us! He can meet all our needs. Our Lord not only said that he is our satisfaction, but that when he satisfies, he makes it possible for us to bring satisfaction to others: "Whoever believes in me, as the Scripture has said, 'Out of his heart will flow rivers of living water'" (v. 38).

What was the effect of this remarkable statement on the lives of those who heard it? What effect has it had on our lives?

Division

Christ's dramatic declaration immediately brought division.

> When they heard these words, some of the people said, "This really is the Prophet." Others said, "This is the Christ." But some said, "Is the Christ to come from Galilee? Has not the Scripture said that the Christ comes from the offspring of David, and comes from Bethlehem, the village where David was?" (vv. 40–42)

There were three immediate opinions about who Jesus was. Some thought he was the prophet referred to by Moses in Deuteronomy 18:15–18. Outside of the land of Canaan, on the plains of Moab, Moses promised the

Jews that Jehovah would give them another prophet like him. He was referring to Christ, as Peter made clear in his sermon in Acts 3:20–22. But the Jews in Jesus' day did not understand that. Others thought, correctly, that Jesus was the Christ, the Messiah. Others said he was just a man. (After all, the Messiah was to be born in Bethlehem, but Jesus was from Galilee. Therefore he could not be the Christ. But their reasoning was misinformed because he *had* been born in Bethlehem. He was just residing in Galilee at that time.)

So there was tremendous division at this point (v. 43). This was no surprise to Jesus. He knew his beautiful, overflowing claim would cause division. He spoke about this in Matthew 10:34, 35.

> Do not think that I have come to bring peace to the earth. I have not come to bring peace, but a sword. For I have come to set a man against his father, and a daughter against her mother, and a daughter-in-law against her mother-in-law.

We see the same thing in Luke 12:51, 52:

> Do you think that I have come to give peace on earth? No, I tell you, but rather division. For from now on in one house there will be five divided, three against two and two against three.

Christ did not want to bring division. But because of the sinfulness of our hearts, because of our fallenness, because of our unwillingness to repent and bow to him, the Prince of Peace is Christ the Divider.

When snow descends upon the Continental Divide, it melts and flows off either to the west or to the east, never to meet again. Christ is the continental divide in our lives. We will either go up with the morning stars or, to use Eliot's phrase, join the valley of the dying stars. Christ brings division to everyday life. We all have experienced this. Maybe we are at the store, in school, or at work, and we are talking animatedly with someone about any number of things—maybe politics or education or sports or the weather. Then someone says something like, "My life has really been different lately because of Christ." Suddenly there is a silence and a shuffling of feet. Someone coughs. Someone else looks at his watch and says, "I have an appointment to get to or I'll be late." Another says, "Oh, yes, I have to go feed the dog. I must be going." But in reality the man who said he had to feed the dog did not have a dog to feed, and the other person's appointment was the next day.

The mention of Christ brings division to life. Talking about religious matters is acceptable as long as you talk about them dispassionately, but talking about them personally is not allowed. G. K. Chesterton illustrates this division in his novel *The Ball and the Cross*. In it a conflict occurs between an atheist and a Christian, both of whom are hauled into court.

> "He is my enemy," said Evan, the Christian, simply; "he is the enemy of God."
>
> The magistrate shifted sharply in his seat, dropping the eye-glass out of his eye in a momentary and not unmanly embarrassment.
>
> "You mustn't talk like that here," he said, roughly, and in a kind of hurry, "that has nothing to do with us."
>
> Evan opened his great, blue eyes; "God," he began.
>
> "Be quiet," said the magistrate, angrily, "it is most undesirable that things of that sort should be spoken about in public, and in an ordinary Court of Justice. Religion is too personal a matter to be mentioned in such a place."
>
> "Is it!" answered [Evan] the Highlander. "Then what did those policemen swear by just now?"
>
> "That is no parallel," answered Vane rather irritably; "of course there is a form of oath—to be taken reverently—reverently, and there's an end of it. But to talk at a public place about one's most sacred sentiments—well, I call it bad taste. (Slight applause.) I call it irreverent. I call it irreverent, and I'm not specially orthodox either."[1]

The result is a comical chase all about England as the atheist and the Christian try to do battle and no one will allow them to because it is not an important matter to fight over. Finally they are committed to an insane asylum. It becomes apparent as time goes on that their captors are insane, not they. Chesterton makes his point very clearly: sincere devotion to Christ always brings division.

Verse 43 says, "So there was a division among the people over him [Jesus]." Christ had just proclaimed his great statement of what he could provide in life, and as a result there was division. Why? Because when one subscribes to what Christ has to say, his life is redirected. His affections are changed. He is seated in Christ in the heavenly places. His values are affected. There comes a division, perhaps even violence. "Some of them wanted to arrest him, but no one laid hands on him" (v. 44). Even in our enlightened age, violence occurs concerning the matter of Christ.

In today's world with its new technology, new individualism, and new geopolitical views, the old orthodoxies may have a hard time in the years to come. The remainder of our text helps us understand why Christ's claims divide men and shows us how to obtain the fullness Christ offers even in such circumstances.

Rejection

First we need to catch the flow of the context. Jesus had appeared in the temple courts at the Feast of Booths. In response, the temple authorities dispatched guards to arrest Jesus but could not. When Jesus came to the temple again, he gave his magnificent invitation: "If anyone thirsts, let him come to me and drink." Though some wanted to seize him, no one did so at that time.

> The officers then came to the chief priests and Pharisees, who said to them, "Why did you not bring him?" The officers answered, "No one ever spoke like this man!" (vv. 45, 46)

What an answer! They could have said, "We were afraid the crowd would riot." That would have been a legitimate response, but the real reason was they were overwhelmed by the presence of Christ and his words. In other words, they came to arrest him, but he arrested them! They came to lay hands upon him, but he laid the spell of his words upon them. In a way, that points out the difference between the Sanhedrin and their guards. The guards did not have the sophisticated preconceptions the Sanhedrin had. They had not discussed the hearsay. They had not decided that Jesus could not be someone of great import, much less the Messiah. And most of all, the guards listened. The men of the Sanhedrin, with notable exceptions, did not bother going to actually hear Jesus. It is much easier to refute your opponents from a distance. The Pharisees then exploded in a shower of words:

> Have you also been deceived? Have any of the authorities or the Pharisees believed in him? But this crowd that does not know the law is accursed. (vv. 47–49)

No one of any account spiritually or academically believed in Jesus. Only the ignorant accepted him. Or so the Pharisees thought. Have you heard anyone talk like that? Rabbinical law records this type of snobbery many times.

When I was a senior in college I was taking a class in Restoration English, and one day William Cowper's hymns were mentioned, and I expressed admiration for "There Is a Fountain." My professor looked up slowly over his glasses, then said with a wry smile on his face, "Mr. Hughes, have you become a tambourine banger?" The Pharisees were sure that no one who was not part of the elite could understand the deeper things of life.

Then entered Nicodemus. He had first come to Jesus by night, but here he openly asked a question: "Does our law judge a man without first giving him a hearing and learning what he does?" (vv. 50, 51). Good question! But the Pharisees responded to Nicodemus by heaping scorn upon him.

> Are you from Galilee too? Search and see that no prophet arises from Galilee. (v. 52)

They were so incensed, they forgot their own history—Jonah had come from Galilee. How ironic! The very Pharisees who said the ignorant masses could not know anything here showed their ignorance.

Dr. Harry Ironside—who liked conflict and verbal confrontation, enjoyed street preaching and had a worldwide ministry—once made an amazing statement. He said, "I have never met an infidel who has ever read one serious book of Christian evidence." Neither have I. Of course there are exceptions, but the point is, many people who reject Christianity do not know what they are rejecting. C. S. Lewis found that to be true at Oxford. A club had been established to debate Christian truths, and Lewis remarked of the club: "We of the Christian party discovered that the weight of the skeptical attack did not always come where we expected it. Our opponents had to correct what seemed to us their almost bottomless ignorance of the Faith they supposed themselves to be rejecting." In other words, we need not be intimidated by what scholars say. The proud men in Lewis's club needed to set aside their presuppositions and discard their fierce invective. They needed to dialogue with and listen to Jesus. That is what we need to do as well, and when we do, we will say, "No one ever spoke like this man!"

Nicodemus, an admirable exception, had listened to Jesus' words. He had come at night to dialogue face-to-face, heart to heart, soul to soul with Jesus. I believe a process of spiritual transformation began that night at the midnight of his life. Twilight came as he spoke up now, enduring scorn for the sake of Christ. And sunshine finally poured into his life as he became one of Christ's followers at the very darkest time of our Lord's life on earth.

I have heard people say, "I reject Christianity because I have not been able to find the answers I need." But in talking to them, I have found that most have not looked very hard for those answers. I tell such persons that if they come face-to-face with Jesus they will find that "No one ever spoke like this man!"

Conclusion

Massive change is taking place today, a complete redirection of our culture. Those who follow Christ are going to find themselves subject to increasing pressure and alienation. The division that Christ brings is going to become more pronounced. The lines will be sharply defined. Christ will be everything to individuals or he will be nothing. Those who drink of the fountains of secularism will be unfilled and empty. But those drinking of Christ will overflow. The changes facing us in society demand that we become great drinkers of the water that only Christ gives, for only those who follow him have great power and vitality in their lives.

But how do we drink the spiritual water Christ offers? John 7:37–39 gives one of the keys. First of all, we have to realize our thirst and our emptiness, the vacuous nature of our lives. We have to admit that nothing we have within us will commend us to Christ. We need to admit we are sinners, throw ourselves upon our Lord, and realize that Jesus Christ, as he claims here, is the sovereign bestower of the fullness of the Holy Spirit. We must ask him to fill us daily, and then by faith we must appropriate the life of Christ, through the Spirit of Christ, within us. Then we will be filled to the uttermost, resting in him.

28

On Having the
Light of Life

JOHN 8:12–20

IN OUR DISCUSSIONS ON JOHN 7 we saw that our Lord was in complete control. His timing was not haphazard when he made his great proclamation ("If anyone thirsts, let him come to me and drink. Whoever believes in me, as the Scripture has said, 'Out of his heart will flow rivers of living water'"). He deliberately chose that moment of silence between the shout of the crowd to the priest to hold his pitcher higher and the chanting of the *Hallel* chorus. We will find in John 8:12–20 that Christ is again in control. We again need to get a feel for the passage to appreciate its drama and the significance of our Lord's words.

According to 8:20, the scene occurred in "the treasury" or, more technically, the Court of Women. That large court was one of the busiest parts of the temple, and at one side of it was a colonnade with thirteen great treasure chests. The chests were called trumpets because they were shaped like trumpets standing on their faces—narrow at the top and rounded out at the bottom. According to William Barclay, these trumpets promoted a program of designated giving. The first two trumpets were for half shekels, which every Jew had to pay for the upkeep of the temple. The second two trumpets were for offerings of pigeons for rites of purification. The fifth trumpet was for wood for sacrifices. The sixth trumpet was for incense. The seventh was for the upkeep of the golden vessels of the temple. Then, if one had any money left, the remaining six trumpets were for love offerings, undesignated giving.[1] Because of the trumpets, this part of the temple was very important and heavily traveled. It was the perfect place for what the Lord wanted to do. He knew just the right moment at which to make his pronouncement—in the treasury on the day subsequent to the festival.

There were two great ceremonies during the Feast of Tabernacles. One, as we have seen, was the pouring out of the water. The other was called the Illumination of the Temple; it took place in the treasury at the beginning of the feast. It was a spectacular celebration—both in its concept and in its annual observance.

In the center of the treasury four great torches were set up. Some accounts say that the torches were as high as the highest walls of the temple and that at the top of these golden candelabra were great bowls holding sixty-five liters of oil. There was a ladder for each candelabrum, and in the evening young, healthy priests would carry the oil up to the top, where they would light the protruding wicks. The great flames that leapt out of these torches illumined the whole temple and much of Jerusalem. It was spectacular! The *Mishnah* describes what happened after the torches were lit:

> Men of piety and good works used to dance before them with burning torches in their hands singing songs and praises and countless Levites played on harps, lyres, cymbals, and trumpets and instruments of music.[2]

They would dance until dawn. It was an exotic festival celebrating the great pillar of fire that led the people of Israel during their sojourn in the wilderness. It was in this place, no doubt with the charred torches still in place, that Jesus chose to raise his voice above the crowd and proclaim, "I am the light of the world. Whoever follows me will not walk in darkness, but will have the light of life" (v. 12). There would scarcely be a more dramatic way to announce one of the supreme realities of Jesus' existence. What a way to focus people's attention on one of the truths they needed to understand!

How can we receive this light, the light of Christ, into our lives?

What Christ Claims for Himself (v. 12)

Notice what Christ announced concerning himself: "I am the light of the world." Those great torches symbolized the *Shekinah* glory. Christ was saying in effect, "Do you remember the pillar that came between you and the Egyptians near the Red Sea, the pillar that protected you and led you on your wanderings in the wilderness? I am the Light of the world. I am identified with that *Shekinah* glory." What a statement! Here Jesus was claiming to be God. His conscious identification with the pillar of fire reveals something about his incarnation. Within the cloud that led Israel through the wilderness, there was always a heart of fire that shone forth at night but was sheathed by day. When our Lord came, he sheathed his glory in flesh so we could look upon him. Time and again God is called light in the Old Testament. Almost the last verse in the Old Testament (Malachi 4:2) says in regard to Jesus:

> But for you who fear my name, the sun of righteousness shall rise with healing in its wings.

When Simeon took the baby Jesus in his arms in the temple he sang:

> Because of the tender mercy of our God,
>   whereby the sunrise shall visit us from on high
> to give light to those who sit in darkness and in the shadow of death.
>   (Luke 1:78, 79)

And John said, "We have seen his glory, glory as of the only Son from the Father" (1:14). I believe John was referring, at least in part, to the Transfiguration, when he was taken along with Peter and James to a high mountain and Christ was transfigured before them. Our Lord's face shone forth like the sun.

Jesus, in John 8, was not only saying he is the Light of the world, but that the benefits and comforts that came with the cloud in the wilderness came from him. What a precious, wonderful truth! He is saying, "I was the One who protected you. I guided you through the wilderness. It was I who enveloped the tabernacle. It was I who came into the temple of Solomon and filled it with such glory that the priests could not serve. I am the *Shekinah* glory." Such was the claim he made for himself.

Living in this dark world, we need to keep this supreme claim before us. Jesus is the light of life in *every* way. He is the answer. Some of us may be stumbling along, wondering what life is all about. We may feel barely able to take another step. We are confused. Christ says to us, "I am the light of life."

What Christ Claims for His Followers (v. 12)

Christ also makes a claim for those who follow him: "Whoever follows me will not walk in darkness" (v. 12).

The Israelites in the desert kept their attention on the cloud. They watched its configuration to see when and where it would move. At night they walked in its light. No matter how dark the night, when they were under the luminous cloud there was no stumbling, no confusion, no fear. Jesus provides similar benefits for those of us who know him, for we have the light of life. Therefore we can have courage though dwelling in a dark world.

Have you ever tried going through an obstacle course blindfolded? The smallest obstacles become difficult obstructions. If we are not walking in the light of Christ, the obstacles that should not be a problem are great stumbling blocks to us. But when we have that light, we understand how to make our way through this dark world.

The whole phrase from verse 12 gives us even more hope: "Whoever follows me will not walk in darkness, but will have the light of life." "Have" in the last phrase is a beautiful word. Christ was saying that not only do we have light coming into us, but there is a sense in which we become shafts of the Lord's light. How beautiful and wondrous!

In one of the churches I served in past years there was a woman whom everyone called a "sunbeam." Her name was Susie Smith. She had a great, contagious laugh and smile and a willingness to do just about anything she could despite her precarious health. She was an uncluttered shaft of light! But how did that come about? She was my daughter Holly's first grade teacher in public school. Day after day my daughter said, "Mrs. Smith, will you come to church with me?" And finally, after several months, she came, then came again. And soon she gave her life to Christ. First a little six-year-old and then Susie Smith had the light!

The light shining in our lives is Christ's light. What a privilege! Ephesians 5:8 says, "For at one time you were darkness, but now you are light in the Lord." We share the very light that Jesus Christ displayed. We are "the light of the world. A city set on a hill cannot be hidden" (Matthew 5:14). Paul told the Philippian Christians that the world is dark, but that they "shine as lights in the world" (Philippians 2:15). We "have the light of life."

Scripture suggests another wonder in this regard as well. Jesus, at the end of the Mystery Parables, states in Matthew 13:43, "The righteous will shine like the sun in the kingdom of their Father." C. S. Lewis once noted that the heavens only reflect or suggest the glory of God, but we share the glory of God with Christ. We will be more glorious than the heavens! In *The Weight of Glory* Lewis says:

> Nature is mortal. We shall outlive her. When all the suns and nebulae have passed away, each one of you will still be alive. Nature is only the image, the symbol, but it is a symbol Scripture invites me to use. We are summoned to pass through nature beyond her to the splendor which she fitfully reflects.[3]

I believe that with all my heart. I do not understand it, but I believe there is a glory awaiting every Christian that involves, in some way, shining forth.

I do not know if we will be 100 watts or 200, 300, or 1,000! We might be like fireflies. But somehow we are going to enter into the fame and approval of God, and we will be glorious beings far beyond all imagination. "We know that when he appears we shall be like him, because we shall see him as he is" (1 John 3:2). John, speaking in the final chapter of the book of Revelation, wrote:

> And night will be no more. They will need no light of lamp or sun, for the Lord God will be their light, and they will reign forever and ever. (22:5)

Not only is the light upon us, but we have the light. What a blessing! We are given light to illumine our steps as we walk through this life. And the light comes into us so it can go out to others, making us to be light and life to them. What wonderful truths!

What Christ Says to Those Who Reject His Claims (vv. 13–19)

Sadly, not all who heard Jesus' claim thought it was wonderful. Some rejected his words. "So the Pharisees said to him, 'You are bearing witness about yourself; your testimony is not true'" (v. 13). They hung their disbelief on a technicality, as do many people who do not want to believe. Within the Hebrew judicial system, truth had to be verified by two witnesses. That was why the Pharisees told Christ he could not establish this truth just on the basis of his own testimony. Their hard-heartedness shows us another reality. When Jesus is loved, followed, and trusted, he becomes light. But when he is neglected, darkness descends.

Hugh Hefner was raised in a minister's home. Joseph Stalin studied for the priesthood. Mao Tse-tung was raised under missionary teaching. The very light of Christ can be obscured.

Jesus replied to the Pharisees' objections in verses 14–19, and his words are an answer for all who disbelieve. In verse 14 Jesus said his claim is above natural laws of verification—one cannot verify judicially the claim that he made. In verses 15–18 our Lord said, in essence, "You ask for two witnesses. There are two. The Father and myself." The Pharisees' immediate reaction was to query, "Where is your Father?" Jesus answered, "You know neither me nor my Father. If you knew me, you would know my Father also" (v. 19). Jesus meant that if you want knowledge of God, you can find it only through him. But if we look to him, the mysteries of Deity will begin to unfold for us.

Having the light of Christ is the ultimate necessity of life. No concern or need is more urgent than that. Without it we will walk into eternal darkness.

Conclusion

"Whoever follows me will not walk in darkness, but will have the light of life." Walking in the light is a matter of following Christ. Listen to the record of Israel and their cloud in Numbers 9:15–22:

> On the day that the tabernacle was set up, the cloud covered the tabernacle, the tent of the testimony. And at evening it was over the tabernacle like the appearance of fire until morning. So it was always: the cloud covered it by day and the appearance of fire by night. And whenever the cloud lifted from over the tent, after that the people of Israel set out, and in the place where the cloud settled down, there the people of Israel camped. At the command of the LORD the people of Israel set out, and at the command of the LORD they camped. As long as the cloud rested over the tabernacle, they remained in camp. Even when the cloud continued over the tabernacle many days, the people of Israel kept the charge of the LORD and did not set out. Sometimes the cloud was a few days over the tabernacle, and according to the command of the LORD they remained in camp; then according to the command of the LORD they set out. And sometimes the cloud remained from evening until morning. And when the cloud lifted in the morning, they set out, or if it continued for a day and a night, when the cloud lifted they set out. Whether it was two days, or a month, or a longer time, that the cloud continued over the tabernacle, abiding there, the people of Israel remained in camp and did not set out, but when it lifted they set out.

We follow Christ by faithful submission and obedience. One of the indispensable ways of living the Christian life is to learn the principle of submission. We must learn this principle again and again. My own experience tells me that sometimes the joy, the power, leaves my life, and then comes confusion and weariness. At such times I find relief only in submitting again to Christ. When I lay everything before God and say, "This is your ministry. It is not my career. It is yours," I find rest, peace, power, and joy.

If you are going through difficult and hard times, if you are confused as a believer, there is a good chance you again need to submit to God. I would encourage you to do what is implied here—to stay under the cloud. You must not run ahead of the cloud or stand behind it. You must stay underneath it. That requires faith and submission to the will of God. "As a deer pants for flowing streams, so pants my soul for you, O God" (Psalm 42:1). The upward look is essential. The word "follows" in John 8:12 is a present participle. It means to continue and keep on continuing.

Perhaps you have never experienced the light of life, and you are asking how to get it. "But to all who did receive him, who believed in his name, he gave the right to become children of God" (1:12). Submit yourself to that truth. Acknowledge that you are a sinner. Submit yourself to the blood of Jesus Christ. Admit that within you there is no good thing that can commend you to God. In that submission you will begin to walk in the light.

As believers, how do we continue to walk in the light? Simply by looking upward and walking continually with him. We want the light of life. We do not want to stumble as we walk through life. We want the light flowing out of us to others. We want to participate in the final glory that awaits us, whatever it may be. "I am the light of the world. Whoever follows me will not walk in darkness, but will have the light of life."

Do you have this light? Are you enjoying the peace, the joy, the comfort that came from the cloud? If not, submit to him now.

29

Ultimate Separation—
Ultimate Union

JOHN 8:21-30

I SOMETIMES THUMB THROUGH my file on funerals, reading a few lines here and there, stopping to reflect on whatever comes to mind. I always experience a wide range of emotion. Sometimes I am dismayed because, as all ministers know, while we have many funerals for believers, we also have many for nonbelievers. At other times I smile because some of my notes call to mind wonderful times—wonderful not because I enjoyed them, but because though the families were experiencing great grief and mourning, there was a sense of God's presence, even a sense of joy.

I think of a young man named Greg Valdemi. Greg was a remarkably handsome boy. When he visited our college department and saw that we had some attractive girls, he stuck around. And as he did, what he heard being taught began to click. In the fall of 1973 Greg unreservedly gave his life to Christ. He was marvelously born again and became an overflowing Christian. He could not get enough of the Bible. He was there whenever the church was open and was always full of questions. He was a witnessing Christian and a great encouragement to me. One New Year's Eve he did what people that age often do—he stayed out all night with the college group. They had breakfast together, and after breakfast they decided they would have a football game— their own Rose Bowl. But as they were out on the athletic field warming up, Greg collapsed. By the time I got there, before the paramedics arrived, Greg had died of heart failure. It was an unspeakably difficult time for his poor mother and a terrible experience for all his relatives and friends. Yet when I recall his home-going and his funeral, the general impression I have is one of joy and of the presence of Christ.

I also think of times I have conversed with a grieving family and have asked all the probing questions I could think of, but could discover no reason to hope the deceased had died in Christ. I remember how I did my very best at those funeral services to say as many nice things as possible in the obituary, but when it came to the message from the Word of God, all I could do was preach to the living. I could make no reference as to where that individual was. There was no hope, no peace.

Those of us who minister the gospel are especially aware that when it comes to the end of life, there is a time of separation when people either go to be with Christ or they do not. Sometimes those who are passing away are aware of this. Thomas Paine was one of the great intellectuals among the founders of our country and an infamous unbeliever. He was a man who led many away from the Scriptures and belief in God. On the day Paine died, these were his final words.

> I would give worlds, if I had them, that *The Age of Reason* had not been published. O Lord, help me! Christ, help me! O God what have I done to suffer so much? But there is no God! But if there should be, what will become of me hereafter? Stay with me, for God's sake! Send even a child to stay with me, for it is hell to be alone. If ever the devil had an agent, I have been that one.[1]

The final words of Thomas Paine—separated from God, desolate—contrast sharply with the experience of Isaac Watts. He was called the evangelical poet and composed some of our great hymns, such as "O God, Our Help in Ages Past." On the very day that he passed away, he said:

> It is a great mercy that I have no manner of fear or dread of death. I could, if God please, lay my head back and die without terror this afternoon.[2]

With great joy Isaac Watts passed into ultimate union with Christ.

In the previous verses in John 8, our Lord has been leading up to this idea of separation. In 8:12 he said he is "the light of the world," implying that either people walk in darkness or they walk in light. Then in verse 21 we read:

> So he said to them again, "I am going away, and you will seek me, and you will die in your sin. Where I am going, you cannot come."

He was saying, "You have been following me all around Jerusalem at the Feast of Tabernacles, taking issue with everything I say. You have rejected me.

There is going to come a time when you will seek me, but it will be too late. There is going to be a separation." Though Christ originally said this to his detractors and enemies, he said it for all people throughout history. There will be a time of ultimate separation. Our Lord's language was straightforward and tough, and the Jews did not respond very well, as we see in verse 22:

> So the Jews said, "Will he kill himself, since he says, 'Where I am going, you cannot come'?"

That was a wicked, sarcastic jibe. The Jews believed that suicide caused a person to occupy the worst place in Hell. Josephus, the Jewish historian, said:

> The souls of those whose hands have done violence to their own lives go to darkest Hades, and God, their Father, will visit the sins of the evildoers on their descendants.[3]

In essence they were saying, "He says we cannot follow him? He must be going to Hell then! And he's right—we won't be following him there!" With scorn they responded to our Lord, and in doing so they confirmed Jesus' words. These men were lost, separated from God, and if that continued to the end of their lives, they would be eternally separated from him. Why were they separated? If we can answer that question, we will find the remedy.

The Basic Reason for the Ultimate Separation

Our Lord began with the overall reason in verse 23: "You are from below; I am from above. You are of this world; I am not of this world." Jesus said they were from different realms or dimensions—one above and one below. And the two could not be joined.

Christ used the word for the cosmos, a word used frequently in the Greek New Testament to refer to the evil world system. Christ was saying that those scoffers were of the evil world system, but he was not, because all that is from above cannot be mixed with that evil world system. Christ and his detractors were from separate realms that could not be mixed. That is why they would seek him but not find him and why where he was going they could not come. Christ was from above, but they were from below.

This point is made in Lewis's great work *The Great Divorce* as strongly as in any literature I have ever read. In that remarkable story, a busload of people is brought from Hell to Heaven so they can choose the latter, but being from the underworld they are not very comfortable in Heaven. In fact, their ghost-like feet experience discomfort just from walking on the grass because the grass pierces them. Lewis makes his point most dramatically, however, in a dialogue between one of the bus's passengers, who was a theologian on earth, and an old acquaintance, Dick, now a resident of Heaven.

"Ah, Dick, I shall never forget some of our talks. I expect you've changed your views a bit since then. You became rather narrowminded towards the end of your life: but no doubt you've broadened out again."

"How do you mean?"

"Well, it's obvious by now, isn't it, that you weren't quite right. Why, my dear boy, you were coming to believe in a literal Heaven and Hell!"

"But wasn't I right?"

"Oh, in a spiritual sense, to be sure. I still believe in them in that way. I am still, my dear boy, looking for the Kingdom. But nothing superstitious or mythological. . . ."

"Excuse me. Where do you imagine you've been?"

"Ah, I see. You mean that the gray town with its continual hope of morning (we must all live by hope, must we not?), with its field for indefinite progress, is, in a sense, Heaven, if only we have eyes to see it? That is a beautiful idea."

"I didn't mean that at all. Is it possible you don't know where you've been?"

"Now that you mention it, I don't think we ever do give it a name. What do you call it?"

"We call it Hell."

"There is no need to be profane, my dear boy. I may not be very orthodox, in your sense of that word, but I do feel that these matters ought to be discussed simply, and seriously, and reverently."

"Discuss Hell *reverently*? I meant what I said. You have been in Hell."

"Go on, my dear boy, go on. That is *so* like you. No doubt you'll tell me why, on your view, I was sent there. I'm not angry."

"But don't you know? You went there because you are an apostate."

"Are you serious, Dick?"

"Perfectly!"

"This is worse than I expected. Do you really think people are penalised for their honest opinions? Even assuming, for the sake of argument, that those opinions were mistaken."[4]

Lewis makes a crucial point. The theologian in his tale is from below and cannot understand what is above. That is what the Lord is saying in John 8. You cannot mix oil and water, or light and darkness, or truth and deceit. You cannot mix that which is from above with that which is from below. There is and must be a separation. Kierkegaard, when he broke up with his fiancée, expressed this very dramatically when he said, "I cannot marry you. You are an eternity too young." Each of us is either from below or from above. There is no in-between.

The answer, of course, is to become part of the upper realm. Our Lord, in his High-Priestly prayer, said of his believers, "They are not of the world, just as I am not of the world" (17:16). When we become part of the kingdom above, we become participants in two dimensions. We still remain *in* the world, though we are not *of* the world. We live by the laws of this world. We participate in the economics and politics of the world. We are involved in its bad days and in its good. But we are not of the world. As long as we are on earth, we experience in varying degrees the implications of what the Scriptures say about our being seated with Christ above. Paul says, "[God] raised us up with him [Christ] and seated us with him in the heavenly places in Christ Jesus" (Ephesians 2:6). Because of that, the above becomes real.

The longer I am in the Word, the more real Heaven becomes to me. The Scriptures tell us that the temporal things we see are not eternal. The unseen things are eternal. The longer I am a believer, the more I look forward to being in Heaven and being with God. I like to say that I can hear the rustle of angels' wings. Some might say I am getting a little carried away, but there must be an upward thrust to our lives. Paul says in Philippians 3:20, "Our citizenship is in heaven, and from it we await a Savior, the Lord Jesus Christ." Are you from above, or are you from below?

The Specific Reasons for the Ultimate Separation

In verse 24 our Lord gets more specific.

> I told you that you would die in your sins, for unless you believe that I am [the one I claim to be] you will die in your sins.

To Jewish ears, that final phrase was literally, "Unless you believe that I AM, you will indeed die in your sins." Those who knew the Old Testament Scriptures thought back to Exodus 3, the story of God's calling Moses to deliver his people from Egypt. When God spoke to him from the burning bush, Moses asked, "What shall I say to them?" (Exodus 3:13). God answered, "I AM WHO I AM. . . . Say this to the people of Israel, 'I AM has sent me to you.'" He revealed himself as the eternal God who has always existed, the eternal predicate, the I AM. When Christ made his statement, he was essentially saying to the Jews that unless they believed he was the eternal God, they would perish in their sins. That is also what Christ says to us.

What we think of Christ is of paramount importance. We can think he is the greatest of teachers and that he is sinless, we can dwell upon his perfection, we can believe he is brave and kind and honest, compassionate and truthful. We can idolize him. We can pray to him. But that is not enough.

Several years ago Dr. Gordon A. Alles, a noted chemist and the man who pioneered the development of insulin for the treatment of diabetes, died of that very disease. His friends who were closest to him came to one of two conclusions. Either he did not know he had the disease or he purposely neglected to use the remedy. What irony—the man who knew more about the cure for diabetes than anyone else in the whole world died of the disease. I do not know what the truth of the matter was, but if Alles knew his condition, the situation was even more tragic. In the same way a person can know that Christ is the "I AM", he can give all of his mind to that, but unless there comes a belief that involves receiving the cure, he will die in his sins. Some Jews lacked that belief.

A dialogue then took place, revealing where many Jews were spiritually. They realized that Jesus was making a tremendous statement, but they decided to reject him. "Who are you?" they asked (v. 25). "Who do you think you are, putting on all these airs?" They again showed him scorn.

> Jesus said to them, "Just what I have been telling you from the beginning. I have much to say about you and much to judge, but he who sent me is true, and I declare to the world what I have heard from him." (vv. 25, 26)

Christ was saying in effect, "Why do I speak to you at all? From the beginning I have been telling you about my unity with the Father. The fact is, when I speak, he speaks, and when I act, he acts. But you haven't responded to that." Why did they not realize that he had been speaking to them of the Father? Because they were from below.

> The natural person does not accept the things of the Spirit of God, for they are folly to him, and he is not able to understand them because they are spiritually discerned. (1 Corinthians 2:14)

Because they rejected Christ's claim to be the "I AM", they could not enter into the realm above and understand its truths.

My friend Greg, when he first came to our college group, used to sit with his eyes wide open, his Bible sometimes open to the place where we were, but he understood very little. It was almost as if his eyes were open, but someone had drawn the shades. But when he experienced Christ, when he looked to the cross, he became a part of the kingdom above, and the Bible became the most exciting book in all the world. He could not get enough.

The Remedy for the Ultimate Separation

The remedy for not understanding is seen in verse 28:

> So Jesus said to them, "When you have lifted up the Son of Man, then you will know that I am he [the one I claim to be], and that I do nothing on my own authority, but speak just as the Father taught me."

Those who heard him say, "When you have lifted up the Son of Man" thought, *When we exalt him, we will know he is the "I AM"*. That is true, but there is more because our Lord spoke with a double meaning here. In 3:14 Jesus said, "As Moses lifted up the serpent in the wilderness, so must the Son of Man be lifted up." That lifting up, on the cross, although so humiliating, was a step to his exaltation. What Christ was saying to the crowd was, "When I am lifted up on the cross, you will know 'I AM'."

Looking back on the long shadow that extends across more than twenty centuries, we can know that he is the "I AM". I have heard that the geographical center of the city of London is Charing Cross. You can find your way anywhere in London if you are at Charing Cross. The story is told of a little boy who was lost. A bobby came along and wiped away his tears. When he had gotten him settled, he said, "Can I take you home, son?" The boy replied, "Oh, no, sir, take me to the cross, and I'll find my way home." When we orient ourselves to the cross, we begin to see the "I AM", the eternity and magnificence of God. By virtue of that undertaking, we enter into the kingdom above by faith.

If only we would keep before us the reality that terminal times do await us, bringing ultimate separation, and that the separation can only be avoided by a radical change bringing us into the realm above. That change comes only by looking in faith to the cross! If only we could keep that before us.

Conclusion

Several years ago as I was preparing to step into the pulpit, I noticed a tall, radiant woman who came into the back of the church and found a seat. She glowed throughout my message. Pastors notice those things. At the end of the service, meeting me at the door, she gave me a big hug. That lady was Greg Valdemi's mother. At my friend's memorial service, Greg's witness and the witness of his friends was clearly presented, and his mother was deeply moved. She returned to her home in Oregon, began attending a little church I recommended, and was marvelously converted. That day in church I saw in her eyes the same light and joy I had seen in her son's. She was a witnessing, dynamic, excited, overflowing Christian. She was involved in Bible study and was leading other people to Christ. In the midnight of her life, she had looked to the cross and had seen Jesus for what he is, the eternal "I AM." Upon believing in Christ, she was lifted from the realm of darkness into the realm of light. She became part of the kingdom above. The same life that had been her son's was now hers.

30

Up from Slavery

JOHN 8:31–36

SAMSON BEGAN HIS LIFE with great expectations. He was to be the deliverer of Israel. In fact, no one was ever born with greater expectations except for the Lord Jesus Christ and John the Baptist. Samson was a man with a fantastic future.

From birth Samson enjoyed special privileges. According to the Scriptures, he was made a Nazirite (even his mother became one when she discovered she was with child). This means, according to Numbers 6, that Samson was especially set apart for God, and as a sign of that, his hair was never to be cut, he was never to touch a dead body, and he was never to drink wine. His never cutting his hair set him apart from other men. His not touching a dead body suggested that he was consonant with the maintenance of his ritual purity. The prohibition against strong drink meant that Samson was to find no other stimulus but God in life. He had fantastic expectations spiritually. And as he began to grow, he exhibited unique physical capabilities as well. It appeared as if Samson could do anything, and indeed when the Spirit of God came upon him, miracles happened.

In Judges 13:25 we read, "The Spirit of the LORD began to stir him in Mahaneh-dan, between Zorah and Eshtaol." God came upon him, and the Jews expected great things. Samson had come of age. He was going to deliver his people. But sadly, his life fell apart. It all began when he pursued a Philistine wife despite his parents' objections. He also made the mistake of having friends who led a dissolute life. He used his powers selfishly, capriciously, wastefully. And then there was his costly liaison with Delilah.

Eventually dissolute Samson, beset by the intrigues of Delilah, decided he would go out as he had done at other times and defeat the Philistines, but this time there was a difference he did not recognize. "'I will go out as at other times and shake myself free.' But he did not know that the L ORD had left him" (Judges 16:20). He had become desensitized to his spiritual situation. His perception was gone. His great potential was unfulfilled.

The sad account continues, "The Philistines seized him and gouged out his eyes and brought him down to Gaza and bound him with bronze shackles. And he ground at the mill in the prison" (Judges 16:21). Life had indeed caved in. How tragic! He was to be the liberator of his people. But now he had fallen into abject servitude. He could not have been any lower.

But the even greater tragedy is that his life has become the agenda for countless thousands of lives down through the centuries—a mirror of those who have had great potential but fell short. I know some like that. So do you. Those who seemed to be free and on the verge of accomplishing great things for God were suddenly in bondage, sometimes right up to the end of their lives on earth. We even see this pattern in our own lives sometimes.

Samson was meant to be a deliverer but instead became a slave. In John 8:31–36 we discover what lies behind slavery and, even better, the prescription and motivation for freedom.

Our Lord was locked in confrontation with the religious authorities. He had proclaimed that he is the Light of the world, implying that his opponents were in darkness. He had also warned the Jews they were in danger of the fires of Hell because they were from below and he was from above—two realms that cannot mix. And as they were reeling from his assault, he carried the argument even further. He even suggested that they might actually be in bondage!

> If you abide in my word, you are truly my disciples, and you will know the truth, and the truth will set you free. . . . Truly, truly, I say to you, everyone who practices sin is a slave to sin. (vv. 31, 32, 34)

The Problem of Slavery

The Jews completely missed his point. Jesus was speaking on a spiritual level, but they were thinking physically. That's why we read in verse 33, "They answered him, 'We are offspring of Abraham and have never been enslaved to anyone. How is it that you say, 'You will become free'?"

In other words, "We haven't been in bondage to anyone. How could you make such a statement?" Not only did the Jews misunderstand Christ, but they were deceiving themselves because they *were* in physical bondage. Their people had throughout history frequently been slaves—in Egypt, in Babylon, under the domination of the Philistines, the Greeks, and now the Romans.

The Jews were slaves, but they would not admit it. That was their problem. The Jews so hated what had happened to them over the centuries that they said in their souls, "History may say it, others may say it, but we are not slaves!" Years later, as the Jewish soldiers were defending the fortress of Masada, Eleazar gave forth the great cry, "Long ago we determined to be slaves neither to the Romans, nor to anyone else, save God."[1] So when all hope was lost, the defenders committed suicide rather than surrender. Jews loathed the idea of slavery. They were so emotional about it that they could not accept the facts.

But of course our Lord was speaking of spiritual slavery, and those who rightly understood what he was saying chose to deny their condition. "Jesus answered them, 'Truly, truly, I say to you, everyone who practices sin is a slave to sin'" (v. 34). Such denial persists today, and not just among the Jews. Although more than two thousand years have passed, there is still much confusion about spiritual slavery. People today do not accept the truth of their condition. If we suggest to someone that he is in bondage, he usually resists the idea. The more enslaved he is, the more he may resent being told the truth. John Calvin said, "The greater the mass of vices anyone is buried under, the more fiercely and bombastically does he extol free will."

Consider as an example a practicing alcoholic. "Me an alcoholic? Not me. I can stop anytime. Where did you hide the bottle?" Suggest to a sensualist that he might be in bondage, and he will probably retort that you are the one in bondage—to archaic conventions and a repressive lifestyle. People do not like to be told they are enslaved. Like the Jews, they are easily desensitized to their true condition. If you place a frog in a pot of water and heat it gradually, the frog will be boiled alive without resisting. The application is obvious.

That seems to have been the case with Samson. In his ever-increasing immersion in the world, he became anesthetized to the fact that God could leave him, that his powers were not unconditionally his. So insensible did he become that even after God had mightily used him, after God helped him defeat one thousand Philistines and marvelously hollowed out a place in the rock and provided water for him, Samson consorted with a prostitute! He did not understand his powers could be taken away. Amazingly, after three attempts by Delilah on his life, Samson told her the secret of his power. His sin had robbed him of his sensibilities. I have no doubt that Samson imagined he was the freest of men, and yet he was the greatest slave.

Some of us may imagine we are on the verge of obtaining freedom as we begin to depart from God's Word and go our own way. In reality, however, we are about to enter the greatest bondage we have ever known. In such a state we resent any suggestions from family or acquaintances that something is wrong in our lives. But we need to wake up and realize that the path to freedom lies in obeying the Word of God.

When we are in bondage, we excel at minimizing our enslavement. "It's not so bad. I just have to make a few adjustments." I once heard a TV news commentator call a societal sin a "cultural neurosis." Nowhere does an insufficient view of sin get more bizarre than in the area of theology, because when we do away with the depths of the hold of sin upon us, we find ourselves in a theological wonderland. I recall hearing an unbelieving preacher, who rejected the Word of God and the divinity of Jesus Christ and espoused a man-made religion, use another frog illustration. His poor frog fell into a large milk can. Try as it would, it could not get out of the milk. It paddled and paddled and paddled but to no avail. There was nothing to do but keep paddling, which it did, until it churned a pad of butter from which it was able to jump out of the milk! Absurd! How tragic to minimize or trivialize the serious teachings of Jesus Christ about our spiritual bondage.

When we do away with the profundity of sin and the bondage it has upon the human soul, trying to achieve happiness and to neutralize our sin is like going after Moby Dick with a pickle fork! It just will not work. A more radical solution is needed. Perhaps some of our Lord's listeners understood his words. And perhaps as they listened, the realization of their bondage swept over them, and they wondered what they should do. If they had listened closely to his opening words, they would have known the answer.

The Path to Freedom

> So Jesus said to the Jews who had believed him, "If you abide in my word, you are truly my disciples, and you will know the truth, and the truth will set you free." (vv. 31, 32)

When our family visited Boston a number of years ago, we took the historical walk from the Boston Common. We started under the great steeple of Park Street Church, walked down past Tremont Temple, came to King's Chapel, took a right to the Old South Meeting House, spent some time listening to a lecture, and then wandered over to Quincy Market and Faneuil Hall, where we had lunch. We had a marvelous time. And in all our sightseeing, there was only one thing required of us—to follow a red line on the sidewalk. If you follow that red line, you will see nearly all the nearby historical sights of Boston. All we had to do was follow the line, pay attention to the signs it brought us to, and obey them. Similarly, only by abiding in the Word of God can we enjoy the liberation Christ offers us.

Abiding in the Word involves two things—studying the Word and obeying it. The result is freedom. Christ showed us the process in the verses we just cited. Christ says first, in verse 31, "If you abide in my word, you are truly my disciples." When one abides in the Word, he becomes a disciple, or literally a learner. "If you abide in my word, you are truly my *learners*." That is, you put yourself in a progressively liberating status if you abide in the Word. If you become a learner of truth, further possibilities of truth open to you that you could never have known before.

Verse 32 shows us the second step: "and you will know the truth." By becoming learners, abiding in the Word, we open ourselves to truth—not primarily scientific truth or historical truth, but truth about spiritual things—our own nature, the nature of God, the way of salvation. These become certainties to us if we abide in the Word. And with truth comes freedom. A man does not become free to know Christ, to have his sins taken away, until he knows the truth. And as he grows in his knowledge of the truth, more freedom is possible. The more we abide in his Word, the more we become learners. And the more open we become to his truth, the more truth he gives to us. And the more truth we learn, the more we can appropriate. It is a blessed spiral. The key, according to our text, is abiding in his Word, holding fast to it.

Abiding begins with being students of the Word of God. If we were to compare the various ages of Protestant church history, we would have to say that today is an age of Biblical ignorance. People do not take the first step in abiding in the Word of God. Yet the importance of basing our lives on the Scriptures is urgent. In Matthew 4:4 Jesus says, "Man shall not live by bread alone, but by every word that comes from the mouth of God." "Let the word of Christ dwell in you richly" (Colossians 3:16). "Do your best to present yourself to God as one approved, a worker who has no need to be ashamed, rightly handling the word of truth" (2 Timothy 2:15).

We all need to know the Word of God. We must be students of the Word—not only the preachers, not just the educated, but *all* believers. And yet even if that takes place, we are not necessarily abiding. To abide in the Word we must obey it. And that is how freedom comes. We learn the Word of God, we obey it, and then we are free. The exhilaration of that freedom motivates us to study the Word of God more, and when we again obey it, more freedom comes. And on and on and on it goes—from freedom to freedom to freedom. The reason many Christians are not experiencing spiritual freedom today is that while they may be Biblically literate, they are not Biblically obedient.

A friend of mine has made it his practice to ask experienced preachers, "I am just a novice pastor. If you could tell me in a phrase what you would most want me to know, what would it be?" He tells me that 90 percent of the time the answer is, to know the Word of God and to obey it. If we are Biblically literate, yet feel bound, perhaps we are not obeying the Word of God.

So Jesus presents the solution of abiding in the Word of God and then in verse 35 gives us a dazzling portrait of the freedom he was speaking of: "The slave does not remain in the house forever; the son remains forever." The spiritual freedom that comes to us is as dramatically different as that of a slave and a son. The son is in the house and has access to everything. He can go wherever he wants to go. He can stay as long as he wants to stay. But the slave has no rights. If you are a slave to sin, the son's freedoms are not yours.

Christ continues his thought in verse 36: "So if the Son sets you free, you will be free indeed." Christ, "the Son," is the One who enjoys freedom par excellence, and he is the One who gives us that freedom. The freedom we enjoy is the freedom that Christ enjoys. The freest being in all the universe pumps freedom into our lives that he describes as "free indeed." Freedom to rise above our sins, freedom to live a holy life. Freedom that we never had before—the freedom to choose the right, the freedom to choose the best, the freedom to keep on growing, the freedom to reach our potential. That is to be free indeed, and it comes, according to our text, from abiding in the Word of God, from knowing and doing God's Word.

Conclusion

One of two words describes us. We are either *bound* or we are *free*. Perhaps some of us have not entered into the initial freedom of being delivered from sin. That initial deliverance comes from acknowledging our bondage and the power of Christ to deliver us, and from personally receiving Christ by faith and repentance.

Others of us may find that even though we have been liberated, the word *bondage* seems best to describe where we are. That may be because we have returned to our old ways. We have become desensitized and anesthetized. God's power is gone from us. What we need to do is repent, turn to God. Samson, in the last moment of his life, despite all his frivolous dissipation, returned to God in faith. It is by faith that we are enabled to turn back to God and become people of his Word. Are you abiding in the Word, feeding yourself on it? Are you obeying the Word? Those are questions of liberation. May God establish these truths in our hearts.

31

Ultimate Ancestry

JOHN 8:37–47

AT THE END OF THE SUMMER OF 1874, an unusual gathering took place. It was remarkably fine weather for September when four or five hundred descendants of Jonathan Edwards poured into the resort town of Stockbridge, Massachusetts, for a family reunion. They lunched under a great tent provided by Yale University, admired memorabilia from the Edwards family—such as Sarah Edwards's wedding dress and the silver bowl from which Jonathan ate his nightly porridge—and poked around the old house, which was substantially unchanged. That gathering teemed with professors, business executives, government officials, ministers, and, according to one account, women of unusual beauty and force of personality. The mood of the reunion was expressed by the initiator of the gathering when he said, "Let God be praised for such a man." His remarks were followed by many laudatory speeches that excited the glee of Jonathan Edwards's descendants. All in all, it was as proud a celebration of ancestry as has ever been held in America. A study by the New York Genealogical and Historical Society says: "Probably no two people married since the beginning of the 18th century have been progenitors of so many distinguished persons as were Jonathan Edwards and Sarah Pierrepont."

Twenty-six years later, in 1900, a man by the name of A. E. Winship did a study of Edwards's descendants. The results have become famous. Winship concluded that from that single union of Jonathan Edwards and Sarah Pierrepont came thirteen college presidents, sixty-five professors, one hundred lawyers and a dean of an outstanding law school, thirty judges, sixty-six physicians and a dean of a medical school, and eighty holders of public office, among them three United States senators, mayors of three large cities, governors of three states, a vice-president of the United States, and a controller of the United States Treasury. Winship concluded:

> There is scarcely any great American industry that has not had one of this family among its chief promoters. . . . The family has cost the country nothing in pauperism, in crime, in hospital or asylum service; on the contrary, it represents the highest usefulness.[1]

The obvious conclusion is: having an industrious, godly ancestry is to one's advantage. But there is another statistic about the family that is rarely mentioned. In 1756 Esther, daughter of Jonathan Edwards, gave birth to a boy. This is how she described her son shortly after his birth:

> . . . very sly and mischievous . . . has more sprightliness than Sally . . . handsomer, but not so good tempered . . . very resolute and requires a good governor to bring him to terms.

Such words could be written about many children, but these were written about Aaron Burr, the man who took the life of Alexander Hamilton and then plotted to crown himself as emperor of Mexico. Aaron Burr was the grandson of Jonathan Edwards!

The poet Constance Carrier summed up the man this way:

> Eight lines of clergymen converged
> to meet in Aaron Burr:
> Edwardses, Tuthills; Pierreponts, each
> a blood-and-thunderer. . . .
> Eight lines of clergymen converged
> as I have said, in Burr,
> but Aaron was Beelzebub
> in mocking miniature.[2]

Those splendid genetic qualities and heritage in the line of Jonathan Edwards seem to have been demonically reversed in Aaron Burr. So we see that while a godly heritage is of inestimable value, it does not guarantee spiritual health.

The Edwards-Burr connection is a compelling story. Many of us had godly parents, and for some of us that godly heritage goes back generation after generation. Some of us, no doubt, have ancestors who were involved in shaping the world's religious thought and tradition and defending the faith. We owe them a great debt. Some of us may be related to someone who is on the forefront of Christian work in the world today. But we must remember that our heritage can be either a curse or a blessing. That is why John 8:37–47 is a very important passage of Scripture. It deals with people who, although they have an outstanding heritage, have come to false conclusions that are detrimental to their spiritual health. Our Lord sets them straight and also gives an outline by which we can check our own spiritual health.

At the point in time in which this passage took place, our Lord was being extremely aggressive. In 8:12 he said, "I am the light of the world," implying that his hearers were in darkness and therefore lost. In 8:23 Christ asserted, "You are from below; I am from above." He was implying that because his listeners were from below, they were in danger of the fires of Hell. Then in verse 34 Jesus said, "Truly, truly, I say to you, everyone who practices sin is a slave to sin."

Now as we come to the Master's words in verses 37, 38, the gloves are off:

> I know that you are offspring of Abraham; yet you seek to kill me because my word finds no place in you. I speak of what I have seen with my Father, and you do what you have heard from your father.

Our Lord indicts his listeners for depending on two things for their spiritual health. One was *physical ancestry* as the offspring of Abraham. The other was *spiritual heritage*. They had assumed that because of their heritage they were children of God. Jesus touched a sensitive nerve here, and the Jews responded just as he knew they would.

Physical Claims Answered (vv. 39, 40)

"They answered him, 'Abraham is our father'"(v. 39). Four words. That was enough of an answer for them: "Abraham is our father." The common belief at that time was that Abraham was so godly and had stored up such a vast treasury of merit that if his descendants would draw upon it, they would attain righteousness. In fact, sometime after this account the Christian Justin Martyr was in dialogue with Trypho the Jew, and Trypho ended that conversation by saying that the eternal kingdom will be given to those who are the seed of Abraham according to the flesh, even if they are sinners and unbelievers and disobedient to God. No wonder the Jews responded confidently with the words, "Abraham is our father." Abraham was their security.

> If you were Abraham's children, you would be doing the works Abraham did, but now you seek to kill me, a man who has told you the truth that I heard from God. This is not what Abraham did. (vv. 39, 40)

When Abraham heard the truth, although he lived in an idolatrous, pagan world, he responded with obedience. That was his distinguishing mark. He heard the truth, took it to himself, and became obedient. But the Jews who confronted Jesus were doing no such thing. They were trying to kill the bearer of truth. They were not spiritual descendants of Abraham. The point is, we may be the descendants of a godly line, but that fact will not bring us eternal life. Have we received Christ for ourselves, and how are we conducting our lives? According to our Lord, that is how we determine who our ancestors are. If we are of Puritan stock, we must be people who love the Word of God, who glorify the sovereign God, and who spend time in prayer and are given to a holy life. If we are of Methodist stock, that means that sometimes we will unexpectedly break into singing, that we are enthusiastic about our faith, that if necessary we will risk our lives for the gospel. Applying our Lord's logic to immediate relationships, it is very possible for a father and son to not really be father and son, at least in the deepest way. It is our deeds that allow us rightfully to say we come from a godly line.

A godly heritage is of inestimable worth. I am a devoted student of preachers and preaching, and I have discovered that often great preachers are third- and fourth-generation ministers. Charles Spurgeon was fourth-generation. G. Campbell Morgan was fourth-generation. If we have learned our prayer lives from our parents, how blessed we are. When we learn to preach from our grandfathers, what a privilege we have. When we get our missionary burden from our grandmother, we are richly blessed. Sublime privileges! A great spiritual heritage is to be highly valued. But if it is not appropriated and made real in individual lives, it becomes a curse.

> His daughter's idol, and his wife's—
> the pictures blend and blur.
> At eighty, unregenerate,
> he died, in character:
> "God's don?" "On that subject I
> am coy," said Aaron Burr.

The words of our Lord Jesus Christ were in essence, "If you are Abraham's children, do the deeds of Abraham." There must be something spiritually substantive in our lives. Is there?

The Lord then intimated that they had a spiritual father other than Abraham: "You are doing the works your father did" (v. 41a). The Jews understood and responded with words to which our Lord had the answer.

Spiritual Claims Answered (vv. 41–47)

"They said to him, 'We were not born of sexual immorality. We have one Father—even God'" (v. 41). What they were really saying was, "We are not concerned about our pedigree. We were not born of fornication like you. We have heard the rumors about you, but we are children of God!" It is so easy to be wrong about our spiritual state when we have a godly heritage. The blessing of that heritage can become a curse. Many of us believe we received Christ as children. However, it does not necessarily follow that because our parents have fondly recounted our infant conversion so often that we can describe it as if we remember every detail, we have truly been converted. And we parents can be guilty of desiring spiritual life for our children so much that we imagine they have virtues they never had.

Edmund Gosse, the famous Cambridge professor, in his autobiography *Father and Son*, tells how he finally rejected the godly heritage and faith of his parents. In one particularly sad chapter he recounts how his loving father was so desirous that his ten-year-old be baptized that he convinced the elders to interview Edmund, who says he ". . . sat on a sofa in full lamplight and testified my faith in the atonement with a fluency that surprised myself (so that my interviewer) . . . was weeping like a child."[3] It was a perfect performance, but Edmund Gosse did not have grace in his life. We too need to examine ourselves. Some of us have well-meaning friends who have spoken in soothing tones about our baptism or our being in the covenant, and we have appropriated false assurance and thus have fallen into the same pit as these ancient Jews. That is possible, and that is why Jesus' answer is so important. In it he revealed what it means to be true children of God.

The first test, he said, is *love for Christ*.

> If God were your Father, you would love me, for I came from God and I am here. I came not of my own accord, but he sent me. (v. 42)

He says, "I am one with God. I am the expression of God. If you say you love God, then you have to love me." The highest test of our faith is whether we love Jesus Christ. We cannot answer that question for anyone else but only for ourselves. In all honesty, does your love for Christ transcend your love for all other things? If the Spirit does not indicate that to you, your heritage may not be working.

Our Lord gave another test in verse 43—*how we respond to God's Word*. "Why do you not understand what I say? It is because you cannot bear to hear my word." And he added in verse 47, "Whoever is of God hears the words of

God. The reason why you do not hear them is that you are not of God." The problem was not that the Jews could not hear physically. They could analyze Jesus' sentences, maybe even diagram them if they had time. But they could not hear him in their souls. Does the Word of God speak to us in such a way that it penetrates and has an effect on our lives? If it does not, that may be an indication we are not in a state of grace.

Then there is the matter of *obedience*.

> You are of your father the devil, and your will is to do your father's desires. He was a murderer from the beginning, and does not stand in the truth, because there is no truth in him. When he lies, he speaks out of his own character, for he is a liar and the father of lies (v. 44).

If we are children of Satan, we will not desire to do God's will. This is not to suggest that Satan's children all consciously desire to serve him. Very few ever come to that. They serve themselves. Nor does it mean that Satan's followers fall to the same level of malevolence to which he fell. What it does mean is that they desire a will other than God's.

Christ says their father is "a murderer," and murder flows out of deceit. Satan is above all things "a liar," and the Lord was saying that those who follow the devil are characterized by deceit. They deceive themselves about their own hearts. They deceive themselves about life. They deceive themselves about Christ. They deceive themselves about God. They deceive themselves about the way of salvation. But the ultimate deception is to imagine you are a child of God when you are not.

Conclusion

We are each of one Father or the other. Regardless of our heritage, regardless of what has been suggested to us by other people, we are either children of Satan or children of God. Do we love Jesus? Does his Word find a place in us? Has it changed our actions substantively?

32

The Way of Seeing

JOHN 9:1–41

JOHN 1—8 records a conflict between Christ and the religious leaders of Judaism, a conflict sustained by Jesus' aggressiveness. That confrontation continues in John 9. We rarely see the Lord as aggressive as he is here.

There was a remarkable setting for this conflict—the Feast of Booths. The final night has taken place, and on that night, as on preceding nights, four huge torches (perhaps as high as the walls of the temple) were ignited. The holy men and the elders of Israel danced the night away in front of those flames. It was before the extinguished torches that Jesus announced, "I am the light of the world. Whoever follows me will not walk in darkness, but will have the light of life" (8:12). The meaning was clear—he was the light, and his enemies were in spiritual darkness. Those were fighting words. And the Lord didn't stop there but went on to tell them they were from below, but he was from above. And as if that were not enough, our Lord also told them that though they prided themselves on being children of Abraham, nothing substantive in their lives validated their spiritual heritage. As a matter of fact, they were serving the devil. When Jesus also stated (8:58), "Before Abraham was, I am" (obviously identifying himself as Jehovah), they attempted to stone him.

Whenever we read the eighth chapter of John we should keep in mind that scene with the great charred torches. It was an unforgettable dramatization of the difference between the realms of light and darkness. And as we come to the ninth chapter, we see that the theme is sustained. The two chapters are meant to be read together because as Christ now leaves the temple, it is a conscious portrayal of what happens when light goes out into the world. As the chapter opens, our Lord immediately encounters one who has never known light—a man blind from birth—and miraculously gives him sight and light.

Notice how John carefully set the stage for this miracle in the opening verses. "As he passed by, he saw a man blind from birth" (v. 1). Jesus evidently fixed his gaze upon the poor man, possibly stopping the whole procession with a contemplative look, because we read in verse 2, "His disciples asked him, 'Rabbi, who sinned, this man or his parents, that he was born blind?'" The disciples probably asked that because it was a common Jewish belief that such defects had immediate hereditary causes. Some even traced deformities to sin in the womb! Jesus' answer is most helpful: "It was not that this man sinned, or his parents, but that the works of God might be displayed in him" (v. 3). In essence Jesus was saying, "I won't be involved in such a profitless discussion. Suffice it to say neither of them sinned. This man is blind so the power of God can be shown forth." Then he concluded:

> We must work the works of him who sent me while it is day; night is coming, when no one can work. As long as I am in the world, I am the light of the world. (vv. 4, 5)

So the stage is set for a great miracle.

The Working of Christ's Light (vv. 6–12)

Here was a man who had never known light. His situation calls to mind the words of Helen Keller: "Gradually I got used to the silence and darkness that surrounded me and forgot that it had ever been different until she came— my teacher—who set my spirit free." Darkness was all the beggar had ever known. He could not conceive of blue, green, red, or orange. A million glories of nature were hidden from him—the green of spring grass, the magic of a sunset. Perhaps there had been a time when, as a child, he had reached up and felt the softness of his mother's face, and possibly even a hot tear upon her cheek, but he did not know what she looked like. He was always dependent either on a friendly arm or his uncertain cane.

Now as he begged outside the temple, he heard someone cry, "As long as I am in the world, I am the light of the world." Then in the unusual silence that followed, he heard that man kneel close to him and gently spit upon the ground. He felt gentle hands apply the damp clay to his eyes and heard the words, "Go, wash in the pool of Siloam" (v. 7).

I wonder how he felt. A bit foolish? Probably. Even though he was blind, he must have had some idea that he was creating a scene as he made his way to Siloam with his eyes covered with mud. But I also think his heart began to pound with the swelling possibility that he might receive his sight. "What if this really works?"

Then, incredibly, as he washed in Siloam, light poured into his being. He could see! Perhaps the first thing he saw was his own reflection, then water, sky, trees, faces. . . .

Do you think he said, "Well, I have to get back to my begging post. It's a competitive business"? No way! It is more likely that as he began to see clearly, he looked intently at the faces of the voices he had known and began to shout, "I can see! I can see! I can see!" Very possibly he began to lope slowly toward home (the context tells us he returned to his neighborhood), and as he gained confidence he began to run faster and faster until finally he burst into the house. "Mom, look, no cane! I can see!" What a beautiful miracle! The whole neighborhood was in an uproar.

> The neighbors and those who had seen him before as a beggar were saying, "Is this not the man who used to sit and beg?" Some said, "It is he." Others said, "No, but he is like him." He kept saying, "I am the man." (vv. 8, 9)

Once he convinced them he really was the man who had been blind, the discussion turned to what had happened.

> So they said to him, "Then how were your eyes opened?" He answered, "The man called Jesus made mud and anointed my eyes and said to me, 'Go to Siloam and wash.' So I went and washed and received my sight." (vv. 10, 11)

What a day! What a miracle! In order to find out more about congenital blindness, I talked to some ophthalmologists in the church I pastor. To a man they said they had no knowledge of anyone who was born blind receiving sight except for someone born with cataracts, in which case the sight is never completely restored. Here we have an eminent miracle, and as a result family and friends began to seek out Jesus and ultimately found salvation.

As we have noted before, miracles in John's Gospel are always signs meant to teach deep spiritual truths. This miracle and the remainder of the chapter teach us how to receive and keep spiritual sight. It begins in verse 1 with a man who is born blind. He receives physical sight and, later, spiritual sight. And in verse 41, the final verse of the chapter, we find men who claim to have spiritual sight but are utterly blind—the Pharisees.

The Controversy of Christ's Light (vv. 13–34)

The intervening drama came in the shape of three ludicrous interrogations. First, the leaders called the man in, and the interrogation quickly broke down. The mini-Sanhedrin dissolved in controversy as they realized that the miracle was performed on the Sabbath. Even making clay on the Sabbath was a sin according to rabbinic law. However, some reasoned that a sinner could not do what Jesus did.

Then they called in the blind man's parents, thinking they would surely find a discrepancy, but his parents were so terrified that all they would say was, "We know that this is our son and that he was born blind" and that they did not know how he could now see (vv. 20, 21).

Finally they called the blind man back again, and this ignorant, uneducated beggar completely turned the tables on his august interrogators with some of the cleverest dialogue in the whole New Testament. Listen to how *The Living Bible* records it in verses 24–33:

> So for the second time they called in the man who had been blind and told him, "Give the glory to God, not to Jesus, for we know Jesus is an evil person." "I don't know whether he is good or bad," the man replied, "But I know this: *I was blind, and now I see!*" "But what did he do?" they asked. "How did he heal you?" "Look!" the man exclaimed. "I told you once; didn't you listen? Why do you want to hear it again? Do you want to become his disciples too?" Then they cursed him and said, "You are his disciple, but we are disciples of Moses. We know God has spoken to Moses, but as for this fellow, we don't know anything about him." "Why, that's very strange!" the man replied. "He can heal blind men, and yet you don't know anything about him! Well, God doesn't listen to evil men, but he has open ears to those who worship him and do his will. Since the world began there has never been anyone who could open the eyes of someone born blind. If this man were not from God, he couldn't do it."

So with oaths and aspersions concerning his legitimacy they tossed him out the door. The Pharisees completely rejected the witness of the light. St. John Chrysostom commenting upon this passage says: "The Jews cast him out of the temple, and the Lord of the temple found him." Jesus came to the man, and his conversion (vv. 35–38) was an even greater miracle in his life, for now he had spiritual light. "The light of the world" had gone out into the dark world with the result that a blind man saw not only with his eyes but with his heart, and those who had vision were blinded because they refused to believe.

Those who know the truth but do not turn to Christ are lost. Why do men who care about spiritual matters (so much so that every area of life is subjected to their beliefs—even more than many Christians) become blind?

The Reception and Rejection of Christ's Light (vv. 39–41)

"For judgment I came into this world, that those who do not see may see, and those who see may become blind" (v. 39). Christ came into this world so that those who *think* they have spiritual insight will be shown to be blind and so those who do not suppose they have spiritual insight will see. The whole argument centers around the idea of need. Those who know they are blind are the ones to whom Jesus can give sight.

> Some of the Pharisees near him heard these things, and said to him, "Are we also blind?" Jesus said to them, "If you were blind, you would have no guilt; but now that you say, 'We see,' your guilt remains." (vv. 40, 41)

Those who go blind are the ones who do not realize their need. Those who receive sight are the ones who sense their darkness. The Pharisees thought they had it all together, that they had arrived. Through their acquaintance with the Law they knew they were not perfect, but they did not understand how deeply infected they were with sin. So they adopted the external appearance of having dealt with sin though actually they had never faced the darkness of their hearts. They were self-satisfied. They said, "We see" when in reality they were blind.

C. S. Lewis writes in the introduction to *Screwtape Letters*:

> Some have paid me an undeserved compliment by supposing that my *Letters* were the ripe fruit of many years' study in moral and ascetic theology. They forgot that there is an equally reliable, though less creditable, way of learning how temptation works. "My heart"—I need no other's—"showeth me the wickedness of the ungodly."[1]

The Pharisees knew none of this. That was not their style. Remember Jesus' parable about two men who went up to the temple to worship—a Pharisee and a tax-gatherer? The Pharisee went into the temple and prayed:

> God, I thank you that I am not like other men, extortioners, unjust, adulterers, or even like this tax collector. I fast twice a week; I give tithes of all that I get. (Luke 18:11, 12)

But the tax-gatherer, unwilling to even lift his eyes up to Heaven, simply prayed, "God, be merciful to me, a sinner!" Self-satisfied people, the religious know-it-alls, believe they see but are blind. For the soul that desires to remain in ignorance of sin, that prefers his own darkened understanding, there is no hope!

The blind man in John 9 knew his need. "I see" was not a part of his vocabulary. He knew he was in the dark, and he knew it was not only physical but spiritual. We can be sure that the disciples' discussion about the cause of his blindness was not his first exposure to the idea of his being a great sinner. And while he did not know whose sin caused his blindness (if indeed anyone's), he did know he was a sinner. Self-sufficient? No. He was a beggar. Proud? Proud of what? His status? His great knowledge? His physique? His accomplishments? Ironically, that is possible. He could have said to himself, "I am the best beggar there is. I am the king of beggars." But the thrust of our chapter is one who sees his need—the blind who want to see.

Possibly the change that Christ initially brought to our lives was quite dramatic too, evidenced perhaps by changed habits and language. But it is also possible that with the change came an unhealthy focus on our "progress" and that ensuing pride began to dull us to the spiritual realities. Darkness then flourished within. It is possible to come to know Christ but to effectively seal ourselves off from the light. As with the Pharisees, our pride in visible change can dull us to the aggressive darkness of our hearts.

The self-satisfied attitude of "we see" is deadly. We comfort ourselves in our ability to "see" the sin of the world. "We see" that Jesus Christ is the answer. "We see" moral problems. "We see" the ethical answers. We focus on what we think we see but never really see into our hearts. It is so easy to focus on our piety or the changes in our habits and speech, but while we congratulate ourselves, we allow evil to spread unrestricted in our souls.

The ground of seeing and spiritual growth is the awareness of how dark our hearts are and how desperately we need Christ! When our Lord in his opening words in the Sermon on the Mount said, "Blessed are the poor in spirit, for theirs is the kingdom of heaven" (Matthew 5:3)—those who realize they have nothing within themselves to commend them to God—he revealed not only what is required to see the kingdom of God, but to keep growing and seeing! It is blind beggars who keep on seeing.

Alexander Whyte, that great preacher of a century ago, was in his study one day when a friend came in to tell him about an evangelist who had come to Edinburgh and was criticizing the local ministers. The man told Dr. Whyte that the preacher had said Dr. Hood Wilson was not a Christian. When Whyte heard that, he leaped out of his chair and said, "The rascal! Dr. Wilson not a converted man!" Then the friend said, "And that is not all. He said you are not converted either." At that, Whyte stopped short, sat back down in his chair, and put his face in his hands. After a long silence he said, "Leave me, friend, leave me! I must examine my heart!"[2] He was poor in spirit.

Oh, how happy are those who realize that within themselves there is nothing to commend them to God. Theirs is the kingdom of God. How happy they are because their emptiness becomes an occasion for his fullness. Oh, how happy are those who mourn over their sins and the sins of others, for they will be comforted. Oh, how happy are the meek—those who allow others to assert that they are poor sinners.

Conclusion

The way of seeing is the way of the blind. Charles Spurgeon said:

> It is not our littleness that hinders Christ; but our bigness. It is not our weakness that hinders Christ; it is our strength. It is not our darkness that hinders Christ; it is our supposed light that holds back his hand.[3]

The way of seeing is essentially a willingness to admit we are blind and naked and hungry. The blind beggar of John 9 is our example. He did not argue with Christ. He acknowledged his blind condition and need. He submitted himself to the hand of Christ and was obedient—and then came the miracle so that he saw with his eyes and with his heart. Remember, great partakers are great beggars. Those who are empty will be filled. The blind will see.

33

The Good Shepherd, Part I

JOHN 10:1–18

PHILLIP KELLER, in his interesting book *A Shepherd Looks at Psalm 23*, describes a danger that is unique to sheep. Shepherds call it "cast down" or simply "cast." It has to do with a sheep that cannot regain its feet. Keller writes:

> Even the largest, fattest, strongest and sometimes healthiest sheep can become "cast" and be a casualty. The way it happens is this. A heavy, fat, or long-fleeced sheep will lie down comfortably in some little hollow or depression in the ground. It may roll on its side slightly to stretch out or relax. Suddenly the center of gravity in the body shifts so that it turns on its back far enough that the feet no longer touch the ground. It may feel a sense of panic and start to paw frantically. Frequently this only makes things worse. It rolls over even further. Now it is quite impossible for it to regain its feet.[1]

Keller then continues to discuss some problems that are unique to sheep. The overall thrust of his book is how utterly helpless sheep are! Among the animal kingdom sheep seem to have come out on the short end. From all accounts they are of limited intelligence. When it comes to finding food, they are definitely uncreative. As creatures of habit, they will follow paths through desolate places even though not far away is excellent forage. Sheep are also given to listless wandering. There are even accounts of their walking into an open fire! Shepherds confirm that they are timid and stubborn. They can be frightened by the most ridiculous things, though at other times *nothing* can move them. They are absolutely defenseless. There is no way a sheep can defend itself. Furthermore, of all the animals subject to husbandry, they take the most work.

267

I remember hearing Dr. Bob Smith, retired professor of philosophy at Bethel College, say that the existence of sheep was *prima facie* evidence against the theory of evolution. There is no way sheep could have survived! I do not know whether that is true or not, but I do know they are an apt emblem for human beings. They represent us so perfectly that the Scriptures frequently appropriate the image. In Psalm 100:3 we read, "It is he who made us, and we are his; we are his people, and the sheep of his pasture." And in Isaiah 53:6 we read, "All we like sheep have gone astray."

Scripture is rich in its imagery as it portrays us as sheep. We twenty-first century North Americans, by virtue of our experience, find ourselves limited in our appreciation of this beautiful image. If you say to me, "Los Angeles," my mind automatically fills with pictures of palm trees, smoggy freeways, and an orange sun setting over the ocean. Our experience helps us understand and relate to the words we read or hear. So when we read about sheep and shepherds we are naturally handicapped. Even if we have had experience with sheep in our own culture, we are still disadvantaged because we undoubtedly think of vast flocks, of men driving them efficiently with their dogs, of co-ops and big businesses. So we miss the richness of the Biblical symbol.

Our twenty-first century image is far from the first-century picture of sheep. In that age shepherding was an intimate occupation. The Palestinian shepherd did not drive his sheep—he went before them, he led his sheep. And while sheep were indeed raised by some for food and sacrifices, more often sheep were raised for wool. A shepherd would typically tend his sheep for years, calling each of his flock by name. It was a highly personal occupation. The very existence of a sheep depended on the shepherd and his twenty-four-hour-a-day care. That is why there was no sharper image of tragedy for the ancient mind than sheep without a shepherd, which our Lord used in Matthew 9:36:

> When he saw the crowds, he had compassion for them, because they were harassed and helpless, like sheep without a shepherd.

The Jews understood Jesus' point. Today we need to catch the flavor of his words because they aptly describe our world. Many people, including many believers, are cast down and in essence without a shepherd. Others are contented members of the flock, enjoying tenderness and attention. We need to grasp the beauty and imagery of John 10, appropriate it for our own lives, and enjoy our "sheepishness." In verses 1–6 we will be talking about the shepherd's *relationship* to his sheep, in verses 7–10 the shepherd's *provision* for his sheep, and in verses 11–18 the shepherd's *heart* for his sheep.

The Shepherd's Relationship to His Sheep (vv. 1–6)

First of all, the shepherd's relationship to his sheep is one of *familiarity*.

> Truly, truly, I say to you, he who does not enter the sheepfold by the door but climbs in by another way, that man is a thief and a robber. But he who enters by the door is the shepherd of the sheep. To him the gatekeeper opens. The sheep hear his voice, and he calls his own sheep by name and leads them out. (vv. 1–3)

Jewish shepherds kept their sheep in two kinds of sheepfolds. If they were out in the country, the sheepfold was like a low-walled corral made of stone with a narrow opening in front. If they were in town, the fold was much bigger and structurally sounder, and it was a communal corral. Often it had a professional gatekeeper. The communal corral is the image our Lord referred to here. He pictured the shepherd coming up to the corral, his automatic recognition by the gatekeeper, his admission into the fold, and his walk among the multitude of mixed flocks. To the uninitiated that would look like an insoluble problem for the shepherd, but the shepherd would begin to talk to his sheep in a characteristic sing-song way to which only *his* sheep would respond. In this way he would separate out his flock, and they would follow him out to pasture.

In verse 3 Jesus said that the sheep "hear his voice." The idea is familiarity. Sometimes travelers to the Middle East have been known to pay a shepherd to exchange clothes with them and then try to call the sheep, but the sheep do not come because the sheep only obey the voice they know. Even though sheep may be stupid, they know their master's voice. Jesus also said in verse 3 that he "calls his own sheep by name." Palestinian shepherds named their sheep according to their characteristics. One might be called Long Nose or Black Ear or Fluffy. This shows how much our Lord cares for us. He calls us by our own characteristics, and we hear his voice and follow him.

But this is just a hint of the familiarity the sheep have with the shepherd. If we look down a few verses (14, 15) we read, "I am the good shepherd. I know my own and my own know me, just as the Father knows me and I know the Father." Jesus knows us just as well as he knows his Father—with intimate knowledge. This is one of the most staggering suggestions to be found anywhere in Scripture. How does the Father know the Son, who is one with him? There could be no more dramatic expression of intimacy than how the

Father knows the Son. But incredibly Jesus says, "I know my own . . . just as the Father knows me and I know the Father." There could be no knowledge more intimate than his knowledge of the Father, and there is no knowledge more intimate than that which he has of us! His knowledge extends into the deepest part of our lives. It even goes back beyond birth.

> My frame was not hidden from you,
> when I was being made in secret,
>   intricately woven in the depths of the earth.
> Your eyes saw my unformed substance;
> in your book were written, every one of them,
>   the days that were formed for me,
>   when as yet there was none of them. (Psalm 139:15, 16)

Jesus knows us in the most profound ways. He knows our past with its failures, its hurts. He knows our present, our unrealized longings. He knows us in the most intimate ways. He knows our idiosyncrasies. He calls us by our characteristics. I sometimes wonder if he calls us some of the things we would not want to be called. It is quite possible he affectionately calls us "Grumpy" or "Fearful" or "Faithless," just as we might talk to our sheep if we were shepherds.

It is encouraging to think that not only does he know us, but we know him! "They will listen to my voice" (v. 16). We know Jesus' voice. We know what it sounds like. "I know my own and my own know me, just as the Father knows me and I know the Father." We probably know him better than we think we do. We hear his voice, and we respond, and he meets our deepest needs.

Os Guinness tells a story about Ingmar Bergman, the great Swedish film-maker who one day while listening to Stravinsky had a vision of a nineteenth-century cathedral. In the vision Bergman found himself wandering about the great building, finally coming before a picture of Christ. Realizing its importance Bergman said to the picture, "Speak to me! I will not leave this cathedral until you speak to me!" Of course the picture did not speak, and that same year Bergman produced *The Silence*, a film about characters who despair of ever finding God. That was Bergman's interpretation of life. But Scripture reveals that Christ knows believers, and they know him in the most deep and satisfying relationships possible.

The Lord adds in verse 4, "When he has brought out all his own, he goes before them, and the sheep follow him, for they know his voice." If you are outside the fold, the shepherd offers you an eternal relationship of peace and joy, a relationship modeled on that between the Father and the Son, a relationship that satisfies. If you are one of his sheep, that relationship is the foundational reality of your existence. If we are believers, we have such a relationship and must appropriate its benefits.

In verse 6 John interjects with the response of those who were listening.

> This figure of speech Jesus used with them, but they did not understand what he was saying to them.

They understood the picture but did not understand the deep spiritual realities. So our Lord began to explain further.

The Shepherd's Provision for His Sheep (vv. 7–10)

> So Jesus again said to them, "Truly, truly, I say to you, I am the door of the sheep. All who came before me are thieves and robbers, but the sheep did not listen to them. I am the door. If anyone enters by me, he will be saved and will go in and out and find pasture. The thief comes only to steal and kill and destroy. I came that they may have life and have it abundantly." (vv. 7–10)

What does the Lord mean by referring to himself as the "door" or gate? When G. Campbell Morgan was traveling across the Atlantic on a steamer, he noticed that among the passengers was Sir George Adam Smith, the most famous Old Testament scholar at the time. The greatest preacher of the day (Morgan) and the greatest Old Testament scholar (Smith) had a great time as they traveled together. Morgan said that among the tales Sir George told of the East was this one:

> He was one day traveling with a guide, and came across a shepherd and his sheep. He fell into conversation with him. The man showed him the fold into which the sheep were led at night. It consisted of four walls, with a way in. Sir George said to him, "That is where they go at night?" "Yes," said the shepherd, "and when they are in there, they are perfectly safe." "But there is no door," said Sir George. "I am the door," said the shepherd. He was not a Christian man, he was not speaking in the language of the New Testament. He was speaking from the Arab shepherd's standpoint. Sir George looked at him and said, "What do you mean by the door?" Said the shepherd, "When the light has gone, and all the sheep are inside, I lie in the open space, and no sheep ever goes out but across my body, and no wolf comes in unless he crosses my body; I am the door."[2]

That is our Lord's meaning in this passage. Jesus was saying, "I am the living door. In order to go into the fold, you must go through me. Likewise, to go out to pasture, you must go through me. As the door I am the protector and I am the provider. When you come in the door, you are not only saved, but you are safe. When you go out through me, you go out to pasture. I am the provider. Nobody is coming through that door except the one who comes through me." In the last part of verse 9, Jesus was saying that the saved go in and out and find pasture, which leads to the claim in verse 10: "That they may have life and have it abundantly." Christ provides abundant life for his sheep. What is abundant life? Many suppose it is an abundance of things. Not so! Money can buy many things—it can even buy a pasture; but it cannot buy satisfaction.

Scripture portrays the great shepherd leading his sheep into green pastures beside still waters, pursuing the strays, keeping them away from the poisonous plants, taking them to the good water, making sure they have life and abundance, providing everything for their health. What is the qualification to obtain all this? Is it to be a brilliant sheep, a beautiful sheep, or an energetic sheep? No. It is just to be a sheep that follows the shepherd wherever he leads, knowing that the shepherd knows what is best for the sheep.

The Shepherd's Heart for His Sheep (vv. 11–18)

I am the good shepherd. The good shepherd lays down his life for the sheep. He who is a hired hand and not a shepherd, who does not own the sheep, sees the wolf coming and leaves the sheep and flees, and the wolf snatches them and scatters them. He flees because he is a hired hand and cares nothing for the sheep. I am the good shepherd. I know my own and my own know me, just as the Father knows me and I know the Father; and I lay down my life for the sheep. (vv. 11–15)

In Matthew 9:36 we read about Jesus having compassion because he saw his sheep scattered and cast down. The word translated "compassion" there conveys the idea that he felt it in his stomach. His stomach turned with compassion. Our Lord is no hireling, like some shepherds who come to us today. His heart was full of sacrificial love. Notice that four times Scripture says Christ laid down his life for the sheep—the last part of verse 11, "The good shepherd lays down his life for the sheep"; the last part of verse 15, "I lay down my life for the sheep"; the last part of verse 17, "I lay down my life that I may take it up again"; and verse 18, "No one takes it from me, but I lay it down of my own accord. I have authority to lay it down, and I have authority to take it up again." This is like a refrain from the Lord's own personal song with each stanza ending, "I lay down my life for my sheep." Such is the Good Shepherd's heart.

Christ devoted his whole life to us each day and finally gave it in an act of supreme sacrifice. He laid it down of his own initiative. The soldiers did not capture Jesus at Gethsemane. He could have called ten thousand angels if he had wanted to. His very words cast them back, but he gave himself up. Also, how does the Scripture describe his death on the cross? "He . . . gave up his spirit" (19:30).

That is the heart of our shepherd. He laid down his life for the sheep.

Conclusion

Jesus says in verse 11, "I am the good shepherd." In verse 14 he repeats, "I am the good shepherd." Two different Greek words are sometimes rendered "good" in our English translation. Often it will be *agathos*, which means "good, morally and intrinsically." Sometimes it will be *kalos*, which has more of the meaning of "beautiful." So some translators render the two phrases, "I am the shepherd, the beautiful shepherd." I think that fits the passage. Years ago Spurgeon caught the feeling of this and proclaimed:

> There is more in Jesus, the good Shepherd, than you can pack away in a shepherd. He is the good, the great, the chief Shepherd; but he is much more. Emblems to set him forth may be multiplied as the drops of the morning, but the whole multitude will fail to reflect all his brightness. Creation is too small a frame in which to hang his likeness. Human thought is too contracted, human speech too feeble, to set him forth to the full. . . . He is inconceivably above our conceptions, unutterably above our utterances.[3]

Such is the shepherd we proclaim. He is altogether lovely—this beautiful Jesus, our shepherd. Why is he so beautiful? Because of the way he relates to us, calls us by name, and knows us, and because we know him and he sees to our every need. Why is he so beautiful? Because he is the door, and when we go in, we find protection and salvation. And when we go out, we find pasture and abundant life. Why is he so beautiful? Because of his heart. Because he laid down his life for his sheep. And he offers us all a place with him.

> I have other sheep that are not of this fold. I must bring them also, and they will listen to my voice. So there will be one flock, one shepherd. (v. 16)

Did you know you are in the Bible? Me, too. I am not a Hebrew, but I am in the Bible. I am one of the "other sheep." Even better than that, before the foundation of the world, my name was in his book, and so was yours if you let Christ be your Savior and shepherd. How do you do that? He says, "I am the door." When he laid down his life, he became the door of salvation and the door of abundant life.

Jesus says, "I am the door." He says in another place, "I am the way." And he is. There is no other way to God but through the door, Jesus Christ. If you have never received this relationship, this provision, this heart, submit yourself to the shepherd as Lord and Bishop of your soul today. And if you are already one of his sheep, God wants you to enjoy the benefits of being in his flock. He is the beautiful shepherd. Worship him in your heart day by day.

34

The Good Shepherd, Part II

JOHN 10:19–30; PSALM 23

AS WE SAID IN OUR STUDY of the first part of John 10, the beautiful Scriptural image of the Good Shepherd and his sheep is a picture of deepest intimacy. Out of that intimacy flows Christ's protection and provision because he is the door or the gate for the sheep. Going in through him, sheep find safety and protection. Passing out through him, sheep find pasture and provision. This image tugs at our hearts because we want to be protected and we want to be provided for.

As we saw earlier, four times our Lord said that he, the Good Shepherd, laid down his life for the sheep. Christ is the Good Shepherd, the beautiful shepherd. He is altogether lovely. Some responded to the Savior's tender invitation, but generally there was a reaction of recrimination and division (vv. 19–21).

Between verses 21 and 22, two months passed. It was time for another great feast.

> At that time the Feast of Dedication took place at Jerusalem. It was winter, and Jesus was walking in the temple, in the colonnade of Solomon. (vv. 22, 23)

The Feast of Dedication took place on the twenty-fifth day of the Jewish month of Chislev, the same month as our December. So this event took place on our Christmas. The Feast of Dedication was the newest of feasts. In fact, some of those there had heard stories from their great-great-grandfathers, who had heard them from their great-great-grandfathers about how in 175 BC a madman named Antiochus Epiphanes came to rule over the area and attempted to mix Hebrew and Greek culture. In doing so, he desecrated the temple, forced pork down the priests' throats, turned the chambers of the temple into a brothel, and converted the altar meant for burnt offerings into an altar for Zeus! But those were also the great days of Judas Maccabaeus, who fought against Antiochus and defeated him. There came a great day when Maccabaeus cleansed the temple and consecrated it. We read his own words in the noncanonical book of First Maccabees:

> That every year at that season the days of the dedication of the altar should be observed with gladness and joy for eight days, beginning with the 25th day of the month of Chislev. (4:59)

In keeping with these words, every house in Jerusalem had eight candles in the window on the 25th of Chislev. It was, in modern terms, Hanukkah.

John's account tells us that on that winter day Jesus was walking in the temple on the porch of Solomon. We can imagine our Lord framed by massive white colonnades rising forty-five feet to a beautifully detailed cedar ceiling, and looking eastward through those colonnades he enjoyed a magnificent view of the Mount of Olives. Our Lord was surrounded by well-wishers, detractors, and enemies. Scripture specifically tells us in verse 24 that the Jews had gathered around him and were saying to him, "How long will you keep us in suspense? If you are the Christ, tell us plainly." They wanted an answer immediately as to who he was. In answering their question our Lord queried their spiritual status and reached back two months to appropriate again the symbol of the shepherd and the sheep.

> Jesus answered them, "I told you, and you do not believe. The works that I do in my Father's name bear witness about me, but you do not believe because you are not among my sheep." (vv. 25, 26)

In other words, "Because you are not my sheep, you do not understand." Notice also verse 27: "My sheep hear my voice, and I know them, and they follow me." Then in verse 28 and following, Christ gives the most powerful and graphic statement of spiritual standing in all the Gospels. In order to appreciate what Christ was saying, we need to consider the background found in the 23rd Psalm, the most unforgettable of all the Psalms. Everyone with any Christian or Jewish heritage at all is familiar with it. It pervades great literature as well. In Shakespeare's *Henry V*, a maid described Sir John Falstaff's death: "Falstaff said, 'God, God, God;' he plucked at the sheet, and then babbled o' green fields." Even though he was evil, the truth of Psalm 23 in his subconscious surfaced as he was dying.[1]

Psalm 23 conveys great comfort. At the end of life we often repeat it, and it is repeated back to us. Our children know that psalm. It is so easy to relate to young David out in the field. As he looked over his flocks, he began to think about them, and his thoughts went to the Shepherd. Then out came his harp, and under the Spirit's direction he composed the magnificent 23rd Psalm.

Psalm 23 is a psalm of status, parallel to John 10. We will consider *the Lord's provision* in the first three verses of Psalm 23, *the Lord's direction* of us at the end of the third verse, *the Lord's protection* in verse 4, and in verses 5, 6 *the Lord's exaltation* of his flock.

The Lord's Provision for Us (Psalm 23:1–3a)

What does our Lord provide for his flock? Look at the first few verses of our psalm:

> The LORD is my shepherd; I shall not want.
>   He makes me lie down in green pastures.
> He leads me beside still waters.
>   He restores my soul.

We discussed earlier a phenomenon that shepherds call being cast or cast down, a situation when sheep get into a position from which they cannot get back on their feet. In 1975 some friends of mine, Clem and Laura Jervis and Clarence and Betty Wyngarden, were vacationing in England. They were in Shakespeare country, in the Cotswolds to be exact. One afternoon they decided to take a drive into the back country. As they navigated a country road, Wyngarden, a medical doctor, noticed a flock of sheep. One of the sheep was away from the rest of them, and he noticed it had all four of its feet up in the air. He assumed it was dead. But as he drove on a little further he began to reflect, "I'll bet that is a cast sheep." He and Clem discussed the matter a bit and finally decided to turn around to investigate, only to discover that the sheep was fat, pregnant, unshorn, overloaded with wool, and lying flat on her back and bleating urgently for help. The task took both of their efforts, but they managed to get that poor old ewe back on her feet, and when they did get her up, she staggered around like a drunken sailor. They steadied her, and Dr. Wyngarden massaged her legs to get her circulation going. Finally she bleated her thank you and wandered off toward the flock.

The men said they learned from that experience that sheep are not theoretically helpless—they are *absolutely* helpless. Medically, being cast is often terminal for the sheep, because as the animal lies on its back its cavity fills with gases that retard the circulation to its limbs. On a hot day a sheep will die in just a couple of hours. In cool weather it may linger for a few days. But the point is, there is nothing the sheep can do for itself. Nothing! It is absolutely helpless. Even without enemies sheep need to have a shepherd attentively watching over them twenty-four hours a day.

Verse 3 ("he restores my soul") pictures a cast sheep with all four feet in the air, an animal absolutely helpless and bleating mournfully. Then the shepherd comes and sets it on its feet. That image is so completely true to our experience because we often get fat and lazy and perhaps grow a little too much wool (or riches or prominence or success), and we find ourselves looking for a place where we can kind of nestle down and let life go by. But when we do this, we suddenly find ourselves cast, and the more we wiggle and squirm, the more difficult and dangerous is the position we are in. Then we begin to bleat, and along comes our Shepherd to set us on our feet again. He massages us and pats us and says, "Won't you ever learn to stay close to me, to not go your own way, to realize the necessity of your dependence on me?" That is what our God is like. Such is our privileged status.

As we move back to verse 1 we read, "The LORD is my shepherd; I shall not want." David knew that as a young shepherd he sometimes failed. Sometimes he did not provide adequate forage. He knew it was possible for one of his sheep to be cast and lost. But as one of God's sheep, he had no fear. "The LORD is my shepherd," said David. If he were alive today, he would probably say, "The Lord God who cast 250 million times 250 million stars across the universe is my shepherd! The Lord, who set me on this little speck of interstellar dust that is so small that from the nearest star with the greatest telescope it cannot be seen, is my shepherd."

The intimacy of Psalm 23 is what draws us to it. Seventeen times it mentions "I," "my," or "me." "The Lord is *my* shepherd." "He makes *me* lie down in green pastures." "He leads *me* beside still waters. He restores *my* soul." "He leads *me* in paths of righteousness." "You are with *me*; your rod and your staff, they comfort *me*." "You prepare a table before *me* in the presence of *my* enemies." "You anoint *my* head with oil; *my* cup overflows." "Surely goodness and mercy shall follow *me* all the days of *my* life." What spiritual intimacy is ours! The Lord is *my* shepherd. Wonders upon wonders! Is he your shepherd? Can you say, "The Lord is *my* shepherd"?

What is the effect of this status in our lives? We lack nothing we need. We may not have riches, but we will not lack. We may not have what our neighbors have, but we will not lack. Our beautiful shepherd supplies all our needs. He makes us lie down in green pastures. He leads us beside still waters. This is important because sheep will not drink from rushing water. Sometimes a shepherd has to dam a stream in order to get the sheep to drink because they are so timid and are frightened so easily. The shepherd also beds them down in green meadows. Putting this in the light of the New Testament, Christ takes us to places where we can feed ourselves to full satisfaction, and then he refreshes us with the Holy Spirit. He restores our soul. He comes to us when we are cast down and depressed. "Why art you cast down, O my soul?" (Psalm 42:5, 11). When we turn to the Lord, he sets us on our feet and gets us going again. Are you cast down? Then these words are for you. Draw on your status. We are sheep. He is our shepherd.

The Lord's Direction of Us (Psalm 23:3b)

When the Lord gets us back on our feet, we can each say, "He leads me in paths of righteousness for his name's sake." Left to ourselves we are all wanderers. "All we like sheep have gone astray; we have turned—every one—to his own way" (Isaiah 53:6). "There is a way that seems right to a man, but its end is the way to death" (Proverbs 14:12). "Prone to wander, Lord, I feel it. Prone to leave the God I love," says the old hymn truly. We are wanderers at heart, but Christ guides us in the paths of righteousness. Sometimes we follow him like good sheep. But at other times he has to guide us by standing in our way, keeping us from making a wrong choice. The Apostle Paul was in Mysia when he decided he wanted to go to Bithynia, but "the Spirit of Jesus did not allow them" to go there (Acts 16:7).

Sometimes the Lord stands in our way to hinder us and keep us on righteous paths, and he does it for his name's sake, to bring himself the glory he so richly deserves. He is acting according to his own character when he keeps us on the right path. He leads us, he hinders us, he uses his staff to pull us into place, all because of who he is. How wonderful it is to realize that the Lord keeps us on paths of righteousness because his reputation is on the line. That truth ought to comfort us.

The Lord's Protection of Us (Psalm 23:4)
> Even though I walk through the valley of the shadow of death,
>> I will fear no evil,
> for you are with me;
>> your rod and your staff,
>> they comfort me.

A valley was a place of danger because it afforded robbers and predators opportunities for ambush. We can be sure David was referring to the fears and dangers that come with death. That is why the psalm is so precious to those who are dying. But the force of the Hebrew also suggests something more, for the phrase can be translated, "The valley of deep gloom" or literally, "dense darkness." Mitchell DeHood says it means "in the midst of total darkness," which suggests David meant those times of gloom and despair when we approach or even enter spiritual depression. Both the spiritual and unspiritual experience this. It happens to the best of Christians.

Martin Luther was a man who was subject to deep, dark depressions, sometimes for several days. Once he was in one of his depressions, and poor Mrs. Luther had just about had it with Martin. She went in, put on her funeral garb, and stood before him. When he lifted up his head, seeing his wife dressed in black, he asked, "What has happened?" She said, "The way you are acting you would think God is dead!" He got the point.

The great G. Campbell Morgan, who for ten years conducted a world-moving ministry at London's Westminster Chapel, said from his pulpit:

> During these ten years, I have known more of visions fading into mirages, of purposes failing of fulfillment, of things of strength crumbling away in weakness than ever in my life before.[2]

Yet he had rescued his church from almost certain failure and established it as one of the great gospel preaching places in all the world! It may be that God's servants who have been most highly favored suffer this gloom more than others. One thing we know for sure—the feeling is common to humanity.

David said: "Even though *I* walk through the valley of the shadow of death. . . ." Characteristic of this despair is a sense of being alone. Although the psalmist pictured himself among a flock of sheep, the word he used was "I," stressing his aloneness. None of us is immune to this. We go to church, we love the people there, we give our friends genuine smiles, but oftentimes within us is a feeling of aloneness and despair. We do not want to spread our gloom, so we pull ourselves together and smile. Many of God's people at any given time are in the valley and are cast down. We need to appropriate again and again the comfort and power of David's opening words: "The Lord is *my* shepherd."

When we look to the Shepherd we will "fear no evil." When we are cast down, one of our biggest problems is fear. When we are cast, we tend to worry about more trouble than ever comes. As an old saying states, "We die a thousand deaths fearing one." But David said, "I will fear no evil." Why? "For you are with me." At a mountain retreat when I was a college pastor some years ago, my young boys were walking with one of the college boys who was quite a character. They were looking at the wildlife—squirrels and so on—and they said, "Rick, are there other animals out here?" Rick answered, "Well, there is the giant tree sloth and the giant sea behemoth." Naturally my boys grabbed on to him. Then he said, "Don't worry, you're with Rick!"

"You are with me." Can we think of a better reason not to fear? We have the Lion of the Tribe of Judah walking beside us! I recall the story of a man who was in a Communist prison. His captors would periodically take him out of solitary confinement, apply hot tongs to his body, then return him to his cell. In the midst of this, he so felt the presence of the Lord and his angels that he regularly danced in his cell—even after months of torture. "I will fear no evil, for you are with me; your rod [a weapon to use against attackers] and your staff [to pull sheep out of the hard places they fall into], they comfort me." This marvelous protection comes from the One who is our Shepherd and our Savior. Are you enjoying that protection? Do you have freedom from fear and want?

As we come to verses 5, 6 we have stretched the sheep-shepherd metaphor to the limit, so David changes the picture to a Bedouin encampment. Also, at this point the feeling of intimacy intensifies because instead of talking about God in the third person, David now speaks to God directly. "You prepare a table before me. . . . you anoint my head with oil."

The Lord's Exaltation of Us (Psalm 23:5, 6)

> You prepare a table before me
>> in the presence of my enemies;
> you anoint my head with oil;
>> my cup overflows. (v. 5)

It sounds as if David had been chased across the desert and had come into a camp where he found friends. In contrast to all of the horror he had been experiencing, he now finds a table bountifully, not scantily, set before him. His hosts pour oil upon his head to refresh him. That is the imagery here. David concludes with a great prospect that comes from retrospect.

> Surely goodness and mercy shall follow me
>> all the days of my life,
> and I shall dwell in the house of the LORD forever. (v. 6)

The word "follow" means "pursue." Instead of being pursued by enemies, he is now pursued by goodness and kindness. David concludes this magnificent psalm with a rapturous ecstasy: "And I shall dwell in the house of the Lord forever."

Conclusion

At the celebration in John 10, on that winter day on Solomon's porch, Christ said:

> My sheep hear my voice, and I know them, and they follow me. I give them eternal life, and they will never perish, and no one will snatch them out of my hand. My Father, who has given them to me, is greater than all, and no one is able to snatch them out of the Father's hand. I and the Father are one. (vv. 27–30)

When my children were little, my wife Barbara and I delighted in taking them for walks. Our children enjoyed it too because they would slip their pudgy little hands into each of ours, and as we walked along the sidewalk, whenever we came to a curb, they could feel our grip tighten so that all they had to do was lift their little legs and they floated right over the obstacle. When we recognize our status as depicted in Psalm 23 and combine it with the words of John 10, we understand that Christ is saying that our safety does not depend on our immature, futile grip upon him, but on his hold on us. How comforting! "No one will snatch them out of *my hand*" (v. 28). Then in verse 29 Jesus says, "No one is able to snatch them out of *the Father's hand.*" One hand (the Son's) is wrapped around us, and another (the Father's) is wrapped around that hand, so that we are doubly safe.

This brings soothing balm to those of us who are true children of God. He holds on to us! The saying "you can't have your cake and eat it too" is true. I have never eaten a piece of birthday cake and had it to eat again. But this rule does not apply to spiritual consolations. You can enjoy a promise, and you can have it again, and you can have it again. In fact, the more you partake of the promise, the more you can partake of it the next time. The greater the sweetness you extract from these verses, the sweeter they will be the next time.

Both Psalm 23 and John 10 were written to people who consider themselves to be sheep. Do you consider yourself one of God's sheep? If so, then appropriate your status as part of the Good Shepherd's flock. Are you going through a dark valley? Are you afraid? Remember that your Shepherd is with you. Are you cast down? All four feet in the air and there is nothing you can do? Depressed? Helpless? Cry out to your Shepherd. He will pick you up, love you, and get you back into the flock.

35

"Lazarus, Come Out!"

JOHN 11:1–46

DR. KENNETH MEYER tells about flying into Chicago's O'Hare Airport on a certain occasion. As the big plane passed over the expressway, Meyer noticed a colossal traffic jam. He also saw that many people were getting out of their cars. Some were standing on their bumpers, straining to see what was going on. As Dr. Meyer glanced northward, he saw what they could not possibly see—the telltale flash of red lights. Meyer knew the problem would be taken care of quickly, so after the plane landed at O'Hare and he proceeded toward his car, he had a completely different perspective from the average traveler on the expressway. He knew he would soon be home. Perspective makes all the difference. We are earthbound creatures, but if we could somehow look down upon the traffic jams in our lives, we would react much differently.

That is precisely the case in the story of the young shepherd David and the armies of Israel as they stood before Goliath. They had fled from Goliath in great fear, but David calmly stood there and said, "Who is this uncircumcised Philistine, that he should defy the armies of the living God?" (1 Samuel 17:26). Before the day was over, with his sling whirling overhead, David was running full blast at that great giant. You know the rest of the story. David let go, and the stone hit Goliath right between the running lights. Israel prevailed that day. The difference was one of perspective. The Israelites saw everything from ground level. David had the divine perspective.

Perspective also brought a turning point in the prophet Habakkuk's life. As he looked at his own people Israel, he saw oppression and ethical impropriety. It looked as if God's sense of justice was gone.

O Lord, how long must I call for help before you will listen? I shout to you in vain; there is no answer. "Help! Murder!" I cry, but no one comes to save. Must I forever see this sin and sadness all around me? (Habakkuk 1:2 TLB)

Then, by faith, he met God, and he then had the divine perspective. Therefore, he concluded his great book by saying:

Though the fig tree should not blossom,
    nor fruit be on the vines,
the produce of the olive fail
    and the fields yield no food,
the flock be cut off from the fold
    and there be no herd in the stalls,
yet I will rejoice in the LORD;
    I will take joy in the God of my salvation. (3:17, 18)

Our perspective makes all the difference! Do we see our problems from above or from ground level?

In the story of Lazarus' death and resurrection in John 11, both perspectives are evident. We see the ground-level perspective in Mary and Martha and the divine perspective in our Lord. This passage is good medicine for our hearts because Lazarus' death is symbolic of the extremities we encounter in life, the difficulties that come to all of us, whether the death of a loved one, the loss of our position, or the erring of a child. Lazarus' death symbolizes all of these things. Our Lord's approach also shows us how our heavenly Father deals with us in the midst of the problems we face. This story teaches us about *perspective*.

Introductory Background to the Miracle (vv. 1–16)

After the final confrontation in the temple, our Lord went to the wilderness to carry on his ministry (10:40). The last verse in John 10 says, "And many believed in him there." His ministry was fruitful. But while he was there, a personal emergency arose in Bethany. We read about it in the first part of chapter 11:

Now a certain man was ill, Lazarus of Bethany, the village of Mary and her sister Martha. It was Mary who anointed the Lord with ointment and wiped his feet with her hair, whose brother Lazarus was ill. (vv. 1, 2)

The emergency involved a special small family of three. Mary loved to sit at our Lord's feet and contemplate him and his teachings. Martha was just as devout but was a busy, kinetic soul who seemed to have the gift of service. Then there was Lazarus. From what we can gather, he must have been their younger brother because he seems to have had no responsibilities in the family. This family was very dear to our Lord. He had a unique personal affection for them. We know from the other Gospels that our Lord liked being in their home. It was a place where he could slip off his sandals and relax and, humanly speaking, be himself. The hospitality of this little home was famous with the apostolic band.

But now things had changed, and the household was in disarray because Lazarus was gravely ill. It appeared that he could die at any time. Pale, worried women were scurrying about the house. No wonder they sent for our Lord. Notice the message in verse 3: "So the sisters sent to him, saying, 'Lord, he whom you love is ill.'"

This was not an invitation or even a request. They did not say, "Lord, please come." They just assumed that as soon as the Lord learned of the situation, he would hurry there. They knew Jesus. They understood his wonderful compassion. The word they used for "love" is the word for friendship. They were saying, "Your good friend whom you love is sick." Of course Jesus would come—to think otherwise was inconceivable. But Jesus' answer in verse 4 gives us a hint of what was going to happen.

> But when Jesus heard it he said, "This illness does not lead to death. It is for the glory of God, so that the Son of God may be glorified through it."

In other words, death would not be the ultimate tragedy here. Something very unusual was about to happen, and it would bring Christ glory. The heart of this text comes in verses 5, 6:

> Now Jesus loved Martha and her sister and Lazarus. So, when he heard that Lazarus was ill, he stayed two days longer in the place where he was.

The word translated "loved" here is a different word than the sisters used. It is the word *agape*—that unstoppable, highest type of love, the love of God. Christ loves us with that kind of love. Knowing this, we might expect Scripture to say, "Jesus, upon hearing that Lazarus was sick, went to one of his disciples, found a horse, and rode as fast as he could to be with Lazarus!" But that is not what our text says. Our text says he loved Mary, Martha, and Lazarus so much that he stayed away. Incredible!

From ground level it sometimes appears to us that even though we are Christ's children and we love him, he does not care about us anymore. At times, humanly speaking, our circumstances seem to admit no other interpretation than that. I think about Joseph being sold by his brothers into slavery. He ended up in Potiphar's household, and by hard work, integrity, and devotion he rose to the top—only to be toppled because he would not compromise himself with Mrs. Potiphar. As a result, he ended up in a foul Egyptian jail. From ground level it appeared that God had forsaken him. Joseph had honored God as a young man, but it seemed God did not care about him any longer. When a child dies in his mother's arms as she cries to God for help and the ambulance lies stalled two blocks away, we wonder if God cares. When a Christian is falsely accused and pleads with God to bring the evidence to clear him, and it is only after his reputation is ruined that the evidence comes, we wonder if God cares. When we plan some great event for God and the whole thing falls through, we wonder if God cares. We must be honest and admit that at ground level there are times when it is very difficult to keep believing in the goodness of God.

But John 11 elevates our perspective. It explains to Christ's praying, devoted children that no matter how it may appear, these inexplicable delays are delays of love. That is what our text says! When we are being ravaged by the events of life, it is very difficult to believe that God really loves us. But John 11 and many other Scriptures clearly claim that these delays are delays of love. God is all-powerful. He can do anything. He knows all. He even knows when a sparrow falls to the ground. He knows our plight, and he cares!

How can we earthbound creatures come to understand God's love, to really believe it despite our crises? First of all, we must recognize that we never comprehend his workings in their completeness. When delays and hardships come to us, we cannot expect to know all the details, all the answers, all the reasons. If we spent all our time asking why, we would be using our time very unprofitably.

The general principle is this: *Christ delayed coming to his faithful, loving followers in Bethany in order to strengthen their love and their faith.* For two days our Lord calmly went about his work far away from his anguished ones. They probably went outside each hour to see if their Lord was approaching, then went back in to Lazarus, whose life was ebbing away, then went out again to look for Jesus. After two days the Lord decided it was time to respond to the sisters' urgent message.

Then after this he said to the disciples, "Let us go to Judea again." The disciples said to him, "Rabbi, the Jews were just now seeking to stone you, and are you going there again?" Jesus answered, "Are there not twelve hours in the day? If anyone walks in the day, he does not stumble, because he sees the light of this world. But if anyone walks in the night, he stumbles, because the light is not in him." After saying these things, he said to them, "Our friend Lazarus has fallen asleep, but I go to awaken him." The disciples said to him, "Lord, if he has fallen asleep, he will recover." Now Jesus had spoken of his death, but they thought that he meant taking rest in sleep. Then Jesus told them plainly, "Lazarus has died, and for your sake I am glad that I was not there, so that you may believe. But let us go to him." So Thomas, called the Twin, said to his fellow disciples, "Let us also go, that we may die with him." (vv. 7–16)

Good old Thomas! Always looking on the bright side! "Okay, men," he said, "put on your mourning clothes because we are going back to Jerusalem so that when they kill the Master, they'll kill us too." He was a bit on the gloomy side, but actually I believe Thomas voiced the thoughts of all the disciples. They could not believe Jesus was heading right back into the middle of trouble to visit a dead man!

And by now Lazarus was indeed dead. His uneven breathing had become less and less regular and finally stopped. His exhausted sisters' cry had gone up from that house to the streets around. They prepared Lazarus for burial, putting a white linen gown on him, poignantly called a traveling dress, and wrapped him lovingly with bandages and spices. Then Martha and Mary led a procession out to the grave. Women were customarily first since it was prejudicially believed that since the woman Eve first sinned, death came through her. At the grave there were some memorial speeches. Then the mourners formed sort of a gauntlet and wailed loudly as the sisters walked slowly toward home. By the time our Lord arrived in Bethany, it was the fourth day, the day when the ritual of mourning reached its highest point because the body was decaying, and there was no hope.

The Lord and Martha (vv. 17–29)

Now when Jesus came, he found that Lazarus had already been in the tomb four days. Bethany was near Jerusalem, about two miles off, and many of the Jews had come to Martha and Mary to console them concerning their brother. So when Martha heard that Jesus was coming, she went and met him, but Mary remained seated in the house. (vv. 17–20)

Martha had evidently been made quietly aware that the Lord was outside Bethany. She probably slipped out unobtrusively and went to the outskirts of town to meet him. There she stood, pale, grieving, weary, no doubt disheveled. Behind her was the shimmering Palestinian countryside in its heat. Before her, heavy with the dust of travel, were Jesus Christ and his men.

Martha looked at the Lord and said, "Lord, if you had been here, my brother would not have died" (v. 21). That refrain had probably come often from Martha's and Mary's lips in the past few days. The wait had been agonizing as they wondered, *When will the Lord get here?* Martha's words were almost a reproof to the Lord. But in verse 22 she caught herself: "But even now I know that whatever you ask from God, God will give you." At first she said what she honestly thought, then she decided she had better sound a little more orthodox.

Have you ever felt that way? "Where were you, Lord? You came too late. Where were you when my loved one died? Where were you when my marriage dissolved? Where were you when my parents divorced? Where were you when my father became an alcoholic? Where were you when I was cheated out of my promotion? Where were you when my child went astray?"

Please notice—the Lord did not reprove Martha for her words! It is not sinful to tell God how you feel. That may sound like heresy in the light of some things we have been taught, and I want to qualify it by saying that we should always be reverent toward God. He is God! We are his creatures and must ever bow to him. But that does not mean we are not allowed to express to him how we feel. Some of us have feelings that ought to be shared with God. The feelings are not necessarily right, but they are feelings that need to be brought honestly before God. But we do not, for fear of losing something. God is more patient and accepting than we realize (not to mention that he already knows our thoughts anyway, so we couldn't hide it even if we wanted to).

The problem here is caused by the misconception that New Testament Christianity requires that "good Christians" never cry or express their inner feelings. This view is in error! King David sorrowed and was disillusioned, and he expressed it to God—and it was canonized in Scripture. God did not reprove David. I cried when my grandmother died, even as I conducted her funeral. Although I had been sorrowing earlier, I had no idea of the grief that would come over me while I stood in the pulpit. It was a terrible experience. It was the longest short sermon I ever preached. Later I asked God some hard questions, and I imagine that if I come to a similar extremity, I will ask some of the same questions. But I will not be sinning by asking them.

God wants us to pour our hearts out to him. That is what he wanted from Habakkuk. That is what he accepted from David. That is what he allowed with Martha. Notice our Lord's response and Martha's subsequent confession: "Jesus said to her, 'Your brother will rise again'" (v. 23). And Martha replied in verse 24, "I know that he will rise again in the resurrection on the last day," as if she were saying, "I know, of course, but, Lord, what about the present? I'm hurting!"

> Jesus said to her, "I am the resurrection and the life. Whoever believes in me, though he die, yet shall he live, and everyone who lives and believes in me shall never die. Do you believe this?" (vv. 25, 26)

This is the sixth great "I am" statement recorded in the book of John. Notice Martha's further confession in verse 27: "Yes, Lord; I believe that you are the Christ, the Son of God, who is coming into the world." She had been tested with grief and loss, and she had allowed her Savior to bring her forth as gold refined in the fire. Her confession was as great as Peter's! This great believer, a remarkable woman of faith, was one of Jesus' favorites. We have to face the fact that even the most spiritual suffer difficulties, the delays of love. They ask the hard questions. But God meets them and elevates them.

While Martha was meeting our Lord, Mary was still in the house. As was traditional with funerals, the mourners were either sitting on the floor or on low stools they had brought. All Mary's and Martha's own furniture had been moved aside. After the sisters had returned from the grave, they had eaten a traditional meal of lentils, boiled eggs, and round loaves of bread, which by their shape symbolized that life was rolling on into eternity. I suspect that Mary had not eaten much since then. She too was probably disheveled in appearance because mourners were committed to not washing themselves or wearing sandals. And the mourning had reached its peak on this day because Lazarus' body had begun to decompose. She, of course, had no idea what had transpired between Martha and Jesus outside the house.

The Lord and Mary (vv. 30–37)

Now notice how our Lord entered into the sisters' grief.

> When she [Martha] had said this, she went and called her sister Mary, saying in private, "The Teacher is here and is calling for you." And when she heard it, she rose quickly and went to him. Now Jesus had not yet come into the village, but was still in the place where Martha had met him. When the Jews who were with her in the house, consoling her, saw Mary rise quickly and go out, they followed her, supposing that she was going to the tomb to weep there. Now when Mary came to where Jesus was and saw him, she fell at his feet, saying to him, "Lord, if you had been here, my brother would not have died." (vv. 28–32)

There was that refrain again. It was the mourning song on their lips. Then came one of the most beautiful and deepest truths in Scripture.

When Jesus saw her weeping, and the Jews who had come with her also weeping, he was deeply moved in his spirit and greatly troubled. (v. 33)

The word translated "was deeply moved" comes from an ancient Greek word that describes a horse snorting. When taken in this text's context, it implies that our Lord let out an involuntary gasp. The wind just went out of him. E. V. Riev translates this, "He gave way to such distress of spirit as made his body tremble." The point is, our Lord was so caught up in both sisters' emotion that he involuntarily gasped. He felt their sorrow with everything he had. Notice that the verse ends by saying he was "troubled." Mary's and Martha's sorrows were taken to his heart.

Verses 34, 35 go on, "And he said, 'Where have you laid him?' They said to him, 'Lord, come and see.' Jesus wept."

Jesus did not wail. That is not the word used here. The word means that tears ran down Jesus' face. We have a great God and Savior who loves us, who delays and stays away, who allows us to go through ultimate extremity, and then he comes and enters into our sorrow. He enters the sorrow that he could have prevented in such a way that he gasps, his whole body shudders, and he begins to weep. That is the perspective Christ wants us to have. If you are hurting, he wants you to know that he weeps with you. Jesus is not a stoic, impassible God. Neither is God the Father. Hebrews 1:3 says Jesus "is the radiance of the glory of God and the exact imprint of his nature." Since Jesus knows our pain, God too feels with us. John says, in the opening verses of his Gospel, "No one has ever seen God; the only God, who is at the Father's side, he has made him known" (1:18). In other words, Jesus is the exegesis of God. That is what the Greek literally says. We do not have a High Priest who cannot be touched with the feelings of our infirmities. Also, the eternal Father shares in our sorrows.

When my wife and I were young parents and our oldest child was in the first grade, we bought her a winter coat. We had intentionally bought a size too large, but it was a marvelous blue fluffy coat with gold buttons down the front. The day after we bought it, a most unusual thing happened in California. It rained. It was a perfect day to wear her coat. I never will forget how she looked as she went out the door—dressed in red boots, a blue coat with gold buttons, a little white knit hat, yellow yarn around her pigtails, and a red umbrella. We were so proud of her. It did not matter that her coat was a little long at the sleeves and at the hem. She was so happy and excited as she walked out the door and down the driveway. Barbara and I stood behind the foggy windowpanes, watching her go.

Then two little friends came down the street. Although I could not hear their words, I saw one of them point at her hair, and I knew what she was saying: "Your hair looks dumb!" Then she pointed at the hem of her coat, and my temperature went up because I knew just what she was saying about it. Then those little gals just walked off down the street. Holly, with her head hanging, walked slowly off to school. I wanted to come through that door and set those little girls straight! Do you know why I did not? My daughter would not grow to her potential if I always stepped in whenever she experienced difficulties with her friends. It would stunt her personal development. As a parent, I tempered my intervention in her life so she would become a whole person.

Do we sometimes feel God is too passive in connection with our trials? We cannot know all the particulars, but we know his delays are for our ultimate development. We also know that when affliction comes, we can pour our hearts out to him honestly and with no fear of rejection or reprisal, and he will weep with us.

> So the Jews said, "See how he loved him!" But some of them said, "Could not he who opened the eyes of the blind man also have kept this man from dying?" (vv. 36, 37)

After these mixed reactions, Jesus asked to be taken to the tomb.

A Miracle at the Tomb (vv. 38–44)

A typical tomb in those days had eight occupants. It was a hollowed-out room, perhaps in a hillside. It had three indentations on one side, three on the other, and two at the end. Lazarus' tomb could well have already been occupied by other bodies from previous years. Jesus asked that the stone be rolled away.

> Then Jesus, deeply moved again, came to the tomb. It was a cave, and a stone lay against it. Jesus said, "Take away the stone." Martha, the sister of the dead man, said to him, "Lord, by this time there will be an odor, for he has been dead four days." (vv. 38, 39)

I can understand how Martha felt. With all this misery, why open the grave and let the stench come out? Why look at the face of a putrefying corpse? She did not understand what Christ wanted to do.

Jesus said to her, "Did I not tell you that if you believed you would see the glory of God?" So they took away the stone. And Jesus lifted up his eyes and said, "Father, I thank you that you have heard me. I knew that you always hear me, but I said this on account of the people standing around, that they may believe that you sent me." (vv. 40–42)

Picture the scene. The stone was rolled away. They could see Lazarus' body, and possibly other bodies. The eager crowd pressed forward. Suddenly they grew quiet. The sisters, who had been weeping, stopped with a sense of expectation. Our Lord's eyes, which before had been weeping, were now aglow. Suddenly Jesus "cried out with a loud voice, 'Lazarus, come out'" (v. 43). He did not have to shout, but he wanted everyone to comprehend the drama.

The man who had died came out, his hands and feet bound with linen strips, and his face wrapped with a cloth. Jesus said to them, "Unbind him, and let him go." (v. 44)

As the crowd stared into the bowels of that grave, they saw movement. They saw Lazarus' body edge off the stone, then stand erect and emerge mummy-like into the sunlight. Mary and Martha feverishly began to unwrap him. Then came joyful carrying on as they wept over him, hugged him, and danced about in their bare feet. The funeral had become a party!

Conclusion

Perspective is everything. As believers, we know that all our times of sorrow will eventually turn into joy. Revelation 21:4 promises:

He will wipe away every tear from their eyes, and death shall be no more, neither shall there be mourning, nor crying, nor pain anymore, for the former things have passed away.

That is a wonderful verse about a fantastic future! But what about right now? We can choose our perspective. We can dwell among the traffic jams, standing on the bumpers, trying to see what in the world is going on, perhaps even discussing it with others. Or we can, choosing to believe Scriptures like John 11, be elevated above the traffic and see that help is on the way, that God is in control. His delays are delays of love! I believe that with all my heart. I believe it on the authority of Scripture. God's silence is a silence of love. He wants us to ask the big questions. He wants us to pour our hearts out to him. He cares so much that he enters into our sorrows. He is not an impassible, stoic God. Rather, he feels our pain and weeps along with our weeping. He understands us better than we understand ourselves. He brings joy and resurrection life into our afflictions. Believing him, we find peace and joy in the delays. What a positive, exciting, wonderful truth!

Where is your perspective? Is it down here in the traffic, standing on a bumper? Or is it from above, where Christ is seated at the right hand of God?

36

Eternal Profiles

JOHN 11:47–57; 12:1–11

JOHN 12:1–11 recounts the celebration dinner commemorating the resurrection of Lazarus, recorded in John 11:1–44. But we also need to be aware of what took place between those two events.

As we can well imagine, Lazarus' resurrection made the religious authorities a little nervous. Put in modern terms, it was *not* one of those incidents where the patient's vital signs temporarily cease and he experiences himself floating out of his body. Rather, this was the resurrection of a decaying corpse. From the opposition's point of view, this was absolutely devastating. Any time your star witness is a resurrected corpse, you have a pretty good case—in this instance, for the validity of Jesus Christ.

John describes the Pharisees' reaction in 11:47, 48:

> So the chief priests and the Pharisees gathered the council and said, "What are we to do? For this man performs many signs. If we let him go on like this, everyone will believe in him, and the Romans will come and take away both our place and our nation."

The dilemma seemed insoluble. They did not know where to look for a solution until Caiaphas came to their help. He was a Sadducee, which meant he did not believe in resurrection under any circumstances, although he was the high priest. Also, as a Sadducee he collaborated with the Romans. He did not want anyone rocking the boat, especially some peasant from Galilee. Having been high priest for sixteen years, he was highly educated, intelligent, but, as we see here, also a cynical and absolutely ruthless man.

> But one of them, Caiaphas, who was high priest that year, said to them, "You know nothing at all. Nor do you understand that it is better for you

that one man should die for the people, not that the whole nation should perish." (vv. 49, 50)

Roughly translated he was saying, "You fools! If you had any intelligence at all, you would see that the answer is very simple. It is better that one die rather than a whole nation." He was a cold, calculating, capable, self-sufficient, shrewd, self-satisfied ecclesiastical climber. He had come to the top of his profession. But I think if he would have felt under his crown, he would have found that his ears had grown long, rough, and hairy, like a donkey's. After all, like Balaam's donkey he was unwittingly giving a prophecy of Christ. John tells us that in verses 51, 52. He also tells us why:

> He did not say this of his own accord, but being high priest that year he prophesied that Jesus would die for the nation, and not for the nation only, but also to gather into one the children of God who are scattered abroad.

Caiaphas had unknowingly given a clear prophecy of the vicarious atonement of our Lord. John adds in verse 53, "So from that day on they made plans to put him to death." During the last days of our Lord's life on earth, he was the supreme outlaw of history!

The Passover was coming, and back in Jerusalem the very air was electric. There were tense conversations everywhere. Some were dangerously loud, others in careful tones. You could hear them on every hand. "Do you think he is really going to come?" "Have you seen those guards over at the temple? I've never seen so many there at one time!" "No, I don't think he'll chance it." "Well, I think he'll come."

Just six days before the Passover, our Lord was approaching Jerusalem. The city was thronged with priests. In just six days our Lord would be stretched on the cross to give his life for those who hated him. That is the setting for the opening verses of chapter 12.

> Six days before the Passover, Jesus therefore came to Bethany, where Lazarus was, whom Jesus had raised from the dead. So they gave a dinner for him there. Martha served, and Lazarus was one of those reclining with him at table. (vv. 1, 2)

Mark tells us that the house belonged to Simon the Leper (Mark 14:3). Matthew reveals that the rest of the disciples were there (Matthew 26:8). So evidently the table was set for at least seventeen. The dinner was a celebration, a "thank you, Jesus" dinner for Lazarus' resurrection. It was certainly a time of great joy, but it was also a demonstration of bravery on the part of the host, and when the authorities found out, they would not be happy.

Martha and Mary (vv. 2, 3)

"So they gave a dinner for him there. Martha served" (v. 2). That was what Martha loved to do. From what the Scriptures tell us about her, she was in her element. She was a guest in Simon the Leper's house, but she was in charge. No doubt she had been up the night before, getting things ready so at earliest dawn she could fire the oven. All day the aroma of a celebration meal had wafted through the rooms of the house. Nothing was too good for Jesus. Martha had used her best recipes, and she loved bringing course after course to Jesus and his men. They loved it too. She was doing her thing, and everybody was happy.

Good old Martha! In the past things had not always been quite so happy. Remember the other dinner for Jesus that Luke records? Remember how Mary had drifted off and Martha had said, "Lord, do you not care that my sister has left me to serve alone? Tell her then to help me"? But Jesus had said, "Martha, Martha, you are anxious and troubled about many things, but one thing is necessary. Mary has chosen the good portion, which will not be taken away from her" (Luke 10:40–42). What an embarrassing time that had been for both Mary and Martha. But at this dinner things were different. Even though Mary, who had no doubt been helping serve the meal, had wandered back to the feet of Jesus, Martha seemed to be at peace. What had happened?

Circumstances had not changed, but Martha had. She had not mistaken what the Lord said on the earlier occasion. He did not say she was supposed to become a Mary. That is good, because if she had, they probably would have starved! She understood that Jesus' insistence that Mary had chosen "the good portion" did not mean that serving in the kitchen and at the table was bad. She understood that Jesus was saying that her harried, depressed, unhappy attitude was separating her from him. She knew that service can be worship, if it is done with the right attitude.

Many of us are familiar with Romans 12:1. There Paul tells us to present our "bodies," our entire lives, as "spiritual worship." Martha understood that true worship also involves service. Preparing a meal can be worship. Fixing a bicycle can be worship. Balancing your checkbook can be worship. Taking a test in school can be worship. Professors' grading a test can be worship. Administering your own business can be worship. Attitude is the defining factor.

Catherine Booth, the wife of the founder of the Salvation Army, was a woman with immense gifts and a remarkable public ministry. Her son wrote in her biography:

> She began her public ministry when I, her eldest child, was five years old. But her own home was never neglected for what some would call—I doubt whether she would have so described it—the large sphere. Both alike had been opened to her by her God. She saw his purposes in both. In the humble duties of the kitchen table, her hands busy with the food, or in the nursery when the children were going to bed, or at the bedside of a sick child, she was working for God's glory.[1]

No matter if she ministered publicly or at home, Catherine Booth realized it was *all* worship for God.

I remember hearing about a sign hanging over a kitchen sink that said, "Divine service held here three times daily." That is really true. It could also apply to laboring over a lathe or a desk. Divine service occurs when the proper perspective is there. Martha knew that when her spirit was right, her service was akin to the dramatic outward worship by Mary.

The options are always before us. We can complain about those who are not doing their job, we can be sour, or we can do our work lovingly and gently. Those are the choices. The transcending point is that loving service is always the characteristic of those who have had their hearts truly touched by Christ.

That meal must have been a success. Good friends. Good food. Can you imagine the conversation around the table? Simon the Leper, or rather Simon the Ex-leper. Lazarus reclining at the table. And of course Jesus and the Twelve.

I can imagine Simon saying, "You cannot imagine what it was like! I saw the scabs fall off my hand! My fingers grew back in place! I reached up, and my eyebrows were there. I was healed!" Then perhaps Lazarus interrupted, saying, "Simon, that was nothing! I mean, that must have been great, but let me tell you what it was like for me. Hey, I died! I was gone *four* earth days. I went to Paradise. Boy, I saw all the biggies—Abraham, Moses, David. But I will tell you, the most amazing thing I saw was when I came back and walked out of that tomb. Peter's eyes were that big around."

As the meal progressed and the familiar glow of contentment settled on the apostolic band, Mary left the room. Mary had been influenced by an incident that had taken place earlier in Jesus' ministry. In fact, Luke described it in the seventh chapter of his Gospel. In that incident Jesus was reclining at dinner at the table of a curious Pharisee. The Pharisee had not been considerate.

He had not washed Jesus' feet or anointed his head, and as they were reclining with their feet away from the table, in came a prostitute. She was clutching a vial, and as she came to Jesus, she was intending to anoint Jesus' head. But she lost control and began to weep, and her tears fell on Jesus' feet, which were all dusty, making quite a mess. The prostitute did not know what to do, so she used her hair to clean his feet. As she did so, she was again overcome with emotion. So, according to Luke 7:38, "She . . . wiped them with the hair of her head and kissed his feet and anointed them with the ointment."

Mary undoubtedly had this incident in the back of her mind. She thought, *I want to do the same thing for Jesus. I want him to know how much I love him.* It was not an impetuous act. It was calculated. She knew exactly what she was doing. She left the room and, according to verse 3:

> Mary therefore took a pound of expensive ointment made from pure nard, and anointed the feet of Jesus and wiped his feet with her hair. The house was filled with the fragrance of the perfume.

What do we learn from Mary's actions? First, her action was very costly. Judas estimated the cost of that genuine spikenard ointment to be about 300 denarii, and a denarius was one day's wages. Calculated at four dollars an hour, which is not exactly high pay, it comes out somewhere in the neighborhood of $10,000! Poured onto Jesus' dusty feet! Whenever we lavish love upon Jesus, he will not reject it!

Mary gave her most treasured possession to Jesus, but our treasured possessions may not be worth as much as Mary's. That was true for Martha. I get the feeling that Martha did not care about perfume. She valued work, acts of service. Her sacrifice to Jesus was perspiration instead of perfume, and it was just as noble and just as valuable as Mary's sacrifice. At one time King David wanted to buy a field that belonged to Araunah the Jebusite. When Araunah found out David wanted it, he said, "All this, O king, Araunah gives to the king." But King David responded, as recorded in 2 Samuel 24:24, "No, but I will buy it from you for a price. I will not offer burnt offerings to the LORD my God that cost me nothing."

What would we give for Jesus? What is our most valued possession? For some of us it is our bank account. For others it is our position. For some it is a relationship. The question is, would we give it? Will we make it available for Jesus' use? Mary humbly gave her best to Jesus. As I understand this, she calculatingly got down on her knees and loosened her hair. Hair in that culture was symbolic of a woman's glory, and she lavished Jesus' feet with her glory.

She was self-forgetting. She was passionate. And the Lord did not restrain Mary (or the prostitute) from what she was doing. I would imagine that when the prostitute came and anointed his feet, our Lord might have been a little embarrassed. But he did not stop her. She and Mary were both passionate in their worship. There are times when we should not shy away from such open, passionate love and worship for Jesus. We should let our tears fall. Jesus said of Mary, "She has done a beautiful thing to me" (Matthew 26:10).

John adds at the end of verse 3, "The house was filled with the fragrance of the perfume." This tells us Mary did not use just a tiny pinch of spikenard to anoint Jesus. She broke the container. The aroma of Christ, so honoring to him and so refreshing to others, does not occur when we give him half our heart or half our pocketbook or half our talents or half our ambition or half our lives or half our boyfriend or half our girlfriend. It comes by giving him *everything*.

When Mary bent over Jesus' feet, she wiped the perfume away with her hair. And when she arose and went about serving, she spread that beautiful aroma around the house. This completely unself-conscious act given to Jesus turned out to be the very means by which the aroma of glory to our Lord was spread to others. As Mary humbly gave herself, with no thought of her own glory, she became a primary means of spreading the blessing.

If you are not a blessing to others, if knowing you does not make others think of Jesus, if your life seems dry and unprofitable, do what Mary did. Get down on your knees before Jesus and give him your all. Pour your life out before him.

Everyone at that meal saw an act of surpassing loveliness, except one. Judas saw it as an extravagant waste. "Why was this ointment not sold for three hundred denarii and given to the poor?" (v. 5). He sounded very impressive, sensitive, not a bad guy. But he was using ethically impressive words to disguise his greed, for Judas was a thief.

> He said this, not because he cared about the poor, but because he was a thief, and having charge of the moneybag he used to help himself to what was put into it. (v. 6)

Mary was a selfless, giving believer, but Judas was a selfish, greedy materialist! To the heart that has never met God, worship seems a most impractical, wasteful pursuit. Judas is a profile of Hell.

> Jesus said, "Leave her alone, so that she may keep it for the day of my burial. For the poor you always have with you, but you do not always have me." (vv. 7, 8)

Many commentators believe that because of her devotion (always sitting at Jesus' feet) Mary saw, more clearly than the rest, Christ's approaching death. I believe this is so. In this respect, G. Campbell Morgan has a beautiful thought: "I would rather be a successor to Mary of Bethany than to the whole crowd of the apostles." Mary certainly had a beautiful spiritual profile.

Lazarus (vv. 9–11)

> When the large crowd of the Jews learned that Jesus was there, they came, not only on account of him but also to see Lazarus, whom he had raised from the dead. So the chief priests made plans to put Lazarus to death as well, because on account of him many of the Jews were going away and believing in Jesus. (vv. 9–11)

Lazarus had become Jesus' star witness. I find that amazing because as I read the Gospels, I cannot find anything outstanding about Lazarus. It seems he never said anything worth recording, and perhaps he never did anything worth recording. Yet he ended up being one of the great witnesses for Christ. Why? The answer is not in what Lazarus did for Jesus. It is in what Jesus did for Lazarus.

Even though we do not possess the faintest trace of genius, and perhaps have little we can bring to Christ, yet if we were dead in our sins, and if over us a voice has cried, "Come forth," and if we have risen to newness of life and the Master has said, "Unbind him, and let him go," so that now we are free, then we have become unanswerable arguments for Jesus Christ. Every believer's life has been so changed that the only way it can be accounted for is the power of Christ. If we have new life and are fellowshiping with Christ, as was Lazarus, we are great arguments for the Gospel, unanswerable proofs of the reality of Jesus Christ.

Conclusion

Martha was serving with all she had. Mary was pouring out all she had before Jesus in compassionate, selfless worship. Lazarus was emblematic of new life in Christ. This is a remarkably complete picture and a microcosm of what happens when Jesus Christ touches the lives of those around him. In our lives, regardless of the breadth of years that separates us from the event; regardless of the years of service; regardless of our mental, intellectual, and spiritual attainments; one thing should be foremost in our lives: Christ has changed our lives!

Mary and Martha both gave their best, and they both spread an aroma— one with mundane acts of prosaic service, the other with exotic spikenard.

But both aromas came by pouring lives out in dedication to Jesus. When we do that, we can expect the fragrance of Christ to follow us.

Do we want our lives to be a fragrance, a blessing to others? If so, we need to get down on our knees at Jesus' feet and anoint them, giving him everything.

37

A New Kind of Royalty

JOHN 12:12–26

ON DECEMBER 4, 1977, in Bangui, capital of the Central African Empire, the world press witnessed the coronation of his Imperial Majesty, Bokassa I. The price tag for that one event, designed and choreographed by French designer Olivier Brice, was $25 million. At 10:10 a.m. that morning the blare of trumpets and the roll of drums announced the approach of His Majesty. The procession began with eight of Bokassa's twenty-nine official children parading down the royal carpet to their seats. They were followed by Jean Bedel Bokassa II, heir to the throne, dressed in a white admiral's uniform with gold braid. He was seated on a red pillow to the left of the throne. Catherine followed, the favorite of Bokassa's nine wives. She was wearing a $73,000 gown made by Lanvin of Paris, strewn with pearls she had picked out herself. The emperor had arrived in a gold eagle-bedecked imperial coach drawn by six matched Anglo-Norman horses. He wore a thirty-two-pound robe decorated with 785,000 strewn pearls and gold embroidery. On his brow he wore a gold crown of laurel wreaths, like those worn by Roman consuls of old, a symbol of the favor of the gods. As the "Sacred March" came to a conclusion, Bokassa seated himself in his $2.5 million eagle throne, took his gold laurel wreath off, and, as Napoleon 173 years before had done, took his $2.5 million crown, which was topped with an 80-carat diamond, and placed it upon his son's head.

Bokassa's reign was not as imposing as his coronation. Just two years later, while Bokassa was out of the country, the French engineered a successful coup. Unfortunately, it was too late for the 200 children who had been executed because they had complained about the expense of their school uniforms.

Bokassa's coronation is a ridiculous story, almost comical if it had not caused so much pain. But at the same time, absurd as it is, it is a painfully accurate portrayal of the longings and methodology of mankind left to itself as it pursues its own exaltation. What a contrast with John 12:12–26, which centers on the events and teachings that surrounded Jesus' Triumphal Entry into Jerusalem as King of Israel.

It was Passover, an exciting and tense time. Only the day before, Lazarus had been raised from the dead. The air was electric. Caiaphas and the other Jewish leaders had their "hit" list, at the top of which was Jesus Christ and now Lazarus. At the same time swarms of people were coming to see Jesus. The situation was explosive. What a context for the presentation of the King.

The King Presented (vv. 12–19)

> The next day the large crowd that had come to the feast heard that Jesus was coming to Jerusalem. So they took branches of palm trees and went out to meet him, crying out, "Hosanna! Blessed is he who comes in the name of the Lord, even the King of Israel!" And Jesus found a young donkey and sat on it, just as it is written,

> > "Fear not, daughter of Zion;
> > behold, your king is coming,
> >   sitting on a donkey's colt!" (vv. 12–15)

"Hosanna" literally means "save" and on this occasion probably meant "save us" or "save, I pray," though some suggest it meant "Lord, save him," similar to the British "God save the King." Whichever, it was an anticipatory cry—they saw Jesus as their deliverer. They quoted Psalm 118, the Psalm that had been sung one hundred years earlier when the warrior Judas Maccabaeus drove out the Greeks. Even the palm branches were symbolic of the crowd's political aspirations, for the palm was the symbol on the coin of the second Maccabean revolt. Waving palm branches was symbolic of a nationalistic spirit. The crowd fully expected to see Jesus issue a call to arms and drive out the hated Romans. In the midst of this tumult, our Lord did something the surging mob did not understand. Five hundred years earlier Zechariah had written:

> Rejoice greatly, O daughter of Zion!
>   Shout aloud, O daughter of Jerusalem!
> Behold, your king is coming to you;
>   righteous and having salvation is he,
> humble and mounted on a donkey,
>   on a colt, the foal of a donkey. (Zechariah 9:9)

As Luke tells us in his parallel account, Jesus had omnisciently directed his disciples to a donkey that had never been ridden. He knew exactly what he was doing when he rode into Jerusalem on it. He was identifying himself with the long-awaited Messiah. At the same time he was saying he was not like other world conquerors past or future—Alexander, Tiberius, Napoleon, or Bokassa. The donkey was a royal beast, but it was an animal of peace, a humble animal. Jesus was a new kind of king, but no one understood that. If they had, they would have cast him aside, which they eventually did. The crowd wanted a king with a sword.

> His disciples did not understand these things at first, but when Jesus was glorified, then they remembered that these things had been written about him and had been done to him. (v. 16)

The masses were swirling and whirling in enthusiasm. The people who had seen Lazarus resurrected from the tomb and those who had heard about it came together like separate tides of the rushing sea. The excitement was immense! The Pharisees summed it up in verse 19: "You see that you are gaining nothing. Look, the world has gone after him."

Now John injects an unexpected event upon which he evidently placed great importance. Some think it took place the next day. Perhaps so. It really makes no difference. The point is, John wanted us to see the events together.

The King Pursued (vv. 20–22)

> Now among those who went up to worship at the feast were some Greeks. So these came to Philip, who was from Bethsaida in Galilee, and asked him, "Sir, we wish to see Jesus." Philip went and told Andrew; Andrew and Philip went and told Jesus.

The presence of Greeks at the Passover was not unusual. The Greeks were inveterate wanderers. In fact, they were the first people to wander just for the sake of wandering. One Greek chided his own people saying, "You Athenians will never rest yourselves, nor will you even let anyone else rest." Also, as Greeks they were characteristically seekers after truth. It was not unusual for a Greek to go through philosophy after philosophy in his search. The force of the Greek behind "we wish to see Jesus" is continuous. The idea is they kept repeating their request. They really wanted to hear Jesus.

John wanted us to see that Gentiles were included in the events of Jesus' incarnation and sacrifice. In the opening chapters of Matthew's Gospel we read that wise men from the East came to see Jesus, and here in John, shortly before the cross, we see wise men from the West coming to Jesus. Gentiles framed both sides of Jesus' life.

With the *presentation* of the king in his Triumphal Entry, and then the *pursuit* of him, we can imagine how shocking Jesus' next words must have been. A hush of expectancy fell on the people, especially when they heard, "The hour has come for the Son of Man to be glorified" (v. 23). The crowd's hearts skipped with excitement. Many, as they listened, remembered Daniel's words about the One who would come to set up a worldwide dominion that would never end. Surely Christ was about to announce his campaign against the Romans and initiate his kingdom, they thought. How disappointing his succeeding words must have been to them.

> Truly, truly, I say to you, unless a grain of wheat falls into the earth and dies, it remains alone; but if it dies, it bears much fruit. (v. 24)

The King's Proclamation (vv. 24–26)

An abrupt hush settled upon the crowd when they heard those words. Jesus was talking about a different kind of king, a king who would rule through death, not conquest. The illustration was so simple. When you hold a kernel of wheat in your hand, you cannot see what is in it. Quite literally each grain contains, if it is a good seed, a million similar offspring. In planting season, a grain is cast forth into the ground as if in a tomb. Then it "dies," is set forth from its encasement, and becomes a resurrection plant, and its many grains are resurrection fruit! Jesus was telling the crowd he would fulfill his kingly role by dying and thereby reproducing his life in others. That was how he was going to rule. Thus his rule would go far beyond those of the Bokassas and the Napoleons, because he would rule not by compulsion but by allegiance of the heart, by love.

Our Lord expanded that principle to include us in verse 25: "Whoever loves his life loses it, and whoever hates his life in this world will keep it for eternal life." Our Lord said that the one who loves his own life destroys it. Was he saying we should cultivate a hatred of life? Of course not. But he is telling us to die to ourselves, that we only find life when we lose it. Whether in this world or the world to come, our potential is never reached except through death to sin and denial of self. Whatever we want to become (God willing) musically, athletically, academically, or whatever, death is the key.

The renowned Paderewski, after finishing a brilliant concert, was told by an admiring woman, "Sir, you are a genius," to which he responded, "Madam, before I was a genius, I was a drudge." His brilliance came through death—

that is, hard work and self-denial. The famous runner Jim Ryun, who set a record for the mile when he was eighteen years old, said about his training, "I would run until I felt I couldn't take another step, then I would run until I felt my lungs were going to burst. When I came to that state, then I would run until I thought I was going to pass out. When I did this, I was making progress." The same principle is true in academics. It is true in marriage as well. Self-denial is the key. The eminent H. P. Liddon, preaching on Palm Sunday one hundred years ago, said, "The errors and miseries of the world are purged with blood: everywhere in the great passages of human history we are on the track of sacrifice; and sacrifice, meet it where you may, is a moral power of incalculable force."[1]

The spiritual life is governed by similar paradoxes. "[God's] power is made perfect in [our] weakness" (2 Corinthians 12:9). Do we want to be rich? We must become poor in spirit. Do we want to be first? We must be willing to be last. "Humble yourselves, therefore, under the mighty hand of God so that at the proper time he may exalt you" (1 Peter 5:6). If we want to rule, we have to serve. If we want to live, we have to die.

"Truly, truly, I say to you, unless a grain of wheat falls into the earth and dies, it remains *alone*" (v. 24). Unless there is death, the vast possibilities inside us will not be released. We will shrivel and remain alone. We must die. Those who are beginning the Christian life or are awakening to their spiritual potential must learn that we live by dying. This has been true in my own life.

> I appeal to you therefore, brothers, by the mercies of God, to present your bodies as a living sacrifice, holy and acceptable to God, which is your spiritual worship. Do not be conformed to this world, but be transformed by the renewal of your mind, that by testing you may discern what is the will of God, what is good and acceptable and perfect. (Romans 12:1, 2)

When I read these verses after coming to know Christ as my Savior, I gave my whole life to him the best I knew how, and I began to grow in my soul. And as the years have gone by, I have learned again and again that dying is a daily requirement for spiritual vitality. If your life is stagnant, if your spiritual potential is going unrealized, it may well be that you need to die, to lay down your life and be released. This was the key to the royalty in Jesus' life, and it is an important principle in ours as well.

George Müller exercised a wide influence for God. When someone asked him, "What has been the secret of your life?" Müller hung his head and said, "There was a day when I died." Then he bent lower and said, "Died to George Müller, his opinions, preferences, tastes, and will; died to the world, its approval or censure; died to the approval or blame even of brethren or friends." The kind of power, reign, and royalty that death brings to life will make the pretenders of this world turn green with envy.

Jesus summed it all up in verse 26: "If anyone serves me, he must follow me." A parallel passage (Matthew 8:35) tells us the royal life does not begin with a coronation but with a crucifixion. What is the reward of death to self? Look at verse 26 again: "If anyone serves me, he must follow me; and where I am, there will my servant be also. If anyone serves me, the Father will honor him." Someone has said that "follow me" is the sum of our duty, and "where I am" is the sum of our reward. That is true! And ultimately this means untold honor. Second Corinthians 4:17 says, "For this light momentary affliction is preparing for us an eternal weight of glory beyond all comparison." First Corinthians 2:8–9 adds:

> None of the rulers of this age understood this [God's wisdom], for if they had, they would not have crucified the Lord of glory. But, as it is written,
>
> > "What no eye has seen, nor ear heard,
> >   nor the heart of man imagined,
> > what God has prepared for those who love him."

Our future coronation will make the world's coronations look like children playing with mud pies.

A group of slaves was being led along in northern Africa, chained to one another at the neck. As they walked, the Arab slave traders and slave masters noticed that all of them were bent over with the heavy iron collars except for one who walked erect and with dignity. Asked why, a trader was told, "He's the son of a king, and he cannot forget it." All who know Jesus Christ as Savior are royalty. But we live the royal life we have been given only as we die to the old way of life and emulate the King of kings.

On that first Palm Sunday when our Lord marched into Jerusalem, the crowds acclaimed him. Gentiles came and said, "We wish to see Jesus." But how did they see Jesus? Through his death for our sins. How did they understand him as King? Through his death. How will those around us see Jesus? Only as we die to ourselves and live for Christ. May God lead us into a royal life, a life of sacrifice, a life that bears much fruit.

38

The Effects of the Cross

JOHN 12:27–36

OUR LORD had just presented himself as a new kind of King, one who rules by a principle no earthly king ever imagined—selfless sacrifice, as exemplified on the cross. Charles Ross Weed captured the idea beautifully in his poem "Christ and Alexander."

> Jesus and Alexander died at thirty-three,
> One died in Babylon and one on Calvary.
> One gained all for self, and one himself he gave.
> One conquered every throne, the other every grave.
> When died the Greek, forever fell his throne of swords,
> But Jesus died to live forever Lord of lords.
> Jesus and Alexander died at thirty-three.
> The Greek made all men slaves, the Jew made all men free.
> One built a throne on blood, the other built on love.
> The One was born of earth, the other from above.
> One won all this earth to lose all earth and Heaven.
> The other gave up all that all to him be given.
> The Greek forever died, the Jew forever lives.
> He loses all who gets and wins all things who gives.

Life comes through death. Kingship comes through serving.

The throng, imagining he was going to call them to arms, were amazed at Jesus' surprising words in 12:24, 25:

> Truly, truly, I say to you, unless a grain of wheat falls into the earth and dies, it remains alone; but if it dies, it bears much fruit. Whoever loves his life loses it, and whoever hates his life in this world will keep it for eternal life.

Our Lord rules from the cross, and so do those who learn to live by his principles. This is the key to the truly regal life.

We are now going to consider the *effects* of Jesus' words on himself, on the world, and on those who first heard them.

The last part of verse 36 is significant: "When Jesus had said these things, he departed and hid himself from them." This was perhaps our Lord's last public discourse before his crucifixion. Significantly, he spoke of the effects of the cross. There was an urgency in what he said as he attempted to capture his hearers' souls. His words were meant to affect us as well, and they will if we allow them to because there is nothing more health-giving than seeing something more of our Savior.

The Puritan Richard Baxter said: "He is the best Christian who has the clearest knowledge of God in his attributes." The more we see of Jesus and what he is like, the smaller our problems become. King David understood this: "Why are you cast down, O my soul, and why are you in turmoil within me? Hope in God" (Psalm 42:11). Considering who God is will make a difference in our lives.

The Effect of the Cross on Jesus (vv. 27–30)

Our Lord now revealed the effects of the coming cross on his own heart:

> "Now is my soul troubled. And what shall I say? 'Father, save me from this hour'? But for this purpose I have come to this hour. Father, glorify your name." Then a voice came from heaven, "I have glorified it, and I will glorify it again." (vv. 27, 28)

Jesus bared his heart, telling his listeners that his soul was troubled. *The Living Bible* renders his words, "Now my soul is deeply troubled." *The New English Bible* says, "Now my soul is in turmoil." The tense connotes a continual state: "My soul is in constant turmoil." Jesus' verbalization of the coming dread suddenly overwhelmed his emotions, tossing them into painful anguish. We can relate to this. Sometimes we have unwittingly verbalized something we were not looking forward to, and our stomachs turned and our palms got cold. Something like this happened within our Lord, for he was truly man. And yet to find a similar response in our Lord (even though in contemplation of the cruel cross) is startling in light of who he is. After all, he is the One who holds the world together. He is the One who healed the leper with a touch, who with a word cast out demons and calmed the seas. He is the One who walked right through crowds intent on his murder. Some say the reason our

Lord was troubled was that he was contemplating the physical horrors of the cross—the cloud of flies buzzing above the cross, his flayed back unevenly pressed against the stake, the nails through the nerves of his hands, the agony of constantly pulling himself up to get a breath. But if that is what we think the Lord was fearing, we do him an injustice, because men in our own time have died more painful, more prolonged deaths than that. If it had been only physical pain he faced, Jesus would have received it with amazing calm.

Jesus said, "Now is *my* soul troubled" because in a few hours he would bear the world's sins and suffer separation from his Father. That is what threw his soul into turmoil. The soul of the very God who holds this universe together was in turmoil because he would bear our sin. Second Corinthians 5:21 says, "For our sake he made him to be sin who knew no sin." His soul, which had never been tainted with sin, would shortly have the sins of the universe poured upon it. He was about to endure the wrath of God as he paid for our sins. As Galatians 3:13 puts it, "Christ redeemed us from the curse of the law by becoming a curse for us." Literally, he was a "cursed one." Jesus cursed! Incredible!

His death was sufficient because as an infinite being in a moment of time he could pay an infinite price for our sin! That is why Jesus was in turmoil. In fact, in the garden of Gethsemane Jesus said, "My soul is very sorrowful, even to death" (Mark 14:34). "Going a little farther, he fell on the ground and prayed that, if it were possible, the hour might pass from him" (Mark 14:35).

The tenses mean he was repeatedly casting himself to the ground as he asked God to deliver him from the cross. And Luke 22:44 says, "And being in agony he prayed more earnestly; and his sweat became like great drops of blood falling down to the ground."

His revulsion was intensified by the thought of his separation from the Father. They created the universe together. They had enjoyed a perpetual intimacy. In the garden he would pray, "*Abba*, Father" ("Dearest Father," "Daddy"), but on the cross he would cry, "My God, my God, why have you forsaken me?" (Mark 14:36; 15:34). "Now is my soul troubled" gives us a look into the very heart of Christ as he anticipated that awful horror and desolation. If we truly see this, we will not, cannot remain the same.

What did Jesus do when faced with such turmoil?

> Now is my soul troubled. And what shall I say? "Father, save me from this hour"? But for this purpose I have come to this hour. (v. 27)

In other words, "No way am I going to turn away from the cross." Jesus knew he was the Lamb slain from eternity. The cross was his ineluctable destiny, his pursuit, his burden. He must go to Calvary. That is why, in the following phrase, he prayed, "Father, glorify your name."

Comparing those words with 12:23 we understand what he was praying. "Father, I am in turmoil, and I do not want to endure the agonies of being the sin-bearer, but give me the cross." Why did he submit to such suffering? First and foremost, for the glory of God. "Glorify your name." But he also endured the cross because he loves us. Lewis captured this in his poem "Love's as Warm as Tears."

> Love's as hard as nails.
> Love is nails:
> Blunt, thick, hammered through
> The medial nerves of One
> Who, having made us, knew
> The thing he had done,
> Seeing (with all that is)
> Our cross, and His.[1]

Such is the loving heart of Jesus! No wonder Isaiah wrote that he is our "Wonderful Counselor" and "Mighty God" (Isaiah 9:6). But the price of our peace was his troubled soul. What a comfort—to know that he loves us like that. Baxter was right when he said, "He is the best Christian who has the clearest knowledge of God." If your soul is cast down, think of the personal pain Christ endured for your salvation and peace, then remember that now, as an object of redemption, he continues to lavish that same self-sacrificing care upon you. If we are going through difficult times, whether the death of a loved one or a painful marital relationship or feelings of worthlessness or uncertainty about our future, we must look to Jesus. When we see Jesus' soul as here portrayed, we will find great strength. As Jesus said in the upper room, "Let not your hearts be troubled. Believe in God; believe also in me" (14:1).

After Christ revealed what was in his heart, the Father did not remain quiet. "Then a voice came from heaven: 'I have glorified it [God's name], and I will glorify it again'" (v. 28).

> The crowd that stood there and heard it said that it had thundered. Others said, "An angel has spoken to him." Jesus answered, "This voice has come for your sake, not mine." (vv. 29, 30)

After the crowd's response, our Lord turned from the effect of the cross upon himself to the effect upon the world.

The Effect of the Cross upon the World (vv. 31–33)

In verses 31–33 we see three effects, the first two negative and the third positive.

The first effect is found in verse 31a when Christ says, "Now is the judgment of this world." When mankind exercised judgment on Christ on the cross, it judged itself. The second effect involves Satan: "Now will the ruler of this world be cast out" (v. 31b). The cross administered the blow that will ultimately still the movements of Satan.

Finally, there is the positive effect.

> "And I, when I am lifted up from the earth, will draw all people to myself."
> He said this to show by what kind of death he was going to die. (vv. 32, 33)

Precisely what was in the mind of our Lord is revealed to us in 3:14: "As Moses lifted up the serpent in the wilderness, so must the Son of Man be lifted up." Numbers 21 tells about the Israelites being bitten by poisonous snakes, causing a fiery fever. Moses interceded with God for the people and was told to make a brass imitation of a serpent and lift it up on a pole outside the camp. Those who had enough faith to look at it would be saved (v. 8). Our Lord was saying, "If I am lifted up on the cross like that writhing serpent, as a sin-bearer, *the* sin-bearer, I will draw all who believe in me to myself." What draws people to Jesus is his being lifted up as our atonement. He is the One who took upon himself our sins.

Many years ago two prominent men made totally contradictory statements. One was the president of Harvard University, the other a graduate of Yale University and the president of the Bible Institute of Los Angeles. The latter, R. A. Torrey, said, "Preach any Christ but a crucified Christ, and you will not draw men for long."[2] The former, Charles Eliot, in a lecture entitled "The Future of Religion," said that while it was okay for ancient man to believe in a divine, atoning Christ, modern man had outgrown that idea. He stated:

> Let no man fear that reverence and love for Jesus will diminish as time goes on. The pathos and heroism of his life and death will be vastly heightened when he is relieved of all supernatural attributes and power.[3]

With the rise of modernism, for a while it looked very much as if Charles Eliot was right. But today Torrey's words ring true. Although men may come for a time to a purely social gospel, they will not remain. Liberalism does not draw. Moral rearmament does not draw. We may proclaim the Lord as a great ethical teacher, but ethics alone will generate no more power than do the Ten Commandments painted on the cold surface of the walls of a church. We may proclaim Jesus as a young reformer, but he will not be able to lift man from his sins if that is all he is. Jesus the radical may draw cheers, but the uplifted Christ draws followers for eternity. "And I, when I am lifted up from the earth, will draw all people to myself." Philippians 2:9, 10 says that every knee will bow to Jesus. Christ was not saying that the whole world would be saved, but that all who will be saved will be saved by looking to and relying upon him. If you are not yet a believer, see his troubled soul as he became a curse for you, as he suffered separation from his Father, as he lovingly bore the penalty of your sins.

My wife and I used to tell our children a story to explain the love of Jesus. A little boy wanted a model sailboat. So he began saving his money until finally he had enough. He went to the toy shop and picked out his kit, making his selection with great care. He spent weeks perfecting that boat, and finally when it was finished, he took it down to the lake. It sailed beautifully—right across the lake and out of sight. Naturally the young boy was distressed and began a frantic search. But despite his efforts he was unable to find his boat. Several weeks later he was walking past a store window and to his amazement saw his boat with a sizable price tag attached to it. He went in and told the owner, "Sir, I would like to have my boat back." The owner said, "Well, I'm sorry, but I paid good money for it. You will have to pay for it." That poor boy worked and worked until he finally got enough money together, again, and bought his boat back. As he walked out of the store, he said, "Now you are twice mine—once because I made you and once because I bought you." Jesus created us, and he purchased us by his death on the cross, and now we can be twice his. How wonderful is the love of Jesus!

The Effect of the Cross on Those Who Heard Him (v. 34)

> So the crowd answered him, "We have heard from the Law that the Christ remains forever. How can you say that the Son of Man must be lifted up? Who is this Son of Man?"

According to their theology, the Messiah could not die. They had read their Old Testament, but they had not remembered or had missed the meaning of important passages such as Isaiah 53, Zechariah 13, and Psalm 22. So they questioned the Lord's words. Confusion and indifference reigned. The Lord responded with an ominous sense of urgency.

> So Jesus said to them, "The light is among you for a little while longer. Walk while you have the light, lest darkness overtake you. The one who

walks in the darkness does not know where he is going. While you have the light, believe in the light, that you may become sons of light." (vv. 35, 36)

Our Lord was saying, "You have heard my message. Light or darkness—take your choice." Which will *we* choose?

Conclusion

Nearly forty years ago I sat next to a young man in a meeting. I was in college at the time. The young man sitting next to me was eighteen years old. As the meeting progressed I felt that I needed to ask him if he would like to respond to the message. I was insecure and shy, and I felt a bit embarrassed, but I finally asked him what he thought about what he was hearing. He replied that he did not understand what I meant. I hesitantly said, "Well, do you know Jesus?" He said, "I don't know if I do or not." I coughed out, "Well, I would like to talk to you about it." That night he asked Christ into his life, and he went on to become a substantial, vibrant Christian. He married a fine young lady, established himself in Mexico City with a business, and became wealthy. A few years later he was killed in an automobile crash in Mexico City. That man had a good life, but he has a better life today—all because he responded to Jesus. Right now he is enjoying "the inheritance of the saints in light" (Colossians 1:12), all because years ago he made the right choice. Have you?

39

On Being People of the Towel

JOHN 13:1–17

AS ONE READS through the Gospel of John, the shadow of the cross grows longer and darker until now the reader stands at the foot of the cross on the evening before the Crucifixion. In just a few short hours (somewhere between fifteen and eighteen hours) our Lord would be suspended between the sky and earth as the sin-bearer of mankind. Before the sun set again he would breathe his last tortured breath.

With the conclusion of chapter 12, there would be more public discourses. Chapters 13—17 record what we have come to know as the Upper Room Discourse. In these five chapters we see intimate teaching about service, love, the Holy Spirit, Heaven, our union with Christ, and prayer. Alexander Maclaren eloquently put forth his estimation saying:

> Nowhere else do the blended lights of our Lord's superhuman dignity and human tenderness shine with such lambent brightness. Nowhere else is his speech at once so simple and so deep. Nowhere else have we the heart of God so unveiled to us. On no other page, even of the Bible, have so many eyes, glistening with tears, looked and had the tears dried. The immortal words which Christ spoke in that upper chamber are his highest self-revelation in speech.[1]

When John 13:1–17 is examined with proper reverential excitement, they will accomplish great good in our lives.

The Upper Room Discourse begins with a dramatic call to follow Christ's example as a servant—to be people of the towel. He tells us, if we are to be his followers, where we must begin, what qualities must be in our lives, and what we must do. John introduces this new section with a few short sentences that form a masterful introduction to the heady atmosphere of the upper room.

The Heart of the Servant (vv. 1–3)

> Now before the Feast of the Passover, when Jesus knew that his hour had come to depart out of this world to the Father, having loved his own who were in the world, he loved them to the end. (v. 1)

The final sentence gives us his heart: "Having loved his own who were in the world, he loved them to the end." The servant's heart is a heart of love. A story about Czar Nicholas I of Russia tells us something of that love. The czar was greatly interested in a young man because he had been friends with the young man's father. When that young man came of age, Czar Nicholas gave him a fine position in the army. He also stationed him in a place of responsibility at one of the great fortresses of Russia. The young man was responsible for the monies and finances of a particular division of the army.

The young man did quite well at first, but as time went along, he became quite a gambler. Before long he had gambled his entire fortune away. He borrowed from the treasury and also gambled that away, a few rubles at a time. One day he heard there was going to be an audit of the books the next day. He went to the safe, took out his ledger, and figured out how much money he had, then subtracted the amount he had taken. As he sat at the table, overwhelmed at the astronomical debt, he took out his pen and wrote, "A great debt, who can pay?" Not willing to go through the shame of what would happen the next day, he took out his revolver and covenanted with himself that at the stroke of midnight he would take his life.

It was a warm and drowsy night, and as the young man sat at the table, he dozed off. Now, Czar Nicholas had a habit of putting on a common soldier's uniform and visiting some of his outposts. On that very night he came to that particular great fortress, and as he inspected it, he saw a light on in one of the rooms. He knocked on the door, but no one answered. He tried the latch, opened the door, and went in. There was the young man. The czar recognized him immediately. When he saw the note on the table and the ledgers laid out, his first impulse was to wake the young man and arrest him. But, overtaken with a wave of generosity, he instead took the pen that had fallen out of the soldier's hand and wrote one word on the paper, then tiptoed out of the room.

About an hour later the young man woke up and reached for his revolver, realizing that it was much after twelve. Then his eyes fell upon his note: "A great debt, who can pay?" He saw immediately that one word had been added—"Nicholas." The young man dropped the gun, ran to the files, thumbed through some correspondence, and found the czar's signature. The note was authentic! The realization struck him—"The czar has been here and knows all my guilt. But he has undertaken my debt, and I will not have to die." The young man trusted in the czar's word, and sure enough, the needed monies came.[2]

The czar's love, paying the price for his guilty young friend, was only a faint shadow of the atoning love of Christ. Nicholas's deed was an easy matter for him—as easy as signing his name. But the atoning love of Jesus cost him everything!

The tenses at the end of verse 1, "having loved his own who were in the world, he loved them to the end," means that in the whole range of Christ's contact with his disciples he loved them! In the upper room he consciously made that the overriding issue.

> A new commandment I give to you, that you love one another: just as I have loved you, you also are to love one another. By this all people will know that you are my disciples, if you have love for one another. (13:34, 35)

And in 17:26 the Savior tells the Father, "I made known to them your name, and I will continue to make it known, that the love with which you have loved me may be in them, and I in them." Teaching his people to love was one of Jesus' overall purposes in the Upper Room Discourse. Specifically, Jesus was saying to his people, "If you want to be my servants, if you want to grow in this authentic aspect of discipleship, if that is what you really desire, you must allow your hearts to deepen in love." Are we willing to do that? Are we willing to grow in love?

Another aspect of the Savior's heart is that Jesus knew exactly who he was. Notice the beginning of verse 1: "Now before the Feast of the Passover, when Jesus knew that his hour had come to depart out of this world to the Father. . . ." Also, "Jesus, knowing that the Father had given all things into his hands, and that he had come from God and was going back to God. . . ." (v. 3). Jesus did not forget he was God and yet humbled himself. Being fully conscious of his supremacy and coming superexaltation, he became the Lord of the towel! Here is the heart of our foot-washing Lord and Savior—a heart that is aware of its royalty while overflowing with a love that loves to the uttermost.

The Example of the Servant (vv. 4–11)

The disciples were alone with Jesus in the upper room. The world was locked out. Only a handful of mortals and honored angels would see what happened there. Because it was a Passover meal, the disciples were reclining in the traditional posture, each with his left arm to support his head and his right arm to reach dishes on the table. Their feet were stretched out behind them away from the table.[3] The Savior rose from the table and performed the last labor of his life. Considering the self-conscious, purposeful drama and the natural intensity it certainly evoked, there were probably a few murmurs and whispers and then silence. Our modern translations use the past tense, but the Greek uses the present. Jesus rises from supper just as in the incarnation he rose from his place of perfect fellowship with God the Father and the Holy Spirit. He lays aside his garments just as he had temporarily set aside his glorious existence. He takes a towel just as he took upon himself the form of a servant. He wraps a towel around his waist, for he had come to serve. He pours water into the basin, just as he was about to pour out his blood in order to wash away human sin. He washes his disciples' feet just as he cleanses his children. On this remarkable occasion Jesus perfectly staged a portrayal of his whole life from birth to death to resurrection! It was a dramatization of Philippians 2:5–9:

> Have this mind among yourselves, which is yours in Christ Jesus, who, though he was in the form of God, did not count equality with God a thing to be grasped, but emptied himself, by taking the form of a servant, being born in the likeness of men. And being found in human form, he humbled himself by becoming obedient to the point of death, even death on a cross. Therefore God has highly exalted him and bestowed on him the name that is above every name.

Jesus' whole life was dominated by service! As Christ said of himself, "The Son of Man came not to be served but to serve, and to give his life as a ransom for many" (Matthew 20:28).

With the uncomfortable quiet in that upper room, undoubtedly all could easily hear the gentle pouring of the water and the Master's breathing as he moved from disciple to disciple. I wonder what he thought. Perhaps as he dried the feet of Thomas and Mark, "These feet will be beautiful on the mountains." And when he came to Judas, "These will soon steal away in the dark." Then he came to a pair of 13Ds—Peter's! Peter said, "Lord, do you wash my feet?" Jesus answered and said to him, "What I am doing you do not understand now, but afterward you will understand." Peter said to him,

"You shall never wash my feet" (vv. 6b–8a). Good old Peter. Sometimes the only time he opened his mouth was to change feet! The Greek here is even more forceful! "Lord, you, my feet do you wash! No, never shall you wash my feet until eternity." Foot washing was a servant's task and not something to be done by the Master! The *Midrash* specified that foot-washing could not be required of a Hebrew slave.[4] The Master dressed in a servant's towel? Absurd! Never!

Jesus answered in verse 8, "If I do not wash you, you have no share with me." Peter replied, "Lord, not my feet only but also my hands and my head!" (v. 9). I like Peter. He was way ahead of Emerson, who said, "A foolish consistency is the hobgoblin of little minds, of theologians and philosophers and divines." "All of me, Jesus!" But now the impetuous disciple was swinging too far in the other direction, as our Lord explained in verses 10, 11:

> "The one who has bathed does not need to wash, except for his feet, but is completely clean. And you are clean, but not every one of you." For he knew who was to betray him; that was why he said, "Not all of you are clean."

When one had bathed and then walked to another's house, he only needed his feet washed in order to be clean. As justified believers, the disciples did not need a radical new cleansing, but rather a daily cleansing from the contaminating effects of sin. Jesus went on to finish washing their feet, and when he had finished, he rose again, put on his garments, and again reclined at the table. Similarly, "After making purification for sins, he sat down at the right hand of the Majesty on high" (Hebrews 1:3).

The Challenge of the Servant (vv. 12–17)

Jesus then asked them, "Do you understand what I have done to you?" (v. 12). I believe they knew! In Luke's account of the last meal we read (22:24): "A dispute also arose among them, as to which of them was to be regarded as the greatest." When the cross was only a few hours away, the disciples were still arguing about matters of pride. Usually when there was no servant present to wash the guests' feet, the first one or two to arrive would perform the ceremony for the rest of the guests. But here the first arrivals were not in the mood. Perhaps the "who's the greatest?" controversy had actually begun as they journeyed there. They were willing to fight for the throne, but no one wanted the towel! Jesus' act was a powerful lesson in servanthood, and they were missing the point!

So Jesus issued a potent challenge in verses 13–16:

> You call me Teacher and Lord, and you are right, for so I am. If I then, your Lord and Teacher, have washed your feet, you also ought to wash one another's feet. For I have given you an example, that you also should do just as I have done to you. Truly, truly, I say to you, a servant is not greater than his master, nor is a messenger greater than the one who sent him.

Jesus employed the compelling logic of a lawyer's *a fortiori* argument: "If it is true for the greater (me), how much more for the lesser (you)."

In 1970 I was among 12,300 delegates to Inter-Varsity's Urbana convention, where we heard John Stott give a masterful application of the truth of this passage. He told a story about Samuel Logan Brengle:

> In 1878 when William Booth's Salvation Army had just been so named, men from all over the world began to enlist. One man, who had once dreamed of himself as a bishop, crossed the Atlantic from America to England to enlist. He was a Methodist minister, Samuel Logan Brengle. And he now turned from a fine pastorate to join Booth's Salvation Army. Brengle later became the Army's first American-born commissioner. But at first Booth accepted his services reluctantly and grudgingly. Booth said to Brengle, "You've been your own boss too long." And in order to instill humility into Brengle, he set him to work cleaning the boots of the other trainees. And Brengle said to himself, "Have I followed my own fancy across the Atlantic in order to black boots?" And then as in a vision he saw Jesus bending over the feet of rough, unlettered fishermen. "Lord," he whispered, "You washed their feet: I will black their boots."[5]

If we are to count ourselves as followers of Christ, there must be humble service in our lives. We must be people of the towel. More specifically, we are to wash one another's feet. While Christ does not exclude washing the feet of those outside the church, it is meant primarily for brothers and sisters in the Body of Christ. That is in some respects more difficult. It is easier sometimes to humble ourselves and wash the feet of those we do not know. But those in our own families? Or fellow believers whom we loathe, to whom we have not spoken for years? But Jesus' instruction was clear: "If I then, your Lord and Teacher, have washed your feet, you also ought to wash one another's feet."

When we do this, it will have a cleansing effect upon other believers. Jesus is saying that the church has received the essential cleansing by him in the forgiveness of sins, but we can help take away the day-by-day dirt of the world by humbly serving one another. We will thus encourage one another to godliness.

Conclusion

"If you know these things, blessed are you if you do them" (v. 17). Jesus did not say we will be happy if we think about these things or learn about them or, as is so often thought, have them done to us. "Blessed are you if you *do* them." Happy are we if we wash our wives' feet! Happy are we if we wash our children's feet! Happy are we if we wash our parents' feet! Happy are we if we wash a detractor's feet! We do not need to learn more about this. We need to do it.

Like its physical counterpart, spiritual footwashing is dirty work! We cannot make people clean by scolding them or lecturing them or patronizing them. We must get our hands dirty if we are going to be involved in a ministry of cleansing.

How do we become people of the towel? First we must observe the marvelous example of our foot-washing Lord and Savior and then listen to Jesus' challenge: "If I then, your Lord and Teacher, have washed your feet, you also ought to wash one another's feet." Perhaps most important, we must have the quality of Jesus' heart. "Having loved his own who were in the world, he loved them to the end." We are to be overflowing with love. Finally, we become people of the towel by realizing who we are. The power, the impetus, and the grace to wash one another's feet is proportionate not only to how we see Jesus but to how we see ourselves. Our Lord saw himself as King of kings, and he washed the disciples' feet. Recovery of a kingly consciousness will hallow and refine our entire lives. We are "a royal priesthood" (1 Peter 2:9).

If you know these things, blessed are you if you do them.

40

Radical Love

JOHN 13:18–35

In my dream I was carried away to a great and high mountain where I saw that great city, the goal of all our hopes and desires, the end of our salvation, the Holy City of God, the New Jerusalem. Around the city, as around the earthly Jerusalem, there ran a wall great and high. There were twelve gates, north, south, east, and west; and every gate was a pearl, and at every gate stood one of the Great Angels. On the gates were written the names of the Twelve Tribes of the Children of Israel, from Reuben to Benjamin. The wall of the city stood upon twelve massive foundation stones, and on each stone was the name of one of the Twelve Apostles of the Lamb; and as I walked around the city, thrilling with joy and rapture at the glory and splendor of it, I read the names written upon the twelve stones—Peter, James, John, and all the others. But one name was missing. I looked in vain for that name, either on the twelve gates or on the twelve foundation stones—and that name was Judas.

The longest night in the history of the world is drawing to a close. The night is passing, but the day has not yet come. Far to the east, over the mountains of Moab, there is just the faintest intimation of the coming day. The huge walls of Jerusalem and the towers and pinnacles of the temple are emerging from the shadows of the night. In the half darkness and half light I can make out a solitary figure coming down the winding road from the wall of Jerusalem towards the gorge of the Kidron. On the bridge over the brook he pauses for a moment and, turning, looks back towards the Holy City. Then he goes forward for a few paces and, again turning, halts and looks up towards the massive walls of the city. Again he turns, and this time he does not stop. Now I can see that in his hand he carries a rope. Up the slope of Olivet he comes and, entering in at the gate of Gethsemane, walks under the trees of the Garden. Seizing with his arms one of the low-branching limbs of a gnarled olive tree, he draws himself up into the tree. Perhaps he is the proprietor of this part of the Garden, and has come to gather the olives. But why with a rope? For a little he is lost to my view in the springtime foliage of the tree. Then, suddenly, I see his body plummet down like a rock from the top of the tree. Yet the body does not reach the ground, but is suspended in mid-air. And there it swings slowly to and fro at the end of a rope.[1]

This is the imaginary vision of Clarence Edward Macartney. It was the midnight of Judas' life. He would never again wake to the sunshine of Christ's countenance. The Apostle John sums this up in the last part of 13:30: "And it was night."

What had driven this follower of Christ to such a humiliating end? The natural supposition would be that the poor man had suffered some great disappointment. Perhaps his business had failed. Possibly it was his marriage. Or perhaps he was one of those poor souls who had never known anything but abuse and belittlement. Maybe it was simply the pressures of life. No doubt it was one of these. But whatever, he was certainly a soul to be pitied, a victim of life, though also a man who chose his wicked path and who will answer to God for it.

As we examine the story of Judas, we will see that not hatred and rejection but reflection on the love of Christ drove him to take his life. Judas' tragic exit into the night (v. 30) divides the movements of our text. Verses 18–30 give us love's demonstration as our Lord reached out to his failing disciple. In verses 31–35 we see love's demand as Jesus challenged his disciples to practice the same type of revolutionary love. Our Lord taught through example, then through specific command, the radical nature and necessity of his love. Here we see love at its most radical.

The setting is still the upper room. Jesus was closeted with the Twelve. The world was locked out. This is as intimate a revelation of Jesus' heart as is found anywhere in Scripture. "Having loved his own who were in the world, he loved them to the end" (13:1). Love is the transcending motif of the upper room. Jesus had just washed their feet in humble service, and now he would demonstrate radical love.

Love's Demonstration (vv. 18–30)

When the Master concluded washing the disciples' feet he explained what he had done, and he probably said it with force.

> Truly, truly, I say to you, a servant is not greater than his master, nor is a messenger greater than the one who sent him. If you know these things, blessed are you if you do them. (13:16, 17)

But as he gave the next phrase, he very likely lowered his voice.

> I am not speaking of all of you; I know whom I have chosen. But the Scripture will be fulfilled, "He who ate my bread has lifted his heel against me." (v. 18)

He was saying, "Men, not all of you who are in this room are blessed, because one of you is going to lift up his heel against me in betrayal." It is significant that our Lord employed a phrase from Psalm 41:9, for it is generally agreed that Psalm 41 refers to the traitor Ahithophel, who hung himself after he betrayed his master, David. Judas would have the same end. Jesus was saying, "Men, there is an Ahithophel in our fellowship."

Then in verses 19, 20 he told them something they were going to need to know.

> I am telling you this now, before it takes place, that when it does take place you may believe that I am he. Truly, truly, I say to you, whoever receives the one I send receives me, and whoever receives me receives the one who sent me.

"There are terrible events ahead," Jesus was saying. "I want you to know this so that you will believe and not stumble. I also want you to remember that when you receive me, you receive the Father. Keep these things before you because you are going to need them."

Then he really got to the point.

> After saying these things, Jesus was troubled in his spirit, and testified, "Truly, truly, I say to you, one of you will betray me." (v. 21)

His voice must have given him away, because John describes him as "troubled in his spirit." That description is important because "troubled" is the same word used in 11:33 as Jesus stood by Lazarus' grave and wept. It also is the same term used in 12:27 as Jesus thought about the coming dread of the cross and said, "Now is my soul troubled."

All the disciples could see his emotion, but they did not know it was because of Judas. Here is demonstrated one of the most remarkable truths about our Lord's heart. On the eve of the cross, just a few hours before he was going to be crucified, our Lord's heart was troubled, not for himself, but for another—and specifically for the one who was going to deliver him to death.

O the deep, deep love of Jesus—
Vast, unmeasured, boundless, free!
Rolling as a mighty ocean
In its fullness over me.

He was troubled over the soul of the one who was going to betray him. While the disciples did not know Judas would be the betrayer, they understood the thrust of Jesus' words, which must have come as a severe shock. Notice their response in verse 22: "The disciples looked at one another, uncertain of whom he spoke." "Lord, is it I? It cannot be me! Lord, who is it?" Judas, reclining at the table alongside Jesus, coolly mouthed the same words.

Judas was as perfect an actor, as accomplished a hypocrite as one can find. Theologians surmise that he was a man of more education and higher social standing than the rest of the apostles. He was not from Galilee but from Kerioth, a much better address. Dr. Ironside said, "Judas was the real gentleman of all the teachers."[2] He had class compared to the rest. Today Judas would wear a Brooks Brothers suit and a Madison Avenue smile. He would know all the right hymns—when to sit down, when to stand up, when to inject the most persuasive cliché, how to ingratiate himself with the power leaders of the church. No one would suspect him of being a traitor, and they did not then either.

Once again we see the Lord's heart because in a tight group like the disciples' circle if there had been any suspicion cast upon Judas, the disciples would have picked it up. In my family a raised eyebrow can mean ten pages single spaced! A pause, an innuendo, the intonation of a voice—we know what is meant. Yet in the upper room the Lord knew Judas' heart, but no one else had any idea. Why? Because our Lord was reaching out to Judas in love. Even though he knew Judas' heart, he wanted to reach him. There was no rejection. What a beautiful illustration of how Jesus reaches out with his accepting love to the world. If you do not know him, the love that Jesus first manifested in the upper room is something to grab and hold on to. It is a matter of life or death.

The upper room was charged with our Lord reaching out to Judas. When he washed the disciples' feet, he washed Judas' feet too. Imagine that! He told Peter as he washed his feet, "The one who has bathed does not need to wash, except for his feet, but is completely clean. And you are clean, *but not every one of you*" (13:10). "Judas, old friend," Jesus was saying, "you're not clean." He was appealing to Judas' conscience, giving him reason to reflect and repent. Can you imagine what it was like when the Lord washed Judas' feet, when those piercing eyes of Jesus met the hollow eyes of Judas? Jesus was reaching out to him. When the Savior quoted Psalm 41:9 about Ahithophel, he was again saying, "Judas, old friend, I have your number. Why do you not turn around?"

Even the way the table was arranged demonstrated Jesus' love. The seating arrangement (from left to right) was Judas, Jesus, and John. Jesus' head was at Judas' breast as they reclined together. John's head was at Jesus' breast. Jesus had given Judas the left-hand side, the place of honor. Evidently when he brought him into the meal he said, "Judas, I want to have a talk with you. Sit in the place of honor to my left tonight." Our Lord was reaching for his heart. Is that not just like Jesus?[3]

Jesus reached out to Judas to the very end. Notice verses 22–24:

> The disciples looked at one another, uncertain of whom he spoke. One of his disciples, whom Jesus loved, was reclining at table at Jesus' side, so Simon Peter motioned to him to ask Jesus of whom he was speaking.

The seating arrangement made it so easy. Peter gestured to John, who had only to turn back a few inches and say, "Who is it?" And Jesus quietly responded:

> "It is he to whom I will give this morsel of bread when I have dipped it." So when he had dipped the morsel, he gave it to Judas, the son of Simon Iscariot. (v. 26)

In the culture of that time, to take a morsel from the table, dip it in the common dish, and offer it to someone else was a gesture of special friendship. Back in the Old Testament we read of Boaz inviting Ruth to come fellowship with him: "'Come here and eat some bread and dip your morsel in the wine.' . . . he passed to her roasted grain" (Ruth 2:14).

Jesus was reaching out to Judas. He was saying, "Judas, here is my friendship. Here is restoration. Judas, here is my heart. All you have to do is take it, old friend. Will you?" But the door had slammed shut. Judas, as Matthew records, replied, "Is it I, Rabbi?" Jesus responded: "You have said so" (Matthew 26:25).

At that moment an immortal soul committed suicide.

> Then after he had taken the morsel, Satan entered into him. Jesus said to him, "What you are going to do, do quickly." Now no one at the table knew why he said this to him. Some thought that, because Judas had the moneybag, Jesus was telling him, "Buy what we need for the feast," or that he should give something to the poor. So, after receiving the morsel of bread, he immediately went out. And it was night. (vv. 27–30)

It certainly was the midnight of Judas' soul. It was the night that would know no morning. Judas had chosen his own place of darkness and doom. I wonder as he left the upper room that night whether he paused and looked longingly back at the light. I wonder if he thought about turning back. How alone he was! He now had to follow the movements of the Eleven, concealing himself as Jesus and his men crossed the Kidron on their way to Gethsemane. How great his loss! He was now separated from the apostolic fellowship, and never again would he sit at table with the Eleven. Their acquaintance and friendship was eternally terminated. Even worse, he was separated from Christ. Never would he see the Master's face except in terror on the future day of judgment. He was separated from peace of mind too, though his soul-anguish was only an earnest of what was to come.

> The tissues of the life to be,
> We weave with colors all our own;
> And the fields of destiny,
> We reap as we have sown.[4]

All in all, Judas was a victim of his own dark heart. He bears the responsibility for what he did. His deeds were his own. Yet he was also a victim of his rejection of Jesus' radical love.

That love makes the rest of our text intelligible. With Judas gone, it seems that our Lord felt somewhat relieved. We have all experienced something like this. There have been times we have been in the presence of someone who has not liked us and we have felt stifled. But then that person left, and the conversation flowed. Now, even though Jesus spoke of the cross, the conversation was brighter as he addressed his purified flock.

> When he had gone out, Jesus said, "Now is the Son of Man glorified, and God is glorified in him. If God is glorified in him, God will also glorify him in himself, and glorify him at once. Little children, yet a little while I am with you. You will seek me, and just as I said to the Jews, so now I also say to you, 'Where I am going you cannot come.'" (vv. 31–33)

With this, Jesus turned from the demonstration to the demand of love as he delivered his deepest teaching.

Love's Demand (vv. 34, 35)

> A new commandment I give to you, that you love one another: just as I have loved you, you also are to love one another. By this all people will know that you are my disciples, if you have love for one another. (vv. 34, 35)

Jesus called this "a new commandment," although the commandment to love was as old as the Mosaic revelation. He did so because his radical love demanded a *new object* and a *new measure*. The object was now "one another." The Jews had watered down the Mosaic teaching so they could love whom they wanted and hate whom they wanted. But Christ changed the object from "neighbor" to "one another." This was a radical new commandment. The world at that time was divided by prejudicial divisions that make many of our differences pale by comparison—master and slave, Jews and Gentiles, and so on. The Greeks regarded Jews as barbarians. The Jews had the reputation of being haters of the world. There was also a vast chasm between men and women. The world seemed helplessly alienated. Alexander Maclaren describes what happened because of Christ's command:

> Barbarian, Scythian, bond and free, male and female, Jew and Greek, learned and ignorant . . . sat down at one table, and felt themselves all one in Christ Jesus. They were ready to break all other bonds, and to yield to the uniting forces that streamed out from his Cross. There never had been anything like it. No wonder that the world began to babble about sorcery, and conspiracies, and complicity in unnamable vices. It was only that the disciples were obeying the new commandment, and a new thing had come into the world—a community held together by love and not by geographical accidents or linguistic affinities, or the iron fetters of the conqueror. . . . The new commandment made a new thing, and the world wondered.[5]

It was as a band of brothers and sisters that the church conquered the world. It was a glorious band of brothers and sisters that sailed the oceans and marched through the continents to both dungeon and throne with the good news of salvation through Jesus Christ! One of the reasons they succeeded is that mankind, severed from one another, longing to come together, witnessed real love among the followers of Christ—and especially among believing Jews, the narrowest, most bigoted, most intolerant nation on the face of the earth.

A number of years ago Johanne Lukasse of the Belgian Evangelical Mission came to the realization that evangelism in Belgium was getting nowhere. The nation's long history of traditional Catholicism, the subsequent disillusionment resulting from Vatican II, and the aggression of the cults had left the land seemingly impervious to the gospel. Driven to the Scriptures, he read John 13 and devised a plan. First, he gathered together a heterogeneous group—Belgian, Dutch, Americans—whoever would come. Second, he had them rent a house and live together for seven months. As is natural, frictions developed as the believers rubbed against one another. This, in turn, sent them to prayer for love and victory. Finally, they went out to witness to others, and they began to see amazing fruit. Outsiders called them "the people who love each other."

Left to ourselves, we seek our own. Movie stars marry movie stars. Doctors seek out doctors. Middle-classers seek out middle-classers. Bikers seek bikers. But when Christ comes, that changes. In the church of Jesus Christ, we discover that the people we love and with whom we fellowship are different from us. The more there is of the love Christ exhorted us to have, a love for one another, the greater will be the diversity within the Body of Christ.

The commandment was new because of its *object*, but also because of its *measure*. If, thought Christ, we are making friends and loving those whom we never would have before we met Christ, praise God—the love of Christ is working in and through us! The measure of this love is, "as I have loved you." Here we clearly see the command's radical nature, for while it is admittedly difficult to love your neighbor as yourself (as the old commandment demanded), it is far more difficult to love others as Christ loves them. That is sacrificial love. On this occasion it was defined by Jesus' dealings with Judas. When Jesus said, "Men, love one another as I have loved you," the disciples naturally thought of Jesus' love, his consistency, his washing their feet. But the disciples were at a disadvantage. They could not then know how Jesus was even loving Judas. Though Judas was his enemy, the Savior reached out to him. Within the church if we are to love one another as Jesus loved us, we must reach out in reconciliation, love, and forgiveness to those who are wronging us. And when that is done, it becomes a convincing argument for the gospel.

Conclusion

In verse 35 Jesus says: "By this all people will know that you are my disciples, if you have love for one another." Possibly the greatest gift that we as the Body of Christ can give the world is to love each other. If we do that, those on the outside will desire to learn more about the gift of gifts, the King of kings himself. The radicalness of Jesus' love in the upper room came as he reached out to one with whom he was not in accord. Will we love likewise, with his love?

41

The Fall and Rise of the Apostle Peter

JOHN 13:36–38

THE LAST THREE VERSES of John 13 center on Peter, a disciple with whom many of us can identify and from whom we can all learn valuable, practical lessons of Christian living and service. If only we did not have to learn lessons the hard way, like Peter did. . . . Perhaps we do not have to, but we do nevertheless.

Peter's Primacy

The Gospels are full of Peter! No disciple spoke as often as Peter. Our Lord addressed him more than any other of his followers. No disciple was reproved by Jesus as much or as strongly as Peter was. He was also the only disciple who thought it his duty to reprove Jesus! He was impulsive, one of those souls who acted first and thought afterward. No disciple ever so boldly confessed and encouraged Christ—and none ever bothered our Lord more than he did.

Christ spoke words of approval and praise (and even blessing) to Peter, the likes of which he never spoke to any other man. At the same time, and almost in the same breath, he said sterner things to Peter than he ever said to any of the other twelve disciples, including Judas! In all four lists of the apostles given in the Gospels, the order of the names varies, but Peter's is *always* first and Judas' is *always* last. All the Gospels testify to Peter's primacy. Peter was always talking, and his verbiage ranged from the ridiculous to the sublime. Sometimes he only opened his mouth to change feet. At other times his words were priceless.

Shortly after his calling, when he observed the miracle of the great catch of fish, he cried out, "Depart from me, for I am a sinful man, O Lord" (Luke 5:8). In answer to Christ's question as to who he was, Peter's immortal response in Matthew 16:16 was, "You are the Christ, the Son of the living God." And yet a few moments later when Christ spoke of the cross, Peter foolishly replied, "Far be it from you, Lord! This shall never happen to you" (Matthew 16:22). Foot-in-mouth disease again! On that stormy night in Tiberias, it was Peter who thrillingly called, "Lord, if it is you, command me to come to you on the water" (Matthew 14:28) and then a few moments later cried, "Lord, save me" (Matthew 14:30) when he began to sink from doubt.

It will always be to his credit that when the others abandoned Jesus, realizing that he was not primarily a material deliverer but a spiritual Savior, and Jesus said, "Do you want to go away as well?" Peter replied, "Lord, to whom shall we go? You have the words of eternal life, and we have believed, and have come to know, that you are the Holy One of God" (6:67–69). But it was also Peter who later on the Mount of Transfiguration, when Jesus shone like the sun, made the preposterous proposal, "Lord, it is good that we are here. If you wish, I will make three tents here, one for you and one for Moses and one for Elijah" (Matthew 17:4).

Now in the upper room Peter said, "You shall never wash my feet" (13:8), then reversed himself, saying, "Lord, not my feet only but also my hands and my head!" (13:9). And after Christ's resurrection Peter's unforgettable tenderness was poignantly expressed in 21:17: "Lord, you know everything; you know that I love you."

When I think of Peter I imagine a broad-shouldered, loud, extroverted, assertive man who is always sweating. Lloyd Douglas's title *The Big Fisherman* says it all. He was a headstrong, unbridled hulk who was always getting into all kinds of trouble and causing his Master plenty of the same. But he also kept turning back to Christ. I love Peter! Sometimes preachers use him as a "homiletical whipping boy." It is great fun to portray "God's clod" slipping below the waters of Galilee! But none of us has walked on water! His passion and honesty and boyishness make him a lovable figure.

Two outstanding characteristics contribute to the primacy of Peter. First, he was a man with a bold, impulsive *confidence*. Even before he met Christ, he was a straight-ahead guy—"full steam ahead." After he met Christ and had something to live for, he was first out of the boat, first with the sword, second to the empty tomb (only because jogging was not his thing). Secondly, *he loved Jesus!* These two qualities combined to produce Peter's primacy. They also contributed to his fateful presumption.

Peter's Presumption

It is night, and the next day Christ will die. Judas has taken the morsel from Jesus' hand and gone out into the darkness, physically and spiritually. The remaining disciples are still reclining with our Lord around the table in the upper room. The seat to Jesus' left is empty. With Judas gone, the Lord exults that the time for his glorification is at hand.

> When he had gone out, Jesus said, "Now is the Son of Man glorified, and God is glorified in him. If God is glorified in him, God will also glorify him in himself, and glorify him at once. Little children, yet a little while I am with you. You will seek me, and just as I said to the Jews, so now I also say to you, 'Where I am going you cannot come.'" (13:31–33)

Evidently Peter heard only the final sentence and missed the famous new commandment in verses 34, 35. So he asked, "Lord, where are you going?" (v. 36). Jesus answered, "Where I am going you cannot follow me now, but you will follow afterward" (v. 36).

Peter did not like that at all! So he protested, "Lord, why can I not follow you now? I will lay down my life for you" (v. 37). This is vintage Peter! "What do you mean I can't follow you? I'll lay down my life as a good shepherd if necessary!" This was not the first time Peter was presumptuous. Now, Peter meant what he said! He was not a flippant braggart. If the Romans had come in right then, he would have barred the door or even told them to put up their dukes. Proverbs 16:18 says, "Pride goes before destruction, and a haughty spirit before a fall." And Peter had a problem!

Peter's presumption came partly from his shallow understanding of what it means to follow Christ and partly from a mistaken estimate of his abilities. Following Christ is perhaps the most difficult challenge in our lives. It requires far more than natural human determination or ability. It requires the life of Christ in us—and Peter did not yet know that in its fullness.

Alexander Whyte comments on this:

> Peter was born a supreme man. Nature herself, as we call her, had, with her ever-bountiful and original hands, stamped his supremacy upon Peter before he was born. And when he came to be a disciple of Jesus Christ he entered on, and continued to hold, that natural and aboriginal supremacy.[1]

It was so easy for Peter to measure everything from the perspective of his own natural strength. "I don't know about the rest of the group, but I know *I* can do it! I've never backed down from anyone or anything!"

A number of years ago Robert J. Ringer's book *Winning Through Intimi-*

dation was a best seller. One of the endorsements on the paperback edition said, "You have hit the nail on the head. *INTIMIDATION* has got to be the greatest book I've ever read." Even Peter did not subscribe to such a crass philosophy, though there in the upper room he was depending on his own human strength—and that was the root of his presumption.

But that was not all there was to Peter—he also had a great love for Jesus, and he could not bear the thought of being separated from him. The poor man was speaking with his heart and not his head. Jesus answered Peter in verse 38: "Will you lay down your life for me? Truly, truly, I say to you, the rooster will not crow till you have denied me three times." Peter did not know how weak he was. Perhaps Jesus' words had an effect because we don't hear another word from Peter in the upper room. Poor Peter. I can see him sulking like a chastened puppy.

Peter's Plunge

The rest of Peter's story goes beyond the passage we are studying in this chapter, but to complete our consideration of this impulsive apostle, we will review what happened afterward. As the night wore on and the meal was finished, Jesus and his men sang a hymn and left the room, then crossed the ravine of the Kidron and ascended the slopes to Gethsemane. Here the Master fell into great agony of prayer so that he shed, as it were, great drops of blood. Repeatedly he came to his disciples (including Peter, of course) only to find them fast asleep. After a time they became aware of an approaching crowd and saw spears and swords and Judas and the kiss of betrayal. Peter had to take action! "Then Simon Peter, having a sword, drew it and struck the high priest's servant and cut off his right ear. (The servant's name was Malchus.)" (18:10). Some have made light of Peter's swordsmanship, saying it was a night when Peter could not do anything right. But there is another explanation—Malchus was wearing the traditional helmet that left the ears exposed, and Peter caught him atop the head and took off an ear. Peter was going for the man's head! In fact, he was ready to take on the whole enemy! We are talking about a brave man. He meant well but was misguided, and so Jesus replied, "Put your sword into its sheath; shall I not drink the cup that the Father has given me?" (18:11). Jesus healed Malchus' ear and then was taken away, with Peter and John stumbling behind at a safe distance.

The procession came first to the house of Annas, where John's connections got them past the first doorkeeper and into the courtyard. But there was a cost—the slave girl who kept the door recognized Peter, saying, "You also are not one of this man's disciples, are you?" (18:17). To which Peter amazingly answered, "I am not."

It was cold, so as Jesus' interrogation continued behind closed doors, those in the courtyard, including Peter, warmed themselves over the glowing charcoal. They probably talked about the Passover crowds, yesterday's fight in the barracks, the new dancing girl, this eccentric teacher from Galilee. Again the girl spoke out: "This man is one of them" (Mark 14:69). Peter again firmly denied it.

About an hour passed, but now the soldiers were getting suspicious too because of Peter's accent. "Certainly you are one of them, for you are a Galilean," they said (Mark 14:70). Then one of the slaves who was a relative of Malchus piped up, "Did I not see you in the garden with him?" (18:26). Peter was trapped! There was no way out except one. His face flushed, his lips curled, and words that had long fallen into disuse poured forth. "He began to invoke a curse on himself and to swear, 'I do not know this man of whom you speak'" (Mark 14:71). At the very least he said, "I don't know what in God's Name you are talking about!" It was probably even stronger than that, for he meant to shock them and thus put them off.

It was the moment of truth. In the heat of his denial, Peter was oblivious to the shuffle of feet as Christ was being led out into the courtyard, and certainly he was not prepared for the excruciation of the next moment. Dr. Luke tells us:

> And immediately, while he was still speaking, the rooster crowed. And the Lord turned and looked at Peter. And Peter remembered the saying of the Lord, how he had said to him, "Before the rooster crows today, you will deny me three times." And he went out and wept bitterly. (Luke 22:60–62)

Christ paused and looked right into the soul of Peter, and the tears coursed down that disciple's face like rain down a rock.

Peter, so filled with presumption just a few hours earlier that he had declared he would die for the Master, had now denied him. Worse, it was not a silent default. And worse yet, it happened not once but three times!

No one would have predicted Peter's plunge. The great apostle had failed precisely at the point of his greatest human strength. This natural extrovert and naturally brave man could not bear the ridicule of the crowd. The shock and strain of seeing evil in apparent triumph over good had shaken his faith, and the censure and estrangement of those around the fire were too much. Our greatest human strengths (no matter what they are) will *never* be adequate for following Christ. What is your greatest natural strength? A winning personality . . . charm . . . discipline . . . speaking ability . . . intelligence . . . wealth . . . attractive or impressive appearance . . . aggressiveness . . . position? Christ can use all these things, but if we suppose we will be able to follow and serve him *because* of our natural gifts, we had better prepare ourselves for a plunge like Peter's. Natural devotion and natural strength will always deny Jesus somewhere or sometime.

No one will ever know the terrible anguish of soul that Peter went through then—the nauseous darkness and confusion of those seventy-two hours of the grave. Something died inside Peter that night! Simon the natural man with all his self-assured presumption was about to die. Peter was beginning to know himself. He was defeated and disconsolate that night, but God was not through with him! As we will see in our study of John 21, our Savior restored Peter over breakfast beside the Sea of Galilee.

Peter's Perfection

The Peter we see in John 21 and in the book of Acts is a different Peter! He was a changed man! On the Day of Pentecost his life displayed the overflowing sufficiency of the Holy Spirit, as we see in his blistering sermon in Acts 2: "This Jesus, delivered up according to the definite plan and foreknowledge of God, you crucified and killed by the hands of lawless men" (v. 23). And before the cynical and sophisticated Caiaphas, who had ordered Christ's death, Peter said:

> "Let it be known to all of you and to all the people of Israel that by the name of Jesus Christ of Nazareth, whom you crucified, whom God raised from the dead—by him this man is standing before you well. This Jesus is the stone that was rejected by you, the builders, which has become the cornerstone. And there is salvation in no one else, for there is no other name under heaven given among men by which we must be saved." Now when they saw the boldness of Peter and John, and perceived that they were uneducated, common men, they were astonished. And they recognized that they had been with Jesus. (Acts 4:10–13)

Peter had become a rock! He was stronger after his plunge than he had ever been! Immediately after Peter's restoration our Lord prophesied of Peter's death:

> "Truly, truly, I say to you, when you were young, you used to dress yourself and walk wherever you wanted, but when you are old, you will stretch out your hands [a phrase that C. K. Barrett believes refers to crucifixion[2]], and another will dress you and carry you where you do not want to go." (This he said to show by what kind of death he was to glorify God.) (21:18, 19)

Our Lord's words are not entirely clear except that at Peter's death he would be a feeble man dependent on the help of others. The traditional view is that Peter was crucified upside-down in Rome because he claimed he was not worthy to be crucified upright, and in that dramatically weakened state Peter was a remarkable demonstration of Christ's power. The rope that is broken is strongest after it is spliced, not because it was broken, but because a skillful hand has strengthened it. "We may be stronger for our sins, not because sin strengthens, for it weakens, but because God restores."[3]

What happened to Peter happened to some degree or in some way to all the apostles, and happens to all who follow Christ today. Paul was one of the greatest minds the church has ever produced. He was the mastermind of the evangelization of Asia Minor. He was the missionary general of the early church. Yet he was not by nature bold. "[Pray] also for me, that words may be given to me in opening my mouth boldly to proclaim the mystery of the gospel" (Ephesians 6:19). But he ascended to the heights of boldness. Acts 14 records his being dragged out of the city of Lystra, stoned, and left for dead and how as the disciples were standing about mourning over him, he popped open an eye and said, "Let's get going!" And they did—right back into Lystra! We also have his emboldened defense before King Agrippa in Acts 26. Consider these words of Paul:

> But he [God] said to me, "My grace is sufficient for you, for my power is made perfect in weakness." Therefore I will boast all the more gladly of my weaknesses, so that the power of Christ may rest upon me. For the sake of Christ, then, I am content with weaknesses, insults, hardships, persecutions, and calamities. For when I am weak, then I am strong. (2 Corinthians 12:9, 10)

Paul understood the source of his power as found in Colossians 2:9, 10: "For in him [Christ] the whole fullness of deity dwells bodily, and you have been filled in him." The great J. B. Lightfoot said: "Your fullness comes from his fullness; his *pleroma* is transfused into you by virtue of your incorporation in him."[4] His fullness becomes our fullness!

That is exactly what happened to Peter. Second Peter 1:4 says, "He has granted to us his precious and very great promises, so that through them you may become partakers of the divine nature." It was the life of Christ in him.

> I have been crucified with Christ. It is no longer I who live, but Christ who lives in me. And the life I now live in the flesh I live by faith in the Son of God, who loved me and gave himself for me. (Galatians 2:20)

Our sufficiency comes from Christ! If we ask him, he will give his power to us. In Luke 11:13 Jesus says, "If you then, who are evil, know how to give good gifts to your children, how much more will the heavenly Father give the Holy Spirit to those who ask him!" Peter had been impulsively confident, but now his confidence was richer and deeper because of the fullness of Christ.

Conclusion

High among the indispensable truths of practical Christianity is this: God is constantly at work to show us that even those things we count as our greatest natural strengths are, by his standards, really weaknesses. When this principle is put to work, our strengths are enhanced and ennobled just like Peter's. But perhaps even more glorious, our weaknesses become occasions for his power! Our shyness, an occasion for his boldness; our weakness of speech, an occasion for his articulation; our lack of imagination, for his creativity; our ignorance, for his instruction; our insecurity, for his assurance. Second Corinthians 4:7 says: "But we have this treasure in jars of clay, to show that the surpassing power belongs to God and not to us." May we lay our lives before him with all our strengths and allow his fullness to work in and through us.

42

"Let Not Your Hearts Be Troubled," Part I

JOHN 14:1–6

THE DISCIPLES WERE NOW TROUBLED MEN. After the euphoria of Christ's triumphal entry into Jerusalem had come his confusing words about imminent betrayal and denial by some of the Twelve. They were dismayed, and the trouble of their hearts was only a shadow of the darkness that lurked nearby.

Knowing their anguish, Jesus spoke to the issue in the opening words of chapter 14: "Let not your hearts be troubled." In the original Greek, this carries the firmness, resolve, and conviction of a command, though from the context we understand these words most likely to have been spoken very gently. Our Lord's statement was not just for his disciples, but for all who would ever follow him. Rightly understood and applied, John 14:1–6 is good medicine for our hearts, for we too live in an age of anxiety.

A good title for our times would be "The Cardiac Age." Many of us have troubled hearts today. Rising crime rates, rising costs of living, international crises, political corruption, escalating violence not only in Third-World countries but in our own neighborhoods—all this and much more brings deep concern to our hearts.

And if that is not bad enough, we also all have the tendency to borrow trouble, to imagine things to be worse than they are. Keats said, "Imaginary grievances have always been my torment more than real ones." Which is worse—the actual hypodermic injection in the dentist's chair or the anticipation as you walk into an antiseptic-smelling office, sign your name, and walk down a long hallway to the dentist's chair surrounded by ominous instruments? Imagined fears can be far worse than reality! Even Christians are not immune from troubled hearts as we struggle with an imperfect faith and seek to help others bear their burdens.

I served as assistant pastor for nine years under a very godly man, and during that time I never saw him lose his temper, say an unkind word about anyone, or lose his cool in public, even under the most trying circumstances. He was a model individual and pastor. His wife told me that one night she woke up and saw her husband asleep on his elbows and knees, with his arms cupped as if holding something and muttering. She said to him, "What on earth are you doing?" Still asleep, he replied, "Shh. I'm holding a pyramid of marbles together, and if I move, they'll all fall down." Even his heart knew anxiety.

When Jesus said, "Let not your hearts be troubled," he used a picturesque word. The idea is, "Don't let your heart shudder." In the preceding chapter, in verse 21, the same word was used to describe Jesus' emotion as Judas went astray. It is a strong word, and he was saying specifically to the disciples (especially in light of the imminent cross), "It may look like your world is falling in and all is lost and the darkness is going to engulf you, but don't let your heart be troubled."

Then he explained how to do this: "Believe in God; believe also in me." The way to have an untroubled heart is to believe in God and believe in Jesus. That is all there is to it. The tenses tell us, "Keep on believing in God. Keep on believing in me." If we would keep in mind the attributes of God—his sovereignty, his omniscience, his omnipotence—our hearts would not be troubled like they often are. The Lord knew we would need a further explanation of what is involved, so he went on to specifically instruct us on the nature of the belief that will deliver our troubled hearts.

Believe That He Is Preparing an Eternal Place for You (v. 2)

In my Father's house are many rooms. If it were not so, would I have told you that I go to prepare a place for you?

An effective guard against having a troubled heart is to believe that Jesus Christ is preparing an eternal place for us as individuals. We all long for Heaven. Many years ago a perpetually barefoot little girl walked across the grass of a housing project, the kind built to house dependents of servicemen during World War II. She was on her way to a Good News Club. She had a dream, and she thought she could make her dream come true because Mrs. White, who taught that group, promised to give her a little book she could read. It was a wordless book, and she had dreamed about that book with its colored pages and its little clasp that neatly snapped shut. She had encouraged her older brothers and sisters to repeat over and over again the words that went with the pages. The black (Romans 3:23), the red (John 3:16), the white (Isaiah 1:18), and, very significantly, the gold (John 14:2, 3). That day she recited her verses, received her book, and sang with the rest of the children.

> Once my heart was black as sin,
> Until the Savior came in.
> His precious blood I know
> Has washed it whiter than snow;
> And in this world I'm told
> I'll walk the streets of gold.
> Oh, wonderful, wonderful day;
> He washed my sins away.

That little girl, now my wife, Barbara, will never forget that day because on that day she met Jesus. In retrospect she says it was the gold page—the promise of an eternal dwelling—that caught hold of her and drew her to Jesus. We all have a longing for Heaven.

On a more sophisticated level, C. S. Lewis calls this the "inconsolable longing."

> There have been times when I think we do not desire heaven, but more often I find myself wondering whether in our heart of hearts, we have ever desired anything else. . . . It is the secret signature of each soul, the incommunicable and unappeasable want, the thing we desired before we met our wives or made our friends or chose our work, and which we shall still desire on our deathbeds when the mind no longer knows wife or friend or work.[1]

We have a longing for Heaven, whether we recognize it or not. We have a desire to live with Christ. We see this in our utopian political philosophies. Marxism, though it thrives on economic woe and injustice, at its core feeds on a longing for Heaven.

Jesus tells us how our unsatisfied longing will be fulfilled: "In my Father's house are many rooms [or dwelling places]." The idea is, he is preparing *permanent* dwelling places for us. When life falls in, when troubles assail us, as they indeed will, we can find comfort and rest for our troubled hearts in the fact that there is an eternal home prepared for us. The psychology of this is impeccable. Paul Tournier, in his book *A Place for You*, says:

> If as a child you have not known a secure home, it is very likely as you go through life regardless of your abode or wherever you are, you will not feel

at home. But on the other hand, if as a child you have been secure and at home, wherever you go will be home.[2]

Having a deep, underlying heart realization that there is an eternal abode for us will bring rest to our souls in the midst of this troubled world. This, I believe, is what made the Apostle Paul such a powerful force even though his world kept falling in. I do not think anyone experienced more trials and tribulations than Paul, and perhaps no one has experienced more of God's sustaining power. But he had an advantage over us.

> I know a man in Christ who fourteen years ago was caught up to the third heaven—whether in the body or out of the body I do not know, God knows. And I know that this man was caught up into paradise—whether in the body or out of the body I do not know, God knows—and he heard things that cannot be told, which man may not utter. (2 Corinthians 12:2–4)

Paul himself did not know if it was a vision or a literal physical experience, but somehow he was caught up into Paradise, and there he saw heavenly realities. The same Apostle Paul who had this vision of Heaven and knew there was a real place for him went victoriously through an amazing list of difficulties (see 2 Corinthians 11). The first certainly fueled the latter. "But our citizenship is in heaven, and from it we await a Savior, the Lord Jesus Christ" (Philippians 3:20). Ephesians 2:6 adds, "Seated us with him [Christ] in the heavenly places." It was that reality that made Paul such a warrior.

John 14:2 tells us that Jesus has gone "to prepare a place" for us. That is a key element of our comfort. Many of us love having guests in our homes, and we lovingly prepare for them. We set out flowers and books we think they will like and lovingly ready a room for them. Jesus is preparing a special place for each of us. I imagine my room will be homey Gothic, lined with books, and it will have a great fireplace with a trophy trout over it! Maybe not, but the point is, Jesus is preparing wonderful homes for me and for you, and that brings us comfort in this troubled world. Some people say this is escapism, that we are being so heavenly minded that we are no earthly good. I do not think so. We may be so pious that we are no earthly good. We may be so religious that we are no earthly good. We may be so impractical that we are no earthly good. But I do not believe we can be so heavenly minded that we are no earthly good. The reality of our heavenly abode helps us guard our troubled hearts. Is our heavenly abode real to us?

When we plan family vacations, do we just drive off with no prior preparation? No way! We obtain brochures, we talk to our friends, we examine maps and pack our bags. How much more we ought to prepare for eternity, for our heavenly home will be wonderful beyond words.

Believe That He Is Coming to Take You to Be with Him (v. 3)

And if I go and prepare a place for you, I will come again and will take you to myself, that where I am you may be also.

In our fallen world, we can gain relief for our troubled hearts from the fact that Jesus is going to take us to be personally with him. *Not just the place, but the person, Jesus, is going to be ours.* "I will come again" is in the present tense—"I am coming again." In the New Testament there are 318 allusions or direct references to the fact that the Lord is going to return to take us to be with him personally. We are going to see him face-to-face. First John 3:2 says:

Beloved, we are God's children now, and what we will be has not yet appeared; but we know that when he appears we shall be like him, because we shall see him as he is.

John Donne said concerning this reality:

I shall be so like God that the devil himself shall not know me from God. He will not be able to tempt me any more than he can tempt God. Nor will there be any more chance of my falling out of the kingdom than of God being driven out of it.[3]

That is why Paul said, "Yet which I shall choose I cannot tell. I am hard pressed between the two. My desire is to depart and be with Christ, for that is far better" (Philippians 1:22, 23).

John 14:1–6 is one of the most comforting passages in all of Scripture. Dr. A. L. Gaebelein used to say that among his family treasures was a German Bible that went back many generations. He said one could open that Bible to some pages and it looked like it had just come off the press, but when opened to John 14, it was spotted, soiled, and worn from the tears of many generations. John Watson, the great preacher, said that if someone in his flock was going through deep waters and was about to die, sometimes he would kneel down next to them and whisper, "In My Father's house are many mansions," and he said that three quarters of the way through the river they would almost turn around and come back, and he would hear them repeating, "Father's house . . . many mansions. . . ." Henry Venn, a Puritan preacher, was dying and, his biography tells us, "The prospect made him so high-spirited and jubilant that his doctor said that his joy at dying kept him alive a further fortnight."⁴ We derive great comfort from the fact that Jesus is coming to take us to be with him.

> But we do not want you to be uninformed, brothers, about those who are asleep, that you may not grieve as others do who have no hope. For since we believe that Jesus died and rose again, even so, through Jesus, God will bring with him those who have fallen asleep. For this we declare to you by a word from the Lord, that we who are alive, who are left until the coming of the Lord, will not precede those who have fallen asleep. For the Lord himself will descend from heaven with a cry of command, with the voice of an archangel, and with the sound of the trumpet of God. And the dead in Christ will rise first. Then we who are alive, who are left, will be caught up together with them in the clouds to meet the Lord in the air, and so we will always be with the Lord. Therefore encourage one another with these words. (1 Thessalonians 4:13–18)

This is to be a great comfort to our souls. Though we live in a world of trouble and tribulation, we "[Wait] for our blessed hope, the appearing of the glory of our great God and Savior Jesus Christ" (Titus 2:13). What a comfort—Jesus will take us to be with him.

Put Your Faith Totally in Him (vv. 4–6)

Our Lord concludes his statement by saying, "You know the way to where I am going" (v. 4). Thomas did not understand, and in verse 5 he asked (probably speaking for all the disciples), "Lord, we do not know where you are going. How can we know the way?" Jesus responded with one of his most-quoted statements: "I am the way, and the truth, and the life. No one comes to the Father except through me" (v. 6). The troubled heart needs to remember that Jesus Christ is everything. He is "the way, and the truth, and the life." Jesus' encouraging words came just before the cross, and there we find further comfort, not only in its saving power, but in its demonstration of divine love. And it is Christ's love that sees us through this troubled world.

Conclusion

We all have repeated experiences of life falling in on us. Job said, "But man is born to trouble as [surely as] the sparks fly upward" (Job 5:7). Trials are part of life on earth. But Christ always says to us in the darkness, "Let not your hearts be troubled." How? "Believe in God; believe also in me." Specifically, this is a command to believe in the substance of verse 6: "I am the way, and the truth, and the life." He invites us to remember that he is coming to take us to be with him, and that will be healing medicine for our troubled hearts.

43

"Let Not Your Hearts Be Troubled," Part II

JOHN 14:12–27

IN JOHN 14:1–6 Jesus told his disciples he was going to prepare a place for them where they would live forever with him. An awareness of that prospect brings comfort to troubled hearts. Subsequent questions by Thomas and Philip led the Savior to reveal new teaching about the Holy Spirit. Significantly, in this second part of this discourse Jesus used words almost identical to those with which he began the discussion: "Let not your hearts be troubled, neither let them be afraid" (v. 27). If we truly grasp the Holy Spirit's ministry, we will find calm confidence in this troubled world.

Without doing injustice to the context, we will in this chapter consider several choice truths from John 14:12–27, though not in the order in which they appear in the chapter.

The Comforting Nature of the Holy Spirit (v. 16)

"And I will ask the Father, and he will give you another Helper, to be with you forever." There is a grammatical point in this verse that we need to understand because it colors everything that follows. It is found in the phrase "another Helper." Two different Greek words can be translated "another"—*allos* and *heteros*. *Allos*, used here, means another of the same kind, while *heteros* means another of a different kind.[1]

The difference would be clearly seen if I held a Golden Delicious apple in front of a church congregation and announced I was going to have the ushers distribute apples to each person present. However, when I went to the grocery store, I was not able to obtain enough Golden Delicious for everyone, so I purchased some Jonathans. The result? Some in the congregation would have Jonathans and some Golden Delicious. Those with the Jonathans would have another of a different kind (*heteros*), but those with the Golden Delicious would have another of the same kind (*allos*)—just like the one I had held up. The word Jesus used to describe the coming Helper was *allos*, which means another helper *just like him!* Jesus was comforting his disciples by assuring them they did not need to be troubled at his leaving because the "Helper" or "Counselor" he would send was just like him. There would be no loss in the exchange. So much are they the same that in Romans 8:9 the Apostle Paul calls the Holy Spirit "the Spirit of Christ."

Have you ever wished you could speak with Jesus face-to-face, so you could share your deepest concerns and fears in his physical presence and see his face as you listened to his understanding and loving feedback? You might tell him, "Master, I thought I would have my life all together by now, but I have never felt more disoriented and confused. What's the answer?" Or perhaps, "I feel worthless. I do my very best, but I always come up short. Lord, what's wrong?" After our personal interview with Jesus, we would without doubt find our self-worth substantiated, our security established, our emptiness satisfied. That talk with Jesus would give us great comfort and strength for our lives.

The logic of our text tells us that having the "Helper" (the Holy Spirit) is the same as having Jesus physically accessible, only better. Imagine he is in Jerusalem. All the airlines would be applying for routes to the Middle East. You would not be able to book a seat on a plane. Steamers, passenger liners, the trains of Europe and Asia would all be moving toward Jerusalem. And even if we ever managed to get close to where Jesus was, there would be long convoys and great crowds of people. We would come to see Jesus, but it would be nearly impossible to get within arm's reach of him. But we have access to the Holy Spirit right now and always. He is at our side. Even better, not only is the Holy Spirit just like Jesus, but his function is to be our "Counselor" or "Helper" or "Comforter." The Greek word used here, *paraclete*, often meant one who was a legal counsel in court, one who argued the case and stood in someone's stead. It always contains the idea of encouragement, one who will shoulder the responsibility of another.

As a father I always tried to help my little ones learn to ride a bike without suffering too many scrapes and bruises. First there would be training wheels and a steadying hand on the handlebars. Then would come the day the training wheels came off, with Dad running alongside the bicycle, one hand under the seat, giving instructions—"Now relax. Keep your wheel straight. Steady! I've got you! You're doing great!" Crash! Time to pick up the child and encourage him to try again. The Holy Spirit comes alongside us, encourages us, holds us up, picks us up, dusts us off when we fall, and gets us going again.

The Apostle Paul wrote in 2 Corinthians that he had been disheartened, "But God, who comforts the downcast, comforted us by the coming of Titus" (2 Corinthians 7:6). Undoubtedly, Titus asked, "How are you doing, Paul, old friend? Not too well?" Then he put his arm around Paul and said, "Paul, let's pray." He prayed with Paul, listened to Paul, reminded him of past battles and victories, and shared some Scriptures with him. Pretty soon Paul started feeling better and was ready to go. That gives us a picture of the Helper, the One who comes alongside. The Latin *advocatus* is the word from which we get our English word *advocate*, used in some Bible translations. Both the *New International Version* and the *Revised Standard Version* say, "Counselor." *The Living Bible* says, "Comforter." *Knox's Translation* very beautifully says, "Another friend for you." If you are going through hard times, it is the work of the Holy Spirit to come alongside and comfort and strengthen you.

A Comforting Relationship with the Holy Spirit (vv. 16, 17, 26)

> And I will ask the Father, and he will give you another Helper, to be with you forever, even the Spirit of truth, whom the world cannot receive, because it neither sees him nor knows him. You know him, for he dwells with you and will be in you. (vv. 16, 17)

Not only does the Holy Spirit come alongside, but the last phrase says, "He . . . will be in you." He abides in us! In verse 23 Jesus expanded that concept when he answered the other Judas (not Iscariot):

> If anyone loves me, he will keep my word, and my Father will love him, and we will come to him and make our home with him.

God the Father and God the Son also reside within us. At the beginning of the chapter Jesus encouraged us not to be troubled because his person and place await us. Now he is saying, "Let not your heart be troubled because I am making a place *within* you." In fact, the word translated "place" in verse 2 and the word for "home" in verse 23 is the same word. Jesus is preparing a dwelling place for us, but he also dwells within us.

One of the most encouraging facts of Christianity is that the Helper not only comes alongside but comes inside of us. One of the most devastating thoughts anyone can entertain when he is going through trouble is, "I am alone." After that comes self-pity, and then the thought that "no one cares."

These are common feelings but unnecessary for the believer. When caring for a sick child the believing parent is never alone. He is not alone in the hospital facing death, or standing over a fresh grave, or at work, or on a missionary compound. Even when we do not feel Christ's presence, he is within us.

Much of the indwelling comfort comes by virtue of the fact that the Holy Spirit in us is, as verse 17 says, "the Spirit of truth." The Spirit of truth indwelling us allows us to begin to understand our inner self and to see and understand something about the course of the world about us. Because of that, we are comforted. He also brings comfort to troubled hearts by reminding us of the Word of God.

> But the Helper, the Holy Spirit, whom the Father will send in my name, he will teach you all things and bring to your remembrance all that I have said to you. (v. 26)

For the unregenerate mind the mysteries of God's purpose in life remain barred, but the indwelling Spirit brings the believer comprehension and thus comfort. He brings before our troubled hearts the Word of God and applies its comforts. When believers stand in a hospital with those whose whole lives are caving in and the Holy Spirit brings to their remembrance the promises of God's Word—how marvelously complete is that comfort!

Jesus promises, "I will not leave you as orphans [literally, "fatherless"]; I will come to you" (v. 18). He is speaking about the Holy Spirit coming to bring comfort. This is perhaps the most healing, certainly the most assuring, of all Biblical doctrines. Although the great doctrine that we hang our faith on is the doctrine of justification, the doctrine of our adoption through the Holy Spirit helps us relate to and appropriate various aspects and applications of salvation.

One Christian told me that for years he had the greatest difficulty in praying to God the Father. He always prayed to Jesus because his relationship with his own father had been so bad. He was terribly insecure. Then he shared how the doctrine of adoption came to him through the ministry of the Word and now he was enjoying a much higher degree of spiritual health. The Holy Spirit had ministered the Word of God to that man's heart. A grasp of our position as God's adopted children is a key to fully appropriating the benefits of salvation. J. I. Packer says in his very helpful book *Knowing God*:

> Some years ago I wrote:
> You sum up the whole of New Testament teaching in a single phrase, if you speak of it as a revelation of the Fatherhood of the holy Creator. In the same way you sum up the whole of New Testament religion if you de-

scribe it as the knowledge of God as one's holy Father. If you want to judge how well a person understands Christianity, find out how much he makes of the thought of being God's child, and having God as his Father. If this is not the thought that prompts and controls his worship and prayers and his whole outlook on life, it means that he does not understand Christianity very well at all. For everything that Christ taught, everything that makes the New Testament new, and better than the Old, everything that is distinctively Christian as opposed to merely Jewish, is summed up in the knowledge of the Fatherhood of God. "Father" is the Christian name for God.[2]

He then continues, "This still seems to me wholly true, and very important. Our understanding of Christianity cannot be better than our grasp of adoption."[3]

God is our Father. We have been adopted by him. A friend of mine who teaches in a seminary has said that the truth of this doctrine came home to him not just because of his New Testament studies, but when he had seen a modern document for adoption. According to this document, the natural parent can disown his children, but an adoptive parent cannot. Beautiful! The Christian life can only be understood in terms of adoption. As God loved his only begotten Son, Jesus, so he loves his adopted children. In 16:27 Jesus assures us, "The Father himself loves you." God had fellowship with Jesus, and he has fellowship with us by virtue of our adoption. First John 1:3 says: "And indeed our fellowship is with the Father and with his Son Jesus Christ." God exalted the Lord Jesus, and he will exalt us.

> Beloved, we are God's children now, and what we will be has not yet appeared; but we know that when he appears we shall be like him, because we shall see him as he is. (1 John 3:2)

When Jesus promised, "I will not leave you as orphans; I will come to you," he was speaking of the comforting ministry of the Holy Spirit as he calls to mind the reality of our adoption. He keeps us conscious, even when we try to deny it, that we are God's children. In this way he gives and builds up faith and joy. Also, he prompts us to look to God as Father with the perfect trust that is natural to secure children. He intensifies "the Spirit of adoption as sons, by whom we cry, 'Abba! Father!'"—dearest Father (Romans 8:15). Finally, he helps us live up to our royal position as children of God by developing a family likeness.

The Comforting Power of the Holy Spirit (vv. 12–15)

During the fighting in the Pacific during World War II a sailor on a United States submarine was stricken with acute appendicitis. The nearest surgeon was thousands of miles away. Pharmacist Mate Wheller Lipes watched the seaman's temperature rise to 106 degrees. The man's only hope was an operation. Lipes told him, "I have watched doctors do it. I think I could. What do you say?" The sailor consented. In the wardroom, about the size of a Pullman drawing room, the patient was stretched out on a table beneath a floodlight. The mate and assisting officers, dressed in reversed pajama tops, masked their faces with gauze. The crew stood by the diving planes to keep the ship steady. The cook boiled water for sterilizing the instruments. A tea strainer served as an antiseptic cone. A broken-handled scalpel was the operating instrument. Alcohol drained from the torpedoes was the antiseptic. Bent tablespoons served to keep the muscles open. After cutting through layers of muscle, the mate took twenty minutes to find the appendix. Two and a half hours later, the last catgut stitch was sewed just as the last drop of ether gave out. Thirteen days later the patient was back at work.[4]

That was especially a magnificent act because the surgery was not done by a trained surgeon in a modern operating room, but rather by a relatively untrained man under the most difficult conditions. "Truly, truly, I say to you, whoever believes in me will also do the works that I do; and *greater works than these* will he do, because I am going to the Father" (v. 12). Because the Holy Spirit indwells us, we do the same works as Jesus—and there is a sense in which they are greater than his works, because of the humble weakness of our instruments. The same power that, through Jesus, brought regeneration and life to many flows through us. The same wisdom that brought healing to the most fragmented relationships is operable in us. The same miraculous love that brought life to impossible situations resides in us, through the Holy Spirit!

Conclusion

> Peace I leave with you; my peace I give to you. Not as the world gives do I give to you. Let not your hearts be troubled, neither let them be afraid. (v. 27)

These words are nearly identical with those with which Jesus began this chapter. He is preparing a place for us. He is giving us his person. We are going to be with him. That is all future. But we also receive present benefits that give us the power to deal with the difficulties and problems of life. We have the same power that Jesus exercised—in a sense, in an even greater way, through the Holy Spirit. What could bring more security in this world than a deepening realization of the fact that the Holy Spirit is indwelling us, not just working alongside us, and that he puts potent spiritual truth to work in our lives.

What is our Helper like? He is just like Jesus. He comes alongside us, encourages us, exhorts us. He picks us up, dusts us off, and gets us going again. So it makes perfect sense for our Lord Jesus to say in verse 27, "Peace I leave with you; my peace I give to you." The same peace the Lord Jesus had is our peace. That is the remedy for troubled hearts.

44

On Bearing Fruit

JOHN 15:1–11

OUR LORD OFTEN USED things at hand to illustrate or explain spiritual truths. At the Feast of Tabernacles as the priest approached the altar and was pouring out the symbolic water Jesus cried, "If anyone thirsts, let him come to me and drink." And the next day as he stood in the temple treasury before mammoth, extinguished torches that symbolized the pillar of fire in the wilderness, Jesus said, "I am the light of the world. Whoever follows me will not walk in darkness, but will have the light of life." He used those dead torches to proclaim that he was the departed *Shekinah* glory.

In John 15:1–11 he used a grapevine as an illustration of spiritual truth. What called this illustration to the Master's mind? Perhaps the closeness of the disciples, or perhaps the moonlit tendrils of a vine at the window. Regardless, the fact that Israel was thought of in terms of a vine reinforced his use of this image. For example, "For the vineyard of the LORD of hosts is the house of Israel, and the men of Judah are his pleasant planting" (Isaiah 5:7). The grapevine was a symbol of national life. That emblem appeared on coins minted during the Maccabean period, their regard for it resembling our regard for stars and stripes. So precious was the symbol to the Jews that a huge, gold grapevine decorated the gates of the temple. The famous old *Calmets' Dictionary* says:

> In the temple at Jerusalem, above and round the gate, seventy cubits high, which led from the porch to the holy place, a richly carved vine was extended as a border and decoration. The branches, tendrils and leaves were of finest gold; the stalks of the bunches were of the length of the human form, and the bunches hanging upon them were of costly jewels. Herod first placed it there; rich and patriotic Jews from time to time added to its embellishment, one contributed a new grape, another a leaf, and a third

even a bunch of the same precious materials . . . this vine must have had an uncommon importance and a sacred meaning in the eyes of the Jews. With what majestic splendor must it likewise have appeared in the evening, when it was illuminated by tapers![1]

It was a grand symbol of national life.

In John 15:1 Christ gives his seventh and final great "I am" statement: "I am the true vine, and my Father is the vinedresser." All the conversation stopped at this powerful pronouncement. The force of his words were, "You all know how Israel is pictured as a vine that is meant to produce refreshing fruit. Well, I am the fulfillment of all that symbol suggests." To Christian believers, this is a wonderfully deep and mystic parable. Christ is the Vine (the trunk), we are the branches, and God the Father is the Gardener. The picture taken together is that of a vineyard with true believers organically related to Christ (the sap that runs in his veins runs in ours) and of the Father walking among the vines lovingly caring for them so they will bring forth fruit.

The overriding emphasis of the passage is fruit bearing, as we see from verses 2, 4, 5, and 8:

> Every branch in me that does not bear fruit he takes away, and every branch that does bear fruit he prunes, that it may bear more fruit.
> Abide in me, and I in you. As the branch cannot bear fruit by itself, unless it abides in the vine, neither can you, unless you abide in me.
> I am the vine; you are the branches. Whoever abides in me and I in him, he it is that bears much fruit, for apart from me you can do nothing.
> By this my Father is glorified, that you bear much fruit and so prove to be my disciples.

Not only is fruit bearing the main emphasis, but our Lord makes it the identifying mark of a true believer. "Every branch in me that does not bear fruit he takes away" (v. 2). Some claim to be in the vine, but the absence of fruit disqualifies them. If there is no fruit in our life, we had better reconsider the authenticity of our Christianity.

Looking for Fruit (vv. 1, 2)

We all need to make a careful examination of our own lives as to fruit-bearing. Most of us immediately think about what we have been doing for the Lord—how many people we have won to Christ or whatever. A preacher received a letter from a girl who was in a state of "spiritual distress" because she had never won anyone to Christ—after all, Christ had promised that she would be fruitful.

Souls can be fruit. I think that was what Paul was referring to in Romans 1:13: "I have often intended to come to you . . . in order that I may reap some harvest among you." But that is not what Jesus had in mind in John 15.

> Let me sing for my beloved
> my love song concerning his vineyard:
> My beloved had a vineyard
>   on a very fertile hill.
> He dug it and cleared it of stones,
>   and planted it with choice vines;
> he built a watchtower in the midst of it,
>   and hewed out a wine vat in it;
> and he looked for it to yield grapes,
>   but it yielded wild grapes. (Isaiah 5:1, 2)

What were these "wild grapes"? "He [God] looked for justice, but behold, bloodshed; for righteousness, but behold, an outcry!" (Isaiah 5:7). The grapes he was looking for were the qualities of justice and righteousness, inner qualities.

Similarly, in John 15 the fruit Jesus speaks of is not primarily evangelism but simply the reproduction of the life of the vine in the branch. Jesus is looking for the fruit of his life in us. If the inward graces of the Holy Spirit are not present in our lives ("love, joy, peace, patience, kindness, goodness, faithfulness, gentleness, self-control," Galatians 5:22, 23), if these qualities are not present (not perfected but present) in our lives, we must face the fact that we may not be true believers. There must be something of the life of the vine in us if we belong to God! There must be Christlikeness. This is a tougher test than outward fruit such as the number of souls saved, people influenced, or money collected. It is possible to have the outward signs without having the life of Christ within. Furthermore, the inward graces of the Spirit will in time bring the outward fruit. The fruit Christ looks for is his own life in us. The question is, how do we get it?

Pruning for Fruit (vv. 2, 3)

"Every branch that does bear fruit he prunes, that it may bear more fruit" (v. 2b). *The branches that are doing well, those that best convey the life of the vine, get the knife.* Anyone who has ever driven through the great northern California vineyards understands what the Lord is talking about. In the winter all you see for miles is bare, twisted trunks. But in the summer, what meets the eye are endless rows of lush green grapevines expanding their foliage so fast you can almost see them grow. Their health is directly proportionate to their pruning. A grapevine will never produce anywhere near its potential without being pruned!

Grape-growers, viticulturists as they call themselves, practice several stages of pruning. There is pinching to remove the growing tip so it will not grow too rapidly, and also topping when a foot or two of new growth is removed to prevent the loss of an entire shoot. Thinning the grape clusters enables the rest of a branch to bear more fruit and better quality fruit. Also, the cutting away of suckers gives more nourishment to the whole plant. The vines are pruned in fall or winter so the main stock will have more advantageous growth and fruit.[2]

It may be that Jesus has this whole process in view. Whatever, it is a drastic process. To the uninitiated eye it looks cruel and wasteful, but to the experienced eye it is the only way to grow healthy, delicious fruit. The same is true in the Christian life.

What is involved in pruning? Pain. Pruning always hurts! David said in Psalm 119:67, "Before I was afflicted I went astray." Psalm 119:71 says, "It is good for me that I was afflicted, that I might learn your statutes." Sometimes the pain of pruning comes because of our sins. Other times it is simply because we are bearing abundant fruit and God wants us to bear more. Whatever the reason for pruning, our natural selves always want to escape it. No one naturally wants the knife. Nevertheless, the results of God's pruning will be beneficial for us and for him.

Often we Christians are subject to what I call the "when syndrome." "When I get spiritually mature, these things won't happen to me." "When I get married, I will not struggle this way anymore." "When I retire, my life will be easier." Afflictions would only stop if they were useless, and that is why they never stop. Without pruning, a vineyard would never be in full bloom.

John 15 clearly teaches that pruning is always good for us. Malcolm Muggeridge in his book *Jesus Rediscovered* says:

> Suppose you eliminated suffering, what a dreadful place the world would be. I would almost rather eliminate happiness. The world would be the most ghastly place because everything that corrects the tendency of this unspeakable little creature, man, to feel over-important and over-pleased with himself would disappear. He's bad enough now, but he would be absolutely intolerable if he never suffered.[3]

Those are true words, and I speak from experience. Some years ago I set off on a grandiose spiritual scheme. I shared it with my friends, and they assured me it would succeed. I had good motives, and the ideas were sound, but

I fell flat on my face, to my great embarrassment. So I called a close friend, whom I could go to when I was discouraged. As we sat in a restaurant, he said to me, "You know what? This is good for you. If you had succeeded at this, you would have started telling others how to do it. Then you would have a seminar, and so on. Failing was the best thing that could have happened to you." Much of what is noble in us has been accomplished by God's pruning in our lives.

A character in C. S. Lewis's Chronicles of Narnia series is named Eustace Scrub, a selfish, immature boy who thinks only of himself. In *The Voyage of the Dawn Treader*, he not only finds himself in a dragon's cave but discovers he has turned into a dragon! He attempts to remove the scales but cannot do so by himself. Finally the Lion, the Christ-figure, comes. Eustace describes what happens next:

> This is what the Lion said, but I don't know if he spoke. "You will have to let me undress you." I was afraid of his claws I can tell you, but I was pretty nearly desperate, so I just lay flat on my back and let him do it. The very first tear he made was so deep that I thought it had gone right to my heart and when he began pulling the skin off it hurt worse than anything I had ever felt. The only thing that made me able to bear it was just the pleasure of feeling the stuff peel off.[4]

That is how it is with pruning. We would rather do it ourselves, but we cannot, and even if we could, we would not remove what really has to go. The truth is, what is noble and attractive in us has come from the cutting we would have avoided. "Before I was afflicted I went astray, but now I keep your word" (Psalm 119:67). "It is good for me that I was afflicted, that I might learn your statutes" (Psalm 119:71). James's experience taught him this truth as well.

> Dear brothers, is your life full of difficulties and temptations? Then be happy, for when the way is rough, your patience has a chance to grow. So let it grow, and don't try to squirm out of your problems. For when your patience is finally in full bloom, then you will be ready for anything, strong in character, full and complete. (James 1:2 TLB)

What else do we need to know about pruning? God's hand is never closer than when he prunes the vine. During those times of severest cutting when, to us, he may seem to have departed, he is the closest. His pruning may pain us, but it will never harm us. When the gardener does his pruning well, he leaves little more than the vine. Similarly, the more we are pruned, the more of Christ there is in our lives! Also, the branch does not bear fruit for itself but for others. The life that has been trimmed by the hand of God sustains others. Consider, for example, Corrie ten Boom, who endured so much and has encouraged so many. "Every branch that does bear fruit he prunes, that it may bear more fruit" (v. 2).

> I asked the Lord, that I might grow
> In faith, and love, and every grace;
> Might more of his salvation know,
> And seek more earnestly his face.
>
> I hoped that in some favoured hour
> At once He'd answer my request,
> And by his love's constraining power
> Subdue my sins, and give me rest.
>
> Instead of this, he made me feel
> The hidden evils of my heart;
> And let the angry powers of hell
> Assault my soul in every part.
>
> Yea more, with his own hand he seemed
> Intent to aggravate my woe;
> Crossed all the fair designs I schemed,
> Blasted my gourds, and laid me low.
>
> "Lord, why is this?" I trembling cried,
> "Wilt thou pursue thy worm to death?"
> "'Tis in this way," the Lord replied,
> "I answer prayer for grace and faith.
>
> These inward trials I employ
> From self and pride to set thee free;
> And break thy schemes of earthly joy,
> That thou may'st seek thy all in me."

Abiding for Fruit (vv. 4, 5)

> Abide in me, and I in you. As the branch cannot bear fruit by itself, unless it abides in the vine, neither can you, unless you abide in me. I am the vine; you are the branches. Whoever abides in me and I in him, he it is that bears much fruit, for apart from me you can do nothing.

What does abiding or remaining in Christ mean? To me (although the text doesn't explicitly say it), the sap that runs between the vine and the branches is suggestive of the Holy Spirit. So remaining or abiding is parallel to being filled with the Holy Spirit. We have already seen that abiding in Christ produces the fruit of the Holy Spirit. We must set aside everything from which we might derive our own strength and merit and draw all from Christ.

Jesus says that abiding in him involves the belief that "apart from me you can do nothing" (v. 5b). Actually there are many things we can do without Christ. We can earn a living, raise a family, and practice generosity. It is possible to pastor a church without abiding. It is possible to counsel people without abiding. So what does Christ mean? He means that we cannot bear spiritual fruit without him. We can tie fruit onto our lives like ornaments on a Christmas tree, but the real fruit of his *character* comes from the vine itself. *We can do nothing without him!* We cannot be loving or patient or faithful or holy. That is why God does not shield us from the assaults of life but rather exposes us to them, so we will learn to hold him fast. Jesus taught, "Blessed are the poor in spirit, for theirs is the kingdom of heaven" (Matthew 5:3). Abiding involves a growing sense of weakness.

Along with this realization we are to consciously, deliberately depend upon Christ. I am not gifted with musical ability. But suppose I sneak into my church's sanctuary on my day off, when nobody is around, and try to play some chords on the piano. Without my knowing it, the great Van Cliburn enters the narthex. The poor man is in pain from my "music," so he walks to the front and says to me, "I would like to help you. I have a power no one else knows about—I can transmit my ability to another person. All you have to do is to look at me and watch me intently." I suddenly get a great idea! I make sure that the next Sunday night all of my church's regular church pianists are away. Van Cliburn is there, but he declines to play. So I humbly sit at the piano, and as long as I look at Van Cliburn, my fingers really fly over those ivories. Nobody has ever played like that at College Church in Wheaton, Illinois! I start feeling pretty good, so I begin looking at the people, enjoying their admiration for my musical prowess. And my ability is suddenly gone! Often we make the same mistake. We fail to keep our eyes on Jesus and to depend on him, to abide in him.

> Therefore, my beloved, as you have always obeyed, so now, not only as in my presence but much more in my absence, work out your own salvation with fear and trembling, for it is God who works in you, both to will and to work for his good pleasure. (Philippians 2:12, 13)

Those who learn to abide stay put for the pruning. We must choose to abide, to get into the Word, to associate with others who are remaining in Christ, to keep growing.

Enjoying the Fruit (vv. 6–11)

What fruit specifically did Jesus choose to mention on this occasion? "If you abide in me, and my words abide in you, ask whatever you wish, and it will be done for you" (v. 7). *An empowered prayer life.* As we pray, we abide. As we abide, we pray more, and more deeply. "By this my Father is glorified, that you bear much fruit and so prove to be my disciples" (v. 8). *The Father is glorified.* Verses 9, 10 add, "As the Father has loved me, so have I loved you. Abide in my love. If you keep my commandments, you will abide in my love, just as I have kept my Father's commandments and abide in his love." *Love will fill our lives!* "These things I have spoken to you, that my joy may be in you, and that your joy may be full" (v. 11). *The joy of Jesus in us!* Chesterton called this "the gigantic secret of the Christian."[5] Peter called it "joy unspeakable and full of glory" (1 Peter 1:8 KJV). Joy to the max!

Jesus is the Vine, we are the branches, the Father is the Gardener. Everything the Father and Son do is geared to enhance our abiding and our fruitfulness. With each trimming, may there be more of Christ in us, for God's glory and the blessing of others!

45

Loving the Branches

JOHN 15:12–17

JOHN R. CLAYPOOL, in *The Preaching Event*, tells a story about identical twin boys.

> The boys' lives became inseparably intertwined. From the first they dressed alike, went to the same schools, did all the same things. In fact, they were so close that neither ever married, but they came back and took over the running of the family business when their father died. Their relationship to each other was pointed to as a model of creative collaboration.
>
> One morning a customer came into the store and made a small purchase. The brother who waited on him put the dollar bill on top of the cash register and walked to the front door with the man. Some time later he remembered what he had done, but when he went to the cash register, he found the dollar gone. He asked his brother if he had seen the bill and put it into the register, and the brother replied that he knew nothing of the bill in question.
>
> "That's funny," said the other, "I distinctly remember placing the bill here on the register, and no one else has been in the store since then."
>
> Had the matter been dropped at that point—a mystery involving a tiny amount of money—nothing would have come of it. However, an hour later, this time with a noticeable hint of suspicion in his voice, the brother asked again, "Are you sure you didn't see that dollar bill and put it into the register?" The other brother was quick to catch the note of accusation, and flared back in defensive anger.
>
> This was the beginning of the first serious breach of trust that had ever come between these two. It grew wider and wider. Every time they tried to discuss the issue, new charges and countercharges got mixed into the brew, until finally things got so bad that they were forced to dissolve their partnership. They ran a partition down the middle of their father's store and turned what had once been a harmonious partnership into an angry competition. In fact, that business became a source of division in the whole

community, each twin trying to enlist allies for himself against the other. This warfare went on for more than twenty years.

Then one day a car with an out-of-state license parked in front of the store. A well-dressed man got out, went into one of the sides, and inquired how long the merchant had been in business in that location. When the man learned it was more than twenty years, the stranger said, "Then you are the one with whom I must settle an old score."

"Some twenty years ago," he said, "I was out of work, drifting from place to place, and I happened to get off a boxcar in your town. I had absolutely no money and had not eaten for three days. As I was walking down the alley behind your store, I looked in and saw a dollar bill on the top of the cash register. Everyone else was in the front of the store. I had been raised in a Christian home and I had never before in all my life stolen anything, but that morning I was so hungry, I gave in to the temptation, slipped through the door, and took that dollar bill. That act has weighed on my conscience ever since, and I finally decided that I would never be at peace until I came back and faced up to that old sin and made amends. Would you let me now replace that money and pay you whatever is appropriate for damages?"

The stranger was surprised to see the old man shaking his head in dismay and beginning to weep. When the brother had gotten control of himself, he took the stranger by the arm and said, "I want you to go next door, and repeat the same story you have just told me." The stranger did, only this time there were two old men, who looked remarkably alike, both weeping uncontrollably.

From this dramatic, true story we can learn several obvious lessons, including how mistrust can poison a relationship and how friendship can be destroyed by suppositions that have no basis in fact.

But the truth that struck me as I first heard the story was less obvious. It can be as true of Christians as of unbelievers. Many of us here know Christians, perhaps even members of the same family or the same church, who have not spoken to each other in years. How sad!

John 15:12–17 focuses on the friendship and love that is to exist among the branches of the vine, among believers. Actually, all of chapter 15 is concerned with the believer's relationships. Verses 1–11 have to do with the relationship between the vine and the branches, between Christ and believers; verses 12–17 with the relationship of branch to branch, or believer to believer; and verses 18–27 with the relationship of the vine and the branches to the world.

The importance of friendship and love between believers is not confined to outrageous situations. Hundreds in the body of Christ are lonely and anxious for friendship. Craig W. Ellison, in his book *Loneliness, the Search for Intimacy*, says:

Loneliness seems to have flooded the lives of millions of modern Americans. It's an emotional epidemic. A recent survey of over 40,000 respondents of all ages found that 67 percent of them felt lonely some of the time. Projected nationally, that amounts to over 150 million Americans who have personally experienced loneliness. Another survey found that over 64 percent of widows over age 50 in several major urban areas mentioned loneliness as a significant problem in their lives. United Methodist men have established a nationwide 24-hour, toll-free telephone line for people wanting to pray with someone. Loneliness is the most frequently mentioned prayer need that they receive. Contact, a nationwide crisis intervention telephone network, received over 18,000 calls due to intense loneliness in one recent six-month period.[1]

Some Christians would give anything for one good friend. Friendship is important. The principles in John 15:12–17 apply to everyone—to those who have friends and those who feel they do not, to the aggressive, the outgoing, the shy—because these principles govern both the initiation, the reception, and the maintenance of friendship. And as friendship develops, these principles take us into deeper and deeper relationships.

Principles That Promote Friendship and Love among the Branches (vv. 12, 13)

In verses 12, 13 we find the principle of *sacrifice* in friendship and love.

This is my commandment, that you love one another as I have loved you. Greater love has no one than this, that someone lay down his life for his friends.

Sacrifice is essential to genuine friendship and love. Verses 12, 13 are a restatement of the "new commandment" given back in 13:34: "A new commandment I give to you, that you love one another: just as I have loved you, you also are to love one another." The idea of sacrifice is found in the phrase, "just as I have loved you," for Christ loved us so much that he gave his life for us. The old commandment was to love God with everything in us, and our neighbor as ourselves. The story of the good Samaritan was Christ's great explanation of that kind of love, and it was a wonderful love. But the new commandment requires us to love as Jesus loved. His sacrifice is our model. Jesus calls for sacrificial love in his church.

Our Lord exemplified this even before the cross. Just before he gave this new commandment, he tried in every way to restore Judas, though he knew Judas was bent on betraying him. He seated Judas next to him, the place of honor. He dipped a morsel and offered it to Judas, a custom offering friendship. Christ was offering restoration. In 15:12, 13 our Lord officially made sacrifice an essential characteristic of love between believers, in imitation of his love for us.

A story from the life of E. Stanley Jones gives a beautiful example of this principle of sacrifice. It occurred when he was preaching his first evangelistic service among the mountaineers of Kentucky, a very poor people at that time. The meetings were held in the schoolhouse.

> At the schoolhouse I was invited to stay with a man and wife, and when I arrived I saw there was one bed. The husband said, "You take the far side." Then he got in, and then his wife. In the morning we reversed the process. I turned my face to the wall as they dressed, and they stepped out while I dressed. That was real hospitality! I have slept in palaces, but the hospitality of that one-bed-home is the most memorable and the most appreciated.

Dr. Jones did not say he became lifelong friends with that couple, but he did reveal his affection for that humble couple who demonstrated so poignantly the sacrificial principle.

Friendship thrives on sacrifice. There is not enough of this in God's family. We must consciously cultivate a sacrificial spirit and must constantly work at being givers.

The Principle of Mutuality in Friendship and Love (vv. 14, 15)

Jesus' words in verse 14, "You are my friends if you do what I command you," speak primarily of obedience, but they also suggest a *mutuality of heart*, the second principle of friendship. Jesus' friends obey him because they share the same outlook and goals. Close friends agree in heart. They will sometimes disagree, but their hearts' aims are the same. Paul uses a very enlightening phrase in Philippians 2:19, 20.

> I hope in the Lord Jesus to send Timothy to you soon, so that I too may be cheered by news of you. For I have no one like him, who will be genuinely concerned for your welfare.

Paul described Timothy as being "of kindred spirit" (NASB), literally "one-souled." We think *soul brothers* is a pop term from the sixties, but actually the concept is two thousand years old! Paul and Timothy's friendship was a friendship of the soul.

Mutuality of heart was also the basis of David and Jonathan's relationship. First Samuel records its dramatic beginning after David killed Goliath:

"As soon as he had finished speaking to Saul, the soul of Jonathan was knit to the soul of David, and Jonathan loved him as his own soul" (1 Samuel 18:1). Their souls were knit together.

Verse 15 tells us that this mutuality of heart is ennobled and promoted by the sharing of personal information:

> No longer do I call you servants, for the servant does not know what his master is doing; but I have called you friends, for all that I have heard from my Father I have made known to you.

Jesus was saying, "Men, I don't consider you slaves, but I call you friends. Therefore, I am sharing personal information with you. What the Father shows me, I show you." Jesus shared the deepest thoughts of his heart with his disciples, and that fostered their mutuality! In the culture of that day, slaves were considered little more than objects. Even Aristotle put slaves on the same level as inanimate objects—agricultural implements. In Jesus' day, typically masters did not share with their slaves, just as typically today employers do not share their deepest thoughts with employees. But in genuine friendship, there are no spiritual barriers.

We all need close friends who can objectify our thoughts. We need the healing that so often comes when we reveal our feelings to another without fear that our confidence will be broken. There is too often loneliness of soul in the Body of Christ. As believers we need to take time to talk about one another's goals, pray about our needs, share, and encourage one another.

The Principle of Promotion (v. 16)

We see the principle of *promotion* in friendship and love in verse 16:

> You did not choose me, but I chose you and appointed you that you should go and bear fruit and that your fruit should abide, so that whatever you ask the Father in my name, he may give it to you.

In this verse we see our Lord's desire to help his friends succeed: "I chose you and appointed you that you should go and bear fruit." He was committed to their fulfilling the ultimate in their calling. Friends rejoice in each other's successes.

> Then Jonathan made a covenant with David, because he loved him as his own soul. And Jonathan stripped himself of the robe that was on him and gave it to David, and his armor, and even his sword and his bow and his belt. (1 Samuel 18:3, 4)

Jonathan gave David the items that represented his station in life. He was the son of Saul and heir to the throne, but he committed himself to make the Lord's anointed—David—king. In the same way and even more so, Jesus is committed to the fulfillment of our ultimate calling. Likewise, we are to be committed to the ultimate fulfillment of our friends, to help them experience all God intends for them. How wonderful it is to have a friend like Jonathan. It is even better to be such a friend!

We don't always feel like kings or like spiritual successes. Sometimes we feel very much the opposite. As Charles Swindoll has written:

> Do you ever feel like a frog? Frogs feel slow and low, ugly and putty, drooped and pooped. I know. One told me. The frog feeling comes when you want to be bright but you are dumb. When you want to share, but you are selfish. When you want to be thankful, but you are filled with resentment. When you want to be great, but you are small. When you want to care, but you are indifferent. Yes, at one time or another each of us has found himself on a lily pad, floating down the great river of life, frightened and disgusted but too frightened to budge.

We all know how the fairy tale goes: Once upon a time there was a frog, except he was not really a frog. He was a prince. He only looked and felt like a frog. The wicked witch had cast a spell on him, and only the kiss of a beautiful maiden could save him. (Since when do cute girls kiss frogs!) So there he sat—an unkissed prince in frog form. But miracles do happen, and one day a beautiful maiden gave him a great big smack! Crash! Boom! Zap! Suddenly he was a handsome prince. And of course they lived happily ever after.

What is the task of the church? Kissing frogs, of course—and allowing ourselves to be kissed! We are to make one another kings and queens! The principle of promotion is beautiful!

Many branches in the body of Christ have never reached their potential because no one ever encouraged them. Others would reach unimaginable heights if only someone would say, "You know, you could really become something." No one has prayed for them, befriended them, or affirmed them. We are called to do just that. That is the principle of promotion.

Conclusion

The Lord did not make the principles of sacrifice, mutuality, and promotion optional. These essential principles are framed by verses 12 and 17: "This is my commandment, that you love one another as I have loved you. . . . These things I command you, so that you will love one another." We might react,

"Why does he command the impossible? Love is a strong, uncontrollable emotion. You can't command it."

What is the answer? First, we must realize that our concept of love has been influenced by Hollywood. It has been sentimentalized and individual-ized into an uncontrollable emotion. The love our Lord commands is *agape* love, which begins with the mind and will. The other part of the answer lies in the context of Jesus' words, which is dominated by the concept of abiding or remaining in Christ. In verse 7 we read: "If you *abide* in me, and my words *abide* in you, ask whatever you wish, and it will be done for you." And in verse 9 we hear him say: "As the Father has loved me, so have I loved you. *Abide* in my love." And finally in verse 10: "If you keep my commandments, you will *abide* in my love, just as I have kept my Father's commandments and *abide* in his love." The initial fruit of abiding is the fruit of the Spirit, and the first of the fruits, according to Galatians 5:22, is "love." Jesus was abiding in the Father, and he loved his own! So it should be with us.

As we abide, we will love the unlovely. We will have loving relationships with one another. As we draw upon Christ, realizing that apart from him we can do nothing, we will love the branches. When our relationship with God is what it ought to be, when we are walking, resting, and relying on him, it is remarkable how loving we can be!

46

"If the World Hates You . . ."

JOHN 15:18—16:14

IN JUNE 1926 A YOUNG CORRESPONDENT, a recent graduate of Harvard, was working in China. In the course of his job, he sought an interview with a shadowy Bolshevik figure named Michael Borodin. Borodin was at that time the cause of considerable chaos in Western trade. The young reporter located Borodin in Canton (now Guangzhou), presented his introduction to the Russian's Vietnamese secretary (later known to the world as Ho Chi Minh), and was ushered into the Russian's presence. The American was surprised by Borodin's reception.

> I found my hand being pumped by a burly six-footer clad in a crumpled white jacket and trousers, with a shock of unruly black hair, a neat handlebar mustache, and a booming voice that bade strangers welcome in heavily accented but fluent and idiomatic American English.[1]

Seated with Borodin, the reporter's mind sped through the scant information available about the man. Borodin had served time in a Glasgow jail. Earlier he had taught school in Indiana and Chicago, and he had been handpicked by Lenin for this job.

Eagerly the novice reporter began the interview, asking questions about the realism of Borodin's goals. But in a short time the tables were turned, and the Russian pressed the attack.

> You forget, young man, that I am not here for my health, or I would not be working in this barbarous heat. I don't spend my time at the bars and the races like the English and French. I am not interested in a career or a fortune like the Americans. I serve an ideology. And with an ideology it is not numbers that count. It is dedication. You Americans would not understand

that. I have lived many years in your country and I know what goes on. You concentrate on comfort and personal success.[2]

Uncomfortable with the Russian's rebukes, the young journalist feebly attempted to divert the conversation. "Do you enjoy your work in China, Mr. Borodin?" he asked.

> "Enjoy!" he echoed scornfully. "A bourgeois question. It is not a matter of whether we enjoy our work here. The work is necessary. That is all that counts. It is of course far from the friends, the concerts, and the theater that mean so much in Moscow. But long ago I made up my mind that Communism alone held an answer for the world. . . . Nothing else matters. Does that answer your question?"[3]

From the first time I read this account, the reporter's question has stuck in my mind. Our society's commitments and pursuits are largely determined by the question of personal enjoyment. That is not wrong in itself, but it should not be the controlling force. Dr. Herbert Hendin, author of *The Age of Sensation: A Psychoanalytic Exploration of Youth in the 1970's*, says:

> It is no accident that at the present time the dominant trends in psychoanalysis [include] the rediscovery of narcissism. . . . The society is marked by a self-interest and egocentrism that increasingly reduces all relations to the question, "What am I getting out of it?"

That attitude has even penetrated the church. Many think Christianity exists only to make us healthy and wealthy and to bring our lives smooth sailing. After the dedication of the Billy Graham Center in Wheaton a number of years ago, one woman was severely critical of blind musician-singer Ken Medema's being included on the platform. His presence, she said, was a slam on the goodness and grace of God—and on the faith of the participants. If he had enough faith, or if the others on the program had enough faith, he would be healed! Yes, a healthy spiritual life does contribute to physical health. And God still heals miraculously. And attention to Scriptural principles often aids one's prosperity. A righteous life does indeed avoid many difficult obstacles. But that is not always the lot of godly believers.

Godly believers are not always wealthy. They sometimes have physical difficulties. Sometimes they suffer and are persecuted. The danger of the health-wealth, smooth-sailing gospel is obvious. When life does not fit our theological box, some toss faith out or deny reality. People react like that every day. John 15:18—16:14 deals with persecution, and it touches by implication on matters of health and wealth.

What are proper expectations and duties as we follow Christ in this fallen world? Jesus' words must have jolted the disciples, for they came in the midst of positive reinforcement that began back in chapter 14. Christ had been speaking about not letting our hearts be troubled, about the benefits of abiding in him, about the love that is to exist between believers, when all of a sudden he turned to matters of trials and the world's hatred.

What Christians Should Expect as They Relate to the World (15:18–25)

> If the world hates you, know that it has hated me before it hated you. If you were of the world, the world would love you as its own; but because you are not of the world, but I chose you out of the world, therefore the world hates you. Remember the word that I said to you: "A servant is not greater than his master." If they persecuted me, they will also persecute you. If they kept my word, they will also keep yours. (vv. 18–20)

What a jolt! A Christian who follows Christ must *expect* to be hated. (The form of the Greek in verse 18 suggests certainty: "You *will* be hated.") Jesus gave several reasons for this. First, the world hated Jesus: "If the world hates you, know that it has hated me before it hated you" (v. 18). And in verses 22–25 he explained why:

> If I had not come and spoken to them, they would not have been guilty of sin, but now they have no excuse for their sin. Whoever hates me hates my Father also. If I had not done among them the works that no one else did, they would not be guilty of sin, but now they have seen and hated both me and my Father. But the word that is written in their Law must be fulfilled: "They hated me without a cause."

Jesus' life, specifically through his word and his works, demonstrated by contrast how sinful the Jews were, and they hated him for that. His inner righteousness drew their abiding hostility because it revealed the shabbiness of their external goodness.

Once an African chief, in this case a woman, happened to visit a mission station. Hanging outside the missionary's cabin, on a tree, was a little mirror. The chief happened to look into the mirror and saw her reflection, with its hideous paint and evil features. She gazed at her own terrifying countenance and jumped back in horror exclaiming, "Who is that horrible-looking person inside that tree?" "Oh," the missionary said, "it is not in the tree. The glass is reflecting your own face." The African would not believe it until she held the mirror in her hand. She said, "I must have the glass. How much will you sell it for?" "Oh," the missionary said, "I don't want to sell it." But she begged until he capitulated. She took the mirror. Exclaiming, "I will never have it making faces at me again," she threw it down and broke it to pieces.[4]

That is precisely what the Jews did with Jesus, and tragically it often happens today. We hate to see what we really are. A good look at Jesus results in either abiding hatred or love, and people have the same reaction toward Christ's followers.

The second reason for the world's hatred is found in verse 19: "If you were of the *world*, the *world* would love you as its own; but because you are not of the *world*, but I chose you out of the *world*, therefore the *world* hates you." "World" (*kosmos*), used several times in this one verse, refers to the sinful world system. The world hates believers because they are not part of that system. It always opposes those who do not conform.

But of course persecution is not always violent, not every godly Christian is constantly persecuted, and not all unbelievers hate Christians. The system *always* does, but not every individual. Persecution wears many faces. Most often it is reflected in attitude and not necessarily in action. Sometimes it takes the form of indifference, and we are treated as nonentities. Other times it is avoidance as antagonists reroute their paths. Sometimes it reaches repulsion or a growing animosity.

When a couple my wife and I know moved into a residential area in California, the people in the neighborhood knew ahead of time they were Christians, and the neighbors greeted our friends with an attitude of criticism and animosity. For example, although dogs ran loose throughout the neighborhood, if our friends' dog got out, someone brought it back within five minutes, with a shovel in hand, saying, "Go take care of it." My wife and I often joke that if you are a Christian moving into a new neighborhood, you had better make sure your dog has had a changed life too. But all joking aside, persecution takes its toll, and many believers stumble.

And of course sometimes persecution is violent. A. T. Robertson says "persecute" in verse 20 has the sense of "to chase like a wild beast."[5] We may not be experiencing this in the United States, but it is happening in much of the world. There were more martyrs for Christ in the twentieth century than ever before. The misery of the early church is being reenacted every day. And it could even happen in the United States. If it does, it will affect believers' health and wealth, notwithstanding mouthings of "I will live in divine health. I'm not willing to be sick."[6] The world persecutes those who are not part of the system.

The third reason for persecution is stated in verse 20, an *a fortiori* statement (that which is true for the greater will be true for the lesser):

> Remember the word that I said to you: "A servant is not greater than his master." If they persecuted me, they will also persecute you. If they kept my word, they will also keep yours.

"If they persecuted me, they will also persecute you." Historically this has proven true. In 1937 Dietrich Bonhoeffer, who was executed at the end of the war (1945) in a German concentration camp, prophetically wrote in *The Cost of Discipleship*:

> Suffering . . . is the badge of the true Christian. The disciple is not above his master. . . . Luther reckoned suffering among the marks of the true church. . . . Discipleship means allegiance to the suffering Christ, and it is therefore not at all surprising that Christians should be called upon to suffer.[7]

Such persecution will be proportionate to the extent of one's identification with Christ.

Jesus' teaching demands that we draw some conclusions. One primary deduction is that smooth sailing is not necessarily a sign that God is pleased with our lives. The absence of persecution may actually indicate something is wrong. Such was the case with Lot. He tired of the separated life in the hills of Palestine and pitched his tents near Sodom until finally he was firmly entrenched in the life of the city, and when the day of judgment came, the angels commanded him to go to his relatives in the city with the message that judgment was coming. But as Scripture records, "He seemed to his sons-in-law to be jesting" (Genesis 19:14). He had lost his credibility along the way.

Most people are not so crass. Rather, they try to find a comfortable spot between the extremes of a godly life and a sinful one—and they achieve this at the cost of their lives. They prefer a smooth sea to being possessed by God! They go through life with little difficulty because they have accommodated themselves to the world.

At the same time, persecution is not necessarily a sign of God's blessing. The godly are not under the sword at all times. Proverbs 16:7 says, "When a man's ways please the LORD, he makes even his enemies to be at peace with him." That is true, though we never completely escape the enmity of the world system.

We must also remember that some of the persecution Christians endure is because of their own sin. An employee of the secular college I attended claimed he was being persecuted for his Christianity. He felt ostracized but said he had dealt with the problem. When I asked what he had done, he said, "I grabbed one guy by the coat and told him if he bugged me any more, I'd let him have it!" After this he reported his persecutors were becoming more "uncivilized." Sometimes we are persecuted because of our stupidity, rudeness, annoying personality, or false piety. Persecution is *not* necessarily a sign that we are following Christ!

A life pleasing to God is a life that by example, word, and deed demonstrates the righteousness of Christ. It thereby condemns the world, and as a result the believer is in some way persecuted. Consider Daniel, the only person in Scripture of whom much is written but who has no recorded sin. He was an exemplary man, so much so that the world system tried to kill him. But God stopped the lions' mouths. William Temple, in *Readings in John's Gospel*, states the third reason for persecution from the Christian perspective.

> The world . . . would not hate angels for being angelic; but it does hate men for being Christians. It grudges them their new character; it is tormented by their peace; it is infuriated by their joy.[8]

For whatever reason, the follower of Christ should expect times of persecution.

> Indeed, all who desire to live a godly life in Christ Jesus will be persecuted. (2 Timothy 3:12)

> For it has been granted to you that for the sake of Christ you should not only believe in him but also suffer for his sake. (Philippians 1:29)

> That no one be moved by these afflictions. For you yourselves know that we are destined for this. For when we were with you, we kept telling you beforehand that we were to suffer affliction, just as it has come to pass, and just as you know. (1 Thessalonians 3:3, 4)

> Beloved, do not be surprised at the fiery trial when it comes upon you to test you, as though something strange were happening to you. But rejoice insofar as you share Christ's sufferings, that you may also rejoice and be glad when his glory is revealed. (1 Peter 4:12, 13)

What, then, does God expect us to do? To retire? To draw back? No! Resentment? Retaliation? Revenge? No! We are forbidden to return evil for evil. Then what is to be our response?

What God Expects of Christians as They Relate to the World (vv. 26, 27)

> But when the Helper comes, whom I will send to you from the Father, the Spirit of truth, who proceeds from the Father, he will bear witness about me.

And you also will bear witness, because you have been with me from the beginning.

Persecution is not an excuse for silence, but it does challenge us to witness, to share Christ lovingly to a hostile world, in the power of the Holy Spirit.

A little boy named Stevie, who was quiet and shy, moved to a new neighborhood. One day he came home from school and said, "You know, Mom, Valentine's Day is coming, and I want to make a valentine for everyone in my class. I want them to know that I love them." His mother's heart sank at the prospect of her son's rejection. Every afternoon she watched the children coming home from school, laughing and hanging on to one another—all except Stevie who always walked behind them.

But at the same time she did not want to discourage her well-intentioned son. So she purchased glue and paper and crayons, and for three weeks Stevie painstakingly made thirty-five valentines. When the big day came, he stacked the valentines under his arm and ran out the door. His mother thought, "This is going to be a tough day for Stevie. I'll bake some cookies and have some milk ready for him when he comes home from school. Maybe that will ease the pain of not getting many valentines."

That afternoon she had the warm cookies and milk out on the table. She went over to the window, scratched a little of the frost off the glass, and looked out. Sure enough, here came all the children, laughing, valentines tucked under their arms. And there was her Stevie. Though walking behind the children, he was walking faster than usual, and she thought, "Bless his heart. He's ready to break into tears." His arms were empty. He was not carrying any valentines.

Stevie came into the house, and his mother said, "Sweetheart, Mom has some warm cookies and milk for you, just sit down." But Stevie's face was all aglow, and as he marched right by her, all he could say was, "Not a one, not a single one. I didn't forget one. They all know I love them."

It isn't a song until it's sung,
It isn't a bell until it's rung,
It isn't love until it's given away.

Figuratively speaking, Christ did not get a valentine, but he did not forget a single person, and we are to be like him! Lovingly we are to "go get 'em" for Jesus. Openly! Lovingly! Vulnerably! Joyously!

Conclusion

> I have said all these things to you to keep you from falling away. They will
> put you out of the synagogues. Indeed, the hour is coming when whoever
> kills you will think he is offering service to God. And they will do these
> things because they have not known the Father, nor me. But I have said
> these things to you, that when their hour comes you may remember that I
> told them to you. (16:1–4a)

"I have told you these things, so that if you have supposed that in following me you will have smooth sailing, you will not be disillusioned. To be forewarned is to be forearmed."

What Jesus prophesied came true, and the disciples did not stumble! All except John, it appears, died martyrs' deaths. They understood. Jesus was hated, and so were they. They were not part of the world order. They were obedient as they lovingly shared Christ.

That young reporter in China saw Borodin once again later, and the Bolshevik was in a more contemplative mood. In the course of conversation they discussed Christianity.

> After a long silence, Borodin, still gazing out the window, began murmuring, half to himself. "You know," he mused, "I used to read the New Testament. Again and again I read it. It is the most wonderful story ever told. That man Paul. He was a *real* revolutionary. I take off my hat to him." He made a symbolic gesture, his long black hair falling momentarily over his face.
> Another long silence.
> Then suddenly Borodin whirled, his face contorted with fury as he shook his fist in my face. "But where do you find him today?" he shouted. "Answer me that. Where do you find him? Where? Where? Where?"
> Then furiously, triumphantly: "You can't answer me!"[9]

We can! Followers of Christ like Paul have been in China—Hudson Taylor and others like John and Betty Stam, who had their faith sealed in blood at the hands of Borodin's followers. Men and women whose lives were like Jesus. Today they are on every continent. Some are suffering persecution, others are not, but their lives all speak about Christ. We are called to follow their example of following the Savior, no matter what the cost.

47

Disclosures of the Spirit

JOHN 16:7–16

SINCE CHRIST'S FOLLOWERS are not of the world system, they can expect to experience enmity from time to time, as Jesus pointed out in the opening verses of John 16. The martyr William Tyndale, who gave us the English Bible, said regarding his persecution, "I never expected anything else."[1] The more authentic our walk, the more likely we will face some form of persecution.

In 16:7–16 the Savior reiterates to his troubled followers that he is going away but tells them his leaving will be good for them.

> But now I am going to him who sent me, and none of you asks me, "Where are you going?" But because I have said these things to you, sorrow has filled your heart. Nevertheless, I tell you the truth: it is to your advantage that I go away, for if I do not go away, the Helper will not come to you. But if I go, I will send him to you. (16:5–7)

How incredible his words must have sounded in that historical context. Judas has already slipped out into the night. The Lord has predicted Peter's denial. Outside, the world is plotting his death. Jesus knows that sorrow has filled the disciples' hearts, that there is a growing panic among them. Now he says, "It is to your advantage that I go away." The advantage was, of course, the coming of the Holy Spirit, "another Helper" (14:16) just like Jesus. The Spirit would be alongside and in the disciples, encouraging and exhorting them and bringing them into an elevated spiritual life. And unlike Jesus, he would not be limited by a physical body but would be everywhere, always available. That is a great advantage.

But there is more. The advantage also includes the comfort that comes with the understanding the Holy Spirit brings, described in verses 7–16. For those who reject Christ, this perception is disquieting. To those who love Christ, it is a great encouragement. This passage is the most extended statement of the Spirit's work of illumination and regeneration in all of Scripture, a source of great encouragement to the disciples and to us. The intended impact of Jesus' words is difficult to overestimate because they are almost his final revelation before the cross. Only his High-Priestly prayer and the agony of the cross are left.

What the World May Perceive through the Holy Spirit (vv. 7–11)

> Nevertheless, I tell you the truth: it is to your advantage that I go away, for if I do not go away, the Helper will not come to you. But if I go, I will send him to you. And when he comes, he will convict the world concerning sin and righteousness and judgment. (vv. 7, 8)

Apart from the Holy Spirit, human beings do not understand spiritual realities. The Holy Spirit's ministry is to bring to the world's consciousness three things—a correct perception of *sin*, a correct perception of *righteousness*, and a correct perception of *judgment*. Verse 9: "Concerning sin, because they do not believe in me." Verse 10: "Concerning righteousness, because I go to the Father, and you will see me no longer." Verse 11: "Concerning judgment, because the ruler of this world is judged." The saying "What you don't know won't hurt you" is certainly not true here!

Jorge Rodriguez was a Mexican bank robber who operated along the Texas border around the end of the nineteenth century. He was so successful in his forays that the Texas Rangers assigned an extra posse to the Rio Grande to stop him. Late one afternoon one of the special Rangers saw Jorge slipping stealthily across the river, and he trailed him at a discreet distance as he returned to his home village. He watched as Jorge first mingled with the people in the square around the town well, then went into his favorite cantina to relax. The Ranger slipped into the cantina as well and managed to get the drop on Jorge. With a pistol at Jorge's head, he said, "I know who you are, Jorge Rodriguez, and I have come to get back all the money you have stolen from the banks of Texas. Unless you give it to me, I am going to pull the trigger." But there was a problem—Jorge did not speak English, and the Texas Ranger did not know Spanish. The two adults were at a verbal impasse.

About that time an enterprising villager said, "I am bilingual. Do you want me to act as a translator?" The Ranger nodded, and the villager proceeded to put the words of the Ranger into terms Jorge could understand. Nervously, Jorge answered, "Tell the big Texas Ranger that I have not spent a cent of the money. If he will go to the town well, face north, and count down five stones, he will find a loose one there. Pull it out, and all the money is behind it. Please tell him quickly." The little translator assumed a solemn look and said to the Ranger in perfect English, "Jorge Rodriguez is a brave man. He says he is ready to die."[2] What we do not know most assuredly does hurt us!

One's ignorance of sin, righteousness, and judgment will ultimately bring eternal hurt. The Holy Spirit is the divine remedy. In verse 8 the word translated "convict" means to cross-examine with the purpose of convincing or refuting an opponent. "He does not simply convict the world . . . but will show that it is lacking in knowledge of what sin and righteousness really are."[3] How does the Holy Spirit do this?

He convicts the world "concerning sin, because they do not believe in me" (v. 9). The Holy Spirit brings the guilt of sin home to the human consciousness so men and women will seek relief through the mercy of God. We see this in the record of Acts 2 regarding the Day of Pentecost. The disciples had been gathered for many days, waiting for the coming of the Holy Spirit. Once that occurred, "Peter, standing with the eleven, lifted up his voice and addressed them: 'Men of Judea and all who dwell in Jerusalem, let this be known to you, and give ear to my words'" (Acts 2:14). Amid accusations of drunkenness, Peter preached a scorcher of a sermon. Hear his concluding words:

> "Let all the house of Israel therefore know for certain that God has made him both Lord and Christ, this Jesus whom you crucified." Now when they heard this they were cut to the heart, and said to Peter and the rest of the apostles, "Brothers, what shall we do?" (Acts 2:36, 37)

The response was amazing. But Peter's eloquence or structure or argument had nothing to do with it. The convicting power of the Holy Spirit elicited those reactions. If Peter had preached the day before, nobody would have believed. But the listeners' hearts were pierced unto salvation. This was the convicting work of the Holy Spirit!

R. A. Torrey in his book *The Holy Spirit* tells how, when he was pastor of Moody Church, the church had a twenty-five-member committee of elders and deacons. They met every Friday night for supper and to go over the church rolls to see which people needed attention. At one meeting, an elder expressed a concern:

> Brethren, I am not at all satisfied with the way things are going in our church. We are having many professed conversions, and we are having many accessions to the Church, but I do not see the conviction of sin that I would like

to see. I propose that, instead of discussing business matters any further tonight, we spend the time in prayer, and that we meet on other nights also, to cry to God to send his Holy Spirit among us in convicting power.[4]

Everyone consented, and they spent not only the rest of that evening in prayer, but a number of the following nights, asking for the Spirit's convicting power. Not long after that first meeting, as Dr. Torrey rose one Sunday night to preach, he saw seated to his left a professional gambler. As he preached, he saw that the man's eyes were riveted upon him. After the meeting one of the church leaders brought the gambler to Dr. Torrey. The man's opening words were, "Oh . . . I don't know what's the matter with me. I feel awful." He revealed how that afternoon he had been out walking and saw an open-air meeting. Among the participants was a man with whom he had formerly associated in his sin. He stopped in to listen, was not much impressed, and went his way. But after he had walked several blocks, he felt moved to return. After the meeting he was invited to church. "Oh, I don't know what's the matter with me. I never felt like this before. I feel awful." He trembled like a leaf and groaned again. Torrey said, "I'll tell you what's the matter with you. The Holy Spirit is convicting you of sin." That powerful man, trembling with deep emotion, that gambler who had never been in a Protestant service before, knelt and cried out to God for mercy. He left shortly afterwards with the joyous realization that his sins were all forgiven.[5]

"When he comes, he will convict the world concerning sin." This describes exactly what happened to me as a twelve-year-old. I remember as if it were yesterday how I sat under the loving preaching of the Word for several months, then became increasingly aware of my sinfulness. One night after a meeting I shyly approached the speaker to talk about my soul, and I found Jesus! All because of the marvelous convicting power of the Holy Spirit.

Verse 9 says the Holy Spirit focuses primarily on the sin of not believing in Jesus: "Concerning sin, because they do not believe in me." The average unbeliever does not look on his unbelief in Jesus Christ as sin, but if one is under the Spirit's conviction, that is the primary focus. Only the Holy Spirit can bring such conviction.

If you are sensing your sin, especially your sin against Christ, grace is at work in your life, and you had better listen and pray as you never have before. Jesus says, "Blessed are the poor in spirit, for theirs is the kingdom of heaven" (Matthew 5:3). That is, "How blessed are those who see their spiritual bankruptcy, for they will see their need and ask Christ to take them to Heaven." Pascal said, "Man is great insofar as he realizes that he is wretched."[6] You need only two things in order to come into new life. First, you need to see your sin. Second, you need to see the righteousness of Christ and the righteousness that God has provided for you in him. Grasping the righteousness provided in Christ is the second convicting work of the Holy Spirit: "Concerning righteousness, because I go to the Father, and you will see me no longer" (v. 10).

The world has a relative view of righteousness, like ascending degrees on a thermometer. For example, a convict's deeds are held to be largely unrighteous, although he may have a little good in him (say, 20 percent). Better men have a little more righteousness (possibly 50 percent). Still better men have more righteousness (maybe even up to 80 percent), while God has the most righteousness of all (100 percent). The logical outcome of this is the unfortunate assumption that there is a degree of righteousness that will be acceptable to God, and if man attains it, he will attain Heaven. This is the Avis syndrome: "We try harder."

But Jesus demonstrated and taught an entirely new standard of righteousness, as is crystal-clear from his Sermon on the Mount. Jesus' made repeated statements revealing the profoundness and depth of the inner righteousness necessary to enter the kingdom of God, made in order to bring men to the end of themselves. The Beatitudes are at the same time extremely inspiring and discouraging. After giving them, Jesus astounded his hearers by saying, "For I tell you, unless your righteousness exceeds that of the scribes and Pharisees, you will never enter the kingdom of heaven" (Matthew 5:20). What a discouraging pronouncement to the common man because the Pharisees were the spiritual superstars of the day! The sum of the Sermon, in Christ's own words, was: "You therefore must be perfect, as your heavenly Father is perfect" (Matthew 5:48). The only righteousness acceptable to the kingdom is perfection!

Our Lord's teaching was vindicated when he was accepted back to Heaven by the Father: "Concerning righteousness, because I go to the Father, and you will see me no longer" (v. 10). When Almighty God raised Jesus from the dead, he was saying, "This is the Man I accept, and all men unlike him I reject." The resurrection was historical evidence of the type of man that God accepts.[7]

The Holy Spirit convinces us that our own righteousness does not come close to Jesus' righteousness. Once we are so convicted, we abandon the Avis syndrome. We abandon all hope of salvation through our 20 percent or 50 percent or 80 percent righteousness. The ground is level at the foot of the cross, and we should pray with Paul that we may

> Be found in him, not having a righteousness of my own that comes from the law, but that which comes through faith in Christ, the righteousness from God that depends on faith. (Philippians 3:9)

Unworthiness is the driving awareness of the man or woman who is in the process of grace. Only the Holy Spirit can bring this awareness. Are you convinced of sin? Are you convinced of Christ's righteousness? If so, you are either saved or will be soon. If the Holy Spirit has convinced us first of sin and second of righteousness, the third conviction is almost sure to follow.

"Concerning judgment, because the ruler of this world is judged" (v. 11). The Holy Spirit convinces the world that there *is* such a thing as judgment. The judgment of Satan and the breaking of his power at the cross is proof of that. While Jesus was on the cross, Satan threw everything he had at him, but after dying for our sins Jesus rose from the dead. And according to Ephesians 4:8, "When he ascended on high he led a host of captives, and he gave gifts to men." He led a victory parade! Satan bruised Christ's heel, but Christ crushed Satan's head (cf. Genesis 3:15)! Therefore, Christ now will bring judgment upon those who are part of the world system.

As a twelve-year-old I knew very little about sin. I had not robbed any banks (although I did steal a box of caps in the first grade). I was not a womanizer (I didn't even know what one was!). And although I had heard all the bad words and acted like I knew what they meant, I really did not. But I knew that I was a sinner, that Jesus' righteousness was something I could never match, and that I was under judgment. Someone might say, "What a terrible load for a young boy to carry." Actually it brought my liberation. "The hardness of God is kinder than the softness of men, and his compulsion is our liberation."[8] Are you experiencing the hardness of God? Are you under conviction of sin? Do you have a compulsion to find relief? You may be approaching liberation.

The work of the Holy Spirit is to convict the world of sin, righteousness, and judgment. It is his work, not ours. There is nothing you and I can do to bring conviction. But amazingly, while it is the Holy Spirit's job to bring conviction, he accomplishes this work through us.

> Nevertheless, I tell you the truth: it is to your advantage that I go away, for if I do not go away, the Helper will not come to you. But if I go, I will send him to you. And when he comes, he will convict the world concerning sin and righteousness and judgment. (vv. 7, 8)

The Holy Spirit comes to the world through us. He is a sovereign God. He can do anything he wants. But his normal method of bringing conviction to the world is through believers.

As far as we know, Thomas Huxley never put his faith in Christ, but he did experience some degree of conviction. Toward the end of the nineteenth century, that great agnostic was a guest at a house party in a country home. Sunday came, and most of the guests prepared to go to church. As expected, Huxley did not desire to go. But he did approach a man known to have a simple and radiant Christian faith and said to him, "Suppose you don't go to church today. Suppose you stay at home and you tell me quite simply what your Christian faith means to you and why you are a Christian." "But," said the man, "you could demolish my arguments in an instant. I'm not clever enough to argue with you." Huxley said gently, "I don't want to argue with you; I just want you to tell me simply what this Christ means to you." So the man did. When he had finished, there were tears in the agnostic's eyes. "I would give my right hand," he said, "if only I could believe that."[9] Huxley had seen something of the spiritual realities through the life of a humble, Spirit-filled believer.

What a breathtaking idea—that God would use us to do this great work. Perhaps this was in the back of Paul's mind when he wrote:

> You yourselves are our letter of recommendation, written on our hearts, to be known and read by all. And you show that you are a letter from Christ delivered by us, written not with ink but with the Spirit of the living God, not on tablets of stone but on tablets of human hearts. (2 Corinthians 3:2, 3)

To be used in this way is not so much a matter of what we say but of what we are.

When I was dating my wife, we lived far enough apart that we corresponded back and forth. When I received one of her letters, I would drop everything and read it, reread it, and reread it again. Our lives are open letters known and read by others. And when they are properly arranged, they convict men of the sin that is theirs, of the righteousness that may be theirs, and of the judgment that they cannot avoid.

This astounding reality was divulged by Christ on the eve of his departure, and he intended it to bring comfort to the disciples' troubled hearts. By virtue of the Holy Spirit, Jesus' convicting power would be theirs. They would have this life-giving force wherever they went. What a powerful thought!

What the Believer May Perceive through the Holy Spirit (vv. 12–16)

> When the Spirit of truth comes, he will guide you into all the truth, for he will not speak on his own authority, but whatever he hears he will speak, and he will declare to you the things that are to come. He will glorify me, for he will take what is mine and declare it to you. All that the Father has is mine; therefore I said that he will take what is mine and declare it to you. (vv. 13–15)

The Holy Spirit guides us into all truth. We will grow as he further illuminates the Scriptures to us. That does not mean we will have all knowledge regarding the sciences, but we will be taken deeper and deeper into the essential truth about God and Christ and eternal life and our souls. The expression "all the truth" connotes increasing liberation, for the truth makes us free (cf. 8:32)! We will increasingly be given the mind of Christ as the Spirit takes what is Christ's and discloses it to us.

> But, as it is written, "What no eye has seen, nor ear heard, nor the heart of man imagined, what God has prepared for those who love him"—these things God has revealed to us through the Spirit. For the Spirit searches everything, even the depths of God. (1 Corinthians 2:9, 10)

All this causes us to glorify Christ!

The mythical Jorge Rodriguez found out that what you do not know can indeed hurt you. In the spiritual realm, that is infinitely more true. The Holy Spirit's work is to open our eyes and enlarge our ability to see. He always begins with sin and righteousness and judgment. Are you convinced of sin? Are you convinced of Christ's righteousness? Are you convinced of judgment? Then you are under the conviction of the Holy Spirit.

If so, there is only one thing left to do if you have not already done it, and that is to come to Christ. Some years ago a certain young woman sat in church. She understood these great doctrines, but she considered herself unworthy of God's salvation. "She was almost in despair and hardly heard the words of the elderly man who was speaking. Suddenly, right in the middle of his address, the preacher stopped and, pointing his finger at her, said, 'You, Miss, sitting there at the back, you can be saved *now*. You don't need to do anything!'" His words struck like thunder in her heart. She believed at once, and with her belief came a wonderful sense of peace and real joy. That night Charlotte Elliott went home and wrote a well-known hymn.

> Just as I am, without one plea
> But that Thy blood was shed for me,
> And that Thou bidd'st me come to Thee,
> O Lamb of God, I come! I come![10]

48

From Sorrow to Joy

JOHN 16:16–33

FEW IF ANY OF US can fully appreciate the misery the disciples experienced in their last night with Jesus, when they saw their Master framed against the rising sun, pathetically agonizing through his last hours, apparently helpless and impotent. The disciples had been up all night, and they'd had no nourishment since the Last Supper. Then came a dizzying whirl of events—the exit from the upper room; the descent from the dark walls of Jerusalem; the ascent of the slopes of Olivet; the vigil at Gethsemane, with the Master repeatedly casting himself down in prayer; Peter's denial and curses. And soon after that would come the growling, ravenous mob and the butchery of our Lord at Golgotha. That was a misery that cannot be fully described.

Nor can the joy be described when, three days after Jesus' death, the disciples learned he was again alive. Matthew's description of the resurrection ecstasy of Mary and Martha gives only a hint: "So they departed quickly from the tomb with fear and great joy, and ran to tell his disciples" (Matthew 28:8). The Greek word translated here as "great joy" is *mega* as in *megaton*.

Can any of us really know what it was like when the sisters charged into the disciples' presence bursting with megajoy? There must have been a lot of whooping and hollering, embracing and weeping, and retellings of the story. The disciples had been cast to the depths of despair but in just a few hours were hurled to the pinnacle of joy! Imagine the relief and joyous release they felt in the following days! As the reality grew, they must have felt like pinching themselves. Because their emotions had run the gamut from misery to ecstasy, their joy was far deeper and more profound than any they had ever known. Jesus did not replace their sorrow—he transformed it! And that is exactly what our Lord had prophesied that last night in the upper room.

Victorious Joy—Sorrow Transformed (vv. 20–22)

> Truly, truly, I say to you, you will weep and lament, but the world will rejoice. You will be sorrowful, but your sorrow will turn into joy. (v. 20)

The Scriptures indicate that Jesus himself experienced the same transformation. His deepest sorrow became the source of greatest joy. Isaiah 53:3 says, "He was despised and rejected by men; a man of sorrows, and acquainted with grief." But Hebrews 12:2 describes him as one "who for the joy that was set before him endured the cross." The miracle of the cross transformed sorrow into joy for Jesus and for his disciples, and it can work the same miracle in us.

R. A. Torrey has given us a memorable testimony concerning the mysterious working of this transformation in his life. One of the great Bible teachers of the past generation, he pastored Moody Church and founded the Bible Institute of Los Angeles. When their twelve-year-old daughter died of diphtheria, Torrey and his wife went through a time of great heartache. The funeral was held on a miserable, rainy day. As they stood around her little grave and watched her body being buried, Mrs. Torrey said, "I'm so glad Elizabeth is with the Lord, and not in that box." But even knowing that, their hearts were broken. The next day as Torrey was walking down the street, the misery came to him anew. He felt the loneliness and heartbreak that lay ahead. In his misery he cried aloud, "Oh, Elizabeth! Elizabeth!"

> And just then this fountain, the Holy Spirit, that I had in my heart, broke forth with such power as I think I had never experienced before, and it was the most joyful moment I had ever known in my life. Oh, how wonderful is the joy of the Holy Ghost! It is an unspeakably glorious thing to have your joy not in things about you, not even in your most dearly loved friends, but to have within you a fountain ever springing up, springing up, springing up, always springing up, springing up under all circumstances into everlasting life.[1]

At that memorable moment Torrey experienced a supernatural touch that transformed his sorrow into joy. I am sure he would say he was not promoted to a state where he no longer missed his daughter, where he no longer mourned. In fact, I am sure he would affirm that the thought of her brought pain as long as he lived. What he would also affirm, however, is that he experienced the transforming power that the cross and resurrection of Christ bring to the believer through the Holy Spirit. If he could speak to us from Heaven today, he would tell us that every tear has been wiped away in fulfillment of the promises of Scripture. Torrey's testimony is proof that the disciples' resurrection experience can be enjoyed today.

In verse 21 Jesus used the phenomenon of giving birth to illustrate what the disciples' transforming experience would be like.

> When a woman is giving birth, she has sorrow because her hour has come, but when she has delivered the baby, she no longer remembers the anguish, for joy that a human being has been born into the world.

Our Lord does not mean that after a woman gives birth, she cannot remember any of the pain of childbirth. Rather, he is saying that the joy of a new child thrusts that pain into the background.

One Monday some years ago a banner was displayed over the door of the Wheaton College (Illinois) Alumni Office—"Welcome Sarah Linnea"—in celebration of the arrival of a baby girl, born to Ed and Marsha Meyer. When Marsha was three months pregnant, she fractured her spine and consequently spent six and a half weeks in a Stryker frame and nine weeks in a body cast. That was an extremely difficult time for Marsha because of her discomfort and her concern for her family and the unborn baby. You can imagine some of the thoughts that ran through her mind. A great amount of prayer from her church and college family rose on her behalf. But after the baby was born, they said, "The joy of our new baby girl makes it all worth it. The memory of the past misery is a small thing in comparison to our great joy." Their sorrow was transformed to joy, and that is precisely what happened to the disciples on Resurrection Day!

We experienced that when we came to know Christ as well. Our mourning over our sins was turned into the joy of new life. For the true believer the sorrows of life are pregnant with potential joy. We see this in the lives of great Biblical heroes. Moses' forty years of discouragement was followed by forty years of powerful ministry (notwithstanding the well-known vicissitudes of that ministry). Abraham's despair over Sarah's barrenness ultimately ended in joyous song. Our present difficulties too bear the potential of joy. True, some of us will never know complete joy until we are with the Lord, but even in life on earth, our sorrows bear the potential of a transformed and deeper joy. In broken families, in times of illness, in spite of financial reversals or outright persecution, our difficulties can bring us new joys.

In verse 22 our Lord tells the disciples that this joy is to be a present possession: "So also you have sorrow now, but I will see you again, and your hearts will rejoice, and no one will take your joy from you."

The disciples experienced exactly what Jesus predicted. That is why Paul could write from prison, "Rejoice in the Lord always; again I will say, rejoice" (Philippians 4:4). He reiterated variations of that thought ten times in that epistle. Nothing could take his joy away! That is the experience of faithful believers. "They have joy and comfort that the angels cannot give and evils cannot take" (Christopher Fowler). But remember, oftentimes that joy rises from the ashes of sorrow.

Jesus shared these words with his disciples not only because the cross was only a few hours away, but because he knew their lives would be filled with continuing difficulty. He warned them of this in both the opening and closing verses of John 16. That is why, along with the promise of sorrow being turned to joy, Christ also spoke about the *maintenance* of that transforming joy and peace through proper actions and mind-set.

Victorious Joy for the Asking (vv. 23, 24)

> In that day you will ask nothing of me. Truly, truly, I say to you, whatever you ask of the Father in my name, he will give it to you. Until now you have asked nothing in my name. Ask, and you will receive, that your joy may be full.

Before the cross the disciples either asked Jesus directly or prayed to the Father, as Christ taught them to pray: "Our Father in heaven . . ." (Matthew 6:9). After the cross a new arrangement was inaugurated—the disciples were to ask in Jesus' name. That is why today we pray in Jesus' name.

Unfortunately, some have interpreted this to mean that by tagging Jesus' name on the end of their prayer, they can ask for what they want and they will get it. It is often used as an excuse to pursue material wealth. "I want a Rolls Silver Cloud and a villa in Majorca, and I'm asking God for it. It says right here, 'Whatever you ask of the Father in my name, he will give it to you. Until now you have asked nothing in my name. Ask, and you will receive!' So, Lord, give it to me now!"

Yes, we are to ask in Jesus' name, and that has everything to do with our joy being made full, but asking in his name brings some constraints. For one thing, it means that we do not come in our own name. Dr. James Boice has said:

> Much modern prayer, even by serious Christian people, is useless and ineffective because the people involved approach God thinking that he is obliged to grant their requests because of something they have themselves done for him.[2]

Praying in Christ's name means coming on the basis of his merit, not ours. Christ's full name is the Lord Jesus Christ, which means Jehovah, the Savior, God's Anointed. That is the name of the One whose merit we depend on for access to God. We cannot think in any way that God will hear us because of our virtue. We cannot come to him in our own name. As the opening verse of the Sermon on the Mount tells us, poverty of spirit is the basis upon which we come to him (Matthew 5:3). If we come in poverty of spirit, relying on Christ and not ourselves, we can expect our prayers to be answered.

The second requirement of praying in Jesus' name is that we must pray in correspondence with Christ's character and objectives. Oswald Chambers interprets praying in Christ's name as asking anything "in my nature."[3] This simply means that we are to ask for what Christ would want, not just our own spontaneous desires. Prayer is not a means by which we get God to do what we want. Rather, it is a means by which God does through us what he wants. Chambers says, "The idea of prayer is not in order to get answers from God: prayer is perfect and complete oneness with God."[4] This happens when we are filled with the Holy Spirit and our hearts are so in tune with the Lord's that we pray for those things he desires for us.

> Likewise the Spirit helps us in our weakness. For we do not know what to pray for as we ought, but the Spirit himself intercedes for us with groanings too deep for words. And he who searches hearts knows what is the mind of the Spirit, because the Spirit intercedes for the saints according to the will of God. (Romans 8:26, 27)

There is a sense in which when we truly pray in his name, we actually articulate the Spirit's hidden intercession. As we pray in his nature, we find answers to our prayer and experience increased joy.

The final requirement involved in praying in Jesus' name is submission to him. Specifically, we must yield to the process of the cross and resurrection. Death and life—sorrow and joy! If we do not submit to this process, we are not submitting to Jesus' name. Alan Redpath said, "When God wants to use a man, he takes him and crushes him." Submission to Jesus allows our sorrows to be turned to joy! Are we submitting to Jesus? Are we praying in his name?

Answered prayer brings joy. In verse 24 Jesus says, "Until now you have asked nothing in my name. Ask, and you will receive, that your joy may be full." Our lives can be transformed by repeatedly asking in his name with the resultant refilling of joy! This is what the disciples experienced, and it has been the repeated experience of countless believers down through the centuries.

What kind of prayer brings this kind of joy? Prayer in his name. Praying in his merit, with a sense of our own unworthiness. Praying in his nature. Becoming so attuned to him that we pray what he would pray. Submitting to his sovereign process of transforming sorrow into joy. Saying, "I yield to you, my sovereign, loving God." This is resurrection joy—megajoy!

Victorious Joy from the Living Source (vv. 25–27)

In addition to prayer, our Lord mentions some other factors that bolster joy and peace.

> In that day you will ask in my name, and I do not say to you that I will ask the Father on your behalf; for the Father himself loves you, because you have loved me and have believed that I came from God. (vv. 26, 27)

Jesus wants his followers to know that we have a direct relationship to the Father and that the Father loves us because we love Jesus and believe in him. This knowledge is meant to bring joy and security. As Ray Stedman said in a sermon:

> There is a three-fold technique in getting up: First, we stretch. That gets the body going. Then, smile. That puts the soul in the right attitude, so that we don't start the day grumbling. And then say, "God loves me" because that sets the spirit right. You are reminding yourself of your identity in that way. And body, soul, and spirit, you are starting the day right. Stretch, smile, and say, "God loves me."[5]

The Father loves us! That is what Jesus is saying. And that is the basis of our joy and security.

Victorious Joy from Belief (vv. 28–33)

Jesus also teaches us there is a relationship between joy and belief. First, he summarizes his mission in verse 28: "I came from the Father and have come into the world, and now I am leaving the world and going to the Father." The disciples responded in verses 29, 30:

> His disciples said, "Ah, now you are speaking plainly and not using figurative speech! Now we know that you know all things and do not need anyone to question you; this is why we believe that you came from God."

They were pleased with themselves. They understood something of the ministry of the Holy Spirit. They knew he would transform sorrow into joy.

They had listened to his teaching on the new arrangement for prayer. They had just been reassured of God's love. But they did not know that their knowledge was a shallow confidence.

Conclusion

So the Lord asked a bigger question: "Do you now believe?" (v. 31). That is a question we must all face. Do we really believe what Jesus said? That is a key question in relation to his joy-transforming process in our lives. Do we believe? That is the ongoing question in respect to his call to joy-giving prayer. Do we believe? That is the constant question in relation to his love. Do we believe?

Christ then spoke his final upper-room words before his farewell prayer:

> Behold, the hour is coming, indeed it has come, when you will be scattered, each to his own home, and will leave me alone. Yet I am not alone, for the Father is with me. I have said these things to you, that in me you may have peace. In the world you will have tribulation. But take heart; I have overcome the world. (vv. 32, 33)

These were courageous, audacious words, spoken in the face of the demonic hordes that would assault him in the following hours. How could Christ say such things? Because he believed in the process he so vividly outlined! He believed that his sorrow would be turned to joy! He believed the disciples' sorrow would also. He believed that as they prayed in his name, their joy would multiply. He believed that the Father loved them.

He says to us today, "Do you believe? Then cheer up! It is a fact—I have overcome the world!"

49

Christ's Prayer for Glory

JOHN 17:1–5

JOHN 17 is one of the greatest chapters in the Bible, and certainly one of the most treasured. Some refer to it as the "Holy of Holies of Sacred Scripture," the revelation of the inner sanctum of Christ's heart as he bared his soul in a final public prayer to the Father before he stepped out into the night and onto the cross. Philip Melanchthon, who along with Martin Luther was the towering intellect of the early Reformation, said:

> There is no voice which has ever been heard, either in heaven or in earth, more exalted, more holy, more fruitful, more sublime, than the prayer offered up by the Son of God himself.[1]

This chapter was read to the Scottish reformer John Knox every day during his final illness and in his final moments.[2] Chapter 17's twenty-six verses have been the inspiration of massive works. Oliver Cromwell's chaplain, Thomas Manton, preached forty-five sermons on it. More recently, Marcus Rainsford, an Irish preacher, wrote expositions that amount to more than five hundred pages. What a privilege it is to study this "Holy of Holies."

Christ's prayer divides easily into three logical, successive sections. In verses 1–5 he prayed for himself. In verses 6–19 he prayed for his apostles. And in verses 20–26 he prayed for the church in the world.

In the opening section, as Jesus prayed for himself, he prayed specifically for his own glorification.

> When Jesus had spoken these words, he lifted up his eyes to heaven, and said, "Father, the hour has come; glorify your Son that the Son may glorify you." (v. 1)

Then in verse 5 he said, "And now, Father, glorify me in your own presence." Personal glorification is the unquestionable thrust of this prayer.

The glory of God is seen in the revelation of who and what he is. The more the revelation, the greater the display of his glory. Throughout history we have seen the glory of God in varying degrees. Everyone sees something of it in nature: "The heavens declare the glory of God, and the sky above proclaims his handiwork" (Psalm 19:1). The stellar marvels surrounding us bear perpetual, eloquent testimony to the glorious power of the Almighty. Some privileged believers have experienced incomplete personal revelations of the glory of God—for example, Moses on Mt. Sinai or Peter, James, and John on the Mount of Transfiguration. By far, however, the most complete revelation of God's glory was in the person of Jesus Christ.

> He is the radiance of the glory of God and the exact imprint of his nature, and he upholds the universe by the word of his power. After making purification for sins, he sat down at the right hand of the Majesty on high. (Hebrews 1:3)

> For God, who said, "Let light shine out of darkness," has shone in our hearts to give the light of the knowledge of the glory of God in the face of Jesus Christ. (2 Corinthians 4:6)

In the upper room Jesus prayed that he would be further glorified, that he would be shown more completely for what he is. How was and is Jesus glorified? For what did he specifically pray? He prayed for his glorification in the cross (vv. 1, 4). He prayed for his glorification in Heaven (v. 5). He prayed for his glorification in the church (vv. 2, 3, 10).

Glorification in the Cross (vv. 1, 4)

Jesus had already glorified the Father by the matchless perfection of his life, as he reiterated in verse 4: "I glorified you on earth, having accomplished the work that you gave me to do." His life was a permanent monument to God's glory. He did this through his many miracles but supremely through the example of his day-to-day life.

Foremost in his mind now was the imminent glory of the cross because the cross would be the supreme revelation of his nature and purpose. So he prayed in verse 1: "Father, the hour has come; glorify your Son that the Son may glorify you." The cross displayed God the Father because, as 1:18 says, Jesus is the explanation or the exegesis of God. What do we learn from the cross? We see the holiness of God in the cross as nowhere else. We see his love of holiness and his hatred of sin and his refusal to compromise with it. We also see his love of justice in his condemnation of sin, even exercising his wrath upon his Son who bore our sins. Finally, we see God's love for us in the vast cost he paid for our redemption. If Jesus had stopped short of the cross, that would have proved there is a degree of love to which God is not prepared to go for us. The cross proves there is no limit to God's love.

We would not have known this without the cross! God who created the universe saw his Son hanging on the tree of Golgotha, covered with the spittle of those he came to save, gasping his final breaths while the sins of the world were showered upon his pure heart. Jesus is "the Lamb of God, who takes away the sin of the world!" (1:29). The cross was the only way we could see the infinite depths of God's love for us.

> In the cross of Christ I glory,
> Towering o'er the wrecks of time;
> All the light of sacred story
> Gathers round its head sublime.[3]

Our Savior had come to glorify the Father by showing what he is like, and the cross would show that as nothing else could. The deeper our contemplation of the tragedy of the cross, the deeper is our understanding of God, and the more profound our glorification of him.

Glorification in Heaven (v. 5)

As Christ prayed, his focus was not only on the glory of the cross but on his coming glorification in Heaven.

> And now, Father, glorify me in your own presence with the glory that I had with you before the world existed. (v. 5)

We can only dimly perceive what Christ's glory was like "before the world existed." We know he was the Creator of a universe so large it would take a person at least fifty octillion years traveling at the speed of light to visit every star. We know he enjoyed perfect intimacy with the rest of the Godhead, that there was always a joyous coming together of the Father and Son and Holy Spirit. Beyond this we know very little. We do know that he "emptied himself" (Philippians 2:7), that he set aside the exercise of his glorious existence of deity in order to plunge so low that he became a feeble creature on a floating sphere in a backwash of space, there to die at the hands of creatures whose resemblance he bore. Lewis likened his plunge to that of a man diving from a great height into a dark pool. As the diver is suspended in the air, he forms a colorful figure, but as he parts the waters, he rushes

> down through green and warm water to black and cold water, down through increasing pressure into the death-like region of ooze and slime and old decay; then up again, back to colour and light.[4]

That is an inadequate but suggestive analogy of our Lord's plunge from and return to glory. The Lord's return to Heaven is a ravishing and a sanctifying thought.

Jesus' prayer here suggests an *acquired* glory because he speaks of that glory as a consequence of his earthly life and suffering.

> Therefore God has highly exalted him and bestowed on him the name that is above every name, so that at the name of Jesus every knee should bow, in heaven and on earth and under the earth, and every tongue confess that Jesus Christ is Lord, to the glory of God the Father. (Philippians 2:9–11)

I agree with Bishop Lightfoot that his new name was "Jesus." Before he was born, the angel Gabriel gave him that prophetic name (Matthew 1:21). The Son of God became Jesus at his human birth. Now he is eternally Jesus. He bears the name that recalls his glorious human life and his glorious death. Today (from our standpoint) our Lord has a greater majesty as he reigns in his glorified human body at the right hand of God, beautified by his scars in the same way a skillful artist makes a figure more lovely than before by the marks of his tools.[5] Infinite glory cannot be increased, but this glory is greater in that there is now a greater understanding by both men and angels. Jesus' prayer for glory was answered, and someday every true believer will experience the dashing ecstasy of it.

Christ's glorification in the cross occurred two thousand years ago, and his glorification in Heaven is only partly comprehensible. If the manifestation of Christ's glory was left only to the heavens and to the cross, we would be greatly disadvantaged because neither of these are perfectly accessible due to time and space. But there is more.

Glorification in the Church (vv. 2, 3, 10)

Between the glorification of Christ in history and in Heaven, there is another glorification here on earth—in his church. Through his church, his glory is comprehensible. The glory that was first seen in Heaven, then in Christ's life and death can now be seen in his church. Christ is glorified in the lives of his earthly followers.

Because Christ is (or should be) manifested in his church, he remembers his followers in the heart of his prayer for his own glorification. (Note that his prayer for glory encompasses verses 1–5. The core of that prayer, in verses 2–4, refers to the church.) Specifically he draws attention to giving his followers eternal life, which he describes as knowing the Father and the Son:

> You have given him authority over all flesh, to give eternal life to all whom you have given him. And this is eternal life, that they know you the only true God, and Jesus Christ whom you have sent. (vv. 2, 3)

What is involved in knowing Christ? And what is involved in gaining a deeper knowledge of him?

First, knowing Christ involves *knowing something about him*. This truth is terribly appropriate today. It is doubtful that even during the Dark Ages there was as much ignorance in the English-speaking world as there is today regarding the Bible and the person of Christ. Hosea said in his day that his people were destroyed for a "lack of knowledge" (Hosea 4:6). Paul spoke of his own people as "alienated from the life of God because of the ignorance that is in them" (Ephesians 4:18). Liberal theology's deemphasis on Bible study has left many people who say they believe the Bible ignorant of its contents and insulated from an encounter with the Christ it reveals. Today new Christians often grow very slowly because everything is so new to them, whereas years ago the newly converted already knew many of the essentials. We must learn about Christ if we are to know him.

Second, knowing Christ involves *intimacy of relationship*. The Old Testament regularly uses the word *know* for sexual knowledge. The idea of knowing suggests a mutual experience and exchange. Knowing Christ is not simply knowing something about him but having a personal knowledge of him. This is repeated with delightful monotony when people are truly converted. They know they know Jesus and that Jesus knows them. Now they see Christ and the Scriptures in living color.

Third, knowing Christ means *a growing knowledge*. (The tenses in verse 3 suggest an increasing knowledge of Christ.[6]) In "The Great Stone Face" Nathanael Hawthorne tells of a boy who lived in a village below a mountain. On the mountain was an image of a great stone face, looking down solemnly upon the people. A legend claimed that someday someone would come to that village who looked just like the great stone face, and he would do wonderful things for the village and would be the means of great blessing. The story so gripped the young boy that he would spend hour after hour looking at that great stone face and thinking about the one who was coming. Years passed, and the promised one did not come. The boy became a young man, and he kept contemplating the majestic beauty of that great stone face. By and by his youth passed, and middle age came on. The man still could not get that legend out of his mind. Finally, he reached old age, and one day as he walked through the village, someone looked at him and exclaimed, "He has come—the one who is like the great stone face!" The old man had became like the object he had contemplated. And so it is with us.

When Moses returned from Mt. Sinai, his face radiated the glory of God. Paul, in expounding on this in 2 Corinthians 3:18, gave us the supreme practical application of Moses' experience:

> And we all, with unveiled face, beholding the glory of the Lord, are being transformed into the same image from one degree of glory to another. For this comes from the Lord who is the Spirit.

Notice that "We all"—not just the Moseses and Elijahs, but *all* of us, including the weakest, poorest, and lowest—can reflect God's glory. "With unveiled face"—God has taken the veil off our hearts, and now we "behold the glory of the Lord"—we see him through the Word and the work of the Spirit. We "are being transformed into the same image from one degree of glory to another." This literally says that a metamorphosis is taking place, a gradual change as we continue growing in glory. The more we look to Christ, the more we are changed.

Why did Christ mention our knowing him within his prayer for his own glorification? Our growing knowledge of Christ means a growing revelation and glorification of him. We all, as true believers, show Christ to some degree and in some way, some more than others.

Sadhu Sundar Singh (the great Christian evangelist of India) once knocked on the door of a village home, and a little girl answered, running back to call her mother. Her mother asked, "Who is it?" The girl replied, "I don't know, but he has such a lovely face, I think it must be Jesus."

> Not merely in the words you say,
> Not only in your deeds confessed.
> But in the most unconscious way
> Is Christ expressed.
> Is it a beatific smile?
> A holy light upon your brow?

Oh no! I felt His presence
When you laughed just now.
To me, 'twas not the truth you taught,
To you so clear, to me still dim.
But when you came you brought
A sense of Him.
And from your eyes He beckons me,
And from your heart His love is shed,
Till I lose sight of you and see
The Christ instead.[7]

That is why Christ prays for us. From ground level, believers are the world's best hope of seeing the glory of God. Jesus made the Father's glory comprehensible, and we are to do so as well. We must be people of the Word, our most accurate source of knowledge about Christ. We must meditate on the cross because it is the clearest demonstration of the love of the Father. We must spend time with those who know him, so that their knowledge will pass on to us. In doing these things we will experience the answers to our Savior's prayer for us.

Conclusion

As verse 1 reveals, when Jesus prayed for glorification, his eyes were wide open and looking up to Heaven, indicating the perfect, unhindered communion he had with his Father. "The hour has come." In the fullest sense, it was his hour, the Father's hour, his enemies' hour, and our own as well.

His prayer for glory was a prayer for the manifestation of his character, his inward being, before the whole universe. He prayed for his glorification in the cross, and never was a prayer so abundantly answered. Never has there been such a display of the inward being of God! He also prayed for his glorification in Heaven. This, too, was abundantly answered. God "bestowed on him the name that is above every name, so that at the name of Jesus every knee should bow." Finally, he prayed for his glorification in the church, a prayer with pressing implications. Is that prayer being answered? The cross was two thousand years ago, and Heaven is not found in this world, but we have a role to play in Christ's glorification in the church.

Are we allowing the life of Christ to flow through us? Shortly after the armistice of World War I, Dr. Donald Grey Barnhouse visited the battlefields of Belgium. It was a lovely spring day. The sun was shining, and not a breath of wind was blowing. As Dr. Barnhouse walked along, he noticed that leaves were falling from the great trees arched along the road. He brushed at a leaf that had fallen against his chest. As he pressed it in his fingers, it disintegrated. He looked up curiously and saw several other leaves falling from the trees. Remember, it was spring, not autumn. Those leaves had outlived the winds of autumn and the frosts of winter. They were falling that day, seemingly without cause. Then Dr. Barnhouse realized why. The most potent force of all was causing them to fall. It was spring, the sap was beginning to run, and the buds were beginning to push from within. From down beneath the dark earth, roots were sending life along trunk, branch, and twig until that life expelled every bit of deadness remaining from the previous year. It was, as a great Scottish preacher termed it, "the expulsive power of a new affection."[8]

How much we allow the knowledge of Christ to fill our being will determine how much of the old dead things will fall away and how much new life will spring forth. We must know Jesus for that expulsive force to work within us. We must look long and intently at Jesus. "And we all, with unveiled face, beholding the glory of the Lord, are being transformed into the same image from one degree of glory to another. For this comes from the Lord who is the Spirit" (2 Corinthians 3:18). Longing for him, we must pray with Paul that we "may know him and the power of his resurrection, and may share his sufferings, becoming like him in his death" (Philippians 3:10).

50

Christ Prays for His Disciples

JOHN 17:11–19

CHRIST'S PRAYER IN JOHN 17 is captivating because it shows us the kinds of prayers he offers for us now in Heaven. The overall thrust of verses 11–19, in which Jesus prays for his disciples, is that the disciples should relate properly to one another and to the nonbelieving world. We do not have to argue the importance of this topic. If there is one area in which we often feel inadequate or are constantly being reminded of our shortcomings, it is in the area of personal relationships. Submission to the teachings contained in Jesus' prayer will be a substantial step in the right direction.

Christians' Relationship with Other Christians (vv. 11–13)

> And I am no longer in the world, but they are in the world, and I am coming to you. Holy Father, keep them in your name, which you have given me, that they may be one, even as we are one. (v. 11)

Jesus prayed that his followers would be "one." He knew his followers would face many trials. Many would be their own fault—for example, childish squabbles such as when James and John through their mother tried to obtain the best thrones in the kingdom. Our Lord also knew Christians would break fellowship with one another over matters like the mode of baptism ("three times forward or one time backward?") or the color of the church bathroom. Every age of the church has known division. The Puritan Thomas Brookes wrote: "For wolves to worry the lambs is no wonder, but for one lamb to worry another, this is unnatural and monstrous."[1]

Our Lord prayed that oneness would be maintained by the disciples' being kept in the Father's name.

> Holy Father, keep them in your name, which you have given me, that they may be one, even as we are one. While I was with them, I kept them in your name, which you have given me. I have guarded them, and not one of them has been lost except the son of destruction, that the Scripture might be fulfilled. (vv. 11b, 12)

The significance of Christ's words comes from the widely acknowledged importance of name to the Jewish people. To them, a name represented a person's whole personality, his character. That is why the psalmist commented, "Some trust in chariots and some in horses, but we trust in the name of the LORD our God" (Psalm 20:7). Today we might say, "Some boast in tanks and airplanes, but we will boast in the character of our God. He can do the job!" Jesus built the disciples' oneness and a sense of security and unity by showing both in his own life and in his teaching the personality and character of the Father. The more the disciples understood the attributes and character of God, the more they experienced unity.

A. W. Tozer wrote:

> Has it ever occurred to you that one hundred pianos all tuned to the same fork are automatically tuned to each other? They are of one accord by being tuned, not to each other, but to another standard to which each one must individually bow. So one hundred worshipers met together, each one looking away to Christ, are in heart nearer to each other than they could possibly be were they to become "unity" conscious and turn their eyes away from God to strive for closer fellowship. Social religion is perfected when private religion is purified.[2]

The more we know of Christ, the more we are drawn to him, and the more we are drawn to one another. While Christ prayed that the whole character of God be kept before his disciples, the emphasis is on the Fatherhood of God: "Holy Father, keep them in your name." Handley C. G. Moule, onetime Lord Bishop of Durham, said:

> "In Thy Name"; they were never to be allowed to wander out of that Name; never to seek another name, one of their own imagining or developing; never to dream of safety or of home for their souls anywhere but within the revealed personal love and life of the holy Father of our Lord Jesus Christ. Within the mystical circle of a knowledge of God as Father they were to be "preserved."[3]

The contemplation and appropriation of the blessed truth that God is our Father thrusts us toward oneness. Those who have the same father long for and love their brothers and sisters.

The result of oneness is joy. "Now I am coming to you, and these things I speak in the world, that they may have my joy fulfilled in themselves" (v. 13). Jesus said, "*my* joy." He was not praying for a joy from below but the joy that has its origin in Heaven. Joy is the occupation, character, and realization of Heaven. It is not dependent on circumstances but on the love of a sovereign God.

As Jesus prayed for our relationships with each other as Christians, he also prayed that we would be constantly kept aware of and growing in the knowledge of God, especially his Fatherhood. In that way we would keep growing in oneness, which will result in joy—his joy. That is how we are to relate to fellow Christians. But what would the world think of all this?

> I have given them your word, and the world has hated them because they are not of the world, just as I am not of the world. (v. 14)

Jesus' followers would have trouble in the world, just as Jesus did. In fact, the more they are like Jesus, the more trouble they will have. The question is, what were they to do?

Christians' Relationship with the World (vv. 14–19)

The answer is in verse 15: "I do not ask that you take them out of the world, but that you keep them from the evil one." First, the Christian attitude toward the world should not be one of withdrawal. Christ does not ask that we be taken away. Withdrawal has always been a temptation for the religious, and in Jesus' time the Pharisees succumbed to that temptation. To be a Pharisee was to be a separatist. The goal of that group was to escape the contamination of fallen society. In the third century Christian hermits fled to the deserts of Egypt. That mentality was perpetuated in the rise of monasticism in the Middle Ages, vestiges of which can still be seen today in such orders as the Carthusians or the hermits of the Eastern Church.

We have all felt this way at times. When I first became a Christian at a summer camp, my treasured hope was to find a way to spend the rest of my life there. The psalmist expressed a longing of all our hearts at times: "Oh, that I had wings like a dove! I would fly away and be at rest" (Psalm 55:6). We all have our escape fantasies—a hideaway cabin in the north woods, burning our neckties, ordering all our clothing from the Bean catalog. We have probably all seen bumper stickers that say, "Have you hugged your hang glider today?" or "In case of Rapture this car will not have a driver."

Our Christian lives can easily become monastic. We often find our lives arranged so that we are around nonbelievers as little as possible. We attend Bible studies that are 100 percent Christian, Sunday schools that are 100 percent Christian, and church services that we hope are 100 percent Christian. We read only or at least primarily Christian books, send our kids to Christian schools or homeschool them, listen only or mostly to Christian radio programs or tapes. None of these things are bad, but it is easy to use these so much that we isolate ourselves in a Christian subculture.

We can even develop a special crypto-Christian language with Christian jokes, Biblical nicknames, and passwords. This can happen in unlikely environments, even on the secular campus. Rebecca Manley Pippert, formerly a national consultant on evangelism with Inter-Varsity Christian Fellowship, writes in her excellent book *Out of the Salt Shaker*:

> We must not become, as John Stott puts it, "a rabbit-hole Christian"—the kind who pops his head out of a hole, leaves his Christian roommate in the morning and scurries to class, only to frantically search for a Christian to sit by (an odd way to approach a mission field). Thus he proceeds from class to class. When dinner comes, he sits with the Christians in his dorm at one huge table and thinks, "What a witness!" From there he goes to his all-Christian Bible study, and he might even catch a prayer meeting where the Christians pray for the non-believers on his floor. (But what luck that he was able to live on the only floor with seventeen Christians!) Then at night he scurries back to his Christian roommate. Safe! He made it through the day and his only contacts with the world were those mad, brave dashes to and from Christian activities.
>
> What an insidious reversal of the biblical command to be salt and light to the world.[4]

We are all susceptible to this. It is possible to go womb to tomb in a hermetically sealed container decorated with fish stickers. It is possible to abandon our culture to the devil. It is interesting to note that though Moses, Elijah, and Jonah all asked to be taken out of the world, not one of their requests was granted (see Numbers 11:15; 1 Kings 19:4; Jonah 4:3, 8). We need to ask ourselves honestly if we have functionally removed ourselves from the world. Christ prays that we will not.

Furthermore, the Christian attitude should not be one of conformity to the world. "That you keep them from the evil one. They are not of the world, just as I am not of the world" (vv. 15, 16). Today the temptation to conform is probably as great as it has ever been, especially with all the criticism Christianity receives about its being so insular. Granted, sometimes conformity has been inspired by a well-meaning desire to demonstrate the fullness of life Christ brings or to draw the unregenerate to Christ. But the result of conformity to the world is assimilation, and in time there is no distinguishable difference between the church and the world system—a secular Christianity. When Lot went to warn his children of the imminent destruction of Sodom, they thought he was joking.

> I appeal to you therefore, brothers, by the mercies of God, to present your bodies as a living sacrifice, holy and acceptable to God, which is your spiritual worship. Do not be conformed to this world, but be transformed by the renewal of your mind, that by testing you may discern what is the will of God, what is good and acceptable and perfect. (Romans 12:1, 2)

Christ prayed that we would succumb to neither isolation nor assimilation, though both temptations are great.

The Christian attitude is also to be one of mission. "As you sent me into the world, so I have sent them into the world" (v. 18). One day a number of years ago I called home late one afternoon to see how things were going around the house. As my wife and I talked, she said, "Oh, by the way, we received a call from the Youth Soccer Association here in town. They were wondering if you might be a coach." I said, "Well, you told them no, didn't you?" She said, "I just didn't have the heart to say no. You'll have to tell them yourself." I assured her I would be firm about that. By the time I got home, I had all my reasons laid out. I did not have time. I did not know anything about soccer. I did not want to do it. I firmly gripped the phone and dialed. As I talked to the poor woman at the other end of the line, I learned there would not be a team if I did not coach. I remember my family chuckling in the background as they heard me say, "Yes, I can do it." The only good thing was that I would get to coach one of my sons.

The next thing I knew, I was up late reading soccer books, trying to understand what a center halfback was, the offside rule, etc. Suddenly I had a coach's whistle, and I was occupied three days a week from four to six and half a day on Saturdays.

The season did not go very well at the beginning. You have probably heard the saying, if the bugle gives an uncertain sound, who will follow? That described my coaching, I am afraid. Fortunately I had some good players, and the team came together as the season went on. In fact, in one of the last games of the season, we beat the number one team in the last second of the game and thus made the play-offs. On the night before the play-offs, I invited the team to my church for a potluck dinner with their parents. Even both sides of divorced parents came. Toward the end of the evening I said to them, "If it is all right with you, I would like to share something from the Word of God." The parents agreed, and I told the boys the story of David and Goliath, with practical applications. The next day we went into the play-offs. We lost in the final minutes, 1-0, but that is not where the story ends. Sunday morning when I stepped into the pulpit, I looked out at the congregation, and there were all my players wearing their orange jerseys, and their parents too—Jews, Muslims, Mormons, and several others with varying backgrounds. That began a ministry in several of those families' lives. I did not want to coach, I did not have time to do it, but because I just did not know how to say no, I ended up coaching. And that turned out to be one of the great experiences of my life.

Despite my reluctance I experienced the truth that our lives are not to be ones of isolation or assimilation but of mission. The Lord gives the method for such mission in verses 17, 19:

> Sanctify them in the truth; your word is truth. . . . And for their sake I consecrate myself, that they also may be sanctified in truth.

The method of mission is sanctification, and that includes two ideas. The obvious one is "to make holy." The other is "to set apart for service." Verse 17 tells us that sanctification comes through the Word. We are to be made holy and set apart for service by a close examination and application of the Word of God. The Scriptures guard us from isolation or assimilation and gear us for mission. Verse 19 indicates that Jesus volitionally set himself apart for service. For him that meant taking on human flesh. In doing this he did not cut himself off from the world, nor was he assimilated. Rather, he accepted the pain and peril of entering the world and made himself vulnerable to suffering and ultimately death. Mission is dangerous! Hebrews 7:26 says he was "separated from sinners," and Matthew 11:19 says he was a "'friend of . . . sinners.'" Christ prayed that his followers would have an attitude not of isolation or assimilation but of mission. For some of us, because of the scheduling of our lives, it will take purposeful, decisive action if we are to meet those who need Christ. But with the Savior's help, we can do this.

Conclusion

Implemented, this might mean taking a class in the park district, taking an active part in the PTA, playing racquetball with non-Christian friends, being a room mother, taking an active interest in the clerks at the businesses we frequent, coaching a team, joining one of the many community clubs or service clubs in town, or befriending a barber or hairdresser.

Christ said, "As you sent me into the world, so I have sent them into the world" (v. 18). How well do we relate to Christians? Are we growing in our knowledge of the Father so that there is a growing unity with our brothers and sisters that engenders a growing joy? How do we relate to the world? Through isolation, assimilation, or mission?

51

Christ Prays for His Own

JOHN 17:20–26

CHRIST'S HIGH-PRIESTLY PRAYER in John 17 contains his final words to his disciples in the upper room, the *terminus ad quem*. There only remains Gethsemane and the cross and then the stupendous resurrection of Jesus Christ. We need this terminal perspective to grasp the full impact of what Christ said in this majestic prayer. We must also sense the spiraling intensity of his words. Christ did not pray this prayer dispassionately! F. B. Meyer says, "As the weight of the jeweled breastplate lay heavy on the heart of the high priest of old, so does it press on him."[1] The burden on Christ's soul for his future children thrust his loving heart passionately upward.

The flow of Christ's thought is: his earthly prayer for his church (vv. 20–23), his heavenly prayer for his church (v. 24), and his eternal vow to his church (vv. 25, 26).

Christ's Earthly Prayer for His Church (vv. 20–23)

> I do not ask for these only, but also for those who will believe in me through their word, that they may all be one. (vv. 20, 21a).

Christ again prayed for the oneness of the church. He was concerned about his people's love, holiness, and mission, but in his final earthly prayer he made unity his transcending concern. Logically, then, this unity must also be his dominant concern today. True, it is not his only concern (the ecumenical movement has used this verse as a proof-text while ignoring the context and theology of the prayer). Nevertheless, it is foremost among Christ's earthly concerns, and we cannot overestimate its importance for today.

First, Jesus is explicit about the *nature* of this unity. He states it three times for emphasis:

That they may all be one, just as you, Father, are in me, and I in you. (v. 21a)

That they may be one even as we are one. (v. 22b)

I in them and you in me, that they may become perfectly one. (v. 23a)

Christ prays for a supernatural unity that is modeled and enabled by the Godhead. This unity is possible because true believers are united in the core of their beings. That is why we often can sense that we have met another believer before words have even been spoken. We share the divine nature!

For in him the whole fullness of deity dwells bodily, and you have been filled in him, who is the head of all rule and authority. (Colossians 2:9, 10; cf. 2 Peter 1:4)

The closer we draw to Christ, the closer we draw to one another. Our unity can be described as an inverted cone, with God at the top and believers around the base. As we ascend the slopes of the cone, drawing nearer to God, we draw closer to our fellow believers. At the pinnacle (in God) we touch one another in deepest joy.

That which we have seen and heard we proclaim also to you, so that you too may have fellowship with us; and indeed our fellowship is with the Father and with his Son Jesus Christ. And we are writing these things so that our joy may be complete. (1 John 1:3, 4)

Christian unity is supernatural because it comes from God's nature and is only experienced in its fullness as we draw close to him: "That they may be one even as we are one."

That unity, though, does not mean uniformity in everything. In the Trinity there exists a unity in diversity—three distinct Persons, yet they are one. Suppose, for a moment, that we could bring some of the great Christians of the centuries together under one roof. From the fourth century would come the great intellect Augustine of Hippo. From the tenth century, Bernard of Clairvaux. From the sixteenth, the peerless reformer John Calvin. From the seventeenth century would come John Wesley, the great Methodist advocate of free will, and along with him George Whitefield, the evangelist. From the nineteenth century, the Baptist C. H. Spurgeon and D. L. Moody. And, finally, from the twentieth century, Billy Graham.

If we gathered all these men under one steeple, we would have trouble! We would be unable to get a unanimous vote on many things. But underneath it all would be unity. And the more the men lifted up Christ and the more they focused on him, the greater their unity would be. There would be unity amid a great diversity of style and opinion.

Christ's prayer for unity does not mean we all should be the same, though many Christians mistakenly assume that. Too many think other believers should be just like them—carry the same Bible, read the same books, promote the same styles, educate their children in the same way, have the same likes and dislikes. That would be uniformity, not unity. We are not called to be Christian clones. In fact, the insistence that others be just like us is one of the most disunifying forces in the church of Jesus Christ. It engenders a judgmental inflexibility that hurls people away from the church with deadly force. One of the gospel's glories is that it hallows our individuality even while bringing us into unity. Unity without uniformity is implicit in Paul's teaching on spiritual gifts.

> Now there are varieties of gifts, but the same Spirit; and there are varieties of service, but the same Lord; and there are varieties of activities, but it is the same God who empowers them all in everyone. (1 Corinthians 12:4–6)

As John Stott has pointed out, the unity enjoined here is not only a unity among present believers, but a unity with the apostolic church and its teaching. Christ says in verse 20:

> I do not ask for these only, but also for those who will believe in me through their word.

Stott goes on:

> It is first and foremost a prayer that there may be a historical continuity between the church of the first century and the church of subsequent centuries; that the church's faith may not change but remain recognizably the same; that the church of every age may merit the title "apostolic" because it is loyal to the teaching of the apostles.[2]

The unity for which the Savior prays is a unity that comes from the indwelling of the Holy Spirit and grows as we draw nearer to God by being rooted and strengthened in his Word. We are never closer to one another than when our hearts are genuinely focused on God.

This Biblical pursuit of unity is extremely important. Our Lord explains why in verses 21, 23:

> That they may all be one, just as you, Father, are in me, and I in you, that they also may be in us, so that the world may believe that you have sent me.

> I in them and you in me, that they may become perfectly one, so that the world may know that you sent me and loved them even as you loved me.

If we have unity, the world will believe that Jesus really came from God. Unity is an evangelistic necessity! We live in a fragmented world. Ever since Adam said to God, "The woman whom you gave to be with me, she gave me fruit of the tree . . ." (Genesis 3:12), things have been going downhill. We cannot imagine how many times Eve asked, "Adam, how could you possibly say that?" Human lives, and marriages, have wrestled with alienation ever since.

Jacques Ellul, the French sociologist, in his book *The Meaning of the City*, says the driving force behind ancient history was the desire to come together and advance in the face of this disunity. Thus the rise of the city. However, he points out, with the formation of cities came the practice of laying the foundation stone on the body of a human sacrifice, a practice, he maintains, we moderns have replaced with the sacrifice of millions of souls.[3] The world's attempts to come together without God are always at the expense of human life.

Christian unity is important because the world's pursuit of unity is futile. When genuine unity is authentically demonstrated, it is irresistible. Real unity between Christians is a supernatural work, and it points to a supernatural explanation—Jesus Christ in us!

Our Lord explains even further what the world perceives when there is a true unity among his people:

> I in them and you in me, that they may become perfectly one, so that the world may know that you sent me and loved them even as you loved me. (v. 23)

Through Christian unity some in the world will come to understand that believers are loved by God even as he loves his own Son! What a breathtaking idea! The Greek translated "even as" means "just as" or "to the same degree that." Jesus is telling us that God loves those who are Christ's *to the same degree* and *in the same way* that he loves Christ! What a tender comfort to our hearts! And some in the world will evidently conclude from this unity and its accompanying love that believers are special objects of a supernatural love. Thomas Manton said, "Divisions in the church breed atheism in the world."[4] The converse is also true: unity in the church builds belief in the world. In view of that, there is scarcely anything more important than Christ's prayer for genuine unity in the church. This unity is a oneness in truth and spirit that comes by drawing close to him and shows itself in love. In verse 22 we see further how the Lord implements it:

> The glory that you have given me I have given to them, that they may be one even as we are one.

What does Christ mean? Leon Morris writes:

> Jesus now says that he has given his followers the glory which the Father gave him. That is to say, just as the true glory was to follow the path of lowly service culminating in the cross, so for them the true glory lay in the path of lowly service wherever it might lead them.[5]

Unity in this world is promoted by humble service to one another. Philippians 2:3–5 capsulizes the glorious attitude Christ enjoins:

> Do nothing from selfish ambition or conceit, but in humility count others more significant than yourselves. Let each of you look not only to his own interests, but also to the interests of others. Have this mind among yourselves, which is yours in Christ Jesus.

Christ's earthly prayer for his church is for unity—unity in apostolic truth, a oneness with the apostolic church, and also a unity that is spiritual, promoted by our walk with God as we seek the heights of spiritual maturity. It is also a unity on earth between brothers and sisters, a unity that comes through mutual humble service.

This unity does not happen automatically or easily. It must be worked at. When a man and woman become one in Christ in marriage, there must be a commitment to oneness—an ongoing commitment to communicate, to share their souls, to spend time together, to have the deepest relationship possible in body, soul, and spirit. Such a relationship is unutterably wonderful when experienced. But many people never attain this, not because they do not want it, but because they are not committed to working toward it with God's help. The same is true of the unity of believers in this world. We must be committed to scaling the heights, committed to the apostolic faith, and committed to humbly serving one another.

Christ's Heavenly Desire for His Church (v. 24)

To frame the picture of this unity, we will look at the heavenly desire in Christ's High-Priestly prayer.

> Father, I desire that they also, whom you have given me, may be with me where I am, to see my glory that you have given me because you loved me before the foundation of the world. (v. 24)

Jesus prayed that one day we would be with him in Heaven and behold his glory, and one day that is indeed going to happen. And when it does, he will say, "Welcome home!" We will arrive at the home we have always longed for, and we will find that we really have never wanted anything else. Christ's prayer asks literally that we will *keep on* beholding his glory, and his prayer will be answered. We will constantly behold his face and will become like him.

> Beloved, we are God's children now, and what we will be has not yet appeared; but we know that when he appears we shall be like him, because we shall see him as he is. (1 John 3:2)

One by one, we will be gathered in. His prayer will come to pass!

Christ's Eternal Vow to the Church (vv. 25, 26)

> O righteous Father, even though the world does not know you, I know you, and these know that you have sent me. I made known to them your name, and I will continue to make it known, that the love with which you have loved me may be in them, and I in them. (vv. 25, 26)

Jesus closes his prayer with a vow to the Father, but it is also a promise to us. He will continue to make his name (meaning all that he is) known to us and also will be increasing the Father's love in us. That is his sovereign vow, and it will be our continuing experience. Blessed be his name!

Some will experience more of this in this life than others. Why? They clearly see the passion of Christ's earthly prayer for his church and perceive their duty to draw near to him, feed on his Word, and humbly serve one another. May we be part of the answer to our Savior's prayer!

52

Who Arrested Whom?

JOHN 18:1–11

THE PASSAGE WE WILL STUDY in this chapter brings us to the arrest of Jesus. The ministry of the upper room is over. The Passover table bears the cold remains of the paschal meal. Judas is gone. The intercessory prayer has ended. With the echoes of the last hymn still floating in the midnight air, Jesus and his disciples have headed for Gethsemane and the cross. The details of these final moments are recorded in John 18, 19. The imminent events are of ultimate importance because none of the wonderful things promised during Christ's ministry would be possible without them. The promise of eternal life, the sending of the Holy Spirit as Helper, Jesus' return for his beloved, the preparation of a place for them, treasures of grace and salvation—all were dependent upon the manner of Christ's death and resurrection. How he would conduct himself in life, especially in these last few hours, would either validate or invalidate his claims.

Christ's life, and especially his death and resurrection, have been interpreted in very different ways by different people. In 1906 Albert Schweitzer published his landmark book *The Quest for the Historical Jesus*. In it Schweitzer concluded that Jesus was a mere man who was dominated by the expectation of the coming of God's kingdom and who finally in desperation tried to force its coming by seeking his own death. Schweitzer describes this in a famous quotation:

> There is silence all around. The Baptist appears, and cries: "Repent, for the Kingdom of Heaven is at hand." Soon after that comes Jesus, and in the knowledge that he is the coming Son of Man lays hold of the wheel of the world to set it moving on that last revolution which is to bring all ordinary history to a close. It refuses to turn, and he throws himself upon it. Then it

does turn; and crushes him. Instead of bringing in the eschatological conditions, he has destroyed them. The wheel rolls onward, and the mangled body of the one immeasurably great Man, who was strong enough to think of himself as the spiritual ruler of mankind and to bend history to his purpose, is hanging upon it still. That is his victory and his reign.[1]

To Albert Schweitzer and, tragically, to the thousands who followed him, Jesus was a mistaken idealist, caught and crushed like a rag doll in the wheels of history, who died in confusion, despair, and rejection. To Schweitzer, Jesus' great contribution was to free mankind of the hope of a future kingdom. A great deal of modern theology has been written to escape the implications of this concept.

Far from seeing Jesus as a helpless figure mangled on the cruel wheel of history, the apostle John portrayed him as one who dramatically exhibited his lordship and control in the terrible events surrounding his death. Christ's actions have encouraging implications for us as we wage lives fraught with trying events. The record of his last days on earth brings encouragement and optimism to those who live in a world that at times *appears* to have no caring Sovereign.

His Lordship in the Symbolism of the Surroundings (v. 1)

We first see Christ's lordship and control in his choice of the place of encounter with his captors. The Lord deliberately chose Gethsemane. John's specific mention of it as a "garden" in verse 1 suggests that the apostle has in mind a deliberate comparison with the original garden of Eden. The symbolism is this:

- The first Adam began life in a garden. Christ, the second Adam, came at the end of his life to a garden.
- In Eden Adam sinned. In Gethsemane the Savior overcame sin.
- In Eden Adam fell. In Gethsemane Jesus conquered.
- In Eden Adam hid himself. In Gethsemane our Lord boldly presented himself.
- In Eden the sword was drawn. In Gethsemane it was sheathed.

This symbolism is not accidental or incidental to Jesus' death. It was an assurance for future generations of readers that Christ was in control.

Enhancing this symbolism, John mentions in verse 1 that "Jesus . . . went out with his disciples across the brook Kidron." A drain ran from the temple altar down to the Kidron ravine to drain away the blood of sacrifices. At this time of year more than two hundred thousand lambs were slain. So when Jesus and his band crossed the Kidron, it was red with the blood of sacrifice.[2]

This divine poetry shows that what was about to take place was not beyond the control of God, regardless of how it appeared.

His Lordship in His Resolve to Endure the Agony

There is a gap between verses 1 and 2 that is filled in by the accounts in the other Gospels. From them we understand that an unspeakable horror overcame Christ in Gethsemane as he wrestled with the reality of what was to come. He experienced intense agony. "He began to be sorrowful and troubled. Then he said to them, 'My soul is very sorrowful, even to death'" (Matthew 26:37, 38). Mark tells us that Christ repeatedly (literal translation) fell to the ground "and prayed that, if it were possible, the hour might pass from him" (Mark 14:35). Evidently he was in such agony that he would cast himself to the ground, then stand up, then again fall to the ground in prayer. No one has known the sorrow our Lord experienced. Luke the physician says, "And being in agony he prayed more earnestly; and his sweat became like great drops of blood falling down to the ground" (Luke 22:44). So great was his agony as the coming dread engulfed him that he actually broke out in a bloody sweat. These and similar verses caused Celsus, a second-century heretic, and others after him to argue that Christ was only a man. After all, they reasoned, he displayed in the garden and on the cross less fortitude than other men have shown in battle or at the stake.

But actually Christ's agony demonstrates that he knew exactly what was involved. It was not the pain that caused the horror. It was not the shame. It was not the imminent desertion of the disciples. It was the fact that he was going to pay the penalty for our sins! The understanding of what that sacrifice meant, which only omniscience could bring, caused our Lord to break out in a bloody sweat. It was the crushing realization of that horror that crushed him. Christ's resolve to endure the agony, even at such a great price, demonstrates his lordship and divinity.

John picks up the narrative after Jesus' formal resolve to drink the cup. The moments are loaded with drama:

> Now Judas, who betrayed him, also knew the place, for Jesus often met there with his disciples. So Judas, having procured a band of soldiers and some officers from the chief priests and the Pharisees, went there with lanterns and torches and weapons. (vv. 2, 3)

It was the middle of a spring night, and it was probably cloudless because John mentions it was "cold" (18:18). The ancient olive trees cast eerie shadows across the encampment. Beyond the ravine lay the scattered lights of Jerusalem, where Judas had earlier made his rendezvous with the Roman cohort of six hundred men from the Tower of Antonia. Matthew later described that cohort as "a great crowd" (Matthew 26:47). The soldiers of the cohort were fully armed, each carrying a short sword. With them came the temple guards with their clubs. Jews and Gentiles were for once united in a common cause. They had carefully chosen the time and place. They wanted to arrest Jesus away from the people, so there would be no riot, but they were prepared for the worst. The sight must have been terrifying as the long line, punctuated by the flickering torches, wound down from the dark, high walls of the Holy City, across the stained Kidron, and up the slopes of Olivet toward the garden. No doubt Judas was in the lead. In a few minutes he, as Mark says, "fervently kissed" the Master as a sign of betrayal (Mark 14:45, literal Greek).

To the unbelieving eye, Jesus' arrest may look like matters were beyond his control. H. G. Wells once said the world is like a great stage production produced and managed by God. As the curtain rises, the set is perfect, a treat to every eye. The characters are resplendent. Everything goes well until the leading man steps on the hem of the leading lady's gown, causing her to trip over a chair, which knocks over a lamp, which pushes a table into a wall, which in turn knocks over the scenery, which brings everything down on the heads of the actors. Meanwhile, behind the scenes God is running around, shouting orders, pulling strings, trying desperately to restore order from chaos. But, alas, he is unable to do so! Poor God! According to Wells, he is a very little, limited God.[3] But this is not the God of our text, for as we take up the narrative again, we see Jesus' lordship clearly manifested.

His Lordship in His Confrontation with His Antagonists (vv. 4–9)

Then Jesus, knowing all that would happen to him, came forward and said to them, "Whom do you seek?" They answered him, "Jesus of Nazareth." Jesus said to them, "I am he." Judas, who betrayed him, was standing with them. When Jesus said to them, "I am he," they drew back and fell to the ground. (vv. 4–6)

Our Lord, instead of waiting to be found, went forward to meet the armed crowd. In response to their question, he openly identified himself. Their reaction was to fall to the ground. John represents their response as a miracle. They did not fall down when he asked them what they wanted, but only after he said, "I am he" or literally "I am." I do not agree with those who partially explain this response by pointing to the moral force that some great and good men and women possess. The Roman soldiers knew nothing of Jesus and had no reason to fear him. Jesus answered in the style of deity, using the divine title, I AM, going back to the burning bush of Exodus 3 when God said, "I AM WHO I AM" (Exodus 3:14). Jesus' response was the last exercise of the power by which he calmed the seas, stilled the winds, and healed the sick. Was Jesus caught on the wheel of history? Hardly! He is the axis of history. In a very real sense the cohort did not arrest Jesus—he arrested them! His words were a gracious warning that they were in way over their heads. Christ could have called ten thousand angels, each sixty feet high and armed with laser beams. But he did not. I wonder what was in Judas' mind as he struggled back to his feet.

Earlier Jesus had said:

> I lay down my life that I may take it up again. No one takes it from me, but I lay it down of my own accord. I have authority to lay it down, and I have authority to take it up again. (10:17, 18)

Christ's lordship is also seen in verses 7–9 of John 18:

> So he asked them again, "Whom do you seek?" And they said, "Jesus of Nazareth." Jesus answered, "I told you that I am he. So, if you seek me, let these men go." This was to fulfill the word that he had spoken: "Of those whom you gave me I have lost not one."

There can be little doubt that the soldiers had intended to arrest the Savior's entire band. As a matter of fact, one had to escape naked (Mark 15:41, 42). But Christ protected all his followers, as promised in Old Testament times. Luther believed that protection was the greatest miracle of all that happened in Gethsemane. Jesus' method was obvious. He asked the cohort twice whom they were looking for, and twice they verbalized, "Jesus of Nazareth." That narrowed their focus. Christ also punctuated his questions by sending the soldiers sprawling to the ground. The end result was to make his suggestion to let his disciples go seem quite reasonable.

Add to this Christ's dealing with Peter's attack, and we see no effete, impotent prophet caught in the gears of history.

> Then Simon Peter, having a sword, drew it and struck the high priest's servant and cut off his right ear. (The servant's name was Malchus.) So Jesus said to Peter, "Put your sword into its sheath." (vv. 10, 11a)

Apparently Judas' betrayal of the Messiah with a kiss was just too much for Peter (cf. Luke 22:48–50). Out came his hidden short sword, and he lunged at Malchus, his sword coming down hard on Malchus' helmet and bouncing down the side, lopping off his right ear. Our primal instincts rejoice that at least one blow was struck for Jesus. The truth is, though, Peter's rash action could have destroyed the church. Calvin comments: "No thanks to him that Christ was not kept from death and that his name was not a perpetual disgrace."[4] Imagine the pounding tension as Malchus stood wide-eyed, blood pouring through his fingers, a hundred steel blades ringing from their scabbards in gruesome symphony. Then came Jesus' words (Luke 22:51), "No more of this!" Then he touched Malchus' ear and healed him. Not only is our Lord powerful and gracious, but he is merciful, even in his final moments.

Finally, note the Lord's majestic summary statement: "Shall I not drink the cup that the Father has given me?" (18:11). The "cup" was the cross, the cup of judgment that we should have drunk. Jesus took upon himself our punishment in those hours of darkness on the cross. We could not have paid for our own sins even if we were punished for them for all eternity.

> Death and the curse were in that cup,
> Oh Christ, 'twas full for Thee;
> But Thou hast drained the last dark dregs,
> 'Tis empty now for me.

Earlier Jesus had wrestled with the terror of the cup, saying, "Not my will, but yours, be done." Now he sovereignly says, "Shall I not drink it?"

Schweitzer's words, though beautifully composed, are pitifully hollow when set beside John's account. "The wheel rolls onward, and the mangled body . . . is hanging upon it still. That is his victory and his reign." John thinks not, and neither do we. The surroundings of Christ's final hour clearly displayed his sovereign control. The intensity of his agony and his sovereign resolve to bear it, his control over his captors, his protection of his own, his grace to the wounded, all proved he is an omniscient, all-powerful God. Christ was in control when life was falling in, when things looked the worst.

How does this relate to us? Though Christ's Gethsemane was infinitely beyond human experience, Gethsemanes are a part of believers' lives.

> Down shadowy lanes, across strange streams
> Bridged over by our broken dreams;
> Behind the misty caps of years,
> Beyond the great salt fount of tears,
> The garden lies. Strive as you may,
> You cannot miss it in your way.
> All paths that have been, or shall be,
> Pass somewhere through Gethsemane.[5]

All of us will have times of ultimate stress in which the cup will appear to be too much for us. We will all experience times when, to the unbelieving eye, we are caught on the merciless wheel of life and are powerless.

Furthermore, just as Christ controlled his own destiny even when the opposite seemed to be the case, so he controls ours. Even when all the "facts" point to a little, limited God, or to no God at all, he controls our destiny.

That is what the patriarch Joseph discovered. After his childhood, he appeared to be caught on the uncaring wheel of history. First, he was sold into slavery, then promoted, then demoted because of his righteousness, then promoted in jail, then disappointed by his friends. Forgotten, alone, he was finally raised to save his people. In retrospect, even the unbelieving eye can see that God was at work, but during the process who saw it except Joseph? And how much did he see? So it was with Moses. It was the same with Paul. So it is for us. God is in control, even in the darkest hour. Men may intend evil, but God intends good (Genesis 50:20).

> All those who journey, soon or late,
> Must pass within the garden's gate;
> Must kneel alone in darkness there,
> And battle with some fierce despair.
> God pity those who cannot say,
> "Not mine but thine," who only pray,
> "Let this cup pass," and cannot see
> The *purpose* in Gethsemane.[6]

Conclusion

Gethsemane was not a tragedy, and neither are our Gethsemanes. This does not do away with the wounds of affliction in this life, but it is encouraging to see that behind human tragedy stands the benevolent and wise purpose of the Lord of human history. Life may be dark at times, tragedy may come, and at times the whole world may seem to be falling apart. The wheel may appear ready to crush us. But this is not the end. "And we know that for those who love God all things work together for good, for those who are called according to his purpose" (Romans 8:28), even in Gethsemane.

53

Pilate before Jesus, Part I

JOHN 18:24–40

IN 1981 I TRAVELED TO ASIA to see the refugee work of the World Relief Commission, especially in Hong Kong, Thailand, and the Philippines. As our plane arrived in Manila from Bangkok, we were informed that we would have to remain on the plane for an hour because our arrival conflicted with the arrival of the Prime Minister of Sri Lanka. As our plane taxied to a stop, I witnessed a memorable sight, especially striking since I had just come from refugee camps in Thailand.

Assembled on the runway, in formation, were several hundred official welcomers, along with Philippine President and Mrs. Marcos. A platoon of navy-clad honor guards wore shining gold pith helmets. Next to them was another platoon, dressed in forest green and mustard, with white gloves and hats. Then came a crimson and gold uniformed band, and finally a group resplendent in white naval uniforms. Add to the scene swaying native dancers in chartreuse and purple, a baby elephant clad in scarlet, a long red carpet, a descending jet with the epigram "Hurray for Hollywood" on its side, a twenty-one-gun salute, and several gleaming black stretch limos and you have the picture. It was an impressive but fleeting scene. A few words, some ringing volleys, and everybody was gone except for those rolling up the red carpet and sweeping the asphalt.

What a parable of earthly power—a big show, a lot of noise, the world in obeisance, then in an instant the spectacle was gone! Shelley expressed the same thought in a poem ("Ozymandias") about a traveler crossing an ancient desert. He comes across "two vast trunkless legs of stone" rising from the desert sand. Nearby, a menacing stone face partially protrudes from the ground. On the pedestal is the inscription:

My name is Ozymandias, king of kings:
Look on my works, ye Mighty, and despair!
Then Shelley comments:
Round the decay
Of that colossal wreck, boundless and bare
The lone and level sands stretch far away.[1]

Whether Babylon, Greece, Rome, the Ottoman Empire, the British Empire, or our own United States, world empires and nations are all ephemeral. They all prove that life is often not what it seems to be. That is one of the abiding truths found in 18:24–40.

Regardless of how things looked in the garden of Gethsemane as Judas betrayed Jesus and an armed crowd came to arrest him, Jesus was in control, and the same is true as the narrative goes on to describe Jesus' trial before Pilate. We see this in Jesus' marvelous self-control before an exasperated Sanhedrin (see Luke 22:63–71). In 18:28–32, as dawn broke and Christ was led before Pilate, we again see his control.

> Then they led Jesus from the house of Caiaphas to the governor's headquarters. It was early morning. They themselves did not enter the governor's headquarters, so that they would not be defiled, but could eat the Passover. (v. 28)

Most likely the Praetorium (or governor's official residence) was in the palace Herod had built, a very impressive structure.

> So Pilate went outside to them and said, "What accusation do you bring against this man?" They answered him, "If this man were not doing evil, we would not have delivered him over to you." (vv. 29, 30)

Pilate asked for the accusation, but Jesus' accusers could not produce one, so they answered with a sarcastic generality.

> Pilate said to them, "Take him yourselves and judge him by your own law." The Jews said to him, "It is not lawful for us to put anyone to death." This was to fulfill the word that Jesus had spoken to show by what kind of death he was going to die. (vv. 31, 32)

John tells us that Jesus even controlled the kind of death that awaited him. Actually, the religious leaders could have gotten away with a vigilante stoning of Jesus, just as they would do with Stephen a few months later. True, there would have been some momentary trouble, but they could have pulled it off.

But Caiaphas, the high priest, wanted Jesus crucified. He wanted him to be displayed to the people as cursed. Deuteronomy 21:23 says, "A hanged man is cursed by God." Caiaphas thought if Jesus was crucified, the Jews would look at him and say, "He cannot be the Blessed One, he's a cursed imposter."[2] Caiaphas failed to remember or did not know that Jesus had prophesied his mode of death when he said, "As Moses lifted up the serpent in the wilderness, so must the Son of Man be lifted up" (3:14). It never entered Caiaphas' diseased mind that he was fulfilling prophecy. Jesus was in control! Jesus was not on trial—Pilate and the Sanhedrin were! Christ was holding court, rendering his judgment, and making provision for all who would come to him.

Pilate was an ambitious opportunist who as procurator of Judea had gotten himself in over his head. He was brutal, politically inept, and anti-Semitic. Originally he was a native of Seville, Spain, and only got his job when, after joining the Roman legions, he met and married Claudia Procula, a granddaughter of the Emperor Augustus. His administration of Judea was noted for political mistakes that revealed severe character flaws. On his initial visit to Jerusalem, he enraged the Jews by having his soldiers carry banners emblazoned with the image of Tiberias into Jerusalem. He dealt with the resulting protests savagely and rashly. On another occasion he foolishly had his soldiers raid the sacred "Corban" treasury of the temple for funds to build an aqueduct. When the citizens objected, he sent plainclothes soldiers into the crowd, who then drew hidden daggers and clubs and attacked the demonstrators. Later he again incensed the populace by having votive shields bearing Tiberias' image placed in Herod's palace. Luke mentions that he even mingled the blood of certain Galileans with their sacrifices (13:1), evidently attacking them as they worshiped. This remarkable series of incidents had not left Pilate in the good graces of Rome. Some evidence suggests that he committed suicide a few years later in Gaul.

For a man of Pilate's background, judging Jesus' case should have been a very simple matter. "If the Jews want this Galilean dead, why not?" But it was not a simple matter.

> Besides, while he was sitting on the judgment seat, his wife sent word to him, "Have nothing to do with that righteous man, for I have suffered much because of him today in a dream." (Matthew 27:19)

Frank Morrison in his book *Who Moved the Stone?* theorizes:

> Pilate and Claudia were probably spending the night together on the evening Jesus was arrested and that Claudia would, therefore, have known

of the visit of Caiaphas (or whoever made up the Jewish delegation) and would have known of his purpose. The result was, of course, as she went to bed her thoughts were quite naturally on Jesus—and so her dream. When she woke in the morning and found that Pilate had already left the palace, she at once guessed his business—so she quickly wrote the warning which Matthew records.[3]

At just what point Pilate received that message we do not know, but we do see its effect—a man torn between the call of two worlds, the material and the spiritual.

Jesus' "Confession" before Pilate (vv. 33–37)

Jesus easily turned the tables on Pilate. We read the exchange beginning in verse 33: "So Pilate entered his headquarters again and called Jesus and said to him, 'Are you the King of the Jews?'" In all four Gospels the "you" is emphatic. Although this is a legal question, it is first an incredulous exclamation. "Are *you* the King of the Jews? You?" It was no wonder Pilate reacted that way: Jesus was in peasant dress, stained with bloody sweat from Gethsemane, his features already swollen. But despite appearances Jesus was still King! No one turns the tables on him unless he allows it, and here he turned them on Pilate (v. 34). "Jesus answered, 'Do you say this of your own accord, or did others say it to you about me?'" In other words, "What about you? Who are you to question who I am?" That question cut right through Pilate's proud exterior. Jesus was after Pilate's heart. Pilate was on trial.

Life is not always as it seems. In God's economy there is often a mighty reversal of appearances—the meek rule, the least are the greatest, the poor are rich, the weak are strong, the unlearned are wise. Here the beaten, defenseless Christ was holding court on Pilate, the Roman Empire, the Sanhedrin, and *us*.

Pilate blustered contemptuously in verse 35, "Am I a Jew? Your own nation and the chief priests have delivered you over to me. What have you done?" But his smoke screen was ineffective, and Jesus went right to the heart of the matter.

> My kingdom is not of this world. If my kingdom were of this world, my servants would have been fighting, that I might not be delivered over to the Jews. But my kingdom is not from the world. (v. 36)

Jesus proclaimed himself to be a spiritual king. A spiritual king does not rule by material force, a fact that Christ had demonstrated in Gethsemane when he reproved Peter's sword and healed Malchus' ear.

Jesus' answer threw Pilate into an agonizing quandary. If Jesus had proclaimed himself an earthly king, Pilate's decision would have been easy—execution. But a spiritual king? Politically, Jesus was guilty of nothing. And spiritually—what if Claudia was right?

What a contrast—Jesus the spiritual king and Pilate the material king. Two completely different approaches to life were thus revealed:

- One would do anything to receive power, honor, and glory. The other gave up his glory.
- One valued only what he could touch, taste, and feel. The other lived and taught that we are not to lay up for ourselves riches upon this earth.
- One ruled by material manipulation. The other lamented, "You are seeking me, not because you saw signs, but because you ate your fill of the loaves" (6:26).
- One was arrayed in royal robes. The other had "no form or majesty that we should look at him, and no beauty that we should desire him" (Isaiah 53:2).

On that crucifixion day, life was not as it appeared. Christ was in control, not Pilate.

In verse 37 we read Christ's kingly confession:

> Then Pilate said to him, "So you are a king?" Jesus answered, "You say that I am a king. For this purpose I was born and for this purpose I have come into the world—to bear witness to the truth. Everyone who is of the truth listens to my voice.

Christ was born to establish a new kind of kingdom. He cried, "For this purpose I have come into the world." This is "the truth" of which he bore witness. Everyone who is "of the truth" (those who realize there is a spiritual kingdom and seek it) hears his voice. Christ calls a materialistic world to seek first the kingdom of God.

The world needs a spiritual Savior but, preferring to satiate its desires, looks to an economic Savior. After Christ fed the five thousand, the people asked him to give them more bread like Moses had given to their ancestors. Jesus told them they needed not physical bread, because they would just get hungry again, but living bread leading to eternal life. When the people responded, "Sir, give us this bread always," Jesus answered, "I am the bread of life; whoever comes to me shall not hunger." After that many people left him and looked for a Savior who would give them the things they wanted. Preferring to remain slaves to their lusts, they forsook life itself. For some, God is a candy machine. They put in a quarter, and if he does not produce, they kick him!

Christ's confession revealed a supreme truth. Immediately Pilate made an unwitting confession, revealing a supreme truth about himself.

Pilate's Confession before Jesus (vv. 38, 39)

"Pilate said to him, 'What is truth?'" (v. 38). It is important to grasp the tone of these famous words. I think Francis Bacon misunderstood when he wrote, "'What is truth?' said jesting Pilate; and would not stay for an answer." Pilate was not joking. He was sarcastic perhaps, but unsmiling, and whatever his exterior countenance, he was confused and despairing. He was a materialist, hungrily pursuing the fantasies of power, celebrity status, and sensual satisfaction. But in that moment he was arrested by his wife's spiritual premonition and the mystical authority of Christ. But we know he did not truly want an answer because he did not wait for one.

Pilate exemplifies modern man. On the simplest level, his is the cry of the modern world. Television in Hong Kong, Bangkok, or Chicago is all the same—materialism and sensuality. I recall a Philippine commercial given in sonorous tones urging Filipinos to watch *Dallas*, saying it was relevant to the common challenges in Philippine life. With his "What is truth?" Pilate stood transparent before Christ, as does the whole world.

After seeing Jesus' innocence, Pilate did his best to escape responsibility (cf. Luke 23:4, 6, 7). Next he sent Jesus to Herod when he realized Jesus was a Galilean. But when Jesus declined to perform any tricks, Herod, in keeping with his cruel nature, initiated his infamous burlesque, dressing Christ in a gorgeous robe, beating him, and sending him back to Pilate.

The Verdict (vv. 38b–40)

Discouraged at Herod's return of Jesus, Pilate was at a loss to know what to do. Then he remembered a Jewish tradition that could perhaps deliver him from his dilemma. Each Passover the people were permitted to ask for the liberation of one prisoner, a symbolic act to remember God's mercifully delivering the Israelites from bondage in Egypt. So Pilate gave them a choice—Jesus or Barabbas. Barabbas was a robber (John 18:40), an insurrectionist, and a murderer (Mark 15:7; Luke 23:19). Matthew tells us he was "a notorious prisoner" (Matthew 27:16). Pilate thought if he gave the Jews their choice, they would pick Jesus, the one in whom Pilate could find no fault, as opposed to the vile prisoner Barabbas. He probably stood before the multitude with a sense of self-congratulation.

But of course the crowd chose Barabbas. Even in this matter, things were not as they seemed. There is divine poetry here. Origen tells us that Barabbas' name was "Jesus Barabbas," meaning "Jesus, son of *a* father." The crowd chose "Jesus, son of *a* father" instead of Jesus, Son of *the* Father. Origen concludes this has always been sinners' choice. This symbolizes man's willingness to resort to murder and theft while rejecting the true spiritual King. This is the way of the world and the way of our hearts before coming to Christ.

Pilate was of course surprised at the crowd's choice. But how did Barabbas feel? Matthew 27 helps us here. The Praetorium was no more than 1,500 feet from the Tower of Antonia. Barabbas, because he was a prominent prisoner, was incarcerated in the bowels of Antonia, awaiting crucifixion. He probably could not hear Pilate, but it would be impossible not to hear the roarings of the crowd. Here is Pilate's dialogue with the crowd.

> Pilate: "Which of the two do you want me to release for you?" (Matthew 27:21).
> Crowd: "Barabbas" (Matthew 27:21).
> Pilate: "Then what shall I do with Jesus who is called Christ?" (Matthew 27:22).
> Crowd: "Let him be crucified!" (Matthew 27:22).
> Pilate: "Why, what evil has he done?" (Matthew 27:23).
> Crowd (shouting all the more): "Let him be crucified!" (Matthew 27:23).
> Pilate, washing his hands: "I am innocent of this man's blood; see to it yourselves." (Matthew 27:24).
> Crowd: "His blood be on us and on our children!" (Matthew 27:25).

But what did Barabbas hear from all this? "Barabbas. . . . Let him be crucified! . . . Let him be crucified! . . . His blood be on us and on our children."

As hardened as he was, Barabbas must have grown faint. He may have stared at the palms of his hands in growing horror of the awaiting agony. He had seen crucifixions. He knew their interminable agony. He heard the sound of the key in the lock, felt even greater terror, and . . . suddenly he was released from his chains and told he was free! He was probably in a daze when he emerged into the sunlight. Slowly the truth unfolded: Jesus Christ was dying in his place.

Dr. Barnhouse says:

> Barabbas was the only man in the world who could say that Jesus Christ took his physical place. But I can say that Jesus Christ took my spiritual place. For it was I who deserved to die. It was I who deserved that the wrath of God should be poured upon me. I deserved the eternal punishment of the

lake of fire. He was delivered up for my offenses. He was handed over to judgment because of my sins. This is why we speak of the substitutionary atonement. Christ was my substitute. He was satisfying the debt of divine justice and holiness. That is why I say that Christianity can be expressed in the three phrases: I deserved Hell; Jesus took my Hell; there is nothing left for me but his Heaven.[4]

Second Corinthians 5:21 says, "[God] made him to be sin who knew no sin, so that in him we might become the righteousness of God." First Peter 2:24 adds, "He himself bore our sins in his body on the tree, that we might die to sin and live to righteousness. By his wounds you have been healed."

Conclusion

What is the truth? Christ is Judge of all. His judgment will fall upon those who have invested their lives in the world with its materialism, its sensuality, its pragmatism. But Christ comes to those who look for a city whose foundation and maker is God.

What is the truth? Christ died in place of all those who will respond to him. A man shared his faith openly with a Jewish merchant friend. The man had not received Christ, but a time came when he was dying. The Christian man went to see him, but the doctor said, "I'm sorry. You can't see him now. He is in too bad a condition." But when things got even worse, the doctor said, "You can go in now. It can't do any harm. But don't say anything." So the man went in and knelt by the bed of his friend. He took his frail hand, and he began to pray silently. The man, just before he expired, opened his eyes and said, "Not Barabbas, but this man."

Jesus Christ has reversed the sentence of all believers. Has he reversed yours? Will you say, "Not this man, but Barabbas" or "I want Christ"?

54

Pilate before Jesus, Part II

JOHN 19:1–16

IF YOU HAVE EVER READ an introduction to a Greek play, you have seen the Latin phrase *dramatis personae*, which means "people of the drama." Under it were listed the choruses, characters, or groups of characters. The *dramatis personae* in John 19:1–16 would make a Greek playwright pale with envy. There are the religious leaders, so blinded by their hatred for Jesus that they do not see the deathly inconsistency of their own lives. They are so scrupulous about the smallest religious details that they will not defile themselves by entering Pilate's residence, and yet they are so unified and intent on trapping Pilate into performing a judicial murder that when questioned they answer with the unison of a Greek chorus, "Let him be crucified! . . . His blood be on us and on our children!" (Matthew 27:23–25). These religious men are so perverted that they prefer the release of a notorious murderer to the sinless Christ and lower themselves to crass political blackmail in order to gain their end.

Also on the list is Pontius Pilate, a representative of Imperial Rome, the greatest power on earth. He was a man to whom success meant everything. He was a native of Seville and came to his position through a fortuitous chain of events. First, he joined the legions of Germanicus, participating in the wars on the Rhine. Then he journeyed to Rome where he met and married Claudia Procula, the youngest daughter of Julia, who was the daughter of Emperor Augustus. James Boice comments concerning Pilate's marriage:

> From the perspective of Pilate's future this was a wise move. Claudia had connections with the highest levels of Roman government. But morally it was a disgrace; for Julia, who thereby became Pilate's mother-in-law, was a woman of such depraved and coarse habits that even in decadent Rome

she was notorious. Augustus, her father, avoided her presence and eventually banished her. It is reported that afterward, whenever someone would mention the name of his daughter to him, Augustus would exclaim, "Would I were wifeless or had childless died!" Unlike Pilate, a man of nobler instincts would not have married into such a family.[1]

The last of the *dramatis personae* is Jesus, our matchless Christ. Description can never do him justice. He is the source and substance of the Eternal Song.

Again, life is often not as it appears on the surface. Christ was not caught up on the tide of history and swept unwilling to his end, but Pilate was. While the tides of life swirled about Christ, he kept his course. On the other hand, Pilate, the man of the earth, the man who had set his mind on things below, was tossed about helplessly, like a twig, on the current of history. He lived according to the course of this world and was thus subject to it. He was proof that the one who fixes his mind on "earthly things" (Philippians 3:19) is not free.

The setting of this final courtroom drama, found in 19:1–16, fluctuates between the bowels of the Praetorium and its portico.

Inside: The Roman Soldiers Scourge and Mock Jesus (vv. 1–13)

Pilate was disappointed. His attempts to escape responsibility for Jesus had failed, for Herod returned Christ, refusing to take him as his jurisdictional responsibility, and the crowd had called for the release of Barabbas over Jesus. So now Pilate attempted another tactic. Luke 23:16 says Pilate informed the multitude that he would "punish and release him." Evidently he thought that if he mutilated Jesus, the mob would pity him and set him free.

> Then Pilate took Jesus and flogged him. And the soldiers twisted together a crown of thorns and put it on his head and arrayed him in a purple robe. They came up to him, saying, "Hail, King of the Jews!" and struck him with their hands. (vv. 1–3)

Scourging was terrible. Many died from it, and others went mad. Ancient authorities as diverse as Eusebius, Josephus, and Cicero relate that scourging normally meant a flaying to the bone. Eusebius tells of martyrs who "were torn by scourges down to deep-seated veins and arteries, so that the hidden contents of the recesses of their bodies, their entrails and organs were exposed to sight."[2] No wonder Jesus did not linger on the cross!

Beyond the scourging, the soldiers carried the "fun" even further. They hated the Jews and saw in Christ a chance to show their contempt for them.

"He is the Jewish King? He wants a crown?" So they plaited "a crown of thorns" and set it on Christ's bleeding head.

Here the symbolism is plain. In 3:14 Jesus said, "As Moses lifted up the serpent in the wilderness, so must the Son of Man be lifted up." He knew he had to bear man's sin, which began through the Serpent in the garden of Eden. Now Jesus received a crown of thorns and briars, which Genesis specifically associates with the curse of the Fall (Genesis 3:18). Even the Roman soldiers conform to an awful symbolism. It was a terrible coronation, yet Christ remained in control.

The gruesome carnival continued as the soldiers "arrayed him in a purple robe," probably using a ragged soldier's robe that had faded from crimson to purple. Matthew and Mark tell us the soldiers also made Christ hold a reed scepter, then repeatedly took it from his hand and beat him about the face. Because the prophetic Scriptures describe this in the extreme, we infer that the soldiers must have gotten carried away.

Outside: Pilate Presents Jesus to the People (vv. 4–8)

The scene switches from the inner recesses of the Praetorium to the morning light of the courtyard pavement. Finally Pilate was about to make a bid for Jesus' freedom. The tone of verse 4 suggests that he was hopeful of his tactic:

Pilate went out again and said to them, "See, I am bringing him out to you that you may know that I find no guilt in him."

Then he presented Jesus. "So Jesus came out, wearing the crown of thorns and the purple robe" (v. 5a). What the crowd saw must have made some of them faint. David, writing prophetically of the cross one thousand years prior, moaned, "I can count all my bones—they stare and gloat over me" (Psalm 22:17). The scourge had done its work. The flesh had been cut away from Christ's ribs as well as from his back. Some ribs were exposed. Add to this the prophetic words of Isaiah 52:14: "His appearance was so marred, beyond human semblance, and his form beyond that of the children of mankind." The soldiers had hit him in the face with the mock scepter until his features were unrecognizable.[3]

Pilate had reason to hope he would succeed. Surely the crowd would be filled with revulsion at the sight, hopefully followed by sympathy. So Pilate shouted, "Behold the man!" Literally, from the precedence of Greek classical examples, this can be translated "the poor man" or "the poor creature."[4] Pilate was saying, "Look at this poor, bruised, bleeding creature. Haven't you hounded him enough?" In saying, "Behold the man!" Pilate said more than he would ever know. It was and is a call to reflect on the incarnation, for it was *the* Man standing before them. God had become a man, and this is what he looked like. And we are enjoined to behold that Man. John says in 1:18:

> No one has ever seen God; the only God, who is at the Father's side, he has made him known.

"Behold the man!"

If we want to see how much God loves us, "Behold the man!" Observe Christ headed for the cross, and hear him as he bears our sins: "My God, my God, why have you forsaken me?" (Matthew 27:46). This is how we are loved. Only the resolution and control of divinity could have accomplished this.

Pilate's ploy was to no avail.

> When the chief priests and the officers saw him, they cried out, "Crucify him, crucify him!" Pilate said to them, "Take him yourselves and crucify him, for I find no guilt in him." (v. 6)

Three times Pilate had judged Christ not guilty. By eventually allowing him to be crucified, he heaped eternal damnation on himself as well as on the multitude.

The exchange continues in verses 7, 8:

> The Jews answered him, "We have a law, and according to that law he ought to die because he has made himself the Son of God." When Pilate heard this statement, he was even more afraid.

By now Pilate was terrified! First, he had encountered Christ's regal demeanor and the reality of his innocence. Then he witnessed the scourging and glimpsed his own guilt, and now he was face-to-face with the nature of Jesus' offense. Now it was Pilate who was dizzy and confused. So he pulled Jesus back into the recesses of the Praetorium.

Inside: Pilate Talks with Jesus about Authority (vv. 9–12)

In this intimate conversation it became apparent that only one free man was in that room—the suffering Jesus. He even controlled the conversation, notably by his use of silence. "[Pilate] entered his headquarters again and said to Jesus, 'Where are you from?' But Jesus gave him no answer" (v. 9). We should note that this silence is even more prominent in the Gospels of Mark

(15:5) and Luke (23:9). It provoked Pilate's telling question that allowed Jesus' supreme reply:

> So Pilate said to him, "You will not speak to me? Do you not know that I have authority to release you and authority to crucify you?" Jesus answered him, "You would have no authority over me at all unless it had been given you from above. Therefore he who delivered me over to you has the greater sin. (vv. 10, 11)

Christ was the free man! Power resided with him, not with Pilate. He alone could do as he pleased. Pilate wanted to release Jesus in the worst way, but he could not. If ever a man was caught and crushed like a helpless doll on the wheel of life, it was Pilate!

Outside: Pilate Yields to the Jews' Demand for Crucifixion (vv. 13–16)

Caiaphas and his friends knew that Pilate was known as the "Friend of Caesar." They also knew, as Pilate did, that Caesar was a paranoid recluse, living on the Isle of Capri, who responded savagely to any hint of unfaithfulness. If such a charge were brought against Pilate, he would stand a good chance of losing his title, even his life.[5]

> From then on Pilate sought to release him, but the Jews cried out, "If you release this man, you are not Caesar's friend. Everyone who makes himself a king opposes Caesar." So when Pilate heard these words, he brought Jesus out and sat down on the judgment seat at a place called The Stone Pavement, and in Aramaic Gabbatha. (vv. 12, 13)

Pilate gave up. He could do nothing else. All his life Pilate had sought success. He was from Seville, located on the still wild Iberian Peninsula. To use a modern-day put-down, he was provincial. Probably as a boy, he had always wanted to be *somebody*. As a young man, he was romanced with stories of Rome and her might. So he became a legionnaire. Still, he was just a soldier. Perhaps he was loyal and brave, but in his own mind he did not amount to much. He longed for success. Finally Pilate came to the fabled city with its seven hills. It was breathtaking—the Forum, the palaces, the splendored arches. He ached to ascend to its power, to be a *success*. So he married Claudia, the depraved granddaughter of the Emperor Augustus. He would do *anything* to succeed. Finally the small-town boy became Procurator of Judea. He had made it! He had reached the heights!

In Arthur Miller's classic play *Death of a Salesman*, success in business is of the highest importance to Willy Loman, the main character. Success is so important that it taints all his relationships, and his obsession with it ends in his suicide. In commenting on Willy Loman, Miller says:

> Willy Loman has broken a law without whose protection life is insupportable if not incomprehensible to him and to many others; it is the law which says that a failure in society and in business has no right to live. Unlike the law against incest, the law of success is not administered by statute or church, but it is very nearly as powerful in its grip upon men. The confusion increases because, while it is a law, it is by no means a wholly agreeable one even as it is slavishly obeyed, for to fail is no longer to belong to society, in his estimate.[6]

Loman's view of success killed him. He was not in control. His son's comments interspersed at his father's graveside say it all.

> There were a lot of nice days. When he'd come home from a trip; or on Sundays, making the stoop; finishing the cellar; putting on the new porch; when he built the extra bathroom; and put up the garage. You know something, Charles, there's more of him in that front stoop than in all the sales he ever made.

In other words, Dad was really himself in those wonderful moments when he forgot his success fixation.

> He never knew who he was.
> Charles, the man didn't know who he was.[7]

Pilate never knew who he was either. His pursuit of success, his death grip on its fantasy, left him with no choice. Even though Christ was innocent, even though Christ had hinted at his divinity, despite the warning from Claudia— "Have nothing to do with that righteous man" (Matthew 27:19), even though he was frantic to see Christ released, he felt he could do nothing but condemn him. He, the man who had set his mind on material wealth, pleasure, celebrity status, and power, was tossed helplessly about on the current of history. It is no different for us. If our mind is set on "earthly things" (Philippians 3:19), we are in bondage, "slaves of sin" (Romans 6:17). We are no freer than Pilate.

The drama concluded out on the pavement. In the sunlight Pilate yielded to the crowd's demands.

> So when Pilate heard these words, he brought Jesus out and sat down on the judgment seat at a place called The Stone Pavement, and in Aramaic Gabbatha. Now it was the day of Preparation of the Passover. It was about the sixth hour. He said to the Jews, "Behold your King!" (vv. 13, 14)

What irony! Christ was still in control. This final rejection took place "about the sixth hour" on Passover Eve, the *very* hour that the priests begin to slaughter the Passover lambs in the temple.[8] The Lamb of God timed his sacrifice to coincide with the paschal lambs. Pilate's words continued to be bent to Christ's control. This time instead of saying, "Behold the man!" Pilate cried, "Behold your King!" Christ was never more regal, more kingly than at that moment. "Behold the man!" Behold divine love! "Behold your King." Yield to his lordship!

Conclusion

> O God, I love Thee, I love Thee—
> Not out of hope of heaven for me
> Nor fearing not to love and be
> In the everlasting burning.
> Thou, Thou, my Jesus, after me
> Didst reach Thine arms out dying,
> For my sake sufferedst nails and lance,
> Marked and marred countenance,
> Sorrows passing number
> Sweat and care and cumber,
> Yea and death, and this for me,
> And Thou couldst see me sinning;
> Then I, why should not I love Thee;
> Jesus so much in love with me?
> Not for heaven's sake; not to be
> Out of hell by loving Thee;
> Not for any gains I see;
> But just the way that Thou didst me
> I do and I will love Thee;
> What must I love Thee, Lord, for then?—
> For being my King and God. Amen.
>
> Gerard Manley Hopkins[9]

Where have we set our minds? That is a valid question for believers. The point of all of this is that as we conform to the ideal spiritual man, we look to Jesus and become like him and become increasingly free. We should not be in bondage but going on to freedom as we are conformed to Christ.

> If then you have been raised with Christ, seek the things that are above, where Christ is, seated at the right hand of God. (Colossians 3:1)

We are called to love Jesus more and more. To be conformed to him is to be free. May God seal this reality in our hearts.

55

Christ's Crucifixion, Part I

JOHN 19:17-22

GRAHAM GREENE, in his novel *The Heart of the Matter*, describes his principal character, Police Lieutenant Scobie, listening in on a dispassionate conversation about the suicide of an acquaintance. The men are discussing whether their deceased friend chose the best way to kill himself. As Lieutenant Scobie examines the man's few belongings and listens, he says to himself quietly, "Through two thousand years . . . we have discussed Christ's agony in just this disinterested way."[1]

Scobie is right. It is too easy to become desensitized to the reality. We hear repeated readings of the crucifixion account. We daily view scenes of real violence as we pass the potatoes and gravy. As Christians we must steel ourselves against desensitization. Christ's passion was real. True, we should not be overcome by a morbid preoccupation with the gore of the cross. Still, Christ's agony must never become a matter of dispassionate interest. His physical sufferings have always been, and will remain, a window through which we see his greater agony as he bore the world's sin.

We will not linger unnecessarily upon the horror of Christ's physical suffering, nor will we underestimate it. We must keep in mind that Christ suffered greatly prior to the crucifixion. In Gethsemane, as he contemplated what he was to undergo, he repeatedly cast himself to the ground in agonizing prayer and suffered the rare but medically documented phenomenon of hematidrosis, or blood sweat. Under great emotional strain, the tiny capillaries in his sweat glands burst, mixing his blood with his sweat.[2]

Christ was first struck in Caiaphas' presence, then was subjected to a series of blows as the palace guards blindfolded him and taunted him to identify them as they passed by, spitting upon him and striking him in the face. Next he was scourged under Pilate. Scourging, nicknamed "the halfway death," involved the soldiers' stripping Jesus naked, tying him down, and using the deadly flagellum to tear skin from bone. In their presentation of the "Comic King," the Roman soldiers again stripped Jesus, robed him in a Roman short cloak as a calculated affront to Jewish modesty, crowned him with thorns, and beat him with a mock scepter until he was unrecognizable. It was then that Pilate presented him to the people, saying, "Behold the man!"—an unwitting call to consider the incarnation.

Finally came the crucifixion. As we consider its opening events, we are going to not only glimpse what Christ underwent for us and the benefits his sacrifice brings but also the demands of the cross.

Christ's Crucifixion: Its Demands (vv. 17, 18)

The crucifixion is described in verses 17, 18:

> [Jesus] went out, bearing his own cross, to the place called The Place of a Skull, which in Aramaic is called Golgotha. There they crucified him, and with him two others, one on either side, and Jesus between them.

The Gospels tell us very little about the crucifixion because everyone involved knew the details too well. Little is said about Jesus' pitiful route to the cross because such processions were as common as funeral marches. Evidently Jesus was placed in the center of a *quarternion*, a company of four Roman soldiers. The crossbeam, or *patibulum*, of the cross was placed on his torn shoulders like an oar (normally it would weigh over 100 pounds). (Chrysostom remarked this was like Isaac's carrying the wood for his sacrifice on Mt. Moriah.[3]) As Christ stumbled along the route to Golgotha, an officer preceded him, carrying a placard describing Jesus' crime. It read: "Jesus of Nazareth, the King of the Jews" (v. 19). Customarily the man to be crucified was led to the site of his execution by the longest route possible, so everyone could see that crime does not pay and also to see if anyone might speak in his defense. As Christ tread the Via Dolorosa, he was so weakened that a bystander had to be drafted to carry his cross the rest of the way.[4]

At the place of execution Christ was laid upon the *patibulum*. Quickly spikes were driven through his hands or wrists, and then the crossbar was hoisted into place. His legs dangled until they were nailed, leaving only enough flex in the knees so he could begin the horrible up and down motion necessary to keep breathing. (The medical assessments of the rhythmic misery are extremely gruesome, so we will not include them here.)

Even with these few details, we can begin to visualize the horror Christ endured for us. Still, that agony was just a shadow of the misery he experienced when our sins were poured upon him, and as a result, the infinitely greater horror of separation from the Father. This was so horrible that he who never complained or reviled throughout the whole ordeal cried out, "My God, my God, why have you forsaken me?" Physical agony was nothing compared with the spiritual horror. In undergoing this, Christ expressed how much he loved us. Lewis said in his great treatise on love:

> The buzzing cloud of flies about the cross, the flayed back pressed against the uneven stake, the nails driven through the medial nerves, the repeated torture of back and arms as it is time after time, for breath's sake, hitched up. If I may dare the biological image, God is a "host" who deliberately creates his own parasites; causes us to be that we may exploit and "take advantage of" him. Herein is love. This is the diagram of Love himself, the inventor of all loves.[5]

We must passionately weave this truth into the fibers of our consciousness. If you do not know Christ, think of this and consider closely what followed.

John is careful to tell us that two others were crucified with the Savior. "There they crucified him, and with him two others, one on either side, and Jesus between them" (v. 18). If the cross is a diagram of his love, the positioning of the crosses is a diagram of how his love is dispensed to the world. The Lord's enemies intended the positioning of the crosses to be his final disgrace—Christ between two convicted robbers as if he were the worst. Instead of being a disgrace, however, that arrangement was a fulfillment of Isaiah 53:12—"Numbered with the transgressors; yet he bore the sin of many, and makes intercession for the transgressors."

One Saturday morning Dr. Donald Grey Barnhouse was working in his study when the custodian came in and announced there was a man outside to see him, giving him the man's card. Dr. Barnhouse read the card, which indicated the visitor was the captain of the *Mauritania*, the largest passenger vessel afloat. So Dr. Barnhouse went out to meet the man. The captain said, "You have a very beautiful church here." Dr. Barnhouse replied, "We are very grateful for all that was done by our faithful predecessors one hundred years ago." The captain went on, "It is very much like the Basilica at Ravenna in Italy." Dr. Barnhouse responded, "Actually, it's an architectural duplication. In fact, years ago they brought workmen from Italy to do the tessellated ceilings and the marble columns and the mosaic. But you didn't come to talk about architecture, did you?" The man said, "No. Twenty-three times a year I sail the Atlantic. When I come down the bank of Newfoundland, I hear your broadcast out of Boston. And as I came in this week I thought to myself, 'I've got twenty-four hours in New York, I'm going to go see Dr. Barnhouse.' And here I am."

Dr. Barnhouse was evidently very straightforward because then he said, "Sir, have you been born again?" The captain replied, "That's what I came to see you about." By this time they had reached a chalkboard in the prayer room, and Dr. Barnhouse drew three crosses on the chalkboard. Underneath the first one he wrote the word "in." Underneath the third he wrote the word "in." Underneath the middle cross he wrote the words, "not in." He said, "Do you understand what I mean when I say that those men who died with Jesus had sin within them?" The captain thought and said, "Yes, I do. And I know Christ did not have sin within him." Then over the first cross and over the third cross Dr. Barnhouse wrote the word "on." He said, "Do you understand what that means?" The captain wrinkled his brow. Dr. Barnhouse said, "Let me illustrate. Have you ever run through a red light?" "Yes." "Were you caught?" The man said, "No." "Well, in running that red light you had a sin *in* you. If you would have been caught, you would have had sin *on* you. The thieves were bearing the penalty of God." Then he wrote another "on" over Jesus Christ and said, "He bore your sins. There was no sin *in* him, but the sin was laid *on* him." Then he took the side of his chalk and over the first thief he crossed out the *on,* drew an arrow over to Christ, and said, "His sins rested on Christ by virtue of his faith in Christ." Then he said, "How about you?"

The captain was a very tall, distinguished man of British carriage, and as he stood there for a moment, Dr. Barnhouse could see he was fighting back tears. He said to Dr. Barnhouse, "By the grace of God, I am the first man." Dr. Barnhouse said, "You mean your sins are on Jesus?" He said, "Yes—God says my sins are on Jesus!" He shot out his hand and said, "That's what I came to find out!" Dr. Barnhouse invited him to lunch and shared further with him, and the man went back to New York City a glowing Christian.

We see the diagram of love and its cost—the Son of God hanging by his arms, his muscles unable to respond. He fights to raise himself just to get one short breath. Finally carbon dioxide builds up in the lungs and the blood-stream, and the cramps partially subside. Spasmodically he pushes himself upward to exhale and gain a little more oxygen. This is the diagram of love. Yet, the true depth and cost of his love resides in his willingness to bear our sins and to suffer separation from his beloved Father. Oh, how Christ loves us!

If we believe in Christ like the repentant thief did, Christ will take our sins upon himself. We gain life simply by faith. That is his offer. That is his demand.

Christ's Coronation: Its Demands (vv. 19–22)

> Pilate also wrote an inscription and put it on the cross. It read, "Jesus of Nazareth, the King of the Jews." Many of the Jews read this inscription, for the place where Jesus was crucified was near the city, and it was written in Aramaic, in Latin, and in Greek. So the chief priests of the Jews said to Pilate, "Do not write, 'The King of the Jews,' but rather, 'This man said, I am King of the Jews.'" Pilate answered, "What I have written I have written."

Jesus' enemies did not like Pilate's inscription. At the foot of Jesus' cross, while they were gloating in his death, the sign stared back at them: "Jesus of Nazareth, the King of the Jews." John's use of the imperfect verb tense suggests that the Jews *repeatedly* asked Pilate to change the sign to read, "This man said, I am King of the Jews." But Pilate would not change it and answered in the Greek perfect tense: "What I have written I have written." Or more literally, "What I have written, I have written, and it will always remain written." In disgust he emphasized the permanence of his statement. Christ was still in control. During his infancy, wise men from the East heralded him as King (Matthew 2:2). At the beginning of the Passion week, the multitudes had cried, "Blessed is he who comes in the name of the Lord, even the King of Israel!" (12:13). Before Pilate, Christ himself bore witness to his "kingdom" (18:36–37). And now his royal title was affixed to his very gibbet.[6] Ultimately he will come back as "King of kings and Lord of lords" (Revelation 19:16).

His rule bears not only eternity but universality. If the Jews had received him, they would have become a light to the nations. Christ's universal regency is implicit in the Aramaic, Latin, and Greek renderings of the inscription on his cross. Christ ruled and rules from the cross. *Every* New Testament reference to Christ's dominion is accompanied by a reference to his cross.[7]

By virtue of his rule from the cross, Christ rightfully made and still makes imperious demands on his followers. Foremost, he demands that we yield to his lordship, which none of us do naturally, as one of Churchill's famous one-liners so well illustrates. It was directed to Sir Stafford Cripps, his austere Socialist opponent. One day as Cripps was passing by, Churchill said, "There, but for the grace of God, goes God." How true—for all of us. If it were not for the constant work of God's grace in our lives, we would assume the lordship of our lives. "There but for the grace of God goes a little god." Christ by virtue of his sacrifice on the cross demands absolute submission. He demands to live our lives for us!

> I have been crucified with Christ. It is no longer I who live, but Christ who lives in me. And the life I now live in the flesh I live by faith in the Son of God, who loved me and gave himself for me. (Galatians 2:20)

Not only that, but he demands that we take up our cross and follow him. Again, the details of the cross were well known to the people of that day. *Take up the cross* was a colloquialism for dying to yourself, which everyone understood.

> Whoever does not bear his own cross and come after me cannot be my disciple. (Luke 14:27)

> If anyone would come after me, let him deny himself and take up his cross and follow me. (Matthew 16:24)

> And whoever does not take his cross and follow me is not worthy of me. (Matthew 10:38)

We must have a spirit of submission and commitment to the rule of Christ in our lives. As Bonhoeffer says, true grace is not cheap.

> Cheap grace is the preaching of forgiveness without requiring repentance, baptism without church discipline, Communion without confession, absolution without personal confession. Cheap grace is grace without discipleship, grace without the cross, grace without Jesus Christ. . . . [Grace] is costly because it costs a man his life, and it is grace because it gives a man the only true life. Above all, it is costly because it cost God the life of his Son: "Ye were bought at a price," and what has cost God much cannot be cheap for us. Above all, it is grace because God did not reckon his Son too dear a price to pay for our life, but delivered him up for us.[8]

We must not forget that the cross was real. The whip and the nails were real, as was each anguished breath. And above all, his love was (and is) real. May God deliver us from ever seeing these things too casually or with cold hearts.

Conclusion

The *benefits* of the cross are infinite. The believing heart, like that of the believing thief, has its sins lifted by the cross and is destined to grow from glory to glory.

The *demands* of the cross are expansive. "Love so amazing, so divine demands my soul, my life, my all."

56

Christ's Crucifixion, Part II

JOHN 19:23–30

Love's as hard as nails,
Love is nails;
Blunt, thick, hammered through
The medial nerves of One
Who, having made us, knew
The thing he had done,
Seeing (with all that is)
Our cross, and His.[1]

Lewis also said that the cross "is the diagram of Love himself, the initiator of all loves."[2] Love is the Son of God hanging by his arms, his muscles paralyzed and unable to respond. Love is God's Son fighting to raise himself in order to get just one short breath. Love is carbon dioxide mounting in the lungs, cramps partially subsiding, allowing our Lord to push himself spasmodically upward for life-giving oxygen. This is a picture of God's love. Still, it is only suggestive of his deeper love, his willingness to bear our sin and suffer separation from his beloved Father.

In 19:23–30 we see our Lord repeatedly agonizing upward for breath, while below him the Roman soldiers divide his clothing.

> When the soldiers had crucified Jesus, they took his garments and divided them into four parts, one part for each soldier; also his tunic. But the tunic was seamless, woven in one piece from top to bottom, so they said to one another, "Let us not tear it, but cast lots for it to see whose it shall be." This was to fulfill the Scripture which says,
>
> "They divided my garments among them,
> and for my clothing they cast lots." (vv. 23, 24)

Since every Jew wore five pieces of clothing—sandals, a turban, a belt, an inner tunic, and an outer robe—it is easy to surmise what happened. First, each soldier chose one of the less expensive articles. Realizing it would be foolish to divide the robe, they then gambled for its sole possession. Unwittingly they were fulfilling the prophecy of Psalm 22:18: "They divide my garments among them, and for my clothing they cast lots." They were cold-blooded men. It is bad enough to take a dead man's belongings, but they were gambling over them while he, in his dying moments, gazed on. The four Roman soldiers were an unwitting picture of a world without God, a capsulization of the world's neglect of Christ's atoning death. This is sometimes calculated, sometimes unthinking, like when a professional baseball player said to his coach, after the coach had lost his temper, "Coach, you need to walk with Jesus." The coach replied, "I'd rather walk with the bases loaded."

Those Roman soldiers also gave a potent reminder that the world is a cold place. Robert J. Ringer described life as a giant poker game with everyone after your chips. There are just three kinds of people in life, he said: 1) those who are after your chips but won't let you know it, 2) those who are after what you have and let you know it, and 3) (the most dangerous) those who are after your chips but do not even know it themselves. It is a cold world!

Jack London said the same thing through his antihero Wolf Larson, who says, "Life. Bah! It has no value. Of cheap things it is the cheapest. Everywhere it goes begging. Nature spills it out with a lavish hand . . . and it's life eat life till the strongest and most piggish is left."[3]

Perhaps this truth has never been made more dramatically than in William Golding's *Lord of the Flies*. In that novel, well-educated British children marooned on an island resort to a nightmare of murder until they are rescued by "civilization" in the form of a British warship that will continue on to hunt its enemy in the same implacable way. We live in a cold world. Just ask the Roman soldiers.

Our text contains a contrast between this group and another group, itself a microcosm of those under Christ's care. Four others, besides the Roman soldiers, stand at the foot of the cross. Verse 25 identifies them as "his mother and his mother's sister, Mary the wife of Clopas, and Mary Magdalene." Four soldiers. Four women. The contrast is unavoidable. I believe this was the purposeful work of our sovereign God so that Jesus' loving heart would be clearly seen in his care and provision for his own.

Jesus' Final Instructions to His Own (vv. 25–27)

Can anyone imagine the pain of those four women? Those of us who have lost loved ones in the spring of life can understand much more than the rest of us. Mary stood there before her son. When Jesus was an infant, she and his father took him to the temple to present him to the Lord. To their delight and surprise, the aged Simeon, a righteous and devout man, was overcome by the Holy Spirit, took the baby Jesus in his arms, and sang of the blessing he would bring. Then he blessed Jesus and said to Mary:

> Behold, this child is appointed for the fall and rising of many in Israel, and for a sign that is opposed (and a sword will pierce through your own soul also), so that thoughts from many hearts may be revealed. (Luke 2:34, 35)

There, on the cross, was the baby Mary had nursed, the boy she had held, the man who had brought her nothing but joy. But now a sword was piercing her heart.

Parallel passages (Mark 15:40; Matthew 27:56) tell us that the second woman, "his mother's sister," was Salome, Zebedee's wife, the mother of James and John. She had been severely rebuffed by Christ for her ambition for her sons, but she had seen love in that rebuke. Now, as Mary's sister, she was experiencing not only personal agony but sister-to-sister filial agony.

We know nothing of "Mary the wife of Clopas," the third woman (though some feel this couple is the same traveling on the road to Emmaus after Christ's resurrection in Luke 24). But we do know much about Mary Magdalene. Seven devils had been cast out of her (Mark 16:9; Luke 8:2). Jesus described her as one who had sinned much and loved much. Mary was the one who had come to Jesus in a Pharisee's house while the Savior reclined at dinner. She watered his feet with her tears, wiped them with her hair, and anointed them with perfume. What misery she experienced at the foot of the cross.

> Love's as warm as tears,
> Love is tears;
> Pressure within the brain,
> Tension at the throat. . . . [4]

Those women were really hurting!

When Jesus saw his mother and the disciple whom he loved standing nearby, he said to his mother, "Woman, behold, your son!" Then he said to the disciple, "Behold, your mother!" And from that hour the disciple took her to his own home. (vv. 26, 27)

The Greek indicates that Jesus was very much in control, almost matter-of-fact as he spoke these tender instructions. His words reveal the depth of his love and care for his own. Jesus was in limitless pain. Hour after hour he desperately strained for another breath, strained tendons like violin strings, experienced joint-rending cramps and intermittent asphyxiation, "searing pain as tissue was torn from his lacerated back as he moved up and down against rough timber; then another agony began. A deep crushing pain . . . in the chest as the pericardium slowly filled with serum and began to compress the heart."[5] Jesus was lingering at the fringes of death. He knew that in the next hour darkness would cover Calvary, and he in cosmic battle would bear the world's sin alone in the darkness—and even with all of that crushing him, he thought of his own. Even as he died, they were all in his heart! And he who thought so perfectly of his own in the time of his extreme suffering bears the same heart, the same depth of love, in his present exaltation. He still cares intimately and completely for his own! We have a Savior who loves us so deeply that when we are hurting, he will come to us without fail.

Jesus' instructions from the cross also reveal just how perfect his love and care are. The phrase in verse 26 describing John as "standing nearby" means John was standing *beside* Mary. Evidently he was the only disciple at the cross, and he stood alongside Mary, supporting her. As R. C. H. Lenski said, "These two belonged together because these two were losing in Jesus' death more than the rest. Mary was losing her son, John the master who loved him beyond the rest."[6]

As John and Mary gazed up in misery at the mutilated form of their greatest love, Christ summoned all his strength and gasped, "John, this is your mother, and, Mary, this is your son," just before his knees buckled, taking him back into the shadowland of semisuffocation. In obedience John took Mary as his surrogate mother.

One extra-Biblical account says John owned a home in Jerusalem at the foot of Zion, Mary stayed there eleven years, and only after her death did John go out to preach the gospel to the Gentile world. Another report says that Mary died in the city of Ephesus while sharing in John's missionary ministry. We really do not know what happened to Mary, but we can be sure that John, being the apostle of love, perfectly fulfilled his new trust. What an encouragement they must have been to one another. Both loved Jesus with all their hearts. Both had poetic spirits. Both were tender. John was young, and she was not. They were now mother and son. Think of the benefits she brought to John's life and later ministry—the hours of conversation, the opportunity for questions. Mary was and is the most blessed of women. Elizabeth's song still applies: "Blessed are you among women, and blessed is the fruit of your womb!" (Luke 1:42). Mary brought sunlight to John's life. The Lord was perfectly caring for each of them.

For John, his blessing came in the form of additional responsibility. After all, John still had his own mother to care for. Delightful as she most certainly was, Mary was undoubtedly at times a burden. She was blessed, but she was a sinner. The Scriptures infer that she could be a little officious and overattentive. There were probably times when John wished she would take her blessing somewhere else! Nevertheless, she was wonderful for John, and he for her. They were God's care to one another.

Christ's care for us may come in the form of responsibility. We would like to think that the more we love God, the less he will ask of us, and the lighter our burdens will become. But that is not necessarily so. If we love Jesus, he will make use of our love. Jesus' care for John came in the form of a burden, but that burden was a blessing. Not all the pressures we bear come because we love. Many are simply due to our own sin and stupidity. Unique responsibilities, however, are placed on those who possess great love for the Lord. Some of our burdens are, in fact, blessings.

The foundation of Jesus' love and care is seen in the words Jesus used (vv. 26, 27). As Jesus made Mary John's responsibility, he called Mary John's "mother." Yet in speaking directly to Mary, Jesus addressed her as "Woman." Some have supposed that Jesus was trying to protect Mary from the possible trouble that might befall her if she was recognized as his mother. Others say Christ did not call her "mother" because he didn't want to make her emotional pain worse. But actually the reason runs far deeper. As Jesus approached the work of redemption, a new relationship was beginning to develop with Mary. At the commencement of his public ministry in Cana of Galilee, he had said to her, "Woman, what does this have to do with me?" (2:4). And now, as the Greek suggests, "on the cross, when emotion was likely to be in evidence, it was in a matter-of-fact manner that Jesus commended his mother to the care of St. John."[7] Their special earthly relationship as mother and son yielded to a higher, holier relationship as he became her Savior. This is the foundation of his love and care for her and for us. Mary, and those with her at the foot of the cross, found their comfort in his atoning work for them. In the ensuing days they would experience the continual refreshment of his having borne their sins, a growing sense of grace and freedom, and an increasing awareness of Heaven. This is the ground of our comfort as well. In this fallen world Christ still offers loving care and provision for his own. His love for us is so deep that he experienced untold agony for us and meets our deepest needs.

We understand from the other Gospels that after Jesus gave his mother to John, darkness fell upon the land from the sixth hour until the ninth hour (Matthew 27:45). Was this darkness meant to hide Christ's hideous *physical* sufferings? No. It hid the agony of the Son as he became a curse for us. In Jewish thinking, to be cursed was to be separated from God, and to have his blessing was to have his face looking upon you with approval. "The LORD bless you and keep you; the LORD make his face to shine upon you" (Numbers 6:24, 25). Jesus had never known anything but the face of the Father. They had worked together in the creation of the universe. They were one another's delight. But now as Jesus bore our sins, he became a curse.

> For all who rely on works of the law are under a curse; for it is written, "Cursed be everyone who does not abide by all things written in the Book of the Law, and do them." (Galatians 3:10)

> Christ redeemed us from the curse of the law by becoming a curse for us—for it is written, "Cursed is everyone who is hanged on a tree." (Galatians 3:13)

At this moment of separation the pain from the nails was nothing to Jesus. Neither was the flayed back and the uneven stake. He may not have even been aware of the physical pain, for there is no experience so painful in the world or universe as separation from God. Jesus cried in the darkness, "My God, my God, why have you forsaken me?" (Matthew 27:46; cf. Psalm 22:1). No human has ever known such terror. A billion crucifixions cannot equal the pain of the curse Christ experienced for you and me.

Jesus' Final Teaching (vv. 28–30)

During the darkness three sayings passed Christ's lips: "I thirst," "It is finished," "Father, into your hands I commit my spirit!" John recounts the first two (vv. 28, 30). The third is given in Luke 23:46.

> After this, Jesus, knowing that all was now finished, said (to fulfill the Scripture), "I thirst." A jar full of sour wine stood there, so they put a sponge full of the sour wine on a hyssop branch and held it to his mouth. (vv. 28, 29)

Paul tells us, "Christ died for our sins in accordance with the Scriptures" (1 Corinthians 15:3). At this moment he fulfilled Psalm 69:21: "And for my thirst they gave me sour wine to drink." Even the unusual use of a branch of hyssop to extend the sponge to Christ's lips suggests Scriptural parallels, because hyssop was the plant prescribed in Exodus 12:22 to be used in the application of the blood of the Passover lamb to the doorpost so the death angel would pass by.

The body of Jesus was by this time *in extremis*. He could feel the chill of death creeping through his limbs. Did he with great effort pull himself up and whisper an additional plea for relief? No. He *shouted*, "It is finished" and "bowed his head and gave up his spirit" (v. 30).

"It is finished" was not a submissive cry but a shout of victory. In the Greek it was only one word, in the Greek perfect tense, meaning, "It is finished and always will be finished!" What had Christ finished? The Law itself (he had completed and fulfilled it). The Old Testament types in the ceremonial law. The Messianic prophecies. But most of all, *he had finished the atonement.*

> Lifted up was He to die,
> "It is finished!" was his cry;
> Now in heav'n exalted high:
> Hallelujah, what a Savior!
>
> Philip P. Bliss

His cry of victory came not because he was dying a horrible death, but because "[God] made him to be sin who knew no sin, so that in him we might become the righteousness of God" (2 Corinthians 5:21). He became a curse for us and was separated from God so we would never have to know the horror of eternal punishment for sin. Not even the most evil man, including Nero or Hitler, has ever known in this life the horror of being completely cut off from God. His presence was always there, if only through common grace. But Christ suffered total separation from the Father as he bore our penalty, then cried out with a joyous shout, "It is finished."

Because he paid for our sins, we must come to him empty-handed. To come to Christ with some of our own work or goodness in hand is to commit the infinite insult. We must come like the thief who hung beside him on the cross.

> Nothing in my hand I bring,
> Simply to the cross I cling.

If we have received Jesus Christ as our Savior, we will never be separated from God but rather will eternally enjoy fellowship with the Father and the Son and the Spirit! God's face will shine upon us forever.

57

The Fact of the Resurrection

JOHN 20:1–31

AMONG THE GREAT THRILLS awaiting the new believer in Christ is the discovery of Psalm 22. Although that psalm was written almost one thousand years before Christ, it graphically—almost technically—pictures the crucifixion of our Lord. The obvious correlations with the descriptions of the Gospel accounts are easily recognizable—Christ's disjointed body, his thirst, his failing heart, his pierced hands and feet, his humiliating exposure. The immortal words he spoke even begin the psalm: "My God, my God, why have you forsaken me?" (Psalm 22:1a). The parallels in Psalm 22 are unmistakable:

> They open wide their mouths at me,
>   like a ravening and roaring lion.
> I am poured out like water,
>   and all my bones are out of joint;
> my heart is like wax;
>   it is melted within my breast;
> my strength is dried up like a potsherd,
>   and my tongue sticks to my jaws;
>   you lay me in the dust of death.
>
> For dogs encompass me;
>   a company of evildoers encircles me;
> they have pierced my hands and feet—
> I can count all my bones
> they stare and gloat over me;
> they divide my garments among them,
>   and for my clothing they cast lots. (Psalm 22:13–18)

The accuracy is absolutely amazing, and even more so when you realize that the Romans did not invent death by crucifixion until 300 years after this psalm was written!

But invent it they did, as John 19 so tragically attests. After Christ knowingly called out, in fulfillment of Psalm 22, "My God, my God, why have you forsaken me?" (Matthew 27:46) and tasted the sour wine, he cried, "It is finished," then "bowed his head and gave up his spirit" (19:30). Christ was dead! The unthinkable had happened. God bore testimony to his death, as Matthew 27 tells us:

> And behold, the curtain of the temple was torn in two, from top to bottom. And the earth shook, and the rocks were split. The tombs also were opened. And many bodies of the saints who had fallen asleep were raised, and coming out of the tombs after his resurrection they went into the holy city and appeared to many. When the centurion and those who were with him, keeping watch over Jesus, saw the earthquake and what took place, they were filled with awe and said, "Truly this was the Son of God!" (Matthew 27:51–54)

As far as the disciples could see, it was all over! They had come against a blank wall. They had not yet associated these events with Psalm 22. They had not believed it would end like this, and they had not yet grasped the truth of Jesus' prophecies of resurrection. There was nothing left except a recurring sense of utter helplessness and the shame of their denials and desertions.

The disciples did not know they were soon going to experience a greater joy than they had ever known. John 20 is the story of that joy. In this passage Christ brings the truth of the resurrection with its accompanying joys to his followers, including us. Their experience is our experience.

The Discovery of the Empty Tomb (vv. 1–10)

John tells us that Joseph of Arimathea, a secret disciple of Jesus, gained permission to bury Jesus' body. With the aid of Nicodemus, he wrapped Jesus' body in linen wrappings and about one hundred pounds of spices and laid him in a new garden tomb (19:38–41). The Lord Jesus lay in that tomb until the resurrection, which took place sometime before dawn on Sunday morning. Shortly after he was resurrected, certain women came from the city to the tomb to anoint Christ's body with spices (cf. Matthew 28:1; Mark 16:1; Luke 24:1; John 20:1). At least four women were there, probably more. Matthew mentions Mary Magdalene and Mary, the mother of Jesus. Mark tells us Salome was present. Luke includes Joanna (Luke 24:10).

These devoted women evidently reached the tomb at daybreak, a time when it was difficult to clearly see. But what they could see shook them: the stone had been removed from the entrance! Had someone broken into the tomb? Had Joseph of Arimathea decided upon another tomb? Where were the soldiers?

Finally the women decided to inform the disciples, and Mary Magdalene left with the message. John 20 picks up the thread of the narrative:

> Now on the first day of the week Mary Magdalene came to the tomb early, while it was still dark, and saw that the stone had been taken away from the tomb. So she ran and went to Simon Peter and the other disciple, the one whom Jesus loved, and said to them, "They have taken the Lord out of the tomb, and we do not know where they have laid him." So Peter went out with the other disciple, and they were going toward the tomb. Both of them were running together, but the other disciple outran Peter and reached the tomb first. And stooping to look in, he saw the linen cloths lying there, but he did not go in. Then Simon Peter came, following him, and went into the tomb. He saw the linen cloths lying there, and the face cloth, which had been on Jesus' head, not lying with the linen cloths but folded up in a place by itself. Then the other disciple, who had reached the tomb first, also went in, and he saw and believed; for as yet they did not understand the Scripture, that he must rise from the dead. (vv. 1–9)

The apostle John "saw and believed" (v. 8). But what did he believe? That Jesus was gone? No. He believed in the resurrection! John was the first in all the world to believe that Christ was alive again.

Why did John believe? Something he saw in the tomb made him believe. Let me explain. First of all, the burial practices of the Jews were distinctive. The Egyptians embalmed their dead. In Roman and Greek cultures corpses were often cremated. In Palestine neither was done. Rather, the dead were wrapped in linen swaddling clothes containing dry spices and were placed on their backs, without coffins, in tombs. Moreover, they were not completely wrapped. As Henry Latham maintains in his book *The Risen Master*, the dead were wrapped, but the face, neck, and upper part of the shoulders were left bare. Typically, corpses were wrapped with their arms folded cross-like across their torso. The head was wrapped separately, with a cloth twirled about it like a turban. This is why, in Luke 7:15, when Jesus raised the son of the widow of Nain as he was being carried to the tomb, the young man sat up and was able to speak. The grave clothes did not cover his face. We see similar evidence in the case of Lazarus in John 11:44. This also explains John's reaction at our Lord's tomb.

John got to the tomb first (fullbacks like Peter are only good for fifty yards). But John did not go in. Verse 5 tells us he stopped and "saw the linen cloths lying there." The word for "saw" (*blepo*) suggests simple seeing. John saw the grave clothes in a cursory manner. When Peter came, he brushed John aside (v. 6), entered the tomb, and "saw the linen cloths lying there." The Greek word there is *theoreo*, from which we get the English word *theater*. Peter took a long, careful look.

> Then Simon Peter came, following him, and went into the tomb. He saw the linen cloths lying there, and the face cloth, which had been on Jesus' head, not lying with the linen cloths but folded up in a place by itself. (vv. 6, 7)

He saw the grave wrappings and turban lying just as they had been wrapped on Jesus. The appropriate space was in between, but there was no Jesus, no body! Then John entered the tomb and "saw" (the word is *orao*, meaning "to see with understanding") and "believed" (v. 8). The cautious C. K. Barrett says, "Here . . . it seems that the body in some way disappeared from or passed through the cloths and left them lying as they were."[1] John Stott says the body was "vaporized" as it became something wonderful and new.[2] John now understood what had happened. "Peter, don't you see it? No one has done anything with the body. It's gone right through the grave clothes! Jesus is risen! He's risen! He's alive! The only reason the stone is gone is so we can see that Jesus is gone. Praise God! Let's go! Last one home washes the feet!"

Yes, Jesus is alive! R. W. Dale's biographer tells us that the great British Congregational minister had long been a distinguished leader in Christendom and was well on in life when one day, while writing an Easter sermon:

> The thought of the risen Lord broke in upon him as it had never done before. "Christ is alive," I said to myself; "alive!" and then I paused—"alive!" and then I paused again; "alive!" Can that really be true? Living as really as I myself am? I got up and walked about repeating "Christ is living!" "Christ is living!" . . . It was to me a new discovery. I thought that all along I had believed it; but not until that moment did I feel sure about it. I then said, "My people shall know it; I shall preach about it again and again until they believe it as I do now." . . . Then began the custom of singing in Carr's Lane on every Sunday morning an Easter hymn.[3]

He is alive! The great goal our text sets before us is to believe as Peter and John believed. If we can obtain that height, our lives will be changed! A living Christ is an all-powerful Christ! A living Christ is a present Christ!

A living Christ is a Christ who gives us life now! A living Christ is a Christ who gives us life in eternity! A living Christ is a Christ who gives victory!

The Appearances of Jesus on Resurrection Day (vv. 11–23)

The apostles believed though they had not seen Jesus alive again. Mary Magdalene was to be the first to have that joy. Probably, when Peter and John sprinted to the tomb, poor Mary Magdalene (who had already run back to inform them) was left in the dust. When they left the tomb, believing, they either overlooked her or departed another way.

Whatever, Mary was shortly afterwards standing outside the tomb, alone, uninformed, and weeping. More accurately, she was sobbing and wailing, because the word used in verse 11 is the same used to describe the mourners at Lazarus' grave. This was the traditional Eastern death wail, and it came from the depths of her broken heart. Jesus had cast seven devils from Mary. She had sinned much, she had been forgiven much, and she loved much. Her heart was in indescribable anguish. On top of the horror of his death came this last indignity—they had taken his body and were undoubtedly going to make further sport of him.

Mary was totally unprepared for what would happen in the next few seconds:

> Mary stood weeping outside the tomb, and as she wept she stooped to look into the tomb. And she saw two angels in white, sitting where the body of Jesus had lain, one at the head and one at the feet. They said to her, "Woman, why are you weeping?" She said to them, "They have taken away my Lord, and I do not know where they have laid him." (vv. 11–13)

St. Chrysostom suggests that at this point one of the angels motioned for Mary to turn around.

> Having said this, she turned around and saw Jesus standing, but she did not know that it was Jesus. Jesus said to her, "Woman, why are you weeping? Whom are you seeking?" Supposing him to be the gardener, she said to him, "Sir, if you have carried him away, tell me where you have laid him, and I will take him away." Jesus said to her, "Mary." She turned and said to him in Aramaic, "Rabboni!" (which means Teacher). Jesus said to her, "Do not cling to me, for I have not yet ascended to the Father; but go to my brothers and say to them, 'I am ascending to my Father and your Father, to my God and your God.'" (vv. 14–17)

As Mary cried "Rabboni," she apparently threw her arms around Jesus. But Jesus cautioned her to not cling to him. He wanted her to realize that a new relationship was in the process of being established. The comfort that awaited Mary and her friends was far more substantial than his material presence could ever give.

It is very significant that here, as in the other three Gospels, Christ first appears to the woman Mary Magdalene—not to an apostle, not to the great in society or in the church, but to a particular woman. Christ appeared first to one who in the culture of the time was oppressed, a woman who had known great sin. What a great comfort it should be to us that Christ always comes first to the poor in spirit. "Blessed are the poor in spirit, for theirs is the kingdom of heaven" (Matthew 5:3). That truth will never change.

How must Mary have felt at that moment? She had been on an emotional roller coaster for days, and now she was deliriously at the top. Off she went on another cross-country run to the disciples. It must have been very satisfying to say to the disciples, "Say, Peter, John, men, I have something to tell you—I've seen Jesus!"

What a day it had been. Multiple trips to the tomb. Multiple retellings. The report of the encounter on the road to Emmaus. Dark threats and rumors too. By now it is Sunday evening. Despite all the excitement, the apostolic band was afraid, and so, in some private room, behind closed doors, they sat together to try to sort it all out.

Suddenly Jesus appeared to the disciples (v. 19). He was in their midst though no one had opened the door. Hearts raced. Adrenaline flowed. Goose bumps appeared on goose bumps. Jesus gave them the supreme greeting, "Shalom"—"Peace be with you." Jesus then displayed his hands and his side, and "the disciples were glad when they saw the Lord" (v. 20b). Luke says, "They still disbelieved for joy and were marveling" (Luke 24:41). Can anyone describe that night? I think not. We reach the heights of mystery when we read in 20:22, 23:

> And when he had said this, he breathed on them and said to them, "Receive the Holy Spirit. If you forgive the sins of any, they are forgiven them; if you withhold forgiveness from any, it is withheld."

What a day. Without a doubt, it was the most dramatic day in the history of the world. But one disciple had missed the whole thing.

The Problem of Disbelief (vv. 24, 25)

"Now Thomas, one of the Twelve, called the Twin, was not with them when Jesus came" (v. 24). We all deal with our emotions differently, and perhaps

Thomas's grief had driven him to go elsewhere to be by himself. He was not a coward. He was the man who had said, "Let us also go, that we may die with him" (11:16), and he meant it. He had probably simply broken down under the pressure of the last few days, and his way of dealing with problems was to be alone. He also was not one to act like he believed when he really did not. So when the other disciples approached him saying, "We have seen the Lord," Thomas answered:

> Unless I see in his hands the mark of the nails, and place my finger into the mark of the nails, and place my hand into his side, I will never believe. (v. 25)

Some say Thomas spoke for the whole world: "Give me proof and I'll believe!" I am not so sure. I think the world's view is more like, "Show me the facts, and I'll invent another theory." Years ago I read Hugh Schoenfeld's *The Passover Plot*, which popularized the ancient swoon theory. That view claims Jesus had not actually died but was unconscious when placed in the tomb. While he lay comatose, the spices and linen bandages provided a helpful dressing for his injuries. Finally the dampness of the tomb revived him and allowed the perpetration of the resurrection hoax.[4] Aside from ignoring the testimony of the text—that the soldiers, hard-boiled professionals, proclaimed him dead, that no human could survive the process of torture and execution as the Gospels describe—this theory foists on the gullible reader more problems than it solves. After all, Jesus was taken down from the cross and carried to Joseph of Arimathea's tomb without any sign of life. There he was washed and bound with one hundred pounds of spices and bandages, then placed in the tomb. After being in the tomb for many hours, according to the swoon theory, he was revived by its icy chill, at which time he extricated himself from the bandages, arranged them neatly for the viewer, pushed the stone away, eluded the guards who were bound by threat of death to keep the imperial seal from being broken, and then, after clothing himself, spent the day and evening playing ghost. It takes more "faith" to believe that than it takes to believe in the resurrection of Christ. Where the swoon theory really falls, though, is in the person of Christ. Had he done as claimed, he could not have been the great ethical teacher he was but rather a liar and a deceiver.

Others say the body was stolen by either Christ's enemies or his disciples. Either alternative is a psychological absurdity. His enemies would not have wanted to encourage belief in his resurrection, and his disciples could never have accomplished it. Besides, they not only believed and preached the resurrection, but they died for it. Who would die for a lie?

The difficulties of belief may be great for some, but the absurdities of unbelief are even greater. The liabilities, I might add, are also far greater, for those who reject a resurrected Christ will never rise to eternal life with him but will rather spend an eternity separated from God because of their delusion.

The Remedy for Disbelief (vv. 26–31)

Praise God, there was a remedy for Thomas, and there is a remedy for us. The Lord gave Thomas time to think about the situation, eight days to be exact, and Thomas did just that. He was fellowshiping with the apostolic band, and I suspect that he became convinced of the resurrection even before the events described in verses 26–28:

> Eight days later, his disciples were inside again, and Thomas was with them. Although the doors were locked, Jesus came and stood among them and said, "Peace be with you." Then he said to Thomas, "Put your finger here, and see my hands; and put out your hand, and place it in my side. Do not disbelieve, but believe." Thomas answered him, "My Lord and my God!"

Thomas may have been slow to believe, but he was not slow to grasp the implications of Christ's resurrection. Jesus was not only his Lord but his God. The evidence was palpable, substantive, and clear. Thomas's faith rested on solid rock.

What about us? The evidence is still just as substantive, just as palpable, just as clear. "Jesus said to him, 'Have you believed because you have seen me? Blessed are those who have not seen and yet have believed'" (v. 29). We can be part of that blessed company. It is not a ship of fools. We have the prophetic Scriptures to confirm our faith, not the least of which is Psalm 22. And we have the testimony of resurrected lives. Apart from the Word of God itself, the truth of this has never been communicated more forcefully than in "Seven Stanzas of Easter":

> Make no mistake: if he rose at all
> it was as his body;
> if the cells' dissolution did not reverse, the
> molecules reknit, the amino acids rekindle,
> the Church will fall.
>
> It was not as the flowers,
> each soft Spring recurrent;

it was not as his Spirit in the mouths and fuddled
eyes of the eleven apostles;
it was as his flesh: ours.

The same hinged thumbs and toes,
the same valved heart
that—pierced—died, withered, paused, and then
regathered out of enduring Might
new strength to enclose.

Let us not mock God with metaphor,
analogy, sidestepping, transcendence;
making of the event a parable, a sign painted
in the faded credulity of earlier ages:
let us walk through the door.

The stone is rolled back, not papier-mache,
not a stone in a story,
but the vast rock of materiality that in the slow
grinding of time will eclipse for each of us
the wide light of day.

And if we will have an angel at the tomb,
make it a real angel
weighty with Max Planck's quanta, vivid with hair,
opaque in the dawn light, robed in real linen
spun on a definite loom.

Let us not seek to make it less monstrous,
for our own convenience, our own sense of beauty,
lest, awakened in one unthinkable hour, we
are embarrassed by the miracle,
and crushed by remonstrance.

John Updike[5]

The Lord pronounced a final beatitude on those who do not see and yet believe. We have great joy now and will someday share in the likeness of his resurrection. In the words of Joni Eareckson Tada, "I know the meaning of that now. It's the time after my death when I'll be on my feet dancing."

58

A Fish Breakfast in Tiberias

JOHN 21:1–14

JOHN 21 is essentially an epilogue to the fourth Gospel, recording occurrences after the resurrection of Jesus Christ. The opening event of this chapter, which focuses on an all-night fishing expedition by the apostolic band, is a living parable of how the risen Lord relates to his servants as they toil in this world. Of course, at the time the disciples had no idea they were actors in a spiritual drama. But when it was over and as the days passed, giving opportunity for reflection, they understood the connection with this and an earlier event. When they were first called to be disciples, they had also been fishing, and Jesus pointed out the symbolism there by saying, "Follow me, and I will make you become fishers of men" (Mark 1:17). Now they were again fishing. The similarity of the two scenes is obvious. Both times there had been a frustrating night of fruitless toil. Both times Jesus commanded them to let down the net once more. Each time there was an instant, great success. These parallels drove the disciples to reflect in the days that followed on the peculiarities of this last miracle in John 21. They saw the care the risen Christ has for his followers as they serve him in the world below.

John gives us a picture of the risen Christ standing on the firm beach in the increasing light of dawn, interested in, caring about, directing, and crowning with his own blessing the obedient work of his servants as they toil on the restless seas of life.

The Church at Work (vv. 2, 3)

The opening words of chapter 21 suggest an idyllic scene:

> After this Jesus revealed himself again to the disciples by the Sea of Tiberias, and he revealed himself in this way. Simon Peter, Thomas (called the

Twin), Nathanael of Cana in Galilee, the sons of Zebedee, and two others of his disciples were together. (vv. 1, 2)

By this time the dizzying whirl of Passover week and the numbing horror of the crucifixion had been replaced by the bounding victory and cheer of the empty tomb. Jesus had even appeared to them through closed doors. Doubting Thomas had cried, "My Lord and my God!" (20:28). The disciples had been vindicated. They felt the surge of new hope. At this moment in time they had traveled the eighty miles from Jerusalem back up to Galilee. They needed that warm sunlit time. The conversation must have been lively. Old mysteries were rehashed, and some were cleared up. The Scriptures were avidly discussed. There was talk about the future. Most of all, there was talk, incessant talk, about Jesus. When would they see him again? What would he say? What would he do? The possibilities were delicious.

Jesus was in Heaven. The disciples knew that because of what he had told Mary when she saw him at the tomb ("Do not cling to me, for I have not yet ascended to the Father"). Later, though, Jesus urged Thomas to touch him (20:27) because he had ascended. Jesus was not hiding behind a rock by the River Jordan. His abode was Heaven. He was ascending and descending as it pleased him. The stage was set for the heavenly Lord to illustrate his earthly ministry to the church.

As usual, Peter's inability to sit still helped create that stage. The aroma of the sea and the addictive rhythm of lapping water were too much for Peter. Finally, he blurted out to his companions, "I am going fishing" (v. 3). The other disciples immediately voiced their approval.

Simon Peter said to them, "I am going fishing." They said to him, "We will go with you." They went out and got into the boat, but that night they caught nothing. (v. 3)

Evening was the best time, so at dusk, after gathering provisions, the whole group left shore with an honest joy in the accustomed feel of ropes and hoisting the patchwork sail and casting and recasting the net, especially in the beauty of the deepening reflection of a million stars over Galilee. It was wonderful—the earth, sky, water, wind, the hearty masculine camaraderie. There was only one problem—they did not catch anything! As the night wore on, the casts became fewer and fewer, and the night got colder and colder. Conversation dwindled—except for Peter's continued comments about pollution, overfishing, the lunar calendar, the inferior net, the landlubbers who were asleep, and the days when "men were men." Like many well-begun fishing trips, the disciples' trip was a real "bummer."

Unknown to the disciples, the seven of them were a microcosm of the church toiling amid a restless world. The fact that the church would have a great work among the Gentiles is seen in that the sea (which in Scripture represents the nations) is in Galilee, the area of the Gentiles. The tiny boat bearing the apostolic band portrays some abiding realities, realities that are important to our spiritual health.

A primary obligation of the church in the world is fishing or evangelism. This specific idea was far from the apostles' minds as they fished that day, but clearly that is what John wanted us to see. Remember the first fishing miracle three years earlier when Christ said, "Follow me, and I will make you become fishers of men" (Mark 1:17). Evangelism is to have a prominent place in the ministry of the church. It should never be eclipsed by social involvement. Today we are facing that danger. Recently a Filipino Christian leader who has pioneered the social witness of the evangelical churches voiced his fears for hard days ahead for evangelism. It used to be much easier, he said, to get money for evangelism than social action, but now it is the reverse. The ideal is "both/and," but history has shown how fragile the balance is. Let us never be lulled into giving evangelism second place! We are to be constantly fishing for men, no matter how dark or cold the night.

Along with the emphasis on evangelism, the picture in John 21 suggests hard work. Fishing, both for men and for food, is exhausting, time-consuming labor. In all of this we are to realize that without Christ we can do nothing. The disciples were pros at fishing. They paid careful attention to equipment, greater attention to strategy. Peter and John knew how the fish surfaced, how to dip the oars quietly, how to cast the net. We know so many things about evangelism and ministry, but the Lord says, "Apart from me you can do nothing" (15:5). It is so easy to think we can do spiritual work on our own. We think that if we are overloaded and busy, God will understand if we do not take time to ask his direction. But Jesus says whatever is done like that amounts to nothing. You can witness and accomplish nothing. You can donate hundreds of hours to the church and see nothing come of it. You can preach, but it amounts to nothing. The imperative of evangelism, hard work, and dependence on Christ are invaluable lessons.

The Church's Lesson (vv. 4–6)

The night was far spent, the blush of dawn was warming the east, and the disciples were tired and heading for home. They probably were not thinking of the Lord, but unknown to them, Jesus was watching them. In fact, he had seen everything.

> Just as day was breaking, Jesus stood on the shore; yet the disciples did not know that it was Jesus. Jesus said to them, "Children, do you have any fish?" They answered him, "No." (vv. 4, 5)

As Bishop Ryle and others suggest, Jesus may have been in a different form (as on the road to Emmaus), and so the disciples did not recognize him. Or perhaps the gloomy mists of dawn and the disciples' weariness shielded his identity. Whatever the case, to the disciples' abiding credit, they admitted they had caught no fish. Generally, if a fisherman is doing well, he will not tell you because he does not want you to horn in on his choice spot. And if he is doing poorly, he does not want to admit it.

The disciples acknowledged their failure. I like to imagine that if the disciples had lied, Jesus would have disappeared or walked on the water to see their catch. But they told the truth. Malcolm Muggeridge has said that failure is the most creative phenomenon of life, and that is true. If we did not fail, we would never make any progress. Failure demands that we assess our past methods to see what we have done right or wrong. Failure helps us discard the moribund and obsolete and opens us to new ideas.

Many years ago a young man ran for the legislature in a large state and was badly defeated. He next entered business, failed, and spent seventeen years of his life paying the debts of a worthless partner. He was in love with a beautiful woman to whom he became engaged, but she died. Reentering politics, he ran for Congress but was badly defeated. He then tried to get an appointment to the United States Land Office but failed. He became a candidate for the United States Senate and was badly defeated. Two years later he was again defeated. It was one failure after another and many setbacks. But he refused to give up and eventually became President of the United States, perhaps our greatest. His name was Abraham Lincoln. Failure is the *sine qua non* of spiritual progress.

Muggeridge beautifully says, "Christianity, from Golgotha onwards, has been the sanctification of failure."[1] Peter, the great rock, rose from the rock heap of failure. Our failures bring us face-to-face with the weaknesses and inadequacies that lie within, so that God's strength can be made perfect in our weakness.

> But we have this treasure in jars of clay, to show that the surpassing power belongs to God and not to us. (2 Corinthians 4:7)

It is in the breaking of these clay vessels, our failures, that the riches of God are exposed for all to see. It is primarily our failures that create in us a poverty of spirit and thus make us fit receptacles for the blessings of the kingdom of God. That is why "Christianity, from Golgotha onwards, has been the sanctification of failure."

We live out a tragedy of the greatest proportions when we will not even admit to ourselves that we have failed, whether it be in devotion to God, in relation to one another, or in our calling to serve. One of the great faults of the church and many Christian organizations is saying souls are being saved when they are not, asserting our effectiveness though we are effete, making claims for a ministry when we should be lamenting its failure, loudly proclaiming our effect on the world when the world does not even know we exist. The creative processes of the Holy Spirit, God's power in our lives, become fully operable when we admit exactly where we are, owning our successes and our failures.

One of the abiding glories of the gospel is that it brings us face-to-face with reality about ourselves and the world. We must face its truth. Christ knew the disciples had not caught any fish. He knew everything about them. It is to the disciples' eternal credit that when asked about their catch, they admitted they had caught nothing. That is what Christ sanctified. Failure can be the most creative thing in life, especially for the believer. But we must have the grace to admit failure and the humility to receive its creative benefits.

The Church's Faithfulness (vv. 6–8)

He said to them, "Cast the net on the right side of the boat, and you will find some." So they cast it, and now they were not able to haul it in, because of the quantity of fish. That disciple whom Jesus loved therefore said to Peter, "It is the Lord!" When Simon Peter heard that it was the Lord, he put on his outer garment, for he was stripped for work, and threw himself into the sea. The other disciples came in the boat, dragging the net full of fish, for they were not far from the land, but about a hundred yards off. (vv. 6–8)

John was ready, and when he saw the net tighten with the great catch, he cried, "It is the Lord!" Peter, as always, was all action. He wanted to give the Lord a respectful greeting, so he threw on his outer garment and performed a cannonball. (People like Peter never dive!) At the original fish miracle, Peter had been so awestruck that he said, "Depart from me, for I am a sinful man, O Lord" (Luke 5:8). But now he not only knew about sin but about God's grace. So there he stood, dripping beard and matted hair, smiling his big, toothy grin.

The fishermen, a picture of the church toiling on the restless seas of life, found it was Christ who brings the increase and that apart from him they could do nothing. They also found that his resources were sufficient, whatever the catch. Morris discusses with great insight the fact that the net did not break.[2] With Christ in the midst directing the work, unlike the first miracle, the resources are never overstrained. Nothing, in a person or a group of persons, is beyond his power and grace. Serving Christ in our own strength, trying to do it our own way, is like going after Moby Dick with a pickle fork. But led and sustained by Christ's strength, the net will never tear.

The Church's Reward (vv. 9–14)

> When they got out on land, they saw a charcoal fire in place, with fish laid out on it, and bread. Jesus said to them, "Bring some of the fish that you have just caught." So Simon Peter went aboard and hauled the net ashore, full of large fish, 153 of them. And although there were so many, the net was not torn. Jesus said to them, "Come and have breakfast." Now none of the disciples dared ask him, "Who are you?" They knew it was the Lord. Jesus came and took the bread and gave it to them, and so with the fish. This was now the third time that Jesus was revealed to the disciples after he was raised from the dead. (vv. 9–14)

The reason there is a mysterious air about this section is that it is figuratively a step into eternity. It happened two thousand years ago, but it pictures the Church receiving her eternal reward. As Alexander Maclaren said:

> All the details, such as the solid shore in contrast with the changeful sea, the increasing morning in contrast with the toilsome night, the feast prepared, have been from of old consecrated to shadow forth the differences between earth and heaven. It would be blindness not to see here a prophecy of the glad hour when Christ shall welcome to their home, amid the brightness of unsetting day, the souls that have served him amidst the fluctuations and storms of life, and seen him in its darkness, and shall satisfy all their desires with the "bread of heaven."[3]

Though we now serve him on the dark seas of life in this age, our risen Lord wants us to focus on the fact that he is on the eternal shore in the ever-increasing light, preparing a table for us.

He wants us to see also that our works for him are of eternal value. He encourages his disciples to bring some of their catch, and he accepts their service and adds the result of their toil to the provision he has already prepared. He did not need their contribution. He could have multiplied what he already had. But he was teaching them, and us, that the believer's works are valued by him and are of eternal consequence. Service rendered to Christ is eternal fruit! The tiniest work done under the inspiration and direction of Christ is more enduring than the Sears/Willis Tower.

The essence of the eternal state is suggested in verse 12: "They knew it was the Lord." The knowledge of the Lord is and will be our increasing reward. As Paul says, "For now we see in a mirror dimly, but then face to face. Now I know in part; then I shall know fully, even as I have been fully known" (1 Corinthians 13:12). Our reward is the knowledge of God in the face of Christ.

Conclusion

If we are believers, we are all in the same boat, riding the same waters. The present age is an age of darkness, and the waters are sometimes cold and harsh, even stormy. All those in the boat are to be involved in fishing and casting and recasting our nets. As Christ's followers, we are all called to face the same realities, to be honest about what is really happening in our lives. And as believers, the most creative, life-giving words we may ever utter are, "I have caught nothing." "Christianity, from Golgotha onwards, has been the sanctification of failure." Fundamental to living productively in this age is an honesty with ourselves and with God.

There also must be obedience, and with obedience comes a great catch, a catch that will follow us right into eternity where we will know the Lord more and more fully. John's words at the realization of the great catch, "It is the Lord!" express the ideal for all of us as we toil through life.

In the darkness, "It is the Lord!"

In our failures, "It is the Lord!"

When our nets are full, "It is the Lord!"

In all of life, "It is the Lord!" teaching us that we must rest and depend on him.

59

The Highest Priority

JOHN 21:12–17

IN THE 1930S MR. IVY LEE, a management consultant and an aggressive and self-confident man, by stealth wangled a private interview with Charles Schwab, then president of Bethlehem Steel, who was no less self-assured, being one of the most powerful men in the world.

During the conversation, Lee asserted that if the management of Bethlehem Steel would follow his advice, the company's operations would be improved and their profits increased. Schwab responded, "Mr. Lee, if you can show us a way to get more things done, I'll be glad to listen; and if it works, I'll pay you whatever you ask within reason."

Lee handed Schwab a blank piece of paper and said, "Write down the most important things you have to do tomorrow." Schwab did so. "Now," Lee continued, "number them in order of importance." Schwab did so. "Tomorrow morning start on #1 and stay with it until you complete it. Then go on to #2 and #3 and #4, and so on. Don't worry if you haven't completed everything by the end of the day. At least you will have completed the most important projects. Do this every day. After you have been convinced of the value of this system, have your men try it. Try it as long as you like, and then," concluded Lee, "send me your check for whatever you think the idea is worth."

This was a very simple idea, and I doubt that it was original to Lee. It might well have been practiced by the Babylonian satraps or officials in the Roman Empire or even some medieval monks. At any rate, a few weeks later Charles Schwab sent Ivy Lee a check for $25,000—an astronomical amount during the thirties. He said it was the most profitable lesson he had ever learned in his long business career. In the cold, hard business world there are few lessons more important than learning how to prioritize and live by those priorities. The degree of one's expertise in this matter is directly related to the success or failure of one's future.

On a much higher level, how well we Christians recognize and maintain spiritual priorities bears incalculable consequences for our entire lives. Sadly, some have never given a second thought to life's priorities. Others have, but have chosen the wrong priorities. Still others have the right priorities in perspective but do not have the self-control or wisdom or whatever to live by them. In 21:12–17 our Lord sets the matter straight for Peter and for all who make up his church.

As the curtain lifts, the backdrop is the morning-lit Sea of Tiberias in Galilee. In the foreground is a rocky beach with a glowing fire. The principal characters in this true-life drama are Jesus Christ, Peter, and six other disciples seated around the fire.

The key to understanding what is about to transpire is an appreciation of Peter's inner feelings, for while Peter made the greatest confession in church history ("You are the Christ, the Son of the living God," Matthew 16:16), he also denied Christ three times just after the Savior's arrest. How the mighty had fallen!

In the wake of his denial, Peter's Master was brought out from the inner chamber, and the meeting of their eyes—the fallen disciple and the eternally loving Lord—was one of the most painful in history. Oh, the agony of that moment when, with the echoes of the rooster still ringing, Jesus' unblinking, guiltless, omniscient eyes looked into the heart of Peter! Peter went out and wept bitterly, but his tears could not wash the image from his mind. He would never forget the awful thing he had done. Could he ever be what he had been again?

All of this was firmly lodged in Peter's psyche. Sure, he had seen the risen Christ and had heard the comforting benediction, "Peace be with you!" But Peter could not forget his lapse of love. Had he disqualified himself from fruitful service? Would his heart ever indeed know peace again? All of that is background to John 21:12–17.

Peter and John and some of the other disciples had traveled eighty miles north to Galilee to take some time to sort things out and recuperate from the whirlwind of recent events. The fishing was therapeutic with its wind, water, and sky. The miracle catch of fish thanks to their Savior's presence on shore was even more therapeutic. And now a dripping Peter stood before the Lord after his fully-clothed plunge and a frantic swim to the Master, an impulsive demonstration of the apostle's love. But Peter was not all better. He had still failed his Lord, even denying he knew him! He doubted his own fidelity, his own ability to walk with Christ or minister to others. He wondered if he could ever be used again. He needed a touch, as we all do sometimes. God has used this very text to touch many of his sons and daughters. I have personally found it to be one of the most helpful passages in all of Scripture because it takes me back to the ground of my faith, helps me assess where I really am, and instructs me on how to set my life straight once more.

The fish breakfast on Tiberias evokes a timeless, ethereal picture—the risen Lord with his back to the glistening blue morning sea, serving breakfast on the beach to the damp crew of disciples, while the smoke wafted between them. Verse 12 hints that there was little conversation. Something was different. The supernatural pervaded everything. It was an awkwardly silent breakfast as they sat huddled around the fire, gazing timidly at the Lord as the morning mists rose from Tiberias.

Peter's Restoration

Finally, breakfast was finished, and Jesus spoke. Peter's heart must have skipped a beat when he heard the Lord's words as recorded in verse 15: "Simon, son of John, do you love me more than these?" The Lord was asking, "Simon, do you truly love me? After all that has happened, and you know what I mean, can you truly say you love me? And do you love me more than these other disciples do?" John does not say what ran through Peter's mind at these cutting words, but from our own experience we can imagine. His heart probably began to race, his stomach churned, his cheeks burned, and his eyes misted. This was a tense moment.

There were several reasons. Jesus had addressed him as "Simon, son of John," which was his name before he met Christ. The way the Lord addressed him intentionally called into question his title of "Peter the rock." His personal message was, "Peter, do you remember your human weakness? Remember what you were like before I met you?" The question, though motivated by love, was calculated to hurt, and it did. Jesus also asked Peter if he loved him *more* than the other disciples did. Here Peter could not help but flash back two weeks to the upper room.

> Simon Peter said to him, "Lord, where are you going?" Jesus answered him, "Where I am going you cannot follow me now, but you will follow afterward." Peter said to him, "Lord, why can I not follow you now? I will lay down my life for you." (13:36, 37)

> Though they all fall away because of you, I will never fall away. (Matthew 26:33)

Furthermore, the fire on the beach undoubtedly reminded Peter of the one before which he denied his Lord. His thoughts were probably a torrent of emotion—the painful aroma of the fire, the same unblinking, innocent eyes, "more than these," "I will never fall away," "do you love me?" The power of the Lord's question was mercifully brutal.

How would Peter answer? "Yes, Lord; you know that I love you" (v. 15). The word that Peter used can be translated "affection" or "friendship." He could not bring himself to profess a full love, so he said, "Lord, I have an affection (a deep personal attachment) for you. I can't say 'love,' Lord, not after all my failures and disgrace." Peter's presumption was gone. The Lord then charged him, "Feed my lambs." In other words, "Then serve me."

Jesus was not through but asked a second question: "Simon, son of John, do you love me?" (v. 16). That is, "Simon, dropping all comparisons, the question is, do you really love me? That is the bottom line." We can be sure there was little movement as the smoke wafted about the apostolic band. Peter carefully and quietly answered, "Yes, Lord; you know that I love you" (v. 16), and again he professed an affection, not a full-blown love. Some would criticize Peter's answer, but 1 Corinthians 16:22 says, "If anyone has no love [a friendship love] for the Lord, let him be accursed." Friendship love is a wonderful love as far as it goes. Again Jesus' gentle response was, "Tend my sheep."

There is stark honesty in the Lord's questioning, but his words were gracious. Jesus was doing something wonderful for Peter. "Simon, son of John, do you love me [literally, do you have a friendship love for me)?" (v. 17). "Do you really have the affection for me that you have claimed?" The Lord took Peter at his word. In his first question the Lord challenged the superiority of Peter's love. In the second question he challenged whether Peter had any love at all. In this final question he challenged Peter's claim to have an affectionate love. Verse 17 says Peter was "grieved," but he steadfastly answered, "Lord, you know everything; you know that I love you [with a friendship love]." "God, you know where I am, but I don't dare claim any more than that." Peter loved Jesus with the deepest of loves, but his illusions, his presumptions about himself, were gone. And the Lord accepted that and said, "Feed my sheep." That response displayed Jesus' deep love for his fallen apostle.

Complete Restoration

The restoration was accomplished, and they had all seen it. And now they probably understood that the Lord had planned it all. Peter's denials happened before a fire, and now Peter's confessions were before a charcoal fire.

There were three denials, and now three confessions, as well as three gracious commissions.

Christ is saying to us through Peter's example that the greatest priority in life is the nature and primacy of our love for God. Here we see a man who had loved God with all his heart but needed to be affirmed in that love before he could again serve fruitfully. Some of us may love him dearly, others may not. But the abiding principle is that before all things, even service to him, we must love him with all our hearts. That is the highest priority in life. It is the first question for every theologian. It is the essential question for every pastor. It is the supreme question for every missionary. It is the number one question for every one of us who wants to please God. Loving God is the highest priority of our lives.

The Priority of Love

Christians are called to serve, but it is all too easy in the everyday following of Christ to put our priority on service rather than on loving God. Techniques and methods can easily become our primary focus. To carry out our methods we need power, and instead of longing for and loving the source of the power, we sometimes lust for power alone. Production or results or success then becomes the center of our thinking. Roy Hession in his beautiful little book *We Would See Jesus* says:

> To concentrate on service and activity for God may often actively thwart our attaining of the true goal, God himself. At first sight it seems heroic to fling our lives away in the service of God and of our fellows. We feel it is bound to mean more to him than our experience of him. Service seems so unselfish, whereas concentrating on our walk with God seems selfish and self-centered. But it is the very reverse. The things that God is most concerned about are our coldness of heart towards himself and our proud, unbroken natures. Christian service of itself can, and so often does, leave our self-centered nature untouched. . . . With those things hidden in our hearts, we have only to work alongside others, and we find resentment, hardness, criticism, jealousy, and frustration issuing from our hearts. We think we are working for God, but the test of how little of our service is for him is revealed by our resentment or self-pity. . . . We need to leave our lusting for ever-larger spheres of Christian service and concentrate on seeing God for ourselves and finding the deep answer for life in him.[1]

The inversion of life's priorities is a deadly trap, especially for those who take their Christianity seriously—both Christian workers and caring laymen—because they want their lives to count, to do something that will make a difference.

The fact is, God has always made the first priority clear. From earliest times he has been explicit, even in the *Shema* sung by ancient Israel:

Hear, O Israel: The LORD our God, the LORD is one. You shall love the LORD your God with all your heart and with all your soul and with all your might. (Deuteronomy 6:4, 5)

Everything we have is to be devoted to loving him. This theme was extended and substantiated by the Lord Jesus himself when a clever lawyer asked him, thinking to trip him up, "Teacher, which is the great commandment in the Law?" To which Jesus answered, "You shall love the Lord your God with all your heart and with all your soul and with all your mind. This is the great and first commandment" (Matthew 22:36–38). Nothing is of greater importance than loving God! If we fail to take this seriously, we may find at the end of our lives that all our works counted for nothing. Ashes on the altar!

This theme was also explicit in our Lord's dealings with Mary and Martha. When Martha urged Jesus to send Mary into the kitchen to help and stop wasting time at the feet of Jesus, he answered, "Martha, Martha, you are anxious and troubled about many things, but one thing is necessary. Mary has chosen the good portion" (Luke 10:41, 42). God wants us to be doers—to feed his sheep. But he wants us to *be* before we *do*. Love first!

We need to reflect honestly upon our lives in the light of Peter's words in verse 17: "Lord, you know everything." In Peter's previous affirmations of Jesus' omniscience (vv. 15, 16), he used a strong Greek word that meant Jesus knew every detail, but here he switches to a word that means intimate, personal knowledge, as if to say, "Lord, you have walked with me, you know me personally in every way." We can bank on that—he *does* know us in that way. If we are honest about our love, he will affirm what exists and will challenge and enable us to higher planes. Some of us may experience constant frustration because our priorities are wrong. Perhaps our job is all we can think about, or our pet ministry, or our season tickets. If so, we need to heed the example of old John Woolman, the mighty Quaker who, when too many customers came, sent them to more needy merchants for Christ's sake. First things first!

Imagine yourself standing alone on the shore with Christ, with the sea of eternity stretching on as a shimmering backdrop. Christ looks at you with knowing eyes and says, "Do you love me? Without comparing yourself with anyone else, do you really love me? Do you have an affection for me?" We must love him above and beyond anything or anyone else.

How do we make our love for Christ the highest priority in our lives? First, we must be absolutely honest about the level of our love. Secondly, we need to spend time with him, because the more time we spend with him, the more we will love him. How much time have we spent with him in the last month? We spend time with those we love.

I think this was the key to Mother Teresa's life. When she was wiping the wounds of someone who would not be in this world much longer, she acted as though she was wiping Jesus' wounds. When she scrubbed a floor, she was scrubbing Jesus' floor. We need to have a conscious sense that we are serving because we love him, so that when he says, "Do you love me?" we can say, "Lord, you know everything; you know that I love you."

60

On Loving and
Following Christ

JOHN 21:18–23

AN EXTRAORDINARY ANECDOTE comes to us from the annals of ancient Mideastern history. As the story goes, Cyrus, the great conqueror of the then known world including Babylon, had a general under his authority whose wife was suspected of treason. She was tried before a great and austere tribunal, found guilty, and sentenced to death. After the sentence was pronounced, the woman's husband (a general) made his way to Cyrus's throne and requested, "King Cyrus, please let me take her place." Cyrus, in awe at what was transpiring before him, said to his court, "Can we terminate a love as great as this?" He then paroled the woman to her husband. As the couple left the court, the general said to his wife, "Did you see the benevolent look in Cyrus's eyes as he pardoned you?" The wife responded, "I only had eyes for the one who loved me enough that he was willing to die for me."

This remarkable story dimly reflects the burning emotion of Peter's heart as he sat across the fire from Jesus on the shores of Tiberias and was drawn by Christ's repeated questions to consciously affirm his love for him. All Peter could see was the One who had loved him enough that he was willing to die for him. Peter loved Jesus with all his heart, and by verbalizing it he not only received restoration but stated for all believers the highest priority in life—loving God. We are to love God with all our heart, soul, mind, and might. Our lives, our service, our good deeds mean nothing without a true love for God.

As we continue on with the story of Peter's restoration, we see that priority extended and clarified. While it is true that serving does not prove we love God, it is equally true that we cannot honestly love him without serving him. Peter not only received a threefold restoration but also a threefold commission: "Feed my lambs" (v. 15), "Tend my sheep" (v. 16), and "Feed my sheep" (v. 17). This is even more significant when we realize that it was a Near-Eastern custom to say something three times before witnesses in order to solemnize it.[1] Now, with his restoration complete, a life of service awaited the apostle Peter.

In 21:18–23 we see what Christ did to infuse Peter with the proper perspective for serving him. This text provides us with universal, unchanging principles for all who respond to his call.

A Life of Service Is a Difficult Life (vv. 18, 19)

Jesus focused the conversation on this matter of service by prophesying of future difficulties that awaited Peter.

> "Truly, truly, I say to you, when you were young, you used to dress yourself and walk wherever you wanted, but when you are old, you will stretch out your hands, and another will dress you and carry you where you do not want to go." (This he said to show by what kind of death he was to glorify God.) And after saying this he said to him, "Follow me." (vv. 18, 19)

There have been, essentially, two interpretations of this prophecy. Some feel Jesus was simply telling Peter that whereas once he was an independent, competent young man who could take care of himself, someday he would be an old man who stretches out his hands to others in order to be dressed and is so dependent that he is taken places he does not desire to go. Nevertheless, he will glorify God by his godly demeanor as he dies of old age. The second interpretation is much preferred, which is that despite his aged infirmity he would die a martyr's death by crucifixion. The giveaway is John's description of Peter's death as a glorification of God, which, according to Raymond Brown, was standard Christian language for martyrdom.[2] Moreover, the church fathers, including Irenaeus, Justin Martyr, and Cyprian, all view the phrase "you will stretch out your hands" as a description of crucifixion, as likewise do the Epistles of Barnabas and the *Didache*.[3] The sense of Christ's prophecy is: "When you were young, you had your own way. You girded yourself and went forth with conscious independence. But a future time is coming when you will be infirm, and someone else will gird you and bind you and even crucify you." Christ was telling Peter very explicitly that his subsequent life of service would be extremely difficult, with the humiliation of his activist ego and even infirmity, and it would culminate in the ignominy of his own personal crucifixion. What a way to encourage one's followers!

Each devoted servant of Christ will bear his own cross. This was dramatically seen in the early years of the Salvation Army. When William Booth began his mission work in East London in 1865, it drew violent opposition, which grew even more violent in 1878 when his "Christian Mission" became the "Salvation Army" and Booth assumed the title of "General."

> One Salvation Army officer came into a meeting loaded down with dead cats and rats; he explained these had been thrown at him; and that he caught and held the dead animals because if he dropped them the crowd would merely pick them up to be thrown again. Pots of human urine were often dumped on the street preachers. Beatings were not uncommon; in 1889, at least 669 Salvation Army members were assaulted—some were killed and many were maimed. Even children were not immune; hoodlums threw lime in the eyes of a child of a Salvation Army member. The newspapers ridiculed Booth. *Punch* referred to him as "Field Marshal von Booth." Soon a band of thugs and ruffians organized themselves into the "Skeleton Army" and devoted themselves to disrupting the meetings of the Salvation Army. They often attacked Salvation Army members as they paraded through the streets or held open-air meetings. They frequently stormed Salvation Army meeting halls by the hundreds, broke out the window panes, and wrecked the inside of buildings. At first the police did little to stop the "Skeleton Army." Instead of helping they frequently harassed Booth and his followers.[4]

William Collier in his book *The General Next to God* says:

> Neither age nor sex proved a barrier, for the mobs were out for blood. In Northampton, one blackguard tried to knife a passing lassie; Wolverhampton thugs flung lime in a Salvationist child's eyes. At Hastings, Mrs. Susannah Beaty, one of Booth's first converts on Mile End Waste, became the Army's first martyr, buried from Clapton's Congress Hall. Reeling under a fire of rocks and putrid fish, she was kicked deliberately in the womb and left for dead in a dark alley of the Old Town. The doctor's prophecy that her injuries could prove fatal came appallingly true.
>   . . . the since-revised dedication of the eighties involved stern and binding promises—"You must be willing that the child should spend all its life in the Salvation Army, wherever God should choose to send it, that it should be despised, hated, cursed, beaten, kicked, imprisoned or killed for Christ's sake."[5]

Why were the Salvationists of one hundred years ago the offscouring of the earth? Why did Peter come to such a difficult end?

> For the love of Christ controls us, because we have concluded this: that one has died for all, therefore all have died; and he died for all, that those who

live might no longer live for themselves but for him who for their sake died
and was raised. (2 Corinthians 5:14, 15)

The love of Christ so controlled them that they no longer lived for
themselves but for Christ alone. The word translated "controls" sometimes
describes one who is "pressed in spirit" (Acts 18:5 KJV), sometimes the tight
hold that men keep on a prisoner (Luke 22:63). The idea is to be "gripped" or
"hemmed in." Christ's love so grips his followers that if they cooperate with
him, they will live for him!

Love so amazing, so divine
Demands my life, my soul, my all.

For Peter and his train this meant obedience. Christ says in 14:15, "If
you love me, you will keep my commandments." Also, "Whoever has my
commandments and keeps them, he it is who loves me. And he who loves me
will be loved by my Father, and I will love him and manifest myself to him"
(14:21). "The love of Christ controls us" (2 Corinthians 5:14). When we love
Christ, we hear his call!

Someone once introduced Hudson Taylor as a great missionary who had
given his life to the Orient because he loved the Chinese. Taylor slowly shook
his head and answered thoughtfully, "No, not because I loved the Chinese, but
because I loved God." The love of Christ controlled him! Love for Christ also
means suffering for him. When God sent Ananias to Paul he said:

Go, for he is a chosen instrument of mine to carry my name before the Gentiles and kings and the children of Israel. For I will show him how much he
must suffer for the sake of my name. (Acts 9:15, 16)

In John 21 Peter was told he would especially glorify God through his
death. When Paul wrote to the Philippians, while he was a prisoner, he said:

For it has been granted to you that for the sake of Christ you should not
only believe in him but also suffer for his sake. (Philippians 1:29)

The love of Christ so grips his followers that they no longer want to live
for themselves but for him, and that will mean obedience and mission and
hardship and suffering.

If our lives are characterized by ease, if we have no problems because of
our Christianity, something is likely wrong. John Stott, preaching on 2 Corinthians 5:14, 15 at All Soul's Church in London, once said:

Now the church is not persecuted so much as ignored. Its revolutionary message has been reduced to a toothless creed for bourgeois suburbanites. Nobody opposes it any longer, because really there is nothing to oppose. My own conviction, for what it is worth, is that if we Christians were to compromise less, we would undoubtedly suffer more. If we were to hold fast the old-fashioned Gospel of Christ crucified for sinners, and of salvation as an absolutely free and undeserved gift, then the Cross would again become a stumbling block to the proud. If we were to maintain the high moral standards of Jesus—of uncorruptible honesty and integrity, of chastity before marriage and fidelity in it, and of costly, self-sacrificial love, then there would be a public outcry that the church had returned to Puritanism. If we were to dare once more to talk plainly about the alternatives of life and death, salvation and judgment, heaven and hell, then the world would rise up in anger against such "old-fashioned rubbish." Physical violence, imprisonment and death may not be the fate of Christians in the West today, but faithfulness to Jesus Christ will without doubt bring ridicule and ostracism. This should not surprise us, however, for we are followers of the suffering Christ.[6]

Christ wanted Peter to know that if he would truly serve him, it was going to be difficult. And that is what he wants us to know too.

A Life of Service Is a Unique Life (vv. 20–22)

Apparently as Jesus and Peter conversed, they left the fire and began walking together with John not far behind, and then Jesus made his startling prophecy. Peter, noticing John nearby, perhaps uncomfortable about his own future, asked Jesus to make a prophecy about John's future.

> Peter turned and saw the disciple whom Jesus loved following them, the one who also had leaned back against him during the supper and had said, "Lord, who is it that is going to betray you?" When Peter saw him, he said to Jesus, "Lord, what about this man?" (vv. 20, 21)

Good old Peter! He loved Jesus with all his heart. He had been restored. He had been commissioned. But he was still Peter. "Jesus said to him, 'If it is my will that he remain until I come, what is that to you? You follow me!'" (v. 22). In other words, "Don't concern yourself with what I choose to do with the lives of my other servants. You just keep following me."

The Lord was not discouraging Peter's interest in the welfare of others but rather the unhealthy habit of measuring one's lot with that of others. A passage in C. S. Lewis's *The Horse and His Boy* beautifully illustrates this point. The boy, Shasta, is conversing with the Christ figure, the lion Aslan, and Aslan recounts his sovereign workings in Shasta's life—how he was the lion who drove the jackals away while Shasta slept and the one who comforted him among the houses of the dead and the one who propelled the boat that bore him to the shore to receive help. As Shasta listened, reflecting on the lion's sovereign claims, he suddenly questioned:

> "Then it was you who wounded Aravis?"
> "It was I."
> "But what for?"
> "Child," said the Voice, "I am telling your story, not hers. I tell no one any story but his own."[7]

Each of our lives is a sovereign creation of God. Our worth and our effectiveness, God's favor in our lives, is not to be determined by comparison with others. We are not to be involved in unprofitable musings about the relative providences of our lives—how one brother has it easier than another, or how one ministry is fraught with hardship and another is not, or why one believer becomes famous and another remains obscure. We are each simply to follow Christ.

A Life of Service Is a Following Life (vv. 19, 22)

No matter what our situation in life, Christ's call to us is, "Follow me." Below the surface of these words there was something very beautiful and meaningful for Peter. This stemmed from the fact that the very first recorded command Jesus gave to Peter was, "Follow me," as Jesus observed him fishing. Peter was younger then. He knew little of what would be involved, but he did follow. Now the command came again. How those words had been deepened by the years! Peter had been in Gethsemane. He had witnessed the sufferings of Christ at Golgotha. He had denied Christ. He had learned the necessity of following Christ. What a depth of meaning the words "Follow me" now carried.

That gracious command rings out to all of us: "Follow me!" If you are a new Christian, this is Christ's abiding command, and you are asked to respond at your own level of understanding. If you have been through the wars, it is still the same—perhaps seemingly infinitely more complex, yet still just as simple. "Follow me!"

"Do you love me?"
"Feed My sheep."
"Follow me!"

Soli Deo gloria!

Notes

Chapter One: The Greatness of Christ

1. C. S. Lewis, *Prince Caspian* (London: Collins, n.d.), p. 124.

2. A note of warning is in order here. Some cultists wrongly translate this phrase to say, ". . . and the Word was a god" (see the Jehovah's Witnesses' *The New World Translation of the Holy Scriptures*). They do this by supplying the indefinite article "a" where there is none in the Greek. While this is proper to do in some situations, it is entirely wrong here because John is stressing the character of the Word. William Barclay's explanation is especially clear: "Now when Greek does not use the definite article with a noun that noun becomes much more like an adjective; it describes the character, the quality of the person. John did not say that the Word was *ho theos*; that would have been to say that the Word was *identical* with God; he says that the Word was *theos*—without the definite article—which means that the Word was, as we might say, of the very same character and quality and essence and being as God" (*The Gospel of John*, vol. 1 [Philadelphia: Westminster, n.d.], p. 17).

3. C. S. Lewis, *The Weight of Glory and Other Addresses* (Grand Rapids, MI: Eerdmans, 1965), p. 15.

4. Quoted in Ewald M. Plass, *What Luther Says*, vol. 2 (St. Louis: Concordia, 1959), pp. 614, 615.

Chapter Three: The Greatness of the Good News

1. C. S. Lewis, *The Weight of Glory and Other Addresses* (Grand Rapids, MI: Eerdmans, 1965), p. 15.

Chapter Eight: The Cleansing of the Temple

1. A. W. Tozer, *The Knowledge of the Holy* (New York: Harper & Row, 1961), p. 13.

Chapter Eleven: "He Must Increase, but I Must Decrease"

1. William Barclay, *The Gospel of John*, vol. 1 (Philadelphia: Westminster, 1956), pp. 134, 135.

Chapter Twelve: The Heart That Ministers

1. Alexander Maclaren, *Expositions of Holy Scripture*, vol. 4 (Grand Rapids, MI: Baker, 1974), pp. 227, 228.

2. C. S. Lewis, *The Four Loves* (Harcourt Brace Jovanovich, 1960), p. 169.

Chapter Thirteen: The Ministering Heart's Message, Part I

1. *Wheaton Daily Journal*, February 6, 1980.

Chapter Fourteen: The Ministering Heart's Message, Part II

1. "Trendier Than Thou," October 1978, *Harper's Magazine*.

2. A. W. Tozer, *The Pursuit of God* (Wheaton, IL: Tyndale House, n.d.), p. 9.

3. C. S. Lewis, *Letters to Malcolm Chiefly on Prayer* (New York: Harcourt Brace Jovanovich, 1964), p. 4.

Chapter Fifteen: Thinking Rightly about God's Love

1. C. H. Spurgeon, "The Immutability of God," The Spurgeon Archive; www.spurgeon.org/sermons/0001.htm

2. J. I. Packer, *Knowing God* (Downers Grove, IL: InterVarsity Press, 1973), p. 113.

3. Leslie Weatherhead, *His Life and Hours* (London: Hodder & Stoughton, 1932), p. 275.

4. A. W. Tozer, *The Pursuit of God* (New York: Harper & Row, n.d.), p. 105.

Chapter Sixteen: The Ministering Heart's Approach to Life

1. Leon Morris' translation of Sbk. II, p. 438.

2. *Mishna*, Aboth 1:5.

3. Charles H. Spurgeon, *Metropolitan Tabernacle Pulpit,* vol. 55 (Pasadena, TX: Pilgrim, 1979), p. 128.

4. H. V. Morton, *In the Steps of the Master* (New York: Dodd Mead, 1984), p. 154.

Chapter Seventeen: Growing Faith

1. C. S. Lewis, *Surprised by Joy* (New York: Harcourt, Brace & World, 1955), p. 229.

2. C. H. Spurgeon, *Metropolitan Tabernacle Pulpit,* vol. 31 (Pasadena, TX: Pilgrim, 1973), p. 571.

3. Maclaren of Manchester, *Expositions of Holy Scripture* (Grand Rapids, MI: Baker, 1974), pp. 234, 235.

Chapter Nineteen: Conflict over the Sabbath

1. Philip Yancey, *Where Is God When It Hurts?* (Grand Rapids, MI: Zondervan, 1977), pp. 103–8.

2. Quoted by James M. Boice, *John*, vol. 2, (Grand Rapids, MI: Zondervan, 1976), p. 32.

3. Lewis Sperry Chafer, *Grace* (Grand Rapids, MI: Zondervan, 1976), pp. 290, 291.

Chapter Twenty: The Claims of Christ

1. C. S. Lewis, *Perelandra* (New York: Macmillan, 1944), p. 198.

2. Phil Donahue, *Donahue* (New York: Simon & Schuster, 1979), p. 94.

Chapter Twenty-One: Receiving the Witness of the Word

1. This account is found in greater detail in J. B. Phillips, *The Ring of Truth* (Wheaton, IL: Harold Shaw, 1977).

2. See Sir Frederic Kenyon, *Our Bible and the Ancient Manuscripts* (London: Eyre & Spottiswoode, 1965), p. 38.

3. Pirke Aboth 2:8.

4. Warren Wiersbe, *Listening to the Giants* (Grand Rapids, MI: Baker, 1980), p. 198.

Chapter Twenty-Two: What Kind of Savior?

1. H. A. Ironside, *John* (Neptune; NJ: Loizeaux Bros., 1942), p. 264.

Chapter Twenty-Three: Appropriating Christ's Power and Sufficiency

1. Elisabeth Elliot, *Worldwide Challenge,* January 1978, pp. 39, 40.

Chapter Twenty-Four: God's Children in the Storms of Life

1. Clarence Edward Macartney, *Great Nights of the Bible* (New York: Abingdon-Cokesbury, 1953), p. 201.

Chapter Twenty-Five: Dining on the Bread of Life

1. *London Times,* April 9, 1978.

2. Dietrich Bonhoeffer, *The Cost of Discipleship* (New York: Macmillan, 1963), p. 20.

3. James Montgomery Boice, *John,* vol. 2 (Grand Rapids, MI: Zondervan, 1976), p. 219.

4. Joy Davidman, *Smoke on the Mountain* (Philadelphia: Westminster, 1954), p. 23.

5. Myra Brooks Welch, *The Touch of The Master's Hand* (Elgin: Brethren Pub., 1957).

Chapter Twenty-Six: Rivers of Living Water

1. Somerset Maugham, *The Summing Up* (New York: Viking, 1978), p. 139.

2. Malcolm Muggeridge, *Something Beautiful for God* (New York: Ballantine, 1971), p. 4.

3. J. Gilchrist Lawson, *Deeper Experiences of Famous Christians* (Chicago: Glad Tidings, 1911), p. 267.

Chapter Twenty-Seven: Christ the Divider

1. G. K. Chesterton, *The Ball and the Cross* (New York: John Lane; 1909), pp. 39, 40.

Chapter Twenty-Eight: On Having the Light of Life

1. William Barclay, *The Gospel of John,* vol. 2 (Philadelphia: Westminster, 1956), p. 11.

2. Sukkah 5:2–3, *The Mishna,* trans. Herbert Danby (Oxford: Oxford University Press, 1933).

3. C. S. Lewis, *The Weight of Glory* (Grand Rapids, MI: Eerdmans, 1965), p. 13.

Chapter Twenty-Nine: Ultimate Separation—Ultimate Union

1. Herbert Lockyer, *Last Words of Saints and Sinners* (Grand Rapids, MI: Kregel, 1969), p. 132.

2. Ibid., p. 119.

3. R. Schnackenburg, *The Gospel According to John*, vol. 2 (New York: Seabury, 1980), p. 198.

4. C. S. Lewis, *The Great Divorce* (New York: Macmillan, 1946), pp. 38, 39.

Chapter Thirty: Up from Slavery

1. Josephus, *War*, VII, 8:6; number 323.

Chapter Thirty-One: Ultimate Ancestry

1. Elisabeth Dodd, *Marriage to a Difficult Man* (Philadelphia: Westminster, 1971), p. 39.

2. Ibid., p. 20.

3. Edmund Gosse, *Father and Son* (New York: W.W. Norton, 1963), p. 145.

Chapter Thirty-Two: The Way of Seeing

1. C. S. Lewis, *Screwtape Letters*, Introduction (New York: Macmillan, 1971), p. xiii.

2. Warren Wiersbe, *Walking with the Giants* (Grand Rapids, MI: Baker, 1976), p. 92.

3. Charles H. Spurgeon, *Metropolitan Tabernacle Pulpit*, vol. 30 (Pasadena, TX: Pilgrim, 1974), p. 489.

Chapter Thirty-Three: The Good Shepherd, Part I

1. Philip Keller, *A Shepherd Looks at Psalm 23* (Grand Rapids, MI: Zondervan, 1977), p. 61.

2. G. Campbell Morgan, *The Gospel According to John* (Westwood, NJ: Revell, n.d.), p. 177.

3. Charles H. Spurgeon, *Metropolitan Tabernacle Pulpit*, vol. 32 (Pasadena, TX: Pilgrim, 1974), p. 3.

Chapter Thirty-Four: The Good Shepherd, Part II

1. Shakespeare, *Henry V*, Scene 3.

2. *Moody Monthly*, September 1974, p. 68.

Chapter Thirty-Six: Eternal Profiles

1. James Hastings, ed., *The Speaker's Bible*, vol. 1 (Grand Rapids, MI: Baker, 1971), p. 31.

Chapter Thirty-Seven: A New Kind of Royalty

1. H. P. Liddon, *Passiontide Sermons* (London: Longman's Green, 1903), p. 105.

Chapter Thirty-Eight: The Effects of the Cross

1. C. S. Lewis, *Poems* (New York: Harcourt Brace Jovanovich), p. 124.
2. R. A. Torrey, *The Uplifted Christ* (Grand Rapids, MI: Zondervan, 1959), p. 21.
3. Wilbur Smith, *Therefore Stand* (Grand Rapids, MI: Baker, 1945), p. 53.

Chapter Thirty-Nine: On Being People of the Towel

1. Alexander Maclaren, *Expositions of Holy Scripture,* vol. 14 (Grand Rapids, MI: Zondervan, 1974), p. 171.
2. James Boice, *Commentary on John*, vol. 4 (Grand Rapids, MI: Zondervan, 1976), pp. 22–24, quoting H. A. Ironside, *Illustrations of Bible Truth* (Grand Rapids, MI: Zondervan, 1978), pp. 67–69.
3. Raymond E. Brown, *The Gospel According to John*, vol. 2 (New York; Doubleday, 1920), p. 551.
4. Midrash Mekilta on Exodus 21:2, quoted in ibid., p. 564.
5. John Stott, *Christ the Liberator* (Downers Grove, IL: InterVarsity Press, 1971), p. 25.

Chapter Forty: Radical Love

1. C. E. Macartney, *Great Nights of the Bible* (New York: Abingdon-Cokesbury, 1953), pp. 85–87.
2. H. A. Ironside, *Addresses on the Gospel of John* (Neptune, NJ: Loizeaux Bros., 1942), p. 565.
3. Cf. William Barclay's commentary on John, *The Gospel of John*, vol. 1 (Philadelphia: Westminster, 1956), p. 169 for helpful details.
4. Macartney, *Great Nights of the Bible*, p. 76.
5. Alexander Maclaren, *Expositions of Holy Scripture*, vol. 10 (Grand Rapids, MI: Baker, 1974), pp. 227, 228.

Chapter Forty-One: The Fall and Rise of the Apostle Peter

1. Alexander Whyte, *Bible Characters*, vol. 2 (Grand Rapids, MI: Zondervan, 1967), p. 38.
2. C. K. Barrett, *The Gospel According to John* (London: SPCK, 1975), p. 487.
3. Alexander Maclaren, *Expositions of Holy Scripture*, vol. 14 (Grand Rapids, MI: Baker, 1974), p. 253.
4. J. B. Lightfoot, *The Epistle to the Colossians* (Grand Rapids, MI: Zondervan, 1965), p. 183.

Chapter Forty-Two: "Let Not Your Hearts Be Troubled," Part I

1. C. S. Lewis, *The Problem of Pain* (New York: Macmillan, 1978), pp. 145–147.
2. Paul Tournier, *A Place for You* (Scranton, PA: HarperCollins, 1968), pp. 9–12.
3. John Donne, quoted by A. J. Gossip in *The Interpreter's Bible*, vol. 8 (New York: Abingdon, 1952), p. 703.
4. John R. W. Stott, *Christ the Liberator* (Downers Grove, IL: InterVarsity Press, 1971), p. 37.

Chapter Forty-Three: "Let Not Your Hearts Be Troubled," Part II

1. Cf. William E. Vine's *Expository Dictionary of New Testament Words* (Old Tappan, NJ: Revell, 1966), p. 60.

2. J. I. Packer, *Knowing God* (Downers Grove, IL: InterVarsity Press, 1973), p. 182.

3. Ibid.

4. Donald Grey Barnhouse, *Let Me Illustrate* (Old Tappan, NJ: Revell, 1967), pp. 358, 359.

Chapter Forty-Four: On Bearing Fruit

1. *Calmets' Dictionary of the Holy Bible,* p. 877.

2. James E. Rosscup, *Abiding in Christ* (Grand Rapids, MI: Zondervan, 1973), p. 50.

3. Malcolm Muggeridge, *Jesus Rediscovered* (Glasgow: Collins, 1969), pp. 158, 159.

4. C. S. Lewis, *The Voyage of the Dawn Treader* (London: Collins, 1974), p. 102.

5. G. K. Chesterton, *Orthodoxy* (New York: Lane, 1909), p. 160.

Chapter Forty-Five: Loving the Branches

1. Craig W. Ellison, *Loneliness, the Search for Intimacy* (Chappaqua, NY: Christian Herald, 1980), p. 17.

2. E. Stanley Jones, *Song of Ascents* (Nashville: Abingdon, 1979), pp. 129, 130.

Chapter Forty-Six: "If the World Hates You . . ."

1. John McCook Roots, *Chou: An Informal Biography of China's Legendary Chou En-Lai* (New York: Doubleday, n.d.), p. 32.

2. Ibid., pp. 33, 34.

3. Ibid., p. 34.

4. H. A. Ironside, *The Gospel of John* (Neptune, NJ: Loizeaux Bros., 1942), pp. 684, 685.

5. A. T. Robertson, *Word Pictures in the New Testament*, vol. 5 (Nashville: Broadman, 1932), p. 262.

6. See *Eternity*, February 1981, p. 22.

7. Dietrich Bonhoeffer, *The Cost of Discipleship* (New York: Macmillan, 1977), pp. 100, 101.

8. William Temple, *Readings in John's Gospel* (London: Macmillan, 1945), p. 272.

9. Roots, *Chou*, pp. 34, 35.

Chapter Forty-Seven: Disclosures of the Spirit

1. William Barclay, *The Gospel of John*, vol. 2 (Philadelphia: Westminster, 1956), p. 221.

2. John R. Claypool, *The Preaching Event* (Waco, TX: Word, 1980), pp. 121, 122.

3. B. F. Westcott, *The Gospel According to John* (Grand Rapids, MI: Eerdmans, 1958), p. 229.

4. R. A. Torrey, *The Holy Spirit* (New York: Revell, 1927), p. 45.

5. Ibid., p. 47.

6. Quoted in Malcolm Muggeridge, *A Third Testament* (New York: Little, Brown & Co., 1976), p. 58.

7. G. Campbell Morgan, *Westminster Pulpit*, vol. 11 (Old Tappan, NJ: Revell, n.d.), p. 162.

8. C. S. Lewis, *Surprised by Joy* (New York: Harcourt, Brace & World, 1955), p. 229.

9. Barclay, *The Gospel of John*, vol. 2, p. 76.

10. James M. Boice, *The Gospel of John*, vol. 1 (Grand Rapids, MI: Zondervan, 1975), pp. 392, 393.

Chapter Forty-Eight: From Sorrow to Joy

1. R. A. Torrey, *The Holy Spirit* (New York: Revell, 1922), p. 95.

2. James M. Boice, *The Gospel of John*, vol. 4 (Grand Rapids, MI: Zondervan, 1975), p. 314.

3. Oswald Chambers, *My Utmost for His Highest* (New York: Dodd, Mead, 1935), p. 150.

4. Ibid., p. 219.

5. "The Abiding Principle," August 12, 1973.

Chapter Forty-Nine: Christ's Prayer for Glory

1. Arthur W. Pink, *Exposition of the Gospel of John*, vol. 3 (Grand Rapids, MI: Zondervan, 1974), p. 90.

2. Ibid.

3. *Worship and Service Hymnal*, p. 57.

4. C. S. Lewis, *Miracles* (New York: Macmillan, 1955), p. 135.

5. C. H. Spurgeon, *Metropolitan Tabernacle Pulpit*, vol. 25 (Pasadena, TX: Pilgrim, 1972), p. 167.

6. Leon Morris, *Commentary on John* (Grand Rapids, MI: Eerdmans, 1971), p. 719.

7. John R. W. Stott, *Christ the Liberator* (Downers Grove, IL: InterVarsity Press, 1971), p. 72.

8. Donald Grey Barnhouse, *Let Me Illustrate* (Old Tappan, NJ: Revell, 1967), p. 97.

Chapter Fifty: Christ Prays for His Disciples

1. I. D. E. Thomas, *Puritan Quotations* (Chicago: Moody, 1975), p. 304.

2. A. W. Tozer, *The Pursuit of God* (Wheaton: Tyndale House, n.d.), p. 97.

3. H. C. G. Moule, *The High Priestly Prayer* (Grand Rapids, MI: Baker, 1978), pp. 101, 102.

4. Rebecca Manley Pippert, *Out of the Salt Shaker* (Downers Grove, IL: InterVarsity Press, 1980), p. 124.

Chapter Fifty-One: Christ Prays for His Own

1. F. B. Meyer, *The Gospel of John* (Grand Rapids, MI: Zondervan, 1950), p. 302.

2. John Stott, *Christ the Liberator* (Downers Grove, IL: InterVarsity Press, 1971), pp. 82, 83.

3. Jacques Ellul, *The Meaning of the City* (Grand Rapids, MI: Eerdmans, 1970), pp. 28, 29.

4. Stott, *Christ the Liberator*, p. 11.

5. Leon Morris, *The Gospel of John* (Grand Rapids, MI: Eerdmans, 1971), pp. 734, 735.

Chapter Fifty-Two: Who Arrested Whom?

1. Albert Schweitzer, *The Quest for the Historical Jesus* (New York: Macmillan, 1959), pp. 370, 371.

2. William Barclay, *The Gospel of John*, vol. 2 (Philadelphia: Westminster, 1956), p. 259.

3. D. James Kennedy, *Truths That Transform* (Old Tappan, NJ: Revell, 1974), p. 16.

4. John Calvin, *The Gospel According to St. John*, vol. 5, trans. T.H.L. Parker (Grand Rapids, MI: Eerdmans, 1974), p. 156.

5. "Gethsemane," C. E. Macartney, *Great Nights of the Bible,* quoted in E. W. Wilcox, *Poems of Power* (New York: Abingdon-Cokesbury, 1953), p. 166.

6. Ibid.

Chapter Fifty-Three: Pilate before Jesus, Part I

1. *The Poetical Works of Shelley* (Westminster, MD: Houghton Mifflin, 1975), p. 366.

2. Leon Morris, *The Gospel According to John* (Grand Rapids, MI: Eerdmans, 1971), p. 766.

3. Frank Morrison, *Who Moved the Stone?* (London: Faber & Faber, 1944), pp. 47–53.

4. Donald Grey Barnhouse, "God's Remedy", *Romans*, vol. 2 (Fincastle, VA: Scripture Truth, 1954), p. 378.

Chapter Fifty-Four: Pilate before Jesus, Part II

1. James Montgomery Boice, *The Gospel of John*, vol. 5 (Grand Rapids, MI: Zondervan, 1979), p. 91.

2. Leon Morris, *The Gospel According to John* (Grand Rapids, MI: Eerdmans, 1971), p. 790.

3. W. E. Vine, *Isaiah* (Grand Rapids, MI: Zondervan, 1946), p. 166.

4. Morris, *The Gospel According to John*, p. 793.

5. Raymond E. Brown, *The Gospel According to John,* XIII-XXI, vol. 2 (New York: Doubleday, 1970), pp. 893, 894.

6. *Arthur Miller's Collected Plays* (New York: Viking Press, 1981), pp. 35, 36.

7. Ibid.

8. Brown, *The Gospel According to John,* XIII-XXI, vol. 2, p. 895.

9. Gerard Manley Hopkins, from St. Francis Xavier, "O Deus Ego Amo Te."

Chapter Fifty-Five: Christ's Crucifixion, Part I

1. Graham Greene, *The Heart of the Matter* (New York: Viking Press, 1948), p. 211.

2. C. Truman Davis, MD, "The Passion of Jesus Christ from a Medical Point of View," *Arizona Medicine*, vol. 22, no. 3, March 1965.

3. *The Nicene and Post-Nicene Fathers*, vol. 14, p. 317.

4. William Barclay, *The Gospel According to John* (Philadelphia: Westminster, 1956), p. 292.

5. C. S. Lewis, *The Four Loves* (New York: Harcourt Brace Jovanovich, 1960), p. 176.

6. Arthur W. Pink, *Exposition of the Gospel of John,* vol. 3 (Grand Rapids, MI: Zondervan, 1974), p. 231.

7. Alexander Maclaren, *Expositions of Holy Scripture,* vol. 11 (Grand Rapids, MI: Baker, 1974), p. 263.

8. Dietrich Bonhoeffer, *The Cost of Discipleship* (New York: Macmillan, 1977), pp. 47, 48.

Chapter Fifty-Six: Christ's Crucifixion, Part II

1. C. S. Lewis, "Love's as Warm as Tears," *Poems* (New York: Harcourt Brace Jovanovich, 1964), pp. 123, 124.

2. C. S. Lewis, *The Four Loves* (New York: Harcourt Brace Jovanovich, 1960), p. 176.

3. Jack London, *The Sea Wolf* (New York: Airmont, 1965), p. 49.

4. Lewis, *The Four Loves*, p. 176.

5. C. Truman Davis, MD, "The Passion of Jesus Christ from a Medical Point of View," *Arizona Medicine*, vol. 22, no. 3, 1965.

6. R. C. H. Lenski, *Preaching on John* (Grand Rapids, MI: Baker, 1973), pp. 47, 48.

7. Nigel Turner, *Grammatical Insights into the New Testament* (Herndon, VA: T & T Clark, 1978), p. 40.

Chapter Fifty-Seven: The Fact of the Resurrection

1. C. K. Barrett, *The Gospel According to John* (London: SPCK, 1975), p. 468.

2. John Stott, *Basic Christianity* (Downers Grove, IL: InterVarsity Press, n.d.), p. 52.

3. A. J. Gossip, *The Interpreter's Bible*, vol. 8 (New York: Abingdon, 1952), p. 792.

4. Hugh Schoenfeld, *The Passover Plot* (New York: Bantam, 1967), pp. 163–175.

5. John Updike, "Seven Stanzas of Easter," *Telephone Poles and Other Poems* (New York: Alfred A. Knopp, 1961).

Chapter Fifty-Eight: A Fish Breakfast in Tiberias

1. Ian Hunter, *A Life* (Nashville: Thomas Nelson, 1980), p. 224.

2. Leon Morris, *The Gospel According to John* (Grand Rapids, MI: Zondervan, 1979), p. 868.

3. Alexander Maclaren, *Expositions of Holy Scripture,* vol. 11 (Grand Rapids, MI: Zondervan, 1965), p. 356.

Chapter Fifty-Nine: The Highest Priority

1. Roy and Revel Hession, *We Would See Jesus* (Ft. Washington, PA: Christian Literature Crusade, 1961), p. 15.

Chapter Sixty: On Loving and Following Christ

1. Raymond E. Brown, *The Gospel According to John* (New York: Doubleday, 1920), p. 1112.

2. Ibid., p. 1121.

3. J. M. Bernard, *The Gospel According to St. John,* vol. 2 (Edinburgh: T & T Clark, 1963), p. 709.

4. Clyde E. Fant, Jr. and William M. Pinson Jr., eds., *20 Centuries of Great Preaching*, vol. 5 (Waco, TX: Word, 1971), p. 204.

5. Richard Collier, *The General Next to God* (New York: E. P. Dutton, 1965), pp. 108–110.

6. John Stott, *Focus on Christ* (London: Fount Paperbacks, n.d.), p. 135.

7. C. S. Lewis, *The Horse and His Boy* (New York: Collins, 1954), p. 147.

Scripture Index

General Index

Index of Sermon Illustrations

Dr. Herbert Hendin: "the rediscovery of narcissism . . . reduces all relations to the question, 'What am I getting out of it?'" 372

Heaven
C. S. Lewis ponders his "inconsolable longing" for Heaven, 343
In an old German Bible, John 14 is worn from the tears of many generations, 345
John Watson kneels at the bed of the dying and prays, "In my Father's house are many mansions," 345
The doctor of a Puritan preacher said that "his joy at dying kept him alive a further fortnight," 345–46

Holy Spirit
A dad teaching his child how to ride a bike, 348
The amazing removal of an appendix by a person who had never performed surgery sheds light on Christ's profound words, "He will do even greater things than these, because I am going to the Father," 351–52
R. A. Torrey's church prays for the Holy Spirit to come with convicting power, 381–82
R. A. Torrey experiences supernatural joy despite the death of his twelve-year-old daughter, 388

Humility
The life of John the Baptist, 44
A humble pastor avoids all pomp as he leads the sunrise service at the Hollywood Bowl, 46
The great conductor Toscanini told his orchestra after a brilliant performance "I am nothing . . . you are nothing . . . But Beethoven is everything," 47
The *shoshben*, "friend of the bridegroom," is a picture of rejoicing in Christ, 97
William Carey's dying words point to Christ, 98
F. B. Meyer exalts fellow preachers, 99
Missionary James Gilmour's sad line in his diary about the difficulties of gospel ministry, 101–2
Ironside's power in ministry came from his exposure to the Bible, 175–76
Alexander Whyte examines his heart after someone said he was not converted, 264
Death to self enabled George Müller to exercise a wide influence for God, 307

Charles Ross Weed's poem "Christ and Alexander," 309
A new recruit to the Salvation Army remembers Christ washing the feet of fishermen, 322

Ignorance
Jorge Rodriguez, Mexican bank robber, loses his life because he cannot speak English, 380–81

Inadequacy
An Arabian fable about a bird that attempts to hold the sky up with its scrawny legs, 82
Long after pole vaulter Brian Sternberg broke his neck, his family still prays for a miraculous healing by God, 157–58
Elisabeth Elliot urges readers to bring whatever they can to the Lord, just like the boy who offered the loaves and fishes, 196
A medical doctor rescues a helpless sheep from a fatal condition, 277

Joy
The doctor of a Puritan preacher said that "his joy at dying kept him alive a further fortnight," 345–46
R. A. Torrey experiences supernatural joy despite the death of his twelve-year-old daughter, 388
The miraculous birth of a girl whose mother had fractured her spine when three months pregnant, 389

Kindness
A businessman comes under the hearing of the gospel coupled with an act of kindness from a young person, 30
C. S. Lewis: "The hardness of God is kinder than the softness of men, and his compulsion is our liberation," 143

The Lamb of God
Edmund and Lucy witness the lamb turn into the lion, Aslan, 67, 74

Legacy
The amazing legacy of Jonathan Edwards and his wife Sarah Pierrepont, 253–54
In an old German Bible, John 14 is worn from the tears of many generations, 345

Anne Ortlund observes that Scripture does not command us to "take it easy," 103

D. L. Moody's bedtime prayer "Lord, I am tired. Amen," 104

Old, feeble John Knox was filled with such power when he preached that he nearly knocked the pulpit into splinters, 136

When William Wilberforce preached, "The little minnow became a whale," 135

Long after pole vaulter Brian Sternberg broke his neck, his family still prays for a miraculous healing by God, 157–58

Elizabeth Elliot urges readers to bring whatever they can to the Lord, just like the boy who offered the loaves and fishes, 195–96

Bonhoeffer: "We will not falter, thankfully receiving all that is given by thy loving hand," 211

Paderewski: "Madam, before I was a genius, I was a drudge," 306

Jim Ryun describes his running regimen, 307

H. P. Liddon: "The errors and miseries of the world are purged with blood," 307

Malcolm Muggeridge on the beneficial aspects of suffering, 358

Ten Boom's poem beginning, "I asked the Lord, that I might grow in faith, and love and every grace," 360

Poem saying all Christians must pass through Gethsemane, 422

The failures of Abraham Lincoln before his election to the presidency, 468

Muggeridge: "Christianity . . . the sanctification of failure," 468

Perspective

A traffic jam looks different from a plane, 283

The author lets his daughter grow through hardship, 290–91

Prayer

Missionary John G. Paton is protected from cannibals by a band of angels as an answer to prayer, 51

George Müller prayed for the salvation of three men converted decades later by someone else, 139

Pride

A humble pastor avoids all pomp as he leads the sunrise service at the Hollywood Bowl, 46

An Arabian fable about a bird that attempts to hold the sky up with its scrawny legs, 82

Dr. Chapin's word association test reveals the highly competitive nature of preachers, 95

Poem about those who reject the truth of Scripture out of pride: "Whatever light man finds they doubt it, they love not light but talk about it," 177

A man in the book *The Great Divorce* takes a bus ride from Hell to Heaven but is totally unaware of where he has come from, actually calling Hell Heaven, 241–42

Calvin: "The greater the mass of vices anyone is buried under, the more fiercely and bombastically does he extol free will," 249

A young Edmund Gosse confesses Christ without believing, 257

The coronation of Bokassa I cost $25 million, 303

Dr. Herbert Hendin: "the rediscovery of narcissism . . . reduces all relations to the question, 'What am I getting out of it?'" 372

The prime minister of Sri Lanka receives a grand welcome, 425

Shelley's poem "Ozymandias," 425–26

Churchill said of Sir Stafford Cripps, "There, but for the grace of God, goes God," 445

Priorities

Charles Schwab writes a $25,000 check for a time-management technique, 473

Hession: Seeking God is our first priority in Christian service, 477

Protection

Missionary John G. Paton is protected from cannibals by a band of angels as an answer to prayer, 51

A four-year-old boy in California is miraculously saved from injury on the highway, 51–52

Moule: Christians are preserved by the name of God their Father, 404

Provision

Author retells of God's miraculous provision for his family at the birth of his firstborn, 201–2

Rejection

A boy sent to college during the Depression later rejects his parents when they visit, 26

Dr. Chapin's word association test reveals the
highly competitive nature of preachers,
which in turn gives rise to *odium theologicum*—the hatred of theologians, 95
George Sanders's sad suicide note, 110
A woman divorces her minister husband
because "I'm not happy. God loves me and
wants me to be happy," 127
Alexander Solzhenitsyn on our worship of
"things," 128
William Beveridge: "my very repentance needs
to be repented oft," 155
Somerset Maugham: "The beauty of life is
nothing but this; that each should act in
conformity with his nature and his business," 219–20
Thomas Paine before his death, 240
The Jewish belief at the time of Christ that
suicide caused a person to occupy the worst
place in Hell, 241
Calvin: "The greater the mass of vices anyone
is buried under, the more fiercely and bombastically does he extol free will," 249
Aaron Burr, the man who shot Alexander Hamilton, was from the bloodline of Jonathan
Edwards, 254
A young Edmund Gosse confesses Christ
without believing, 257
Helen Keller: "I got used to the silence and
darkness," 260
C. S. Lewis: "My heart—I need no other
'showeth me the wickedness of the ungodly,'" 263

Substitution
Jesus died in our spiritual place, just as he died
in the physical place of Barabbas, 431
A general in King Cyrus's army is willing to
die in the place of his condemned wife, 481

Success
In *Death of a Salesman*, Willy Loman's view of
success kills him, 437–38

Suffering
Malcolm Muggeridge quote illustrating the
beneficial aspects of suffering, 358, 468
A boy in the Narnia series, after becoming a
dragon, allows Aslan to painfully remove
the scales, 359

Ten Boom's poem beginning, "I asked the
Lord, that I might grow in faith, and love
and every grace," 360
Bonhoeffer: "Suffering . . . is the badge of the
true Christian," 375
Poem saying all Christians must pass through
Gethsemane, 422
The failures of Abraham Lincoln before his
election to the presidency, 468
The extremely rough beginnings of the Salva-
tion Army, 483

Temptation
A little girl knows where sin comes from as she
kicks her brother in the shins, 41

Thankfulness
Bonhoeffer: "We will not falter, thankfully
receiving all that is given by thy loving
hand," 211

Trust
Identical twins—business partners and best
friends—are torn apart for twenty years
over one lousy dollar bill, 363–64

Unity
Brookes: "For wolves to worry the lambs is no
wonder, but for one lamb to worry another,
this is unnatural and monstrous," 403
One hundred pianos are tuned to one fork, 404
Stott: Our unity with the apostolic church, 413
The ancient practice of laying the foundation
stone of a city upon a human sacrifice, 414

Witness
Missionary letter laments that some used
money to "buy" the happiness of their
"converts," 182
C. S. Lewis tells of attacks against Christianity
at Oxford, 229
Belgium, Dutch, and American Christians
learned how to love each other in the Belgium Evangelical Mission, 331–32
Communist leader Borodin asks, "Where do
you find a man like Paul today?" 378
Poem with the ending line "Till I lose sight of
you and see the Christ instead," 400–1
Pippert: We must not become "a rabbit-hole"
Christian, 406

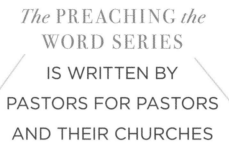